ROADSIDE MEETINGS

ROADSIDE MEETINGS

By

HAMLIN GARLAND

MEMBER OF THE AMERICAN ACADEMY

Decorations by

CONSTANCE GARLAND

New York

THE MACMILLAN COMPANY

1930

SET UP BY BROWN BROTHERS LINOTYPERS
PRINTED IN THE UNITED STATES OF AMERICA
BY THE FERRIS PRINTING COMPANY

ROADSIDE MEETINGS OF A LITERARY NOMAD

AN EXPLANATION BY THE AUTHOR

In taking up the purely literary side of my experiences during the last forty-five years, I shall parallel, necessarily, the general line of advance taken in my "Middle Border" books, but as the chief characters in those chronicles were pioneers, a group of migrating families, so in "Roadside Meetings" I present the vicissitudes of a man of letters. All matters pertaining to my family history have been excluded —only so much of my personal history is retained as may be needed to put the records in sequence and to clarify them.

This book, whatever its demerits, has the quality of history in that it is based upon dated records, and in its later portion on actual diaries. I began keeping a notebook in 1885, and an accurate daily chronicle in 1898, and it was my original plan to select and arrange these entries and print them without comment, under the heading "Red Letter Days," but my friends all assured me that I should indicate, in outline at least, my personal situations and fortunes in order that each comment might have its full significance. "We must have a thread of narrative," they said. "You can not expect the reader of 'Roadside Meetings' to refer to 'A Son of the Middle Border' in order to clarify the records. This book must be able to stand by itself and justify itself."

v

In accordance with this advice "Roadside Meetings" presents by way of a loosely strung series of literary and artistic portraits my concept of the various esthetic invasions which have from time to time set in from overseas, agitating (each in its own way) our alert and devoted intellectuals. Without claiming for it the dignity of history, this chronicle will, I trust, illustrate our progress—if it can be called progress—from 1880 to 1900. It will present portrait sketches of the men and women who represented and vitalized literature and art during this period. Many of them were known to me and some of them were my friends.

The book is, as its name implies, a series of meetings with artists, authors, public men and women, together with some revelations as to the sources of my previous books, confidences which may have some slight interest to my readers. However, all passages failing of interest can be skipped.

HAMLIN GARLAND.

CONTENTS

viii

CONTENTS

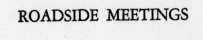

ROADSIDE MEETINGS

ROADSIDE MEETINGS

CHAPTER ONE

THE KNOCK ON MY DOOR

ONE Sunday afternoon in the summer of 1884 whilst I, a young man of twenty-three, was sitting with my mother and father in our home in Ordway, a minute village on the treeless plain of South Dakota, I heard a knock on the door. Thinking it the hand of a neighbor, I called out heartily, "Come in!"

The visitor proved to be a stranger, a tall, fair-skinned, blue-eyed man of thirty-five, who said, "My name is Bashford. I am a Methodist minister and I have just been speaking in your little church. Some one spoke of you as a Wisconsin family and I have called to have a chat with you."

My father gave him a chair and while he talked as freely as a neighbor I studied him. He was humorous, kindly, and understanding, a lovable character who sensed our situation and did not count it against us.

My father, who had been one of the first to settle in Ordway, three years before, owned a farm some two miles out but was keeping a general store at this time and my mother and sister were housekeeping in a building which ran alongside the wareroom—camping out while waiting for something better. The land was a level, treeless, arid plain and the hopefulness of early settlement had begun to fail.

The talk fell at once upon the climate. Mr. Bashford confessed that he had been lured into buying a near-by claim. "I am here to look at the pig-in-the-poke I have purchased," he said with some humor. "I am a native of Dane County, Wisconsin, but I went East ten years ago and am now the pastor of a church in Portland, Maine."

His manner was winning, so winning that he soon had my confidence. I confessed to him that I was sick of the country and in despair of its future. "I've had enough of it," I said. "It's too hot and dry in summer, too cold and desolate in winter. I am planning to sell my claim and spend a year or two in some Illinois normal school and fit myself for teaching. I want to teach literature and oratory," I added in a still deeper confidence.

This appeared to surprise him. He studied me reflectively. "Why don't you go to Boston and take special work along those lines? No other place offers the same advantage."

"Oh, I couldn't do that," I declared. "I *daren't* do that. I haven't money enough and I am afraid of cities. I couldn't earn a living in a city."

"Nonsense," he genially retorted. "You can earn a living anywhere. I went East without money, planning to work my way through Boston University, and I did it, easily. I found the Eastern people very kind, and so will you. I'll give you a letter of introduction to the head teacher of Oratory and also one to the Professor of English Literature. They will advise you and make your course easy."

Although I protested that I would never use the letters, he sat down at a desk and wrote them out then and there and when he went away he said with a smile, "I shall expect to see you in Portland. Write me when you reach Boston."

This chance meeting altered the course of my life. I began to dream of Boston and to figure the cost of a year amid its splendors. I felt a singular weakness in the pit of my stomach as I dwelt upon the glories of this adventure.

For nearly two years I had been "holding down a claim" in McPherson County, some forty miles west of Ordway. It was a handsome piece of velvet-green upland sod in May, but in August it became hot and hard as a brick pavement, and in winter it was a wind-swept, desolate, arctic plain. I had lived out several blizzards in my little shack, but I now hated the sight of it. The endless, level plain no longer interested me. My pioneering enthusiasm had cooled and I longed for the trees and streams of Iowa, and the hills of my native valley in Wisconsin. "I am wasting my time here," I said to my mother.

With only a preëmption title to my land, which had recently been surveyed, I now planned to "prove up" on it in September, sell my equity in it, and use the money toward my education in Boston. At most, my cash return above the government price of a dollar and a quarter per acre would be less than two hundred dollars, and the lowest railway fare would take nearly one-fifth of that sum. I figured that I could land in Boston with one hundred and fifty dollars, which would not carry me far. Nevertheless I assured my father that I would not ask help from him. "If Mr. Bashford is right, I'll find some way to earn my way through the school."

In truth my plans were all ludicrously vague; I was like a child groping in a fog. Fully warned of my audacity, I was also aware that I was running counter to the spirit of the Border and to all the instructions I had hitherto received. Horace Greeley's *Go West, Young Man, Go West* had been the marching orders under which the Garlands and McClintocks and all their neighbors had been moving for forty years. No one, so far as I knew, had ever gone East from choice. All promise, all romance was in the sunset sky, and I now realized that in facing the sunrise I was encountering the astonished or amazed glances of all the westward-marching millions. Had I said, "I am going to Montana—or Colorado or California," no one would have wondered and many would have expressed a fervent wish to accompany me; but a migration to Boston—that was unthinkable!

Despite all this I left Ordway in October bearing a second-class ticket for Chicago, and occupying a seat in the smoking car. Late the next day I reached Chicago, where I stopped long enough to buy a twenty-dollar suit of clothes, a suit of which you will hear more. The coat, a Prince Albert frock of a purplish color, was mostly cotton but it fitted me well and I was rather pleased with it. I was a stalwart, brown-bearded young man of middle height, wearing a broad-brimmed black hat and carrying an imitation leather valise which contained a few shirts and socks. I also owned a pasteboard trunk containing some books and a few extra articles of clothing.

The train was very slow. I spent two long nights and one day in that smoking car, living on lunch-counter sandwiches, doughnuts, and coffee; so that when I landed in the Hoosac station one rainy autumn day I was so sick that I could hardly stagger under the weight of my valise. Ignoring the street car, partly because I could not afford the fare, and partly because I was afraid the driver would not permit me to take my valise inside, I started toward the

Common. No aspiring youth ever entered this capital in less exultant mood. The weeping skies overhead and the mud under my feet, were in perfect harmony with my feeling of weakness and despair.

CHAPTER TWO

DR. HALE AND EDWIN BOOTH

I

BOSTON in 1884 was still the chief literary center of America. Its roll of writers included Oliver Wendell Holmes, James Russell Lowell, William Dean Howells, Thomas Bailey Aldrich, and many others, while Edwin Booth, most highly honored of tragedians, was an occasional resident. Although in reality a small city, it was to me a splendid capital, overpowering with the grandeur of its historic monuments and the wealth of its records of great men and greater events. To a youth from the plains, its innumerable red, yellow, and green horse-cars tinkling along the streets and its thunderous horse-drawn trucks were confusing. At night arc lights sizzled menacingly at certain corners but ancient lamplighters still went their rounds lighting with a long pole the gas jets in iron lanterns. By contrast with Ordway, it was appallingly splendid.

There were no high buildings on Tremont Street, but the trees on the Common were majestic, and the golden dome of the Statehouse was to me, as to other literary pilgrims, "the Hub of the Universe," as Dr. Holmes had affectionately named it. Beacon Street was a synonym for grandeur, and the Public Library, a plain brown building on Boylston Street, a palace. To be near it, I secured a room in Boylston Place, which led off the Common just beyond it.

The Parker House was the outstanding hotel. Depart-

6

ment stores were few. Music Hall and Tremont Temple were shrines of music and oratory and the Boston Museum and the Howard Atheneum were still centers of drama. The *Transcript* was the chief evening paper, and the *Herald* the most widely circulated morning journal. Houghton & Mifflin, the leading publishers then as they still are, owned the *Atlantic Monthly*, of which Thomas Bailey Aldrich was the editor. Book advertising, like other forms of publicity, was keyed low, and while an increasing material traffic thundered distractingly over granite cobbles, the city's intellectual life was low-toned and the pace of its citizens sedate.

Some of these things I am describing from my present standpoint, for at that time I was too awed and too humble to achieve any well-defined comment on the town's intricate and ceaseless tumult. My concern was to find the least expensive coign of safety. With less than one hundred and forty dollars in my pocket to carry me through the winter, and with no hope of earning another dollar till spring, I pinched every penny. I was a bewildered plainsman, a scared rustic in the midst of a gigantic metropolis. With but two clear ideas in my head, one to make my money go as far as possible, and the other to get all the learning I could while it lasted, I settled into place.

That it was a kind of insanity, I knew, a blind following of a desire to see and know the capital in which my father had lived and which he had taught me to venerate; but here I was in the center of a vaguely alluring literary universe. New York meant little to me then, whereas Massachusetts connoted Emerson, Hawthorne, Whittier, Longfellow, and other of my boyhood idols whose writings had created a longing to see the places they had made illustrious. Here, too, was the center of lofty oratory; Faneuil Hall suggested Daniel Webster, Wendell Phillips, and William Lloyd Garrison. A stir of wonder ran through my brain each morning when I woke and remembered where I was. "I must make the most of it while I am here."

Of literary Boston I knew a little; of the actual city, nothing. No Jason ever sought a Golden Fleece with less knowledge of the seas before him. All waters were to me uncharted. It is impossible that any young man of to-day could be so ignorant and so venturesome, for I was utterly without help in time of trouble. I knew but one man in all New England, and he, a Methodist preacher in Portland, Maine, was only a chance acquaintance. Furthermore, his introductory letters did not help me to any new friends. I was in much more difficult case than "Lemuel K. Barker, from Willoughby Pastures," the chief character in Howells' story, "The Minister's Charge," for Lemuel could walk back to his farm in a few hours, whereas I was more than fifteen hundred miles from my father's door.

My share in the city's glory consisted of a sunless, narrow hall bedroom in Boylston Place, a dismal blind alley whose only advantage was its nearness to the Public Library. I had discovered that the reading room was always lighted and warmed and as my room was usually cold, I found much comfort in Bates Hall, as it was called, and spent most of my waking hours there.

The Professor of English at Boston University and the head of the dramatic school to whom I presented my letters took no interest in me, and when I went to Harvard to see if I could share courses of lectures in some way, I was told that they had no place for outside students. I was not precisely shown the door in these three institutions, but I came away from them bitterly aware of my folly in taking

Bashford's letters so seriously. There was but one thing to do, and I did it. I went every day to the great hall in the library, and there read with desperate intensity, resolved on becoming as learned as possible before my money was utterly gone. All this I have outlined in "A Son of the Middle Border," but it is necessary to repeat it here, for the benefit of a new generation of readers.

In the resolution to stay as long as possible I adopted a rigid regimen. For breakfast I allowed myself a three-cent cup of coffee and two doughnuts which I ate standing at a little booth just around the corner; and for noonday meal I went to a restaurant on Pleasant Street where rough work-men ate, and where for fifteen cents I could get a meal of bread and meat. In going to this place I passed a house in which Hawthorne was said to have lived for a time, and in the fact of his poverty I took comfort. For supper I bought a glass of milk and two buns or rolls. My room and laundry cost me about two dollars per week. In this way I was able to keep within my budget of twenty dollars per month and could count on lasting through till May.

Naturally I went only to such places as could be reached on foot—I had no nickels for carfare—and I attended only such lectures and concerts as were free. With no money to pay tuition in any school, I made the Public Library my university, and it was in this connection that I first met a distinguished man.

The rules of the circulating department (very properly) did not permit readers without endorsement to take books to their homes, and I, who was neither a pupil in a school nor an employee in a business house, could read only in the hall under the eyes of attendants. In consequence of this rule all my Sundays and other holidays were lost hours.

I cast about to see what could be done to get a regular
reader's card. Judge Chamberlain, the librarian, after quoting the rules, said, "See Dr. Edward Everett Hale. He is
one of the directors and can help you." I decided to follow
his advice.

One of my Sunday diversions had been attendance upon
historic churches and their notable preachers, and Edward
Everett Hale was first among those I had heard, for indeed
his name had been one of the cards in our set of "Authors,"
in my boyhood. He was a tall, shaggy-haired, deep-eyed
New Englander with a booming voice, beloved by his con-
gregation and widely known for his philanthropy. His home
was in Roxbury, but his study was in his South End Church.
I decided to call upon him at his study.

It took courage to do this, but I did it! He opened the
door himself and greeted me with the bluff kindness of a
man whose duty it was to aid the destitute and comfort the
sorrowing. As he towered above me, I would have been
utterly intimidated but for the compassionate look in his
deep-set gray eyes and the genial lines on his broad brow.

"Take a seat and tell me how I can serve you," he said.
I stated my case plainly, and I fear, bitterly.

"Well, well," he exclaimed in a resounding baritone.
"This surprises me. In theory our library is free to any
student. You are precisely the reader we wish to attract."

"The librarian says there are twenty thousand young people like myself in Boston with no one to endorse them."

His surprise deepened. "No one has explained that fact
to me. We'll look into the situation. Meanwhile I'll see
that you are taken care of."

Writing out a card to the chief librarian, he sent me away
confident that in him I had a friend whenever I should need

one. This was my first literary contact in New England, and in my letters home I described my visit and the effect of that card with gratitude and pride. "I am a privileged reader in the library now!"

II

My only extravagance during this winter was the purchase of tickets to the Boston Museum, where Edwin Booth as "visiting star" was playing a special six weeks' engagement. By paying thirty-five cents I could stand at the back of the first balcony, and from this place I saw ten of the principal rôles which this noblest of tragedians then enacted. I saw everything and remembered what I saw. I was filled with admiration of his face, his voice, his enunciation. He taught me the glory of the English tongue. I became conscious of my Western burr, and I began to study the laws which govern cultivated speech. I made notes of his accent, his emphasis—justifying my extravagance by calling this a part of my education. Each day I made record of the Shakespearean characterizations I had seen the night before with an attempt at their literary interpretation—looking at them as living people.

By day I read, in the library, books on the evolution of the drama, the rise of the minstrel, the development of the novel, and the like; but on the nights when Othello, or Iago, or Macbeth, or Hamlet walked the stage, I was to be found leaning upon the backs of the rear seats in the first balcony, ready to slip down into a vacant seat, if one offered, intensely eager to be nearer the marvelous face of the man who meant more to me, at this time, than any other citizen in Boston. In course of time the boy ushers came to know me and to pity me, and one of them often helped me to a vacant seat. This he did without a tip, realizing that I was in his class, with no dimes or quarters to waste. What an education that was! With reckless disregard of the expenditure I paid my thirty-five cents and stood night after night in the semi-dark of my position taking no account of aching limbs. I was only a brain. My mind was at once a photographic plate and a phonographic film. Nothing escaped me. The grace, the majesty of Booth's movements, the velvet smoothness of his voice, the beauty and precision of his speech were precious revelations to me. Each night I staggered down the stairs, my limbs benumbed, my mind in a tumult, and found my way home across the Common to my den like a sleepwalker, so profoundly stirred that nothing physical mattered.

On one glorious night a man in the very front row of the balcony was obliged to leave, and one of the boy ushers led me down to this seat; and there I sat for two acts so close to the face of my tragedian that I could note every subtle shade and fleeting line of his marvelous characterization. It chanced to be Sir Giles Overreach, and at the moment when stricken with paralysis he mutters, "Some undone widow sits upon my sword," one of the actor's eyelids drooped and the muscles of his cheek sagged, a marvelous simulation of the physical paralysis which the dramatist had imagined.

As I write this I have before me the little notebook wherein I set down my memories of Booth's gestures, inflections, and above all his emphasis and the matchless music of his voice. Fresh from the silence of the Dakota plain, and filled with worshipful admiration of a noble artist, how could I fail of being translated into a new world by this interpreter of the great dramatist? Harvard University would have given me much, but I am not sure that all its professors, no matter how learned, would have given me so much and in so short a time.

Edwin Booth taught me the power and the glory of English speech. He made me feel very rude and small and poor, but he inspired me. He aroused my ambition. I bear witness to his wizardry, for I was sustained by its spell. If you say that this wizardry was mostly in my imagination I shall not contend with you; the fact remains: Booth and his Shakespeare were the greatest educative influences in my life at this time. Outwardly seedy, hungry, pale and lonely, I inhabited palaces and spoke with kings.

III

It was this aroused interest in speech which led me to attend a series of lectures on the laws of expression, by Professor Moses True Brown at the Young Men's Christian Union on the corner of Tremont and Boylston streets. These lectures were free, and I attended the entire series.

The speaker, who was advertised as "The principal of the Boston School of Oratory," delighted me, and at the close of the final talk I was moved to go forward and tell him so. "I've just finished reading Darwin on 'Expression in Man and Animals,' and I am greatly pleased to hear you quote it with approval."

Brown, who was a large man with a full beard, genial gray eyes, and a pleasant voice, appeared interested, and we exchanged a few quotations from the book. "It is too late to go into the matter here," he said. "Come to my study to-morrow after four. I'd like to discuss the subject with you."

This invitation meant a great deal to me, for up to this

time I had talked with no one—my interview with Hale could hardly be called a talk; and to be asked to visit the principal of the Boston School of Oratory was a triumph.

Brown's office was at No. 7 Beacon Street at the top of a four-story building, without an elevator, and as I climbed the stairs, I found my breath shortened by something other than the exertion of the ascent. I was almost as intimidated as I had been in Dr. Hale's study.

Brown met me as a fellow student of the science of oratory and I soon lost my timidity. After outlining my studies in comparative literature and my reading in modern biology, I ended by declaring that Edwin Booth was my chief admiration and that I was making a study of his art.

Brown listened to my torrential outgiving with an amused but sympathetic smile, and when I paused for breath—or possibly for shame, he explained that he was just finishing a volume called "The Philosophy of Expression" wherein he sought to define the physical or natural basis for every gesture and tone. "I am not a mystic," he said; "I base myself on the laws of evolution." He showed me the manuscript of this book and read some of it to me, and my comment so pleased him that at last he said, "I want your comment. I'd like to read it all to you and get your notion of it in detail, and if you care to enter my school I will put your work with me over against the charge for tuition."

This was my second literary contact and I went away from it with a feeling that I had found another friend, happy in the tone of comradeship which this good and successful man had used throughout our interview. That such a scholar should respect my reasoning powers and value my comment was heartening. No doubt he saw that my shoes were

almost without soles and my overcoat threadbare, but he
did not undervalue me on that account.

In the mornings which followed I sat with certain of his
classes and every afternoon I worked with him on his book.
For him I translated several French authorities on Expression, and one by Mantegazza, which I transcribed as well
as translated for him. These hours in his study were very
precious to me, for I had no other conversational outlet.
With no youthful friends at all—the people I met at my
rooming house did not interest me—I allowed nothing to
interfere with my reading. Concentration was intense. Aside
from an occasional walk, I kept rigidly to my studies.

Each morning I read the *Herald* and each evening the
Transcript. I heard every free lecture in the Young Men's
Union, and I knew the voice and mannerisms of every
notable preacher in the city; and whenever a public meeting
in Faneuil Hall took place I was there. I read all the book
reviews in the daily papers and in the magazines and at last
began to feel at home in the midst of Boston's literary
activity. Its writers were remote and radiant stars in my
sky, but I had acquired some conception of their relative
orbits in the world of letters.

In short, I made every necessary preparation for the writing of this chronicle, my hall room being a logical substitute
for an attic, but I can not say that it was a joyous winter.
I was hungry most of the time, and from a tanned young
athlete weighing one hundred and eighty pounds I declined
into a gaunt and bearded student, infesting the library, and
walking carefully to save my shoes. With no definite plan
for the future, I cut my living expenses down to the irre-

ducible minimum in order that my savings should last out
the winter.

Brown, I think, would have asked me to his house, but
his wife, a rather handsome woman, regarded me askance.
To her I was merely one of her husband's seedy, unsavory
pupils, all well enough in the schoolroom but impossible at
a dinner table—a decision which I considered, even then,
to be well taken. I had no clothing suitable for a drawing-
room, and no conversational pleasantries whatsoever. I was
a raw plainsman undergoing training (without knowing it)
for a literary career.

CHAPTER THREE

FRIENDS IN TIME OF NEED

I

Upon invitation from Mr. Bashford, I spent the holidays at his home in Portland, and while there he gave me a letter to a friend in Jamaica Plain, saying, "Dr. Cross is a good man for you to know. He is one of the kindest men in the world and will look after your health."

For some reason, probably because I could not spare the carfare, I did not present this letter till late in April. I am sure of this, for I have the most vivid memory of that ride into the suburbs. Pear trees were in blossom, the apple buds were showing pink, and robins were hopping about on the green lawns. After passing Roxbury I rode on the front end of the horse car, rejoicing like a man released from prison, and in truth I was sadly depleted in vitality as well as in weight. I had not been outside the region of the Common since my arrival in Boston. My robust frame had shrunk, my face was pallid, and my garments many degrees seedier than when I had visited Dr. Hale. My money was gone and in spite of my brave resolution I had been forced to borrow twenty-five dollars from my father.

Dr. Cross' house was a small frame cottage on a commonplace street, but it seemed very sweet and homelike to me. The doctor told me afterward that he was alarmed by my pallor and at once suspected that I was in need of food.

No doubt my joy in his dinner helped out his diagnosis. It was a glorious midday meal—just the sort I had been accustomed to in the West; and afterward he invited me to ride with him while he made some calls. He drove a high-headed, intelligent brown horse hitched to an old-fashioned buggy (how long ago all that seems!) and as I sat beside him, looking out at the lovely trees and lawns, I was saddened by the thought that I should probably never see them again.

My stay in Boston was at an end. With no ability to earn a dollar in the city, I was facing the necessity of giving up my studies and returning to some sort of manual labor in the country. As a carpenter, a handy man, I had once been able to earn good wages, and it was with this plan in mind that I went into Professor Brown's office one afternoon and bluntly said, "I've come to say good-by. I'm leaving to-morrow."

He was amazed by my tone as well as by my words, for I was hardly able to speak—so bitter was my sense of defeat. He asked me why I was leaving. I told him that my money was gone and that I had no way of earning any more, "except by working on a farm or at the carpenter's trade." I explained, "I can shingle as well as any man—and I'm going out into some small town and get a job with a builder."

As he grew to a clearer understanding of my situation he began to chuckle, his fat middle shaking with amusement. "Shingle!" he said explosively. "Can you shingle?"

"You bet I can," I replied.

This set him off into a genuine ha-ha! which angered me. "It may be funny to you," I retorted, "but it isn't a bit funny to me. It means giving up all my work here." This sobered him. He ceased to laugh. "Let's discuss your situation," he said earnestly. "A man who can think and write as you have done should not be forced to shingle. I'll find something for you to do." He thought a moment. "I must get out circulars for my summer school at once, and you can help me on that. Then we will announce a class in American Literature conducted by Professor Garland. All you take in shall be yours. I don't believe shingling will be necessary this summer."

This offer argued a confidence in my ability and a warmth of friendship which lightened my dark outlook. Accepting this offer, I set to work upon the task he had put into my hand. I helped to write and mail his prospectus, and when he suggested that I announce a lecture of my own, I put before him one of the papers I had written on "The Art of Edwin Booth."

He liked this and put it on his schedule; and so I not only went into his catalogue as "Professor Garland" conducting a class in American Literature, but as a special lecturer at the close of the term. I was on the way to earn my living in Boston, a condition I had hitherto considered quite impossible.

On the Sunday following this most important interview with Brown I went again to dine with Dr. Cross and during the afternoon, as we were jogging around the shore of Jamaica Pond, he said, "My wife and daughter are going away in June, to be gone all summer. I shall be alone here. Why don't you come and stay with me during their absence? You need the change."

To many of my readers this will seem a trivial incident, but I assure them that it opened a shining vista to me. To escape from my sunless den in Boylston Place, to have three good meals each day, and to walk and ride about these beautiful, quiet streets was to be uplifted, translated. Coming in connection with Brown's offer, Dr. Cross' invitation changed my outlook on Boston and the future. I accepted but insisted that I should pay the cost of my keep—"I can't pay much, but I will not come for so long a time without paying something."

He smiled. "Very well. We'll agree that you are to pay five dollars per week when you can."

He offered me a room on the same floor with him, but I insisted on taking an unused attic room—a chamber with a sloping ceiling in which was a small bed, a desk, and a chair. "This is all I deserve at present."

II

One of the first to enroll in my American Literature class was a little lady from a suburb who had achieved the singular conviction that I was worthy of promotion. Her name was Payson and she deserves a high place in this chronicle, for she not only brought other pupils to me, she organized a series of four lectures to be given at her home in Hyde Park during August, the last month of Brown's summer term. For two weeks she went about among the most distinguished of her friends dragooning them into buying tickets. She levied with equal success upon her immediate neighbors; so that when I faced my first audience in her sitting room I was aware that Parker Pillsbury, the famous Abolitionist, Professor Churchill of Andover, and Professor Raymond of Princeton were sitting with several Boston editors among my auditors.

As I think back upon this venture, I wonder what my audience really thought of me, a bearded Westerner in a long frock coat and a Windsor tie, assailing their ears with strident voice. The room was crowded. Chairs jostled the foot of the little platform on which I stood and the air was so close that Mrs. Payson went about mopping her face with a handkerchief while her guests sweltered in most astonishing patience; but I was exalted far above the atmosphere!

My paper was on "Edwin Booth as Iago," and as I began my reading I observed almost under my stand a small, brown-bearded, pale-faced man of middle age who sat with bowed head, one hand shading the light from his eyes. He never once looked up at me and his bored attitude stimulated me to my very best expression.

At the close of my reading, this indifferent auditor came up to congratulate me, and Mrs. Payson introduced him to me as "Mr. Charles Hurd, literary editor of the *Transcript*." He surprised me and in a sense shocked me by treating me as an equal. "I am, myself, a Booth idolator," he said in a soft, rather hurried, utterance. "I would like to talk with you about your very original paper. Come in some afternoon and see me. My office is just opposite the spire of the Old South Church."

Others praised my lecture that night, but Hurd's brief comment was of more importance to me than all the others, for was he not a man of letters, a critic in close touch with the world of writers? One other comment of a differing sort lingered in my mind. I overheard Churchill of Andover say to my hostess, "He's a diamond in the rough," a fact which I myself dimly appreciated. I also felt that I was proving the prediction of my friend Bashford who had said, "You will find New England people sympathetic and helpful."

It remains to say that the other essays in this course were

equally successful and enabled me to pay Dr. Cross for my July board.

The thought of penetrating to the sanctum of a New England literary editor was highly exciting and as soon as I decently could I climbed the long three flights of stairs which led to Hurd's office on Washington Street. It was a tiny room, hardly larger than a closet, containing a tall desk, cluttered with books and papers, and one chair for a visitor—also burdened with books—not at all the kind of workshop I had expected to see; but the magic of the *Transcript's* high reputation transfigured it, made it the seat of power.

Hurd looked paler, smaller, and seedier than I had thought him. He wore a threadbare black coat and gray trousers, and was writing on a long sheet of orange-colored paper with a pen—no one used typewriters in those days—and I marveled at the beautiful regularity of his manuscript. Untidy, jumbled, and dirty as his surroundings were, his mind, as expressed on these yellow sheets of copy paper, was orderly, lucid, and graceful.

For lack of something better to say I asked, "Do you always use that colored paper?"

"Yes, I find it easier on my eyes," he replied and I realized why he had shielded his eyes from the light of the lamps on my reading desk at Mrs. Payson's. His poor eyes were overtaxed like his pen hand.

He was more than politely interested in me—that was evident. He asked me how I came to be in Boston; and I answered him without reservation in the conviction that he would prove not only another understanding friend but a helpful critic. In his small office I breathed a literary atmosphere, coming close to the making of books and the building of reputations—and as I reluctantly rose to go he said with sincere intonation, "Come and see me whenever you can. I am always here, but three in the afternoon is the best time for a chat."

Taking him at his word I called upon him thereafter as frequently as I dared, rejoicing in his companionship, for I found him a true lover of literature, one who lived and wrought in the presence of authorship. He showed me grateful letters from poets, young and old, and many volumes autographed to him by famous novelists. He knew all the young American writers and understood their aspirations. He had also a thorough knowledge of Scandinivaian language and literature, and could talk of Ibsen, Björnson, and other of the great figures of the North. To most of his acquaintances he was just another overburdened newspaper hack; but to me he was a fellow spirit as well as a teacher. There was something large and fine in his attitude. Tired as he was, sad and worried as he seemed, he was always quick to do a favor and sensitive to every youthful aspiration. I am glad to pay tribute to him as one of my most valuable friends at a time when I was in need of friends.

As autumn came on, new books came pouring in upon him. Each time I went in his face looked whiter, his eyes more bloodshot, and one day I said, "I'll review some of these books for you—if you'd like me to do so."

He thanked me warmly but added, "I can't pay anything, I wish I could."

Here again—if my readers are interested—is a partial answer to the question, "How did you get your start?" My meeting with Brown led to an acquaintance with Mrs. Payson, a devoted advocate, and my lecture at her house introduced me to Hurd; and my offer to review a book for Hurd led to an acquaintance with the editor of the *Transcript*, and a letter of introduction to the author of "The Minister's Charge."

It must have been in the early autumn that Hurd gave me this book to review (he was rather opposed to Howells) and so it chanced that I had been reading more than one of Howells' books, before I read "The Minister's Charge" as it appeared in the *Century Magazine*. I had been converted by it, and whatever Hurd thought of the book, he valued my review of it. He not only gave it a prominent position, printing it in larger type than the other reviews, but sent me a note saying, "Mr. Clement, the editor in chief, would like to see you when next you are in the building."

This message, coming close upon the excitement of seeing my essay in print, was profoundly disturbing. Did it mean that I was to be given a place on the paper? With wondering expectancy, I mounted to the chief's door. He was seated at a roll-top desk, busied with slips of proof. He nodded at me with noncommittal gravity, saying, "Take a seat," and went on with his work, while I studied him. He was a handsome man with white hair and mustache, a florid complexion and a pleasant glance.

Calling a messenger he turned over some papers to him, then turned to me and said, "That was a noble review of yours. You are quite right in your defense of Howells' methods. It is evident that you know his people, as I do."

He went on to speak of the judgment of the man at his club who professed to believe that Lemuel's relations with Statira Dudley and Amanda Grier were less innocent than Howells represented them. "Aldrich takes this view, but Howells knows American youth better than that. You

should meet Howells. I have sent your review to him, and
I'm going to give you a letter of introduction to him." He
interrupted himself, and mused a moment. "No, on the
whole you'd better not see him now. There is a fight being
made on him and your readers will say you have been influenced by him. He's very charming. You'd better do your
writing about him before you see him."

CHAPTER FOUR

BOSTON PAINTERS AND WRITERS

I

AMONG the interesting people whom I met at Mrs. Payson's house was a tall, red-bearded, bushy-haired man, named John Enneking, a landscape painter whose home was in Hyde Park and his studio in Boston. His friendly and jovial comment pleased me, and when he invited me to visit his studio I accepted, and a few days later sought him out.

The hour I spent with him that afternoon made many changes in my thinking. He took me into a strange new world, a world wherein men were wholly concerned with harmony of color and grace of line. For the first time in my life, I heard the language of the studios and breathed the odor of paint. As he exhibited his pictures he talked, incessantly but deliberately, commenting on each canvas with blunt candor. Some he commended heartily, speaking of his canvases as if they were the work of a friend, others he criticized with equal freedom, squinting at them with keen blue eyes. "This is all right as far as it goes, a good, direct slap-dash sketch, but it must be carried further. Now this is more what I'm trying to get—tone, depth, mystery."

It was a revelation of beauty to me. His studio was packed with portraits of New England's loveliest features, for he was a tremendous worker, a swift and powerful craftsman. Here was the land of my forbears. Here were

26

low, elm-defended mansions, with hills for background. Here were rocky sheep pastures with delicate lambs lying like pink flowers in the hollows of rocky ledges, half submerged in sea fog. Here, too, were rude water mills and colorful interiors of dusty barns and Colonial kitchens, all translated into something rich and fine by the artist's love and skill. There was a manly directness in his method and a naturalistic charm in his coloring which appealed to me more strongly than any other paintings I had ever seen. I apprehended in him something akin to Whittier and Lowell. His work was wholly American.

He talked of his predecessors, of the "Hudson River School," and of Winslow Homer and Inness, but he had a glowing enthusiasm for George Fuller. "Art has always had a hard time in America," he said. " 'No one buys an American picture,' the dealers say, and they're about right. We all have to teach or paint potboilers to make a living. I get along better than most of my fellows. I paint portraits of places, scenes people know and love, and put a price on them that people can pay. The average man likes to recognize something familiar in a painting."

He was a rugged, soil-encrusted philosopher, and notwithstanding a certain bungling of his words at times, he possessed the eloquence of truth. I could not follow his depreciatory remarks of certain of his pictures, but I understood the essential modesty underneath his candid confessions. One of the stories he told to illustrate the relations of colors remains in my mind.

"I had a preacher friend who used to come in here and talk theology, trying to convert me to his way of thinking. He interrupted my work and riled me so that I lost a half day's painting every time he came in. Finally one day I got tired of it and I said, 'What are you comin' in here for? You can't tell me what's true and what ain't. You don't know black from white.' This made him sit up. 'What do you mean by that?' he said. 'I'll show you what I mean,' I said. I was working on a sketch of an orchard in blossom and under it I had painted a goat. 'What color is that goat?' I asked. 'Why, it's black,' he said. 'All right,' I said, 'now you put your thumb over it and don't take it off till I tell you.' So he put his thumb over this goat and I slashed some paint all round his thumb. 'Now what color is it?' He took his thumb off it, stood a minute—then, 'You're the devil!' he said and fled. I haven't been bothered with him since." He chuckled at the memory of it.

Through him I came to know several other painters, among them William Halsall, who painted ships and mid-sea waves, Robert Vonnoh, a portrait painter, and Jerome Elwell, who wrought on imaginative themes like "Childe Roland to the dark tower came" with dragons stretching over leprous sand dunes, a handsome, slender, brown-haired young man with a love for literature. His fellow painters called his paintings illustrations. He interested me and we became friends. One of his Venetian scenes inspired me to write a verse upon it—I recall only a few of the lines:

"Like falling plover's lifted wing
The gay sails in the ominous air hang fluttering."

It was a very slight little poem, but Elwell was delighted with it. He asked for a copy of it and carried it about with him, a habit which gratified the author of the lines, however much the reading of them may have bored the other artists.

Another painter to whom Enneking introduced me and

who interested me exceedingly was a man named Collins, a smooth-faced, bright-eyed young fellow of commanding figure. He had a beautiful smile and a dimple in his chin, and as he worked or talked he smoked innumerable cigarettes, a habit I had not hitherto known. He was entirely French in his theories of art and in his habits, but he had been powerfully moved by Edward Bellamy's recently published romance, "Looking Backward," and we had many arguments concerning Socialism with which I had no sympathy. I was an individualist and a believer in Henry George's land-value tax.

In spite of our differences, I liked Collins, and it was at his house that I met George Pellew, a lover of Howells, who was to me an even stranger type. He was small, fair-skinned and red-lipped and parted his hair in the middle, but his brain was alive with vigorous ideas. He could not utter the letter "r" and this gave his speech a childish coloring. He said "wode" for rode and "sowwy" for sorry and yet he commanded respect, for he was a powerful and original thinker. I find among my notes of that day these lines, "Pellew is an amazing contradiction in terms. He looks and speaks like a lah-de-dah loafer, but he reasons like a philosopher. After this I shall distrust outside appearances."

Both these men captivated me and I often sought their company. Pellew was a valiant defender of Howells, and Collins was equally outspoken in his disgust with social conditions. I recall his saying with tragic accent, "As I came along the street I saw a man laying a gas main, and I said, 'What right have I to the enjoyment of good clothes and soft white hands whilst my fellow men are wallowing in mud and breathing the fumes of a broken gas pipe?'" a remark typical of the arguments voiced by the readers of

Bellamy's novel—arguments which did not impress those of us who had an exact scientific method of doing justice.

My association with these artists resulted in a complete change in my personal appearance. I secured a Van Dyke cut to my brown beard and wore a loosely knotted Windsor tie. I became a regular caller at studios and joined in their discussions. I entered into the technical problems which engaged painters and sympathized with their resentments.

They were all strugglers. Some taught drawing, some painted portraits, others lived on borrowed money. It was a discouraging period in American art. Like fiction and poetry, painting was in process of change.

A new technique in the use of color was being developed and I heard much violent criticism of the "Old Hat" schools of Munich, of "landscapes done in brown gravy," of "mud" —"Oh, the Munich kind of thing!" was a frequent scornful remark. All the younger men fresh from Paris were open-air painters at war with "the bitumen school" who had studied in Germany and Holland, a war which I enjoyed without fully understanding its significance. Enneking's position was midway. He was an open-air painter but not an imitation Monet.

In calling on Dennis Bunker, a powerful young artist of a type not unlike Collins, I heard him say to Enneking, "I'm in a hole. I don't know how I shall come out but I show no more canvases till I have solved my problem."

His seriousness convinced me that his struggle was as real as mine, although I could not understand it. A little later Lilla Cabot Perry, one of Bunker's friends, brought back from Paris a group of vivid canvases by a man named Breck and so widened the influence of the new school.

If I am not mistaken I was taken to her house by Pellew,

but however it came about, I recall seeing the paintings set on the floor and propped against the wall, each with its flare of primitive colors—reds, blues, and yellows, presenting "Impressionism," the latest word from Paris. They were un-American in subject as in treatment, and while they interested me, I held to my opinion that Enneking was the sounder artist, and I am certain that I would think so still although Enneking has been surpassed and subordinated by many of our later men.

My preparation for the acceptance of the blue and purple shadows of impressionism was singular in that it was scientific, for in a chapter on Architecture by Herbert Spencer I had happened upon a description of blue shadows on a marble building, and a discussion as to their probable cause. Furthermore I was a man of the outdoors. I had seen the blue shadows on snow when lit by the morning sun and it was easy for me to see lavender shadows on the sidewalk or on the beach.

This exhibition opened the campaign for Monet, Sisley, Pizarro, and other of the European painters who had sternly banished black and brown from their palettes, claiming that all the effects of nature could be obtained by the use of red, blue, and yellow pigment, a claim which rested on the scientific constitution of light.

Bunker died soon after, and when his paintings were exhibited, I understood something of the struggle which he had undergone in changing from "the school of mud" to the school of the open air, and the use of primary colors. In fact I began to write and to lecture on impressionism, a service which carried me ever deeper into the camp of the young revolutionaries. I retained, however, my admiration for the naturalistic art of those who granted the blue shadows and went calmly on completing a noble transcript of New England's hills, orchards, and streams.

II

Meanwhile, in carrying on a fight for truth in American fiction, I had adapted Veritism as the word which best described my theory, a word which I gained from reading Eugène Véron's "Esthetics" and Max Nordau's savage "Conventional Lies." Howells was the leader in the school of writers whose work was verifiable, and all the romantic novelists and their admirers had risen in bitter and vociferous opposition. It was a lively contest, and being strong for native art, I naturally took a fist in it.

This brings me back to Charles Hurd, for in his gentle way he influenced me more than any other of my acquaintances at this time. Through him I met Edgar Chamberlin, who conducted a column in the *Transcript* called "The Listener."

Though a hard-working journalist, Chamberlin was a loyal lover of nature, and spent every holiday in the country. He was a short man with brown hair and close-clipped mustache, low-spoken, thoughtful, and gentle. Despite his modest manner he was a determined individualist and had little patience with any socialistic scheme.

He came to hear me make my first speech on the Single Tax and filled his column in the *Transcript* next day with kindly criticism of my arraignment of our land system, a blaze of publicity which rather terrified me. In a letter to him I complained a bit of his stressing the poetry of my address rather than its logic, ending by saying, "We shall meet—at Philippi."

To this he responded: "I had a serious misgiving yesterday lest my account of the meeting might have wounded you; but I feel now that even if it did wound you, you have forgiven me. I was impressed with the meeting and wanted to tell the story of it and couldn't really describe it except as it appeared to me. As to the meeting at Philippi, I shall be glad to have it take place as soon as practicable. I am no good at an argument. I expect to be beaten."

This meeting took place in his home at West Medford, where I met Mary E. Wilkins, Bradford Torrey, Gertrude and Minna Smith, and a number of other young writers, a jolly and informal company. Chamberlin and his wife were ideal hosts and had the one open fire known to me and I recall that as we all sat about the hearth on this night, Mary Wilkins told ghost stories in the light of it, and my admiration of her grew with acquaintance. She was a fair, small, blue-eyed girl at this time, just beginning her work as a short-story writer. She was quiet, almost shy in the presence of strangers, but in Chamberlin's home she was ready, in her low-voiced way, to do her share of the entertainment.

In spite of my plaid Windsor tie and frock coat I think Chamberlin's friends liked me, and when I learned that he had spent his boyhood in Wisconsin and was filled with poetic recollections of it, I sought him out whenever possible, and often went walking with him. I read his column with care and valued his comment for its quiet depth of feeling. To the readers of the *Transcript* he was only an essayist, but to me he was a thinker of unusual powers, tenacious yet reasonable. With him I discussed American fiction and drama with greater freedom than with any other man. He was less remote, less of the desk than Hurd, with whom I never quite reached the same sense of comradeship.

Miss Wilkins was a charming talker, humorous in her

laconic way, but her succinct, low-voiced comment was often lost in the joyous clamor of less important voices. Boston was just becoming aware of her rare quality and *Harper's Magazine* was printing her stories almost month by month. Her success, although marvelous in my eyes, aroused no envy. We had only admiration for her artless art.

Her home was in the suburban village of Randolph and I recall visiting her in a small white Colonial cottage, exactly appropriate to her. Her home might have been used as a typical illustration for her stories, and the supper which her companion served me was equally in character. Its cakes and pies, its hot biscuits and jam were exactly right. I felt large and rude like that man in one of her tales, who came into the well-ordered sitting room of his sweetheart with such clumsy haste that he overturned her workbasket and sat down on the cat. That she was taking my measure at the same time that I was taking hers was certain. Her keen glance was almost as intimidating as that of Howells. As a student of minute forms of conduct, she had no superior. The amazing part of her genius lay in her ability to see the near-by life of her neighborhood in artistic perspective. In her ability to characterize elderly folk she had no superior.

In a letter to her I put certain questions concerning her work which drew forth this highly significant confession: "Yes, I *do* consider that I am writing about the New England of the present day and the dialect is that which is daily in my ears. I have, however, a fancy that my characters belong to a present that is rapidly becoming *past* and that a few generations will cause them to disappear. Still this may be only a fancy."

Her only competitor in the New England short-story field was Sarah Orne Jewett, a graceful figure in Boston society.

I read her stories, but I never met her. In fact I only saw her once at a public meeting. Her work was related to the school in which Mary Wilkins was an exemplar but she was more adroitly literary. There was a little more of the summer visitor in her stories of the New England villages which she celebrated. I greatly admired her work and once wrote to her to say so.

I received the following reply:

"I thank you for your letter and am much interested in what you say. I have often wondered why we read realistic sketches with such delight, when the scene is laid in foreign countries, and are apt to find equally truthful and truly artistic sketches of our own neighborhood a trifle dull. But perhaps I do wrong in insisting that we are always as artistic in our work as our foreign neighbors. It is not the accuracy of the likeness but the artistic quality of the work that does count and should count most.

"Octave Thanet's and Mrs. Cooke's and Mr. Chase-Wymans' and Miss Wilkins' stories are so much better than all but the very best of Russian and French stories.

"I listen to all that you say of the dark and troubled side of New England life. Mrs. Cooke has felt that and written it, but her Connecticut people are different from those I have known and thought most about. It is a harder fight with nature for the most part, and there were not such theologians in the old days here as in that part of New England. Yet the types of humanity are the same varied by the surroundings. I am often struck by the fact that the old-fashioned people here have small vocabularies and are sure to say least when they feel most."

There were others in this Boston group of writers who wrote occasional sketches with the color of New England in them, and so related themselves to the local-color movement in the South where Thomas Nelson Page was doing for Virginia something like the same work that Harris was doing for Georgia and Cable for Louisiana, a work in which Bret Harte and Joaquin Miller were leaders for the Coast. The importance of this local-color fiction increased with every month, for Gilder in the *Century* and Alden in *Harper's* welcomed it and encouraged it.

The reader will begin to understand how helpful Hurd, Chamberlin, and Enneking were in extending my knowledge of artists and writers, but it is only fair to say that I was spending from ten to twelve hours of each day in the library reading in preparation for my classes in literature. Furthermore, I had begun to write a book to be called "The Evolution of American Ideals," a sufficiently inclusive subject, you will say, which had been suggested by the writings of Herbert Spencer, De Tocqueville, and Walt Whitman. It was based on my reading but its philosophy was derivative.

III

My first attempt at story writing was highly sensational —at least in title. I called it "Ten Years Dead." It was a short story, a very short story—so short that it hardly got under motion before it stopped. I suspect it stopped because my invention gave out, but it is all so long ago that I had but a dim recollection of it as I was writing "A Son of the Middle Border."

Though so sensational of title it was studiedly veritistic. I met the man who had been ten years dead in the Boston Public Library—I mean that is the way the tale opened; and the calm current of the narrative was in careful contrast with the theme, which was the return to familiar scenes of a man who had in some singular fashion been as one dead for a space of ten years.

It was published by a Boston weekly periodical, and I don't remember being paid for it though perhaps I did receive a five-dollar check. It was a column or two in length, perhaps about fifteen or eighteen hundred words, and was written about 1885. I hope nobody will look it up, for it was a very boyish performance. I was only fumbling around with material. Some of my verse of this time I am still able to read in public, but that story would seem comical if not disconcerting to me now.

It comes to me dimly that it was a dream story; that is to say, the theme came to me in a dream. It was after Hawthorne—a long way after—and I only mention it now because it really was my first attempt and I can not tell a lie; that is to say, I consider it more interesting to tell the truth about it.

Meanwhile, more important still (as it afterwards proved), I had begun to do a little in the way of Western local color. One evening in November while at work in my attic in the home of Dr. Cross just at dusk, I heard the ring of a scoop shovel in the alley under my window (it was a truckman unloading a ton of coal) and this sound, combined with the moan of the wind in the elm trees over the roof, put me back into the gloom of an autumn sunset on an Iowa farm. Instantly I was shoveling corn from a wagon box into the crib at the close of a day's husking in a broad, bleak field.

Thinking back into those desolate days, I experienced a singular desire to relive them, painful as they had been, and as I could not do so in reality, I was inspired to do so in imagination. I began at once an article descriptive of Western corn-husking, in the belief that no such word-picture had ever been made.

At the end of the sketch, which contained some four or five thousand words, I began to reflect on its value. I had read many poems and stories of New York and New England in which the husking bee was a charming social frolic, but no one, so far as I knew, had ever described the stern and solitary task of harvesting corn in the prairie West. With something of the spirit of the historian as well as the pioneer, I revised my article, making it still more exact, and finally sent it to the editor of the *New American Magazine*. I can not recall just why I selected this magazine, but it may have been because it was making a brave attempt at being American, or it may be that I lacked the courage to try the *Century*. Whatever my reasons may have been, I was surprised and heartened by a letter of acceptance from the editor, William Wyckoff, who not only praised the truth and novelty of the essay but urged me to keep on. "I am a native of a corn-growing community, and I recognize the truth of your picture," he wrote.

He apologized for not being able to pay promptly or adequately, but that did not destroy the value of his letter, which had an inspiring effect. It confirmed me in my historic mood. "Why don't you take up other phases of your life on the prairie?" he suggested a little later, and this I did. During the winter I wrote some six articles dealing with haying, wheat-harvesting, threshing, winter sports, and the like.

Wyckoff wished to use all of them, but as he could not pay for them, and as his magazine seemed in danger of retirement, I sent some of the remaining ones elsewhere.

Even when accepted they brought me only a few dollars, but that did not greatly dishearten me. It was a keen satisfaction to see them in print.

With no confidence in the value of my writing, I kept to my teaching, which enabled me to pay my board at Dr. Cross' kindly home. I clung to my attic room with desperate zeal.

At about this time I wrote a long poem, "Lost in a Norther," for which John Foord, editor of *Harper's Weekly*, paid me twenty-five dollars, a marvelous evidence of power. I was feeling my way toward a delineation of life in Iowa and Dakota, a field in which I had no predecessor.

IV

The *Atlantic Monthly* and Houghton & Mifflin's publishing business occupied an ancient three- or four-story house on Park Street near the corner of Beacon, and I never went by it without a feeling of awe. This feeling is rather comical to me now, for it was not an imposing building and the offices were far from luxurious; nevertheless it was rich with memories of Emerson, Holmes, Howells, and many other great personalities. I recall two visits to this famous house, once to see Thomas Bailey Aldrich, and again to have a word with Frank Garrison, who was connected with the book-publishing department. My errand to Aldrich was the result of a highly ambitious plan. After finishing four of my studies of "Edwin Booth as a Master of Expression," I had sent them to the *Atlantic Monthly* in the hope that the editor would find them worthy, and I had received a brief note from Aldrich requesting me to call at his office. I entered his room in great expectation yet humbly, for to me he was a prince in the literary hierarchy of New England. I knew his poetry as well as his prose and admired its graceful lightness.

He was standing as I entered and received me with cold aloofness but gave me a chair. His office was a square room which seemed very large and very luxurious to me, quite in keeping with his position. He was a man of middle size with dark hair and long mustaches the ends of which were waxed. He was courteous but curiously restless. As he talked he walked back and forth across the room, scarcely looking at me. Fastidiously clothed and barbered he looked almost the beau from my point of view and I felt that he had a rather poor opinion of me, due to my speech as much as to my unfashionable coat and tie. As he went on I perceived something antagonistic in his attitude. After tepidly praising my article, he began to criticize it and to point out this or that mistake, faults due to the fact that I did not know the great actor. He explained that my studies were not available, and then let the cat out of the bag by saying, "Booth is my friend and neighbor. I have known him for many years, and I have already written something about him which I intend to use in the magazine."

This ended the session for me. I went away with the boyish belief that this great editor was trying to keep my articles from being published, an absurd concept on my part, for my articles had no literary quality, they were valuable only for their observation. Young and aspiring authors get such notions of their elders and betters.

I saw Aldrich afterwards only in public places. His articles on Booth never came under my eyes and so far as I know he was never aware of my later work. The last time I saw him was at the Players. He was gray and rather fat, and was sitting alone waiting for a friend who had agreed to take him to the theater to see his poetic drama Judith produced. I did not speak to him and he, of course, did not recognize me. He had largely outlived his fame and no one in the club seemed to know or to care who he was. To this complexion must we all come—if we persist long enough!

CHAPTER FIVE

LOWELL, INGERSOLL, AND BOOTH

I

ONE of my most admired authors at this time (1886) was James Russell Lowell, whose literary essays had vastly stimulated me. His poetry, other than his dialect verses, had never appealed to me—I found it rather cold and formal —but he was a great figure in Boston, and as ambassador to Great Britain had won high place in the estimation of the English. Therefore I read with joyous anticipation the announcement that he was at home and had promised to deliver a course of lectures at the Lowell Institute, although his subject, "The British Dramatists," was not of vital interest to me.

These addresses were for the public, and on the opening night of the series I was in my seat eager to hear and to see the great writer and honored diplomat. The hall was completely filled and among the auditors were many distinguished citizens who had gathered to do him honor.

As he came on the platform I was shocked to find him an old man with a long, gray beard and a sadly ashen complexion. He moved stiffly, almost painfully, to his desk, opened a thick bundle of manuscript, shuffled the pages about, and began to read.

His voice was feeble, and his accent, to my thinking,

un-American. Bending low over his paper and peering closely at it as though the light were poor or his glasses dim, he went monotonously on in a mumbling rumble, a disappointment to us all. Being directly before him I should have heard every word of his essay, but I did not. I heard only snatches of it. I was troubled also by the masklike immobility of his countenance. Only his lips moved. The muscles of his face appeared atrophied. His cheeks were as rigid as those of a Japanese mask. Furthermore he took very little account of his audience, but appeared to be talking to himself—or to the people in the front now. As most of his auditors were unable to follow him, they slipped out by twos and threes, and when he closed his lecture less than half of his audience remained. As an orator he had drearily failed.

All this was sadly shocking to me. I went away musing on the chasm between the shining, confident James Russell Lowell of my imagination and the mumbling graybeard of the platform. The second lecture was a still more depressing attempt. The hall was only half filled at the beginning, and most of those present withdrew after a few minutes of silent resentment. Only a handful of the faithful remained to the end.

This ended it for me. I attended no more of the talks, but I heard that the course was a complete failure. The truth was none of his hearers were greatly interested in his subject and on finding themselves unable to follow his words, took little joy in watching him plod painfully through his manuscript. Had he spoken of the English authors he had known, or characterized the leaders in English politics at that time, we might all have stayed to the end. However, these were the topics he avoided, and it was in reporting some of his remarks concerning the court that Julian Hawthorne drew upon himself an undeserved reproof.

I never saw Lowell again. He lived several years longer, and in private life continued to hold the admiration of Howells and other of his friends, but so far as I know, he never attempted another course of lectures.

II

Lowell's direct opposite in every way was Robert Ingersoll, whom I heard at about the same date. My interest in Ingersoll had begun when, as a lad of sixteen, I read some of his speeches, but I had never been able to hear him speak. Now that he was announced to lecture at the Boston Theater on "Myths and Mythmakers" I had my chance. I decided that one of my precious dollars should purchase a seat. Like Booth, he was a part of my education in oratory, and so, with nearly three thousand other enthusiasts, I found my way to the theater one Sunday evening, tensely expectant of a marvelous address, but with only the vaguest notion of the orator's personal appearance.

He came on the vast stage alone, as I recall the scene, a large man in evening dress, quite bald and smoothly shaven. He began to speak almost before he left the wings, addressing himself to us with colloquial, unaffected directness. I say "to us," for that was precisely the effect he produced. He appeared to be speaking to each one of us individually. His tone was confidential, friendly, and yet authoritative. "Do you know," he began, "that every race has created all its gods and all its devils? The childhood of the race put fairies in the breeze and a kobold in the stream. Every religion began in exactly the same way."

These were not his exact words, of course, but such was

the manner of his beginning. The stage was bare and he had no manuscript. Standing with his hands clasped behind his back, and speaking without effort, he made his words clear to every auditor. I was not especially concerned with his religious antagonism, but I enjoyed the beauty of his phrasing and the almost unequaled magic of his voice. He was a master of colloquial speech. Unlike Lowell, he eyed us, and laughed at us and with us. He bantered us, challenged us, electrified us. At times his eloquence held us silent as images and then some witty turn, some humorous phrase, brought roars of applause. At times we cheered almost every sentence like delegates at a political convention. At other moments we rose in our seats and yelled. There was something hypnotic in his rhythm as well as in his phrasing. Now and again he became the poet, chanting his marvelous lines like a Saxon minstrel. His power over his auditors was absolute. His voice had no melody such as that of Booth possessed, but he had the singular power of making me oblivious of its quality. In the march of his ideas, in the pictures he drew, I forgot his bald head and his husky voice. As he spoke, all barriers between his mind and mine vanished. His effect on his hearers was magical, but the magic lay in his choice of words, rather than in beautiful enunciation.

As I studied him I came to the conclusion that a large part of his power lay in the fact that he vitalized every word, every syllable. He thought each sentence out at the moment he gave it utterance. He was alive to the tip of his tongue. He did not permit his organs of speech to proceed mechanically. He remained in control.

After more than forty years, I can still repeat some of his lines which I have arranged as verse:

"Strike with the hand of fire, O weird musician, thy harp
Strung with Apollo's golden hair:
Blow, Bugler, blow till thy exalted notes
Do touch and kiss the moonlit waves
And startle the lovers wandering amid the vine-clad hills.
Fill the vast cathedral aisles with thy sweet symphonies
Hushed and dim, deft toucher of the organ's keys:
But know, thy sweetest music,
All is discord compared to childhood's happy laugh,
The laugh which fills the eyes with light
And the very heart with joy.

Oh, rippling river of laughter, thou
Art the blessed boundary line
Betwixt the beasts and men
And every wayward wave of thine
Doth drown some fretful fiend of care."

He taught me the value of speaking as if thinking out
loud. After hearing him, the harsh, monotonous cadences
of other orators became a weariness.

For two hours I listened, rapt with interest, and when I
went away I had no regret for my dollar, a condition of
mind very like that with which I always left the theater
after seeing Edwin Booth. I was content. I had heard
Robert Ingersoll, our greatest orator, as Edwin Booth was
our greatest actor.

The fame of an orator, like that of an actor, rests largely
on the testimony of those who heard him and I gladly bear
witness to the reality of Ingersoll's marvelous eloquence.

As I studied his printed addresses I found them filled
with passages of singular beauty, lines of true poetry. His
so-called "infidelity" meant less to me than to many others
of his auditors, for I was a student of Spencer and Darwin,

but his skill as a phrase maker satisfied my sense of form. As I go over them to-day I find them as I remember them, well written and vibrant. Only last summer I read one of them to an audience of young people of literary training, and its English, crisp and clear and vital as when I first heard it more than forty years ago, aroused the applause of my auditors.

Although I heard him speak six or eight times, I grew rather slowly to a full understanding of his method. First of all came his fearless humor. It is this quality which made his "Mistakes of Moses" irresistible even to his opponents. I recall his roguish look when after he had computed that in order to produce a flood which would cover the tops of the mountains in the space of forty days and forty nights, it would be necessary to have something like ten feet of rain per hour, he suddenly asked, "How is that for dampness?" He was not merely humorous; he was witty. He had an Irishman's ability to answer on the spot.

The second source of his power was his naturalness, his colloquial tone, and his informal manner. He ignored oratorical conventions. He had something to say and he said it as directly as possible. He had small use for a chairman. I once saw him enter the theater alone and it gave me a feeling of surprise, almost a shock, to see him thus unattended. He walked into the vestibule as quietly and as inconspicuously as any of his auditors.

My only personal meeting with him came some years later, when as a member of a committee I went to his office in a downtown New York block, to ask him to speak at a meeting. He was kindly but a little remote and preoccupied. He was older and whiter than when I had last heard him speak and his hair was thinner, but his eyes were undimmed, and his smile winning. He denied our request, but did so with such a kindly tone that we went away without resentment.

III

In spite of my admiration of Ingersoll, Beecher, and other great orators, Edwin Booth remained my chief exemplar of noble speech. Whenever he came to Boston I went again and again to see him and especially to hear him, for certain of his readings in Macbeth and Hamlet had a subtlety of intonation which meant more to me than any other music. I noted down and analyzed his gestures and his inflections, with intent to use them some time in print. I made especial study of his greatest rôles—Iago, Macbeth, Hamlet, and Lear—and during his second season I went so far as to mail to him one of my studies (the one on Macbeth) with a letter which informed him that I was writing a book upon him as an interpreter of Shakespeare. I did this in a mood of exaltation which soon passed, leaving me scared and humble.

A few days later the manuscript came back, redolent with tobacco smoke and showing signs of having been carefully read. With it was a letter in Booth's own hand thanking me for my interest:

"I am very 'poor in thanks' and know not how to express the gratification which your mention of those seldom noticed effects of tone, eye, and gesture have given me. It is more encouraging to know that such delicate lights and shades are appreciated and not wasted (as I have often feared they were) than in loudest applause bestowed on the bolder effects of one's art work. But as this seems to come too near the praising of myself, I will say no more than that I thank you sincerely for the pleasure you have given me in the knowledge that the more careful part of my labor is not lost."

Emboldened by this letter, I wrote him again:

"I saw your magnificent presentation of Macbeth last Saturday and it was one of the greatest artistic successes anybody ever made. It was absolutely above criticism.

"I saw you during the week in Hamlet and as Brutus, in which you played easily. I take it you could not stand the strain of playing each time as you did Saturday evening. I shall have little to change in my study of your Macbeth. It seems to me I got at its core, but I would like to ask you what you conceive Macbeth's motives to be when he returns from the chamber of the king with Lennox, saying, 'Had I but died an hour—' etc. I observe you use a low, strained, dispirited tone, a little tremulous as if constraint was laid upon it, as if the speaker wavered between two emotions or more—(How clumsy and inadequate words are in attempting to describe these subtleties of the voice!) I cannot get a firm hold upon that reading.

"Again, what do you conceive Iago's mind toward Desdemona to be when he leans over her in illy-assumed sympathy during her long speech? I note you stand with calm countenance, expressing little, the habitual noncommittal face of Iago, but with a keen, watchful eye fixed a trifle obliquely down upon her.

"You may remember my somewhat elaborate study of your Iago. I think I caught the leading phases of the presentations, but one or two places like this I am not decided upon. Whether Iago really loved, in his measure, Desdemona or whether he readily acceded to Othello's determination to kill her as well as Cassio, is still debatable with me. I am not quite sure how much genuine entreaty you mean to express in the line, 'Let her live, I beseech you.' 'But let her live' is the exact line; if my memory serves, you use the additional words, 'I beseech you.'

"If you can find time I should like to have you write me of these points."

To this he replied:

"It is highly gratifying to know that the delicate touches by which I endeavor to illustrate my rendering of Shakespeare's text are not made in vain. They must escape the notice of many, even close observers, and only sympathetic eyes and ears can detect and appreciate the value of a glance or tone. All that I dare say in regard to your admirable essays on my performances of Iago and Macbeth is—I thank you. This is but scant encouragement, but the subject is of so delicate a nature that it would seem like self-praise to say more. If I may suggest an alteration, it is the word *couch* for *floor*, where Othello shrinks from his base suggestion to Iago, 'set on thy wife to observe,' etc. Also I do not like the action of tapping his heels in your description of Iago. I must correct that fault. In Macbeth I shudder at the wine offered me by the murderer in the banquet scene, as though its color suggested blood and I make the eight kings wear 'gory locks' as well as gold crowns, the former to remind Macbeth of Banquo's ghost, not the latter, which Banquo never wore. 'Thy (bloody) crown doth sear mine eyeballs,' etc. All the apparitions similarly marked with bloody hair recall the blood-battered Banquo 'with twenty trenched gashes on his head' who at last appears and points at them for his 'line of kings.' I think this passage has bothered the Shakespeare critics somewhat. This explanation may be a poor thing, but ' 'tis mine own' and is submitted for what ' 'tis worth.' "

Surely I had a right to be proud of this letter, whose every word I studied as with a mental microscope, finding in its careful phrasing ample justification for all the labor I had put into my lecture. That he regarded me as a professor of standing and assurance was evident, and at the moment I felt myself to be, at least, a conscientious observer and student.

Reëxalted as I was by this letter from my revered instructor, I had no slightest hope of ever meeting him, but the unexpected often happened to me in those days, and when one morning I read that the veteran actor, James E. Murdoch, was to read at a hall on Park Street, and that Edwin Booth and Lawrence Barrett, as old friends of the reader, were to be there, I hastened to buy a ticket, no matter what the cost.

The hall was small and I was sure that I should glimpse the great tragedian somewhere in the audience. Perhaps he would sit on the platform with the speaker. I knew Murdoch only as the man who first recited "Sheridan's Ride" to an audience, and while I was interested in him, I would not have paid a dollar to hear him read.

Being early at the hall I got a seat near the middle of the center aisle and facing the door so that I could watch the notables as they entered. As the hour came and Mr. Booth had not yet appeared some of my neighbors openly doubted his intention of coming, and it did seem quite impossible that the most illustrious actor of his time should fill a seat in this small audience, select as it undoubtedly was.

Murdoch and his sponsor seemed troubled, and, after waiting a little beyond the hour, the reading began. The veteran actor was gray and dignified, a tall, handsome man who read sonorously and with taste, but none of us really listened; we were all watching the door at the side, hoping to see Edwin Booth.

"There he is!" some one said. Murdoch paused, a soft hand-clapping and murmur arose, and Lawrence Barrett, a bit pompous in bearing, appeared followed by a smaller man with beautiful, downcast head, a shy, almost timid man, negligently clothed—Edwin Booth!

No one could have been less like Richelieu, or Macbeth, or Iago. He tiptoed down the aisle like an embarrassed girl, apologizing in every motion for such a belated and spectacular entrance. He ignored all the applause, all the greetings of his friends, and sank into his seat with such evident relief that those who knew him smiled. So far from being on the platform he was several rows back of where I sat and I could not see him after he was in place.

It was to me a very strange fact that this man adored by thousands, who had addressed millions of his fellow citizens from behind the footlights, should be so shy when confronting a few hundred worshipful spectators many of whom were his personal friends, but this was the impression he made upon me at the time.

In a little notebook formed of soft paper and sewed with a black thread, I find the record made that day of this great event. I quote it to show how accurate my memory is:

"Mr. Booth came into the room as unobtrusively as possible, looking a little embarrassed, tiptoed down to his seat and slipped into it hurriedly. Only a few saw him enter. I spoke with him after the reading. His hair is quite gray and flung gracefully back from his fine, high forehead, under which glow his wonderful eyes. He does not look old in the face and there is a gentleness in it which is Hamlet. His dress is simple, almost poor, and his necktie was the most commonplace.

"But his marvelous eyes! You think of nothing else as you look at him. They are said to be like the eyes of Nathaniel Hawthorne, and are his most remarkable feature. He has a long and very flexible upper lip, and his nose is straight and cleanly cut. His voice is gentle and unassertive, full of the same rich tones he uses on the stage. Save for his beautiful face and the dignity and sweetness of his manner no one would know that he was a great actor earning several thousand dollars each night. No man could be more unobtrusive and natural. You can understand Mr. Barrett's face and voice, but the face of Mr. Booth baffles scrutiny. There is a depth, a shadow there which none other of our actors possess."

At the close of the reading, many of his friends gathered about him where he stood and with a courage for which I cannot account, I approached Mr. Barrett and told him that I was the author of the lecture on Macbeth.

Plucking Mr. Booth by the sleeve he said, "Edwin, this is Mr. Garland, who wrote that valuable paper on your work."

I had no awe of Barrett, but when Booth turned his beautiful dark eyes upon me, my tongue failed me utterly. Never had I looked into such eyes or upon a gentler, more sensitive face.

He smiled with kindly interest, murmured his thanks for the minute and authentic record I had made of his methods, and then another idolator intervening, he turned away and I went away down the stairs and across the Common, ennobled by his praise and his thanks.

The last time I saw him play Macbeth was in the Boston Theater and it was one of the most moving of all my youthful experiences. Through his courtesy I had a seat in the orchestra and every subtle shadow of his face was visible to me. Never before had I been so near, never had I looked upon him at such an angle. An enormous audience filled the theater, applauding madly, but he seemed aware only of his fair young daughter, Edwina, who sat in a lower box at the right of the stage, and when called again and again before the curtain, he ended each appearance by bowing to her while she clapped her small hands in adoration. His voice that night was more beautiful, more profoundly melancholy than ever before, and when he read those majestic lines, "My way of life is fallen into the sere, the yellow leaf," he uttered them as if they were a prophecy of his own approaching death.

I had been told by those who knew him that he had gone beyond any desire for money or applause, and as I studied him that night, I could well believe it. Like Macbeth he seemed a-weary of the world, interested only in that slender young girl in the box, and this thought running beneath his conception of Macbeth gave to his performance a poignant quality which has never left me. He voiced the Macbeth of the text, the troubled dreamer, the poet who had been forced by circumstances into a life of warfare and murder. His eyes were dark as midnight, and his voice like liquid topaz.

Long afterward, I came to know that daughter, when she was a gentle, elderly lady and I a man of graying hair. I could not relate her to that radiant young princess of the stage box, but I was still the loyal worshiper at the shrine of her noble father, Edwin Booth.

CHAPTER SIX

MEETINGS WITH HOWELLS

I

DURING the summer of 1885 Howells became the subject of much literary gossip. It was reported that he had gone over to Harper's and that all his work was to appear under their imprint. The newspapers also announced that he was to write regularly for a department of *Harper's Magazine* called "The Editor's Study," discussing any book or subject which interested him.

He was recognized as the chief American realist. His "Modern Instance," "Indian Summer," "The Minister's Charge," and "Silas Lapham" were valued as the most original and highly skilled pieces of writing America had known. They were being read aloud in thousands of home circles, and clubs and social gatherings rang with argument as to whether or not his women characters could be found in New England society. It was agreed that his men existed, but their wives and daughters were woeful exaggerations— according to his critics. To use a good old phrase, his method and works created a "regular katouse" in Boston and vicinity, as I well knew, for it echoed in my classes and raged in every home I knew.

This attack and defense of the great novelist gave me a livelier sense of his power than before and increased my desire to see what manner of man he was. I had Clement's assurance that he was charming, but this newspaper din cre-

ated in my mind a wholly different conception. His opponents, who probably had never seen him, represented him as
a ruthless, intellectually arrogant, and destructive critic, a
personality hard to reconcile with his delightfully humorous
and graceful writing. That he was the chief figure in American literature was indisputable even by those who disliked his
fiction. His influence on the American reader as well as upon
the American critic was very great.

All this was implied in Clement's remark that a fight was
being made on him, and it was not until October that I
raised my courage to the point of setting forth in search of
him. He was reported to be spending the autumn in Auburn-
dale, a near-by suburb, and early one afternoon I boarded
a train in greater excitement than I had known since coming
East. There was a wide difference between calling on a
minister who wrote stories, like Dr. Edward Everett Hale, or
a hard-working literary editor, like Hurd, and a man who
was not only admittedly a great novelist but the most talked-
about critic in all America. His utterances on the side of
the realists had made him hated as well as loved.

It is probable that no young writer of to-day could feel
for any author the same awe, the same boyish worship
which filled my heart and weakened my knees as I inquired
the way to the hotel where Howells was staying. I fervently
hoped that the hotel would not be too magnificent, too
intimidating, for I had felt very small and very shabby
at the start, and every rod of my advance sensibly decreased
the little fund of self-confidence with which Clement's letter had endowed me. My knowledge of what was fashionable was rudimentary, but I knew my coat was seedy and
my Western hat spectacular; nevertheless, I kept on with a
feeling that I could turn back at any time.

As I came opposite the entrance of the hotel grounds, I entered a state of panic, for the towering portico of "The Elms" made it appear a palace for millionaires. In saying that my resolution almost entirely failed me, I am not exaggerating for literary purposes. I did in simple truth walk past the gate twice before I found heart to turn and enter. What an entirely unwarrantable and presumptuous act it was—this call on a great author! What excuse had I for intruding on his time? It was too late to retreat, however, and so, outwardly at ease, I marched sternly up the graveled walk.

Entering the wide central hall, I advanced warily across the rugs on its polished floor to the desk behind which stood a highly ornate and haughty clerk, and asked in a husky voice, "Is Mr. Howells in?"

"He is, but he is at luncheon," the young despot on the other side of the counter coldly replied, and his tone expressed the opinion that Mr. Howells would not relish being disturbed by a seedy individual wearing a Prince Albert frock coat, a plaid Windsor tie, and a broad-brimmed hat, one who did not even know the proper hour for an afternoon call. In fact I didn't. I thought everybody lunched between twelve and one o'clock.

However, my Western blood was aroused. Producing my letter of introduction I said, "You send this in to Mr. Howells and let him make the decision about seeing me."

The clerk quailed, not through fear of me, but out of respect for the *Transcript* envelope. The colored porter who took my letter in to the dining room soon returned with the information that Mr. Howells would be out in a few minutes. "You are to wait," he said, and led the way to a small and very formal room near the front of the building.

For several minutes I waited, sitting on the edge of a fringed and gilded chair, with my eyes on the portières, vainly trying to swallow a frog in my throat. I do not believe I could have uttered a word at the moment. "How will he receive me? What will he look like? What shall I say to him?" I asked myself, without another coherent phrase in my head. My visit seemed, at the moment, wholly unauthorized. All this may appear very old-fashioned and romantic to the present-day student, but so it was that day with me.

A light step reached my ears. I rose. The curtain parted and a short man with a handsome head stood before me. His face was impassive but his glance one of the most piercing I had ever encountered. In that single instant, before he smiled, he discovered my character, divined my state of mind, and probably inventoried my clothing. It was the glance of a student of men, of the author of "Silas Lapham."

His appraising scrutiny took but a second's time. Then his face softened and he smiled winningly. "I am glad to see you," he said, and his tone convinced me of his sincerity. "Won't you be seated?"

He indicated a seat at one end of the sofa. I took it, finding him like his portraits, only kinder. He began by thanking me for my reviews, then proceeded to inquire concerning my own work and my purposes. It took but a moment to start the story of my coming to Boston. In truth I was bursting with talk. I hurried on with rushing flow, developing my early antagonism to his realism and my recent conversion to it. I outlined my theory of criticism, and seeing that he listened intently, I described a work which I had in manuscript called "The Development of American Ideals." I was a torrent, a whirlwind, and a spring overflow.

I analyzed the local-color novel and spoke of its growing importance in American literature, and this appeared to interest him. He permitted me to enlarge upon my reasons for believing that this novel was the most important literary form of the day, and that it would continue to grow in power and insight, for it had in it the seeds of greatness.

I said in substance what I was saying to my classes, "In my judgment the men and women of the South, West, and East are all working, without knowing it, in accordance with a fundamental principle which is this: American literature, in order to be great, must be national, and in order to be national must deal with conditions peculiar to our own land and climate. Every sincere writer must write of the life he knows best and for which he cares most. "Thus," said I, "the stories of Joel Chandler Harris, George W. Cable, Sarah Orne Jewett, and Mary E. Wilkins, like the work of Joaquin Miller and Bret Harte, are but varying phases of the same movement, a movement which is to give us at last a vital, original, and national literature."

In the heat of my argument, I harangued like a political orator running on at top speed. I didn't know how to stop —I don't think I did stop. I imagine he applied the brake, but if he did, he was so deft and so kindly in action that I did not understand exactly how he made use of it.

"You are doing a fine and valuable work," he said, and I was sure he meant it. "Each of us has had some perception of this growth of local-color fiction, but no one, so far as I know, has correlated the various groups as you have done. I hope you will go on and finish and publish your book."

This judgment, uttered perhaps out of kindliness, brought the blood to my face and filled me with pride and gratitude and joy. The lightest meed of praise from the lips of this widely accepted critic was like a medal of fine gold to me, for I had good reason to know how discriminating he was in his use of words. To gain even a hint of commendation from the author of "The Modern Instance" was rich reward for a youth who had but just escaped from the drudgery of a Dakota farm.

Emboldened by his gracious manner, I confessed that I was ambitious to do a little in the way of recording the manners and customs of my native West. "I don't know that I can do this in stories," I said, "but I intend to do it in essays and poems."

He was kind enough then to say that he would like to see something of mine. "Whatever you do, keep to the West," he urged. "You have almost a clear field out there. Why don't you regularly go in for it? I am sure you could give us something that would be typically Western."

How long he talked, or how long I talked, I cannot now recall (the clock stopped for me), but at last, in some deft way, he got me outside, and as we walked down the street toward the station he became still more friendly. He treated me not merely as a literary aspirant, but as a critic in whom he could confide. He spoke of his aroused interest in the Russian writers and asked my opinion with regard to certain questions in debate at the moment, and I answered with joyous vigor. I was, I fear, a mad orator, exalted and presumptuous, but in his gentle way he governed me and finally headed me for my train.

As we neared the depot he turned to me with a camaraderie which touched me, and asked, "What would you think of my doing a story dealing with the effect of a dream on the life of a man? I have in mind a tale to be called 'The

Shadow of a Dream' or something like that wherein the principal character is to be influenced in some crisis, I don't quite know what, through the memory of a dream which is to pursue him in actual life and have some share in the final catastrophe, whatever that may turn out to be. What would you think of such a plot?"

·Filled with pride at this evidence of his trust and confidence, I managed to stammer out a blunt judgment. "It doesn't sound at all like you," I said. "It's more like Hawthorne."

He caught at my full meaning and quickly replied, "You think it is out of keeping? You are right. It is rather romantic, and I may never write it." He smiled in reassurance. "But if I do, you may be sure it will be treated in my own way and not in any other man's way."

I would not let it rest at that. "There are plenty of men, Mr. Howells, who can do 'the weird kind of thing,' but there is only one man who can imagine 'The Modern Instance' and 'Silas Lapham.' "

That any praise of mine, or any criticism of mine, could have any lasting effect upon a man whose fame was international, I could not believe, but to have him desire my impression of the fitness of a chosen theme, was like feeling on my shoulder the touch of a king's ennobling blade. I went away like a young squire who had won the accolade. My apprenticeship was over, I had been accepted by America's chief literary man as a fellow, a literary historian.

II

With this recognition the current of my ambition changed. I began to hope that I, too, might some day become a novelist and embody in fiction some part of Middle-Western life. As often as I dared thereafter I went to call upon him, and always his taste, his judgment, his exquisite yet simple English produced in me the profoundest admiration. An hour of his incisive, humorous talk sent me away in mingled exaltation and despair—exaltation over his continued faith in me, despair over my own blunt and graceless speech. His talk, while never formal or ornate, was so much better than any dialogue I could ever hope to write that I went back to my pen with a kind of desperation. He was my standard in all matters literary. No one but Edwin Booth filled so large a place in my thought.

As I came to know him better he revealed to me some of the swift, emotional transitions to which a Celtic man of letters is liable. Irish humor and Welsh pathos mingled in his talk. His comic spirit, always close beneath the surface, rose with a chuckle like a gentle, bubbling spring, close upon his most somber mood, to break in some crystal phrase which lingered in my memory for weeks.

One day as we were walking across the Common together we met an old vagabond who whined out a plea for money. Howells with an instant look of pain and indignation put his hand into his pocket and gave the man a coin, and for a moment thereafter we walked in silence. At length Howells said, "We are warned not to give to these street mendicants, and yet"—and here he smiled again—"I don't suppose they are perfectly *rolling in wealth.*"

His emphasis on the phrase "rolling in wealth" and his subtle smile meant that even if this beggar were a fraud his daily walk was by no means a path of roses through a world governed by the rich. I who was almost as poor as the tramp was less indulgent—I had no half-dollars to hand out even to deserving mendicants.

He spoke often of the poverty which was all about us in

Boston and charged our social system with its production. "It is a reproach to our lawmakers that poverty should persist in the midst of our plenty."

These conditions seem almost medieval as I write this sentence, for six dollars for an eight-hour day is the wage of sewing women, and scrubwomen are almost as haughty as cooks—the poor are almost obsolete. 1929.

Speaking of cooks reminds me that Howells once told me that his farce, "The Albany Depot," was suggested by an experience of his own in hiring a cook for Mrs. Howells.

I once said to him, "It comforts me to know how simply you lived while editor of the *Atlantic*. I hunted up your house the other day and found it about like the home of a village carpenter."

He laughed. "Yes, we all lived like villagers in those days. Even the great were not above taking home a beefsteak in a brown paper parcel."

I cannot, of course, report his exact, delicious phrasing, but I can express the spirit of it. In acknowledgment of one of my radical poems he wrote (in that small, illegible script which his typewriter produced) the following revealing note:

"This is a very beautiful and far-reaching poem. It says some things not attempted before and says them well. I am truly sorry that I can not think with you about those less or greater things for I love you, and would like to be of one mind with you, but wherever there is competition there will be the oppression of the weak by the stronger, and wherever there is unequal wealth there will be the world, the flesh and the devil."

That he was deeply moved by the social injustice of which we were all aware was evident, and sometimes as we walked he discussed Bellamy's "Looking Backward" and the growing contrasts between the rich and the poor, while I, in turn, dilated upon Henry George. I could never quite get him to see the difference between his program and mine. He was fixed upon some communistic reform, whilst I was perfectly clear that land monopoly was the fundamental cause of poverty and must be destroyed first of all.

His voice was sad, poignantly sad, when reviewing the sorrow and injustice of the world, and yet he always had himself in hand. He never argued, never monologued, as I often did.

I recall visiting him at Little Nahant in 1886 and of spending several hours lying on the sunny slope of a hill which fronted the sea, dreaming out an ideal world in which poverty would be unknown. He said to me that day many of the things which he afterward recorded in "The Traveller from Altruria." I remember wondering at the moment how poverty and sickness and crime could exist in a world so beautiful as that upon which we looked, as the dusk began to fall, and the lamps burst into bloom along the beach across the bay, and yet at the moment the illness of his eldest daughter was filling his heart with almost intolerable anxiety.

As the hour of parting came he led me down to a small rustic gate at the corner of his garden and as we stood there, entranced by the splendor of that sunset, he contrived to express his appreciation of my youth and his confidence in my future. With a wave of his hand toward the starry roadway, he said with a smile of shy sweetness and friendship, "*There* lies your path!" And in his voice vibrated the suggestion that I was about to enter upon a way of light. Alas! How far I have fallen short of the ambition which filled my heart at that moment!

CHAPTER SEVEN

JAMES A. AND KATHARINE HERNE

I

As I think back into my busy Boston days, I am persuaded that my mental windows stood wide to every intellectual Old World breeze, no matter how unexpected. As in the past, though in somewhat lesser degree, New England was still a literary province whereon successive waves of European culture beat, and in Boston the high-thinking few prided themselves on being sensitive to each newest theory. French Impressionism and Russian Veritism were still in debate when the doctrine of dramatic realism swept upon us from the north, embodied in Henrik Ibsen's austere plays, and I, being already instructed in northland literature by Hurd of the *Transcript*, became its advocate.

I well remember the day when Edgar Chamberlin and I attended the first performance of "The Doll's House" (or The Doll Home, as Hurd declared it should have been translated) and saw Nora played by Beatrice Cameron, wife of Richard Mansfield. She had put the play on for a special matinée while engaged in another piece with her husband, but this afternoon was something more than a pleasing experiment to me. It was a revelation of the power, naturalness, and truth of the great Norwegian's methods.

Hitherto, in reading his plays, I had found the lines almost devoid of grace, dull and flat, but I now understood very clearly that they were only surface guides for the players.

65

As in life, so his dramatic meanings lay below the lines, for these dull scenes when played by good actors gave the effect of life itself. Furthermore, the absence of all asides, soliloquies, and sensational climaxes made the conventions of the ordinary stage ridiculous. "This performance marks an epoch in American dramatic art," I said to Chamberlin. "It moves me more deeply than Shakespeare," he replied.

I left the theater that afternoon converted to the new drama, and like all recent converts I began to talk and write on Ibsenism as I had been talking and writing on Impressionism and Veritism. It became another "cause" for me.

There was method in my folly, however. In my poor, blundering fashion I was standing for all forms of art which expressed, more or less adequately, the America I knew. As I had welcomed the paintings which discarded the brown shadows of the German studios, so now I responded to the dialogue which aimed at representing life. That our artists in painting purple shadows were merely exchanging masters, I conceded, but Monet's canvases were more akin to the meadows and hills of New England than those of Corot. Similarly, Ibsen's method, alien as his material actually appeared, pointed the way to a new and more authentic American drama. "If we must imitate, let us imitate those who represent truth and not those who uphold conventions," was my argument.

Tea tables at once resounded with a new dramatic clamor. Those of us who scorned stage conventions, heard with eager attention descriptions of "The Independent Theater" in London and "The Free Stage" in Berlin, and deplored the absence of similar aspiring managers in New World cities, while earnest actresses announced their desire to uplift the stage.

All this has its amusing aspect now, but we were all very serious. None of us admitted that Ibsenism was just another wave of Old World influence sweeping over a bored provincial capital. America had been subject to such literary trade winds for two hundred years. Sometimes they came from Germany, sometimes from Italy, sometimes from France. Instructed by Howells, we had read the novels of Valdes, Tolstoy, and Flaubert. Now, through William Archer, we studied the dramas of Ibsen and Björnson. All these enthusiasms were natural phases of our development, but some of us said, "Ibsen will be a foolish fad if we do not advance the truth and power of our own writers. We are not to imitate Ibsen. We must accept his theory, but do our own work in our own color."

II

One afternoon in January, 1888, as Hurd and I were discussing plays, he handed me two theater tickets and asked if I had ever seen Jim Herne act. I told him I had not.

"Do so at once," he said, "for he is a local-color realist after your own heart. He's not an Ibsen, but he is trying to represent New England life."

I accepted the tickets with pleasure and that night witnessed the performance of "Drifting Apart" by James A. and Katharine Herne. They were playing at that time on a second-rate stage in the South End and their surroundings were cheap and tawdry, but I can still recall the profound impression which they made upon me by their action as well as by the play.

The plot of the piece was very simple. In the first act, Jack, the middle-aged husband of Mary Miller, was shaving himself in preparation for a trip to the village to purchase some Christmas presents, and all through the scene, which was charmingly set, Herne moved unaffectedly, joking, chuckling, making quaint gestures with a naturalism I had never before seen upon the stage; and Katharine was almost equally delightful as the wife, and when at the close of the joyous act her sailor husband returned from the village, his arms full of holiday presents, hopelessly drunk, her expression of grief, of shame, of despair formed a complete and piteous contrast to the homely comedy which preceded it.

The second and third acts, being a dream, were less moving, but the fourth act, which brought Jack back to tender sobriety in his own home, restored the reality of the opening scene, and was almost equally colloquial. The play closed on Christmas morning with a satisfying glow, with Jack repentant and Mary forgiving.

The quiet naturalism, the unaffected humor of the play so moved and interested me that I wrote immediately to Herne thanking him for the pleasure it had given me. I also expressed my admiration for the acting of "Miss Herne" and went on to say: "By such writings as that in the first and last acts of 'Drifting Apart' you have allied yourself with the best local-color fictionists of New England and deserve the encouragement and support of the same public."

A day or two later I received a modest and earnest letter in which he said:

"Your kindly conceived and earnestly written letter lies before me. I have read and reread it, and each perusal has added strength to the already firm conviction I had in the ultimate success of my play. By success, I mean that by which the managers measure—'financial,' for be the play or player never so fine, when there is no cash, there are no open doors. Your letter demonstrates the fact that as you saw my work, others will see it also, not so readily, nor so clearly—but they will see it. My task, and a difficult one at first, is to secure the attendance of the fine auditor—the others will follow. . . . It was, as you say, a daring thing to present such a subject in such a delicate form, but I have received many letters concerning it—none perhaps that I prize so much—for none bear such evidence of having given the subject deep thought. They are written from the heart, yours from the head *and* the heart. You say you would like to know more of me. I can only repeat that the desire is mutual. It will, however, be impossible for me to meet you during my present engagement. The past week has been devoted to *nine* performances of 'Drifting Apart' and six rehearsals of next week's production, 'The Minute Men' (please see that play), no small task you will admit, but when my season is ended and I return home, I will feel honored if you will spend a few hours and dine with Katharine C. (Mrs.) Herne, myself, and our three babies."

The wish was fulfilled some months later, when in answer to a cordial invitation I hastened to call upon him at his home. It was a small, plain, frame cottage such as a village carpenter might build, but Mrs. Herne, daintily gowned and looking quite like Mary Miller of the play, met me with charming grace and presented me to her sister and to her three little daughters, Julie, Chrystal, and Dorothy. They made me almost instantly a member of the family and listened to me with such respect that I hardly knew myself.

Our first evening, filled with cordial explanations and tumultuous debate, is still vivid in my memory. It was in effect a session of Congress, a Methodist revival, and an Irish comedy. Our clamor lasted far into the night, and when I went away at last, it was with a feeling that I had met people of my kind. I had never known such instant and warm-hearted understanding and sympathy. My head rang with their piquant phrases, their earnest and cheerful voices.

Still an active and, I fear, a pestiferous advocate of Henry George's land theories, I managed at our next meeting to switch our discussion to the single tax. Then having converted them to "Georgism," I fell upon the constitution of matter and outlined Spencer's theories of evolution. Mrs. Herne, a thinker of intuitive subtlety and a special lover of astronomy, took an active part in all our excited debates, wherein, beating the arms of our chairs, we warred over the nebular hypothesis with entire unconsciousness of the clock.

These extraordinary theatrical folk brought to me a wholly new world—a world of swift and pulsating emotion, a world of aspiration, and the story of brave battle for an art. It is difficult for me to express in a few lines how much they and their lovely children meant to me during the years that followed. They were at once a puzzle and a provocation.

Herne, I soon discovered, was only halfway on the road toward a finer form of dramatic art, and the tragic result of his aspiration seemed to be that just in proportion as his writing increased in truth and his acting gained in subtlety, he failed to interest the public, even the public he had already won in other plays. He confessed that he was deep in debt and sinking deeper day by day, and I dimly perceived that my influence was not helpful at this moment. My criticism rendered him discontented with the plays which had hitherto given him comfort, but did not materially aid him in his effort to achieve something better.

He had made a great deal of money with Hearts of Oak,

his first play, which was obviously only partly American, but he had lost heavily on his second play, "The Minute Men," a picturesque study of Colonial times, and was steadily dropping money on "Drifting Apart." Naturally he was discouraged, though never embittered.

"The managers all admit the good points of my play," he explained to me. "In fact they say it's too good. 'The public doesn't want a good play,' they say. 'It wants bad plays. Write a bad play, Jim. Not too bad but just bad enough.' Meanwhile I must play in theaters which are not suited to my way of doing things and am obliged to insert into my lines tricks and turns which I despise."

He related these experiences with a smile, but admitted that he was disheartened and with deepest sympathy I at once offered to assist him in finding an audience and a better theater. "There is a public for your plays if we can reach it," and I bluntly added, "You can do better work than any you have done and no play can be 'too good.' I want you to write a play in which there are no compromises at all."

Under the influence of my optimism, he took heart and began to revise "Drifting Apart" for the third time. It was stated at one time that I was working with him, but as a matter of fact I never suggested a line in any of his plays, though he read them to me scene by scene. In this case I followed his revisions day by day, encouraging him to cut out the very lines which his theatric advisers considered most vital. As he afterward wrote me, I upheld his elbow.

"I never was so much encouraged in the work I have laid out to accomplish as I have been by you," he wrote. "You have as it were endorsed my judgment, and showed me that it is possible to succeed and to force acknowledgment in spite of the opposition I have met with and the obstacles I have yet to overcome."

On August 5, 1889, he wrote me from Maine, "I will do no more with 'Drifting Apart' until I see you. I have done about all I can with it. After I have heard you fully and got closer to your idea, I will then scribble a little more on it, and try to get it nearly right by the time it gets to the stage again. I've finished 'The Hawthornes'—'rough finished' —and you'll like some of it."

This fixes the date of the first draft of the play which later became his enormously successful Shore Acres.

III

My admiration for Mrs. Herne's art was almost unbounded. I felt that she could play other and much more important parts than Mary Miller, although there was in "Drifting Apart" a scene, in the dream, wherein the poor little mother sits holding her child in her lap while it dies of cold and hunger, which tested her art. The exquisite restraint, the marvelous fidelity to nature, and the grace with which she played this tragic episode convinced me that she was one of the subtlest actresses in America. The music which accompanied this scene, a wailing melody, came to embody, for me, all the pathos and defeat which lay in the failure of "Drifting Apart" and "The Minute Men."

My happiest days in Boston were associated with the Hernes. I loved the children, those vivid and dramatic little tow-haired girls, while their mother's lambent wit and their father's glowing humor enthralled me. I had never known such people. They were subject to all that is most typical in the Celt. Their extravagances of phrase and change of mood entranced me. They brought me to know many other figures in their strange world. They introduced me to William Gillette, Mary Shaw, and Robson and Crane, and before long I was not only thinking in terms of the theater but planning a general reform of the stage. I became one of the committee organized to promote the first Independent Theater Society in America. Herne, Flower, and Mary Shaw were among the promoters.

Having discovered the Hernes, I was eager to let all my friends know how fine, how important they were, and to that end I dragged Mr. Howells down to see the play and I insisted that Clement should comment upon it. I was a most indefatigable press agent and soon all my literary friends knew what the Hernes were trying to do, but my efforts proved of little financial value to them. They left the South End Theater, discouraged but not defeated. James A. had most marvelous resiliency. Just when I thought he was beaten to the earth, he rose with a chuckle and went at it again.

My brother Franklin joined the company in the autumn and during the next year we both shared the play's bewildering "ups and downs" on the road. I was present at the opening of the season in Troy, and when they reached Brooklyn I went on to New York to interest Gilder and Stedman in the Hernes. I suffered with them when the houses were small and exulted with them when the sales were large. I traveled with them to Buffalo, spending long hours on the train discussing why the play had no appeal in the East, and forecasting its chances of success in the West. I experienced the desolating effect which the sounds of slow-dropping seats in a half-filled auditorium has on a manager. The deep discouragement of watching streams of people pass the open door was another scarring experience.

In after years, when skies were fair, we were all able to laugh over these drab experiences, but they were not funny at the time, or at least if they were funny it was because Herne's irrepressible humor made them so. I suffered more than he—apparently, for I was wholly unaccustomed to the abrupt changes of mood which mark theatrical life and deceived by the readiness with which he turned a mood of defeat into laughter. I took his depressions (which always had in them a touch of exaggeration) to be despairs, and came slowly to a knowledge that his humorous sallies were meant to conceal from me the more poignant of his griefs. Altogether his friendship was a painful as well as a most beautiful experience. It gave me a deeper insight into that singular and passionate world in which the Hernes lived and had their being.

CHAPTER EIGHT

OTHER PLAYS AND PLAYERS

I

In the summer of 1890, Herne decided to give up "Drifting Apart" and produce a new play upon which he had been working called "Margaret Fleming." In this venture I was instantly and profoundly concerned. A volume of Ibsen's plays had just been translated and the discussion of "the Independent Theater" was in full swing. To every one I met I described Herne's new play, and I interviewed several managers, urging them to put it on—all to no purpose. The producers of Boston, like those of New York, would not consider it for a moment, although up to that time it was by all odds the most original of Herne's plays.

One day at a luncheon given to Herne by Howells, the dramatic situation was thoroughly gone into and James A. with boyish frankness confessed that he was at his wits' end. "All the theaters in New York and Boston have refused to consider my new play," he said, and to this I was able to bear corroborative testimony, for I had been personally rebuffed by five Boston managers.

Howells then spoke of a like situation in Berlin, and related the story of Sudermann and his associates, who secured a hall on a side street and made production of their plays there. "They brought the public to them by the sheer force of their dramatic novelty," said Howells. "Why don't you do as they did—hire a sail loft or a stable and produce your play in the simplest fashion? The people will come to see it if it is new and vital."

Poor Herne did not instantly take fire at this suggestion, for he had reached almost the last ounce of his courage and pretty nearly the last dollar of his savings, but he went away with me, revolving the idea in his mind. "I'll do it," he said. "I'll hire Chickering Hall and remodel it into a little theater."

Of this music room which seated less than five hundred people (counting its small balcony) Herne made the first of the so-called "Little Theaters" in America, and all our dramatic reformers looked forward to the experiment with intense eagerness. In it Herne promised to produce effects hitherto unknown on our stage, and in all the rehearsals of the play he and Katharine had this in mind. They always and everywhere schooled their actors in a naturalism which, while not precisely the way in which the characters would speak in life, nevertheless produced that effect upon an audience.

To give up my own work and serve as press agent (without pay) was a joy, and while Herne carried on the rehearsals and supervised the construction of the stage, I bustled about the city, interesting the young men of the press and all my literary friends in the venture. Complimentary seats were sent to many of the most distinguished literary and artistic men and women of the region, and when, one night in the early autumn, the curtain rose on the first scene, the Hernes had one of the most notable audiences ever drawn together for a dramatic entertainment in Boston.

The performance was worthy of the audience. Not merely Herne but Mrs. Herne, and every one of the actors seemed to be actually presenting the unexaggerated gestures and accent of life. Katharine was especially moving in the title part, and the close of the play involved a touch of art which up to that time had never had its equal on our stage. After having refused reconciliation with her husband, *Philip Fleming, Margaret* was left standing in tragic isolation on the stage, and as the lights were turned out one by one, her figure gradually disappeared in deepening shadow, and when the heavy, soft curtains, dropping together noiselessly, shut in the poignant action of the drama, no one moved or spoke. The return to the actual world in which we lived was made silently.

There was a little pause, a considerable pause, before the applause came, and then the audience rose and slowly filed out. I saw Mr. and Mrs. Howells, Mr. and Mrs. Thomas Bailey Aldrich, Mr. and Mrs. Deland, Mrs. James T. Field, Sara Orne Jewett, William Lloyd Garrison, Mary E. Wilkins, John J. Enneking, and many others of the literary and artistic personalities of the day. Some of them spoke to me of the "wonderful play" and others of the "marvelous" acting, and, to my inexperienced mind, the Hernes had won. It seemed to me that the city must ring with applause of this courageous and distinguished performance.

Without question it was the most naturalistic, the most colloquial, and the most truthful presentation of a domestic drama ever seen on the American stage up to that time, and I am free to say that in some regards I do not think it has been surpassed since. But alas! while some of our most distinguished auditors came night by night, the general public could not be induced to flock in sufficient numbers to pay expenses, and after four weeks of losing business, poor Herne was obliged to leave the cast and go to New

York under contract with a big commercial manager to produce a commercial success, The Country Circus.

On October 7, 1891, he wrote me from New York:

"Klaw & Erlanger have no faith in the ability of 'Margaret Fleming' to pull out at Chickering Hall. They will probably close it there at the end of next week. Of course I have not the means to keep it on. They have not told me positively that they will close, but say 'It is madness to keep on,' etc. They talk of trying to get time in a theater for it, but you know if it fails in the hall the theaters will not have it at all. Our only hope lies in a success in Chickering Hall. Klaw got back this morning, and I presume, after they have conferred together, I'll get a decision. I feel what that decision will be. . . . If I had the means I would run it at the hall for another six weeks myself. It can be done for nine hundred or a thousand dollars, but I haven't got it and so there is an end. . . . Of course they only look at the money loss they've made. I look at the failure of my life. . . . The author of 'The Country Circus' read his play to the company to-day. *Oh, God!* But it'll go, I suppose. Oh, how I'd like to see such rot where it belongs!"

It was this letter which decided B. O. Flower to underwrite the extension of the play and I was glad to continue as "man in front" for another four weeks.

Naturally the play was widely discussed. Some could see no virtue in it, but others felt in it the beginning of a new and higher type of drama. Concerning Mrs. Herne's art there was no diversity of opinion. Praise was general. We could not then foresee the effect of our experiment, but we were satisfied. It had cost the Hernes several thousand dollars, but it had lifted them into the honorable position they deserved to fill.

II

Herne spent the winter in New York, working for a producing firm, and the following summer returned to Ashmont. For several seasons he had been in the habit of spending July and August at East Lemoyne on the coast of Maine, and being a close observer of life, had become keenly interested in his gnarly neighbors. He now began to think of putting them into a play. In a note to me I find this sentence: "I shall also try to do something more on 'The Hawthornes,' " and in all his letters, as well as those of Mrs. Herne, are humorous references to the curious and interesting characters they had met along the coast.

On his return in September he read to me the first act of "The Hawthornes." Later he spoke of it as "Uncle Nat" and finally as "Shore Acres." But the plot under all these names remained the same. The action involved two brothers, one, the elder, sweet, patient, self-sacrificing; the other discontented, sullen, and resentful, eager to make money without labor. The play was, in fact, the record of a bitter struggle over the question of "cuttin' the old farm up into buildin' lots," and as Herne read it to me scene by scene, the lines appealed to me as having something of the quality which made Mary E. Wilkins' stories so amusing and so vital.

It was by far the best play Herne had ever done, for it was written out of love for New England united to a thorough knowledge of coast characters. He tried all winter to get his new play produced, and it was not until the following spring that the manager of the Boston Museum, being in sore need of something to fill out the tag end of his season, yielded to Herne's plea, and put on "Shore Acres" for two weeks.

The opening night found me once more on hand as unofficial "man in front." Herne always declared that I stood in the door of a saloon opposite the entrance in order to gloat on the crowds filling the stairway and I guess I did. The piece was an instantaneous success. It drew great audiences from the first, and before the end of the first week half the managers in New York had written offering their theaters.

Among those who anxiously wired for the play was Harry Miner, a well-known New York theater owner, one of Herne's old acquaintances, and with him James A. signed a contract for the production of "Shore Acres" at the Broadway Theater the following autumn. Herne told me that in making out the contract he had insisted on the play being kept going for four weeks, no matter what the receipts were. "A most important proviso," he explained, "for 'Shore Acres' must have time for our kind of people to find out what sort of a play it is."

Naturally I was in New York to witness this opening, and my brother was in the cast. The play was greeted by a good house but fell off, as usual, on the second and third nights, and as I was behind the scenes a good deal of the time, I found Miner an interesting study. The first night he was jubilant. He posed in the lobby, glorious in evening dress, a shining figure. "We've got 'em coming, Jimmy, my boy," he said to Herne after the first act. But James A., whose face remained an impenetrable mask while Miner was looking at him, winked at me with full understanding of the situation.

"Watch him to-morrow night," he said after Miner left the dressing room.

Tuesday's house was light and Wednesday's still lighter, and on Thursday Miner fell into the dumps. "We've got to take it off, Jim," he mournfully announced.

"You'll do nothing of the kind," retorted Herne. "You'll keep it on four weeks according to contract, if it doesn't bring in a cent."

Miner was furious. He stormed about, declaring himself on the verge of ruin—all to no effect. Herne's face was stern as a New England granite boulder.

"You'll keep your contract," he calmly repeated.

Miner's attitude during the second week was comical. He became morose and was seen no more in the lobby. He brooded over the contract as though Herne had done him a grievous wrong, and all his employees came ultimately to share his resentful attitude. The house acquired a dank, depressing, tragic atmosphere and then, magically, came a change. The people began to come—our kind of people. At the end of the second week the house was filled. Miner ordered the lobby lighted up and reappeared in evening dress. He strutted once more in dazzling, confident splendor. He expanded. He appeared taller, larger. He clapped Herne on the back. "They're coming back, Jimmy, my boy!" he shouted, forgetting all his resentment, all his hard words, all his tragical gloom. "We'll be turning them into the street next week," he exultingly ended. "Your fortune is made."

This was almost literally true. The play ran the remainder of the season at the Broadway Theater and all the next year at Daly's, which was a phenomenal run in those days. It put Herne on his feet financially, as "Margaret Fleming" had established him artistically. He was now in the forefront of stage realists, quite independent of cheap theaters and cheaper managers and I was mightily relieved that he had succeeded in spite of my sinister influence.

III

Meanwhile Katharine had bought a handsome house on Convent Avenue in Harlem, and my brother and I were often there of a Sunday, and when we all came together in those days the walls resounded with our clamor. Herne was a great wag and story-teller and one of the most accomplished masters of dialect I have ever known. He could reproduce almost any accent and could dramatize at a moment's notice any scene or dialogue his wife demanded of him. Nevertheless, he took his art very seriously and was one of the best stage directors of his day, though his methods were so far in advance of his time that they puzzled or disgusted some of his subordinates. That he profoundly influenced the art of acting is admitted.

He was not only a good father in the ordinary sense, but an accepted comrade with his children. He played with them as if he were their own age, and was forever planning some new joke, some enterprise for their amusement. And yet with all his apparent simplicity and humor, he was a very complex and essentially a very sad character. In other words, he was a Celt. One of my friends upon seeing him for the first time in private life said, "His face is one of the saddest and sweetest I have ever seen." He was the Irish bard whose songs are compounded of laughter and a wailing keen.

Katharine Corcoran, his wife, was not merely of Irish temperament, she was Irish born and her laugh was one of the most infectious I have ever heard. Her speaking voice was very musical and expressive and her face could pass instantly from gay to grave like a sunny field over which the cloud shadows swiftly pass. Mr. Howells once said of her art, "I have never seen so many subtle expressions appearing in the lines of a woman's countenance."

"The both of them," as an Irishman would say, were capable of enthralling, spontaneous comedy on the stage and they were forever "guying" each other at home. Jim could not be trusted for one moment, but Katharine usually gave him as good as he sent. Indeed he was a little afraid of her keen wit, and often when she loosed her verbal arrows he quite frankly dodged.

He admired her profoundly, and generally remained silent during the call of a chance acquaintance or of a stranger. Only in the presence of intimate friends did he abandon his attitude of smiling and interested reticence. At the same time, his love and admiration for Katharine did not prevent him from observing every peculiarity which could be turned against her. One of his tricks was to rise gravely just as she had reached the middle of an eloquent period, and solemnly pretend to reverse a little switch at the top of her shoulder.

Sometimes she frowned for an instant at this outrage, but usually she acknowledged the justice of his action and broke into a ripple of laughter, with full appreciation of the fact that she had been "going it again."

They both held from the first an exaggerated notion of my importance in the world of letters and listened to me with a respect, a fellowship, and an appreciation which inspired me to better work. They called me "The Dean" on account of my supposed learning and often after dinner Herne would say, "Now, Dean, for the salt cellar."

In this way he always referred to an early discussion in which I had used a salt cellar to illustrate Spencer's theory of the constitution of matter. "We do not know what matter is. We cannot say this glass is solid, neither can we say it is made up of invisible molecules, etc."

We often harangued till long after midnight. Sometimes my brother was with me, sometimes not, but we were all flaming with hatred of land monopoly in those days, and when we were not advocating realism in fiction or impressionism in painting, we were quoting "Progress and Poverty."

Those were beautiful days to me and very successful days for the Hernes. Katharine in a recent letter refers to them as "the good old Convent Avenue days. But dearest of all we hold the little home in Ashmont."

In one of Herne's later letters I find the following reference to our first meetings:

"Yes, those Ashmont days were indeed glorious days. They laid the foundation of what success we have since achieved by strengthening and encouraging us in our work and making us steadfast to a purpose that we felt was the true one. And we believe that you, too, got something in your work and for your future out of them. They are gone but not forgotten. They change but cannot die."

IV

Inevitably I tried my hand at writing plays. Not to have done so would have been phenomenal stolidity, but I was never able to forget in those days that I was a reformer, so my first play dealt with land monopoly and was called "Under the Wheel," and my second was based on a celebrated investigation of the lobby by the legislature of Boston. I named it "A Member of the Third House." Whatever my plays possessed in the way of dramatic power, they were absolutely unsalable by reason of their austere content. Herne sympathized with them as documents, but was too wise to attempt to produce them.

In addition to these attempts I worked with him on a melodrama called Fall River, he writing one act and I another, but they came to nothing. Then I worked with Katharine on an Irish comedy for her, which we named "Mrs. Crisp," but that also ran into the ditch. Then I induced Mr. Howells to work with me on a dramatization of "A Modern Instance." The net result of which is a manuscript, partly print and partly his own writing, nothing more.

Through Herne I met William Gillette, one of the handsomest and most talented of all the actor-dramatists of that day. I had seen him in "The Private Secretary," in which he appeared to be a forlorn, ganglionic individual about seven feet tall, and it was a pleasant shock to meet the man himself, so graceful and shapely, notwithstanding his height. I was greatly delighted by his alert and humorous mind and his clarity of expression.

Through Mrs. Herne I came to know Mary Shaw, whose voice had always delighted me. I had seen her several times in support of Julia Marlowe and considered her a better reader of Shakespeare than the star herself. She was in the fullness of her powers at this time, a noble actress and a cultivated woman. She had been a teacher in a Boston school and her taste and judgment made her impersonations among the best on the stage. She was of Irish parentage, blonde, gray-eyed, and humorous. She could tell a story with more effect than any of my acquaintances except Herne. She made fun of herself like a man and yet was essentially feminine.

One of the subjects of her monologues at our first meeting was an actor she called "Plim" and as I listened to her I was led into new regions. It did not seem possible that such amusing, carefree people could exist. They were characters in a novel. One of Herne's friends was a man he called "Putt," who was subject to illusions of grandeur. He had much to say of his "man Petah" and of his "paddock" and his "cobs." He went so far as to detail the way in which he shipped his horses to and from New York and how valuable "Petah" was. I met Putt one day and could not believe that he was the hero of Herne's stories, but he was! In truth he had no farm, no horses, and no paddock. They were all imaginary and "Petah" turned out to be a small boy of about fifteen. No character in fiction could surpass this braggart, who was a tall and graceful Englishman of fifty.

Up to this time the men and women of my world in Boston, as in the West, had been serious, restrained souls. Jesting of a quiet sort was common in my mother's family, but my father, although he told a story with dramatic power, was never comic, and most of the women I had known up to this time had been long-suffering and patient. Lambent spirits like Mary Shaw and Katharine Herne were new to me. I listened to their laughing comment with wonder and delight. That they did not openly make fun of me is proof of their kindly natures. No doubt they had their private opinion of me, but they never failed to treat me with highly flattering expressions of respect, even when I was most ponderous.

In order to be quite fair to myself, I must admit to being fairly well clothed at this time, and although a colossal bore when preaching the single tax or defining the local-color school in fiction, I had moments of being companionable. At times I laughed, especially when in the presence of Mary Shaw and Katharine Herne. In short, I was on my way to a mellow old age.

A relentless idealist in general and a Veritist in particular, I continued to uphold the fiction represented by Howells and to advocate similar drama. I commended Edward Harrigan for his attempts to put Harlem's shanty town on the stage and openily declared that Denman Thompson's "The Old Homestead" was also headed in the right direction.

Herne's use of my name in connection with that of Howells always made me wince. How little they knew of me! I tried to tell him that I was only a free-lance instructor and that no one would buy my stories, but he and Katharine continued to listen as though I were a philosopher and poet as well as a devoted friend. I repeatedly warned them against my cranky notions, but they persisted in seeking my judgment and while I did not suggest a line of Shore Acres, Herne declared that I had profoundly influenced the structure of it.

We spent hours discussing plays like "Shenandoah," "My Partner," "Davy Crockett," and "The Henrietta," as well as farces like "The Hole in the Ground," "The Brass Monkey," and "Mulligan's Ball," assessing their value in terms of their truth to life. "I want to be truer than any of them," said Herne. "I want my 'Shore Acres' to be as true as Mr. Howells and Miss Wilkins." He included one or two of my short stories in this category, but as I had no book to my credit at this time, his judgment of me was based on faith in what I might do some time, rather than upon anything I had done.

As a writer, I included Augustus Thomas, Bronson Howard, and William Gillette among the forerunners of a new school of dramatists. They fitted into my lecture on "Local Color in Fiction and the Drama." It didn't harm them and it gave me and my pupils a great deal of satisfaction to have their plays arranged and classified. Moreover, Thomas and Herne both lived up to their label, Thomas with "In Missouri" and "The Hoosier Doctor" and Herne with "Shore Acres" and "Sag Harbor."

V

My interest in Herne, Gillette, and Thomas did not lessen my admiration for Edwin Booth. He was still the reigning king in my dramatic world, but each time I saw him play I sensed a decline in his vitality. He was growing old all too swiftly. He moved less alertly, and his voice, though beautiful as ever, was burdened with the tragedy of age, and when he uttered Macbeth's somber soliloquies he filled me with poignant regret that his day was falling "into the sere and yellow leaf."

Booth's founding of the Players and his retirement was soon followed by his death. Although I became a member of the club it was not till 1897, and so I never saw him there, but many of my friends have described to me how he came and went from his rooms on the second floor, a slight figure with a beautiful, sad face. He usually ate alone, not in austere mood but in gentle aloofness, and only his intimate friends ventured to join him. Occasionally when some question concerning the reading of a passage from Macbeth or Hamlet came up, his dark eyes flashed with remembered fire and his glorious voice was heard again for a moment. Mainly he was a shadowy figure, haunting the club he had created.

The rooms in which he died are preserved by the Players

as a memorial, just as they were when he laid down his book and took to his final, bed, and it is the custom of those who knew him to show visitors this chamber, together with the costumes and books which he bequeathed to the library. To those of us who remember him in these garments, the robe of Richelieu and the cloak of Hamlet bring glorious memories. They make the Players, small as it is, the most distinctive club in the New World, and in the square before the club, a beautiful bronze statue of him by Edmund Quinn stands as an evidence of the beauty of his face and the grace of his form as he appeared in Hamlet, a characterization which we all admired and in which we saw most of Edwin Booth the man.

CHAPTER NINE

VERNACULAR POETS AND NOVELISTS

I

IN my studies of early American literature, I was irritated by the aloofness of fiction and poetry from the realities of common life and speech. That our Colonial authors wrote as if in violent distaste of their surroundings is evident, for they found poetic exaltation only when musing on Rome or Egypt or when recalling their former English homes. In early days of the Republic skylarks and nightingales sang in their landscapes, palms and pyramids adorned their verse, and lords and ladies rode through the pages of their pale and feeble novels. As the bobolink, the partridge, and the mocking bird, like the native flowers, were not worth mention, so the speech of the farmers, carpenters, sailors, and other workers was considered beneath the level of literature. Sermons and exhortatory letters fill the volumes of that time.

I could discover very little concerning the actual speech of the Colonial villager or the Virginia planter and yet scholars reported that localities differed markedly in pronunciation and idiom and that the members of the first Continental Congress had some difficulty in understanding one another. Without doubt a realistic novelist or dialect poet would have made a most entertaining chapter from the contradictory oral peculiarities of Washington and Adams, and yet the first hint, and it is only a hint, of this New World's vernacular is to be found in the work of James Fenimore Cooper, whose conception of the speech of hunters and sailors is a spasmodic and uncertain note set in the midst of tall talk of a conventional English kind. Only now and again (as when Deerslayer pleads for his freedom) does the speech of the characters ring true. The dialogue of common folk is not easy to record, but in Cooper's case it was not so much a lack of perception as a lack of valuations.

The actual speech of rural New England did not enter American verse till James Russell Lowell in his "Biglow Papers" came frankly and with zest to the task of representing it. With the advantage of a scholarly training in criticism and a love for Robert Burns, he perceived and was ready to defend the wit and flavor of the Yankee vernacular.

His "Biglow Papers," while mainly political in their content, won wide recognition at the time and are entitled to long life by reason of their report on the cracker-barrel oratory of the forties. Rhymed political essays though they are, they still possess truth enough and humor enough to make them readable even though the Mexican War and its causes are almost as remote as the campaigns of Cyrus. We sympathize when the orator says to the recruiting officer:

> "Jest go home an' ask our Nancy
>   Whether I'd be sech a goose
> Ez to jine ye—guess you'd fancy
>   The etarnal bung was loose!
> She wants me fur home consumption,
>   Let alone the hay's to mow—
> Ef you're arter folks o' gumption,
>   You've a darned long row to hoe."

In another poem, "The Courtin'," Lowell conceived and wrought out an enduring genre picture of Colonial life, a charming idyl which has truth and loveliness:

"Zekle crep' up quite unbeknown,
    An' peeked in thru the winder,
An' there sot Huldy all alone,
    'Ith no one nigh to hender.

The wa'nut logs shot sparkles out
    Towards the pootiest, bless her,
An' leetle flames danced all about
    The chiny on the dresser.

Agin' the chimbly crooknecks hung
    An' in amongst 'em rusted
The ole queen's-arm that gran'ther Young
    Fetched back from Concord busted.

The very room coz she was in,
    Seemed warm from floor to ceilin',
An' she looked full ez rosy agin'
    Ez the apples she was peelin'.

'Twas kin' o' kingdom come to look
    On sech a blessed cretur;
A dogrose blushin' to a brook
    Ain't modester nor sweeter."

Whittier also quite frankly acknowledged his debt to Burns, and in his second period wrote beautifully of Massachusetts farm life, but made no attempt at representing the dialogue of his neighbors. Expressing his own emotion in his own way in poems like "The Barefoot Boy," "Telling the Bees," and "Snowbound," he embodied in simple form the homely signs and scents and sound of the farm life he knew, but only once or twice, as in "Skipper Ireson's Ride,"

did he attempt to suggest the accent of his characters. He
caught the spirit but not the accent of his region.

When I was a youth at school, I used to recite on Friday
afternoons "The One Hoss Shay" and "How the Old Horse
Won the Bet" by Oliver Wendell Holmes, finding in them
lively stories in verse suggesting scenes and men I knew.
His horse race was not so very different from those at our
county fairs, but they contained only a few words of dialect.

The vernacular of the toiler appeared first in the newspapers and later was reported in the stories of travelers in
the South and on the Border, but it was not till the early
seventies that Bret Harte in "Dow's Flat" and "Jim" faith-
fully recorded the actual speech of the Western man. An
old miner coming into a saloon calls out:

> "Say thar! P'raps
> Some o' you chaps
> Might know Jim Wild?
> Wal! No offense.
> Thar ain't no sense
> In gettin' riled.
>
> Jim was my chum
> Up on the bar;
> That's why I've come
> Down from up thar—
> Lookin' fer Jim."

"Dow's Flat" is equally adroit and contains a story as
well as a characterization, but to value these poems properly
the reader should bear in mind the fact that Harte had no
American predecessor in this attempt to present actual men
and their accent.

John Hay at about the same time, stimulated by Harte's
success, composed his "Pike County Ballads" and in poems

like "Little Breeches" presented certain salients of the common speech of Illinois. I can not imagine any Colonial or New England poet writing such lines as these:

> "You may resoloot till the cows come home,
> But ef one of ye teches that boy,
> He'll wrassle his hash in hell tonight
> Or my name's not Tilman Joy."

Unimportant as these poems of Harte and Hay may appear to-day, they were immensely significant of a new country, a new freedom, and a changing people. They were all as far from John Winthrop, Cotton Mather, and Peter Stuyvesant in thought, as the prairies of Illinois and the cañons of California were from the pavements of Boston and Manhattan. They were without precedent and, hence to me, have a touch of the miraculous. I know how difficult it is to create in the image of life.

It was inevitable that somewhere in my study of the groups of local colorists in fiction and poetry I should ask "Where is the representative for the great mid-West?" No one had come to the support of Eggleston, who was essentially a Hoosier. The prairie West had no novelist till a young man named Howe, editor of the *Globe* in Atchison, Kansas, published "The Story of a Country Town," a singularly gloomy, real yet unreal, narrative written in the tone of weary and hopeless age. Howells, quick to recognize its originality and power, wrote of it, and when another story, the "Moonlight Boy," came out I wrote the author a letter part of which is worth quoting as an expression of my feeling concerning the prairie West at that date.

"JULY, 1886.

"DEAR SIR: I have just finished reading the 'Moonlight

Boy,' and after careful attention to your first works, I want to say that I like your stories. Your delineation of the monotonous and provincial life of the rural West compels my admiration, though it grieves me to think how unavoidable the most of that life is. You speak of these people not as one who coldly looks on them as 'picturesque' but in an earnest, sincere tone *as from among them.* Your work has an *indigenous* quality which appeals to me very strongly, perhaps more strongly than to most critics. I can value your strong, idiomatic, Western prose, I think, better than one who has not heard it spoken. . . . Among representative names standing for 'local scene and character painting,' in which category you stand alone in representing the great West (myself your only rival, not having published yet). In the midst of my press of study and writing upon critical lines, I am myself striving to express some of the unuttered thought of the Western prairies.

"Pray do not think I ask for a biography or anything approaching it, but if you see fit to give me some sketches of your boyhood, residence, schooling, etc., I could at the least give you a column in the *Transcript*, which would be something. I shall have some hand in the review of the 'Moonlight Boy,' which, by the way, is puzzling Eastern readers—myself included. 'All the conventional novelist would have done he has avoided,' is one of the notes I sent in when I returned the book to Mr. Hurd of the *Transcript*.

"It is not so tragic, so powerful, of course, as the other two, but it has a charm of its own. I like it for its faithful treatment of homely, prosaic people in their restricted lives."

From his reply and from other sources I learned that he was born near Wabash, Indiana, in a log cabin, that his father was a Methodist circuit rider, and that "The Story of

a Country Town" accurately presented his recollections of
the Fairview neighborhood, although he came away from
it when a boy of twelve. The original of "Davy's Bend"
was Brownsville, Neb., a town the author visited only once,
during high water in the Missouri River.

He wrote "A Moonlight Boy" in five months, at night.
The two other books were written in the same way.

"When I quit the newspaper I will write my best book, but
I am successful at newspaper work and am afraid to give
it up."

The author had shot his bolt in "The Story of a Country
Town." None of the stories which he published afterward
equaled it in significance, and his representative position
was lost.

II

One day whilst I was deep in the study of these changes
in vernacular literature, I happened to call on Hurd of the
Transcript and as we were chatting he picked from his desk
a small parchment-covered volume and said, "Here's a book
of dialect verse you should know—if you haven't already
read it."

It was a tiny volume about four inches square entitled
"The Ole Swimmin' Hole and 'Leven More Poems by Benj.
F. Johnson of Boone," and whilst I was turning its pages,
Hurd went on to say that the author's real name was Riley,
and that his home was in Indiana. "Out there they call him
'The Hoosier Poet.' As an advocate of local color you must
take him into account."

This was on the tenth of September, 1886. I am sure of
this, for Hurd signed the book over to me and dated his
signature. It was a little book, less than fifty pages, and I

read it in a few minutes, but the originality and humor, and the music of its lines came to me with such appeal that I committed many of them to memory. It is significant to note that this little volume now brings several hundred dollars.

The preface, which was short and as unassuming as the volume, was dated "Indianapolis, July, 1883." The copyright was in the name of James W. Riley and in his foreword the poet wrote, "As far back into boyhood as the writer's memory may intelligently go, 'the country poet' is most pleasantly recalled. He was, and is, as common as the country fiddler, and as full of good old-fashioned music."

I found the verses all written from the standpoint of an Indiana farmer, and utterly unlike any other I had read. Here were subjects no one else had ever used. "The Frost Is on the Punkin and the Fodder's In the Shock" and "Watermelon Time" were joyous memories to me as well as to old Benjamin. I rejoiced in such phrases as "the husky, rusty russel of the tossels of the corn," and "the moon a-hangin' o'er us like a yaller-colored slice." Some of the expressions were strange to me, but I recognized the truthful humor and simple beauty of the work, and at once wrote to the author expressing my delight in his book.

His reply, embodied in graceful script, was so modest and so grateful withal that I took it to Hurd with a sense of its being a revelation of the poet's character. The letter bore the date October 10, 1887, and was written from Indianapolis.

"Many thanks for your good opinion of 'Benj. F. Johnson of Boone.' The old feller is jes' plum' tickled to have his work appreciated for the reason of its fidelity and homely truthfulness to Nature. Am heartily glad our good friend

Mr. Hurd has joined our hands. Give my thanks and warm regards to him for this new favor.

"Just now am rather chased with lecture engagements, but, just prior, a gracious illness has given me time to get another book into the printer's hands. Poems—serious and dialectic—a collection of fifty or more, which the Bowen-Merrill Co., Indpls., will issue for the Holidays. My _complete_ work, you speak of, I will not put together _soon_, though in time will.

"Replying to your request for any newer poems since last published books, I have no way, until coming volume, of answering. Most of my work is printed in newspapers, and I do well to get copy oftentimes, myself. However, if you will so favor me on the nick o' Christmas, I will be glad to send you the new book where directed to."

During the year 1888 he published another volume, and was renowned on the platform as a reciter of his own verse. Indeed he was in such demand by editors as well as by lecture committees, that I, still an attic dweller and humble teacher of literature, regarded him with wonder, and when he was reported to be at the Parker House, I was amazed. Generals, senators, and bankers put up at the Parker House and the fact that Riley could spend several days in such splendor quite overwhelmed me, and, after sending up my name, I awaited his answer with a sense of uncertainty. Was I justified in doing this? He had written to me pleasantly, but suppose he should refuse to see me?

Happily the message which the boy brought back was reassuring. "Come right up," he said, and soon I was at the poet's door. He met me in a red undershirt and black trousers, busily adjusting gold studs in the bosom of a hard-boiled shirt.

"Come right in, p'fessor," he called in a drawl which was as characteristic of Indiana as Mark Twain's utterance was of Missouri. "Take a cheer and don't mind my 'dishabilly.' I'm just dressin' fer dinner." His smile was cordial, but his mouth was puckered at one corner for the reason, as I soon discovered, that he was carrying a quid of tobacco in that cheek, and while he went on with his toilet he proceeded in a quaintly querulous monotone. "Yas, I'm dressin' fer dinner—'pears like I'm always dressin' fer dinner nowadays. When I was young and had a good digestion, could eat anything at any time, no one asked me to dine, but now when I'm old and feeble, stomach all gone, can't eat a thing but crackers and milk—look at that!"—Here he put his hand on a heap of invitations. "Don't it beat hell?"

He asked this gravely, solemnly, while from his eyes a gleam of elfin humor shone.

"It surely does," I replied. I might have added that I could take some of those dinners off his hands, but I didn't. I only laughed in complete understanding of him, while he rambled along in a most amusing, poetic and individual monologue, now quoting some of his own lines, now uttering a droning stream of shrewd comment on Western writers and Western literature. He described comical incidents of his lecture tour, and quoted criticisms of his recent verse, comment which I could not chronicle at the time and could only faintly remember afterward. That it was all "copy" of high commercial value I knew, and in the midst of it and through it all I was studying him with unwavering attention.

He was a short, blond man, with square shoulders and a long, bald head which he himself described as "of the tack-hammer variety." Although he wore pinch-nose glasses, his round gray eyes were plainly visible at all times, and whilst they possessed a comical light, his face remained as blank as the side of a china bowl. He was purposely amusing me and I watched and listened in a glow of delight.

He quoted one of his descriptive poems cautiously, opening one corner of his flexible mouth, and his utterance, in spite of his quid, was singularly musical. Taking from his dresser a manuscript, he read with frank delight "Knee Deep in June," keeping one eye fixed upon me obliquely as if enjoying the effect of his performance, and I, keenly sensitive to dramatic reading, was a delighted auditor. He talked of the country fiddler, of the tin peddler, and called my attention to certain phrases which he had caught from life. He was at once character actor, comedian, and poet. Howells had delightful humor, swift wit, and an exquisite use of words, but he was never droll. Riley was always the wag.

I had never known any one so individual, so amusing, and so thought-provoking, and as we went down in the elevator together we were like comrades of long association.

"You and I are voices cryin' in the Western wilderness," he said. "We're obliged to keep neighborly," and his smile, now that he was rid of his quid, displayed fine, even teeth. "So long!"

His success on the platform that night was phenomenal. He had the ability of the actor to characterize, and one of his most amusing "acts" was an imitation of a professor addressing a Sunday-school class on the subject of a peanut. He read his serious poems musically yet with fine restraint.

Thereafter Whitcomb Riley, as I called him, was a beloved figure in my literary world. His verses had larger place in my lectures on "Vernacular Literature," and I kept in touch with him by correspondence and by way of his books which he autographed to me as they came out year by year.

From other Indianapolis friends I learned that he was a bachelor and that his home was a room in a hotel. He was said to be an inveterate joker like James A. Herne and everybody in Indiana knew him and loved him.

One of my friends, who attended an authors' reading in New York, described to me the effect of Riley's first appearance there.

"All the big ones were seated on the platform—Howells and Aldrich, Gilder and Stedman—and they all came forward one by one and read their compositions or poems, in calm and rather feeble voices which hardly reached the back-seat auditors, and at last, about eleven o'clock, just when everybody was tired out and ready to leave, Gilder, who was presiding, said, 'And now I have the pleasure of presenting Mr. James Whitcomb Riley, the Hoosier poet, from Indianapolis.'

"Thereupon a short, blond, bald, wide-mouthed man who had been sitting at the back of the platform came forward and, without book or manuscript, began to recite a poem. With his first line he woke that tired audience. There was something at once human and dramatic in him. He had humor and pathos and the quality we call magnetism, and he also possessed the art of the true comedian. As they used to say of English actors, 'the pit rose at him.'

"When he finished every hand applauded with a vigor which had nothing polite about it. It was a spontaneous tribute to genius."

Riley was known to the critics and editors of New York City, and thereafter all its halls and magazines were open to him. He had arrived.

My admiration for the man and my liking for his work led me to write a lecture on vernacular verse in which he was the chief exemplar of the newer, truer Hoosier dialect. I sent this to him for his approval and soon after received the following characteristic letter:

"DEAR MAN. I 'ben away fhum home, 'at's why. Now tell me where to send it, so's it'll be *shore* an' reach ye. Seriously, though, I'll tell you what's the matter with it. It's *too* good, —as even I forecast when I felt the grip o' your hand and thawed in the blaze o' your eyes. You want to stand firm as 'John Maynard' at the helm of yourself, and not root up the sea so or you'll founder us both. That's all! When I return article, you just jump into me with both feet and sqush me through your toes every once in a while! I'll stand it better, and so will your general audience. Write me *where* and I'll send lecture as promptly as I hear from you. Am swirled in a vortex of things. Getting ready for coming lecture campaign. Mr. Nye and I are billed together. Solely, steadfastly yours—and God cuff you with great palms of grace!"

J. W. RILEY.

"Your poem 'Ladrone' just now escapes my finding. It is safe, however, and I'll return it soon as I can search further. I don't wonder at all that Edgar Fawcett finds in it, and all your work, such marrowfat for praise. Don't you be other than reposeful as to your worth. Your work is *religion*. Keep it always that, and no fear then of anything."

The reference in this letter to Edgar Fawcett brings to mind a novelist of New York City—now utterly forgotten— with whom I corresponded and whose work, in my judgment, then, made him one of the representatives of "the urban group"—as I was moved to name them as a part of my scheme. Fawcett's novels were indeed saturated with the color of old New York—"The House at High Bridge," for example. I still think his books significant.

III

One night at the Authors' Club in New York City, I met the two most distinguished writers of Southern dialect, Hopkinson Smith and Thomas Nelson Page. I think Gilder introduced me to them, and also to John Burroughs, whom I remember as a small, dark-bearded, handsome man who kept shyly in the background. Will Carleton, whose "Betsey and I Are Out," had been one of my recitations at school in the West, was also there—a tall man with pleasant smile— but the figure which stands out most clearly in my mind was that of "Hop" Smith, slim and graceful, who did a "stunt" for the amusement of the members.

Rising gravely from his seat, he laid aside his coat, and bowing low on all sides in recognition of applause leaped upon an imaginary tight rope and there trod to and fro, balancing a long pole (also imaginary) in clever simulation of a circus acrobat. When we applauded he bowed again right and left with the mechanical grin of the professional, kissing his hands to imaginary ladies and then at the end he leaped to the ground with catlike grace, smiling and gen-uflecting in grateful acknowledgment of our approval.

To me, a serious reformer, this was an amazing exhibition of what I later came to call "the spirit of the studio." Never having seen any of Smith's paintings, and knowing little of his career as a lighthouse builder and novelist, I conceded his skill as an actor. Like Riley, he was a most successful platform reader.

Thomas Nelson Page recited a short story which was so filled with negro dialect that I could not follow it and several others spoke, but the two men I most vividly recall are Burroughs for his shy reticence and "Hop" Smith for his assured and graceful fooling.

There was a cult of the vernacular in 1888 and Gilder was its high priest. Not that his own poems were in that manner, but as an editor he welcomed it, and printed it, gladly. In almost every issue of the *Century,* either in the body of it or in the "Lighter Vein" at the back he carried dialect by Riley and other writers in the vernacular with illustrations by A. B. Frost or some other sympathetic artist and Alden of *Harper's* was almost equally hospitable. With their aid fiction as well as poetry was basing itself on the common earth.

Coincident with this demand on the part of the public for local-color literature came a call for local-color recitals on the platform, and a flock of corn krakes and woodland thrushes arose. George W. Cable spoke and sang from the platform (like Riley) in the vernacular of his native city, which was New Orleans, and Clemens of Missouri went on the circuit with him, a curious pair to draw to—as Mark said. Cable, small, refined with a high, soft, almost timid voice, was the exact opposite of Clemens, his profane and shaggy partner. I saw them several times together and the contrast always caused me to wonder how such a combination came about. Howells was unable to tell me, but he chuckled over the reports which Clemens gave him.

Cable, gentle, religious, and rather effeminate, was always courteous and considerate, but Clemens, a merciless practical joker, made life very uncertain for his kindly companion for a while. Ultimately he came to like him and let up on his shocking remarks. Cable used to illustrate his stories by singing the Creole songs of the French Quarter of New

Orleans and his audiences liked his clear, musical chanting. Clemens told negro stories marvelously and read selections from his far Western books.

Bill Nye and Riley made another team which was highly successful for several seasons. Nye's humor was not always to my taste, but some of his numbers I still recall as very funny. One of these was a burlesque of a story in an old-fashioned school reader and the boy who was called upon to read it. Riley was always effective, for he had the art of the poet as well as that of the reciter. He was a full program all by himself and was "chased" by lecture committees.

John Fox was almost equally successful as an exponent of the Kentucky mountaineer, and in "Hell Fer Sartain" and other sententious monologues pleased many audiences East and West. Hopkinson Smith who had created "K'yernel C'yahter of C'yahtersville" was as adroit on the platform as he was in lighthouse building, painting, and fictionizing. He was the most versatile man of all my acquaintances, and a delightful companion. Of robust build, with powerful head and shoulders, a mustache with wide sweeping wings, and a pleasant smile, he made a handsome figure in any company. There was nothing quaintly humorous about him; his success came from his choice of words and the dramatic quality of his inflection. He was the Southern gentleman telling a good story in the way of a negro or Virginia planter.

Thomas Nelson Page who occasionally joined the ranks of these entertainers, did not make regular tours as a reader. Stedman and Gilder did not utterly refuse to appear as readers of their own verses, at least in New York City, and many lesser men like myself were only too glad to be called upon to contribute our voices to this chorus of larks and thrushes, and as a result every corner of our wide land

yielded up its most characteristic accent. The lecture platform, like the theater, became an exponent of local-color
art, and so these sayers, actors, and singers came at last to
the point of fulfilling, to some degree, the prophecy of
Whitman who had cried out, "I see all America singing."

IV

When in 1886 Hurd asked me to review a novel called
"Zury" by a man named Joseph Kirkland of Chicago and
I found it recording the dialect of the early Illinois "sucker"
I tackled it with some misgivings. The author was unknown,
the region ugly, but I was soon convinced of the book's truth
and power. While it was a trifle too meticulous in the statement of its facts, and its values were too evenly distributed,
it nevertheless appealed to me as the best picture of pioneer
Illinois life yet written. It was less fantastic than Eggleston,
and its characters were wholly unrelated to Dickens or any
other writer. Its style, curiously sprightly, was equally uncon-
ventional, and the speech of its chief character, "Zury, the
meanest man in Spring County," phonetically exact.

I wrote of it with enthusiasm as one of the first veritistic
novels of the mid-West and called especial attention to the
story's most appealing feature, its recognition of the fact that
upon the wives and mothers of the border fell the heaviest
burdens of pioneering. Not only did they suffer from loneliness and poverty, but they were often called upon to see their
children die for lack of food and competent medical care.

My review of this book drew from the author a letter of
grateful appreciation:

"DEAR SIR: Many, many reviews of 'Zury' but none that
went quite so straight to my heart as yours in Monday's
Transcript. How could you, an Eastern man, enter so com-

pletely into my views, aims, principles? . . . Well, whether 'Zury' sells or not, I have at least the book itself and your review of it, so fate and I are not far from square."

My reply not only explained that I was a Western man myself, but that after three years of life in Boston I was going West on a visit, and to this Kirkland responded on May 31st:

"Your second letter has arrived and I have been waiting for it in order to carry out my wife's command to ask you to hasten your visit westward so as to spend a week with us. I recognize the justice of your criticism of my dialect, but if this lingo, now spoken by some ten millions of people, is to be crystallized, it must be done by taking an average and sticking to it. It is a composite photograph establishing a type. I took it (modified, of course) from a country district in Central Illinois, where I spent ten years and whence I drew my subject.

"By this mail I send a copy of 'Zury' with my emendations made in preparation for a second edition. The main corrections are those from pp. 219 to 232, where I have added a word to relieve my beloved Anne from any suspicions of wantonness such as (to my surprise) I find some women harboring against her.

"If Mr. Howells (name to conjure with) has not yet read 'Zury' I should like him to have the use of this amended copy. Also Mr. Baxter. Perhaps it would not be asking too much to beg you to get another copy or copies (chargeable to me, of course) from Houghton, Mifflin & Co. and scribble in the new matter for the use of either of these gentlemen or any other literary person who may be interested. I can not bear to have any one see that poor girl in a false light. I am more than pleased to hear that you are coming westward. Please let me know just when to expect you, that I may prepare to entertain you at home unless my house shall be closed for the summer. But even if it be so, I shall be 'camping' in it and we can perhaps make life tolerable there.

"More reviews come pouring in. Still I think yours holds first place even above one from San Francisco, which declares 'the book bears strong internal marks of having been written by a woman' and speaks of the author as 'she.' That makes me fancy that all my loving labor on Anne was far from wasted."

This invitation interested me and I at once replied, promising to stop on my way Westward.

CHAPTER TEN

A RETURN TO THE WEST

I

DESPITE the aid and endorsement of considerate friends, and my teaching and writing, I found myself, after three years, still clinging to my attic room in Jamaica Plain. Although paying for my housing with increasing regularity, I permitted myself only now and again a gallery seat in the theater. Walking wherever I could to save carfare I denied myself many needed things in order to pay for a visit to my father and mother in Dakota and to my old home in Iowa.

For this purpose I had, on June 15th, 1887, exactly one hundred dollars. As this sum was the result of three years' labor, I cannot claim to have been a literary success. However, I was at home in Boston, which I considered the most distinguished city of America, and felt a growing, slowly growing, confidence in my ability to make a living. With no extravagant hopes of my future, I acknowledged that I would have been on the rocks several times but for my good friends, Professor Brown and Dr. Cross.

New York was an unknown, terrifying jungle to me. Its millions oppressed me. As a single taxer I saw in it a dreadful example of progress and poverty. I was in no sense drawn to it. Equally ignorant of Philadelphia and Washington, I was content with New England, my ancestral home, and with Boston, its storied capital. Chicago was negligible, interesting only as the home of Joseph Kirkland, my newly discovered friend.

These admissions are necessary to define the intellectual fog (if one can define a fog) in which I lived and worked. I had developed a notion, a fuzzy notion, that I could in some fashion put certain phases of my boyhood into literature, and with intent to record my impressions I carried in my pocket a small notebook in which I designed to set down my observations and my mental reactions.

This absurdly feeble little book is before me as I write, and its brown pasteboard cover (broken at the corners), its leaves yellowed with years, bring back to me the highly wrought emotion with which I bought my round-trip ticket to Ordway, Dakota, that summer morning. According to this record I spent two nights in the day coach, dozing the long hours away in company with the men and women of my financial status, snatching poisonous sandwiches at Buffalo and other ten-minute station stops, so that when I reached Chicago I was by no interpretation a triumphant literary critic. I presented myself at Kirkland's door on Rush Street with sadly wrinkled coat and a headache.

The author of "Zury" was a small man, alert and humorous, with keen, black eyes and thick, dark eyebrows, and his home, a four-story mansion on the north side of the Chicago River, still further subdued me. He received me in his ground-floor study with cordial interest and after thanking me for my review of his novel, began to quiz me. "What are you doing out here?"

Briefly (I was too sick to be verbose) I gave him a history of my life while he leaned back in his chair and smilingly regarded me. He could hardly restrain his laughter, and yet I was the *Transcript* reviewer of his novel and his fine eyes grew sympathetic as I confessed that I had been two nights in a day coach with only such sleep as a hard seat permitted, and then, remembering my mission, I turned interrogator. "How did you come to write 'Zury'?"

He explained that he had lived almost all his life in Illinois, part of the time in a small town. "I am the son of a pioneer woman writer, Caroline Kirkland," he said, "and I know farm life. All the characters in 'Zury' have their prototypes in my down-state acquaintances. The book is as true as I could make it. Many of its incidents are literally exact."

I then spoke of Eggleston's work, and he agreed with me that it was the truest fiction of the mid-West yet written —"excepting 'Zury,' of course," he said with a humorous lift of his eyebrows. "Howe is too melodramatic. His country town never had existence outside of his tired brain. Why shouldn't our prairie country have its novelists as well as England or France or Norway? Our characters will not be peasants, but our fiction can be close to the soil."

He then showed me a tall pile of manuscript. "Here is my sequel to 'Zury,' a story I call the 'McVeys.' I want you to read it and tell me what you think of it."

His was the keenest mind I had ever met in the West, for he was a lawyer as well as a man of letters. We discussed my favorite subject, "The Local-Color Groups in American Literature," and he admitted that he had not taken it so seriously. "I have been a part of it without knowing it," he said with another flash of understanding. "I am afraid my eyes were fixed on Eggleston's 'Hoosier School-master' and 'The Circuit Rider' as examples to be improved upon."

He, too, was reading Tolstoy. "I have a great admiration

for Howells," he said, "but I can't follow him in his exaltation of the Russian novelists. I find a pose in all of Tolstoy's praise of labor and the nobility of the peasant."

We went over the ground covered by our local novelists. I told him of Miss Wilkins and Miss Jewett, some of whose work he knew, and we discussed Cable in New Orleans and Page in Virginia. "Why is it?" I demanded, "that the great State of Illinois has no novelist but you—and you of recent date?"

"For the same reason that the noble State of Iowa has no writer but you; in fact I know of none in the whole Northwest. We of the prairie are just reaching the articulate stage, I guess."

"That's what I had in mind when I began my articles descriptive of boy life on the prairie," I replied. "New England had many poems and stories descriptive of farm life, but the West had not a line, so far as my reading went, which dealt with corn-husking and wheat harvests on the prairie. So I've tried to put some of my boyhood experiences into essays and verse."

"Your articles on Western farm life are good as far as they go," he said, "but you should move on into fiction."

"Fiction is out of my line," I declared. "I can write descriptions of things, but I can not do dialogue."

"Nonsense!" he replied, with a mocking note in his voice. "You're lazy, that's all. It's easier to tell about people than it is to dramatize them, but you'll come to it. You *must* come to it."

II

"You're lazy, that's all!" This accusation stuck in my mind.

It was true. All the way across Iowa I pondered the problem. "Can I move on into the short-story field? Can I put the life of Wisconsin and Iowa into fiction as Eggleston has done for Indiana and as Kirkland is doing for Illinois? Miss Wilkins and Sarah Orne Jewett are recording the life of New England by means of the short story. Why can not I do something of the same sort for Wisconsin?"

I arrived in Osage about sunrise of the Fourth of July, weary with another sleepless night in a common coach with grimy skin and wrinkled clothing, but alert to all that was going on inside of me as well as to all that was going on around me. That I was in process of change is made evident by some dated notes which I have before me. I didn't make many—I hadn't sense enough, for my point of view was plainly that of one who, having escaped from this sad life, was now a pitying onlooker. That my old neighbors were in a mood of depression was evident. Things were going badly with them. Wheat was very low in price and dairying had brought new problems and new drudgery into their lives. Six years had made little improvement in farm conditions. The trees they had planted had grown up around their homesteads, but new houses were few.

My mind was in a tumult of readjustment. I had gone far in the years of my absence. Three years in Boston had not only given me perspective on these farms and villages, they had made me a reformer. There was nothing humorous about the lives of these toilers. On the contrary, I regarded them as victims of an unjust land system. An immense pity took possession of me. I perceived their helplessness. They were like flies in a pool of tar. By some miracle I had escaped this enslavement, and while I rejoiced in a wider, happier life I had no desire to satirize those less fortunate.

The records which I made on the spot are valuable to me as revelations of contemporary moods:

"Osage, July 4, 1887.

"The dress of all the farmers I met seemed unkempt, miserable. Perhaps they can afford no better. George A.'s house showed rude comfort, but not a trace of beauty. Rag carpets, old gunny sacks on the floor. George and his family were eating their Sunday dinner of bread and milk. He was in his shirt sleeves with bare feet. The table was covered with blue oilcloth with vast pitchers of milk and dishes of pickles. The steel forks and the use of steel knives brought back disagreeable memories. The irritable women dragged their tired and ugly bodies around, unlovely, characterless, finding comfort only in the Gospels."

On another page I find a still more depressing note:

"At Blank's house I came upon the ghost of a once happy girl. . . . The dumb old man and his guinea hen of a wife. . . . The flies, the poor food, the narrow room, the crude and ignorant husband who knew nothing but the care of his cattle, unthinking, irreligious. . . . The white, drawn face of the girl-wife—'I do not find time to play the organ now,' she said. She gazed upon me with wondering eyes while two little brats tugged at her knee. The yard was full of weeds. As I drove away I felt that I had looked upon the tragic end of a happy girlhood.

"The lives of these farmers are hard, parched by the sun and tanned by the wind. They wear filthy clothing the year round. I heard no words of affection in their homes. All is loud, coarse, but rudely wholesome. They fear to be polite. They consider it a weakness. They are all pack-horses and they never lay down their burdens. No wonder the boys are discontented and that the girls marry early. No beauty, no music, no art, no joy—just a dull and hopeless round of toil. What is it all worth?"

In these lines, authentic of mood, the reader will get, as I do, a very clear notion of my state of mind as I said good-by to these friends and took the train for the James River Valley in South Dakota. Nothing that I saw on my long ride west and north lightened my gloom. On the contrary, the farther I got into the sun-smitten treeless plain, the deeper my gloomy concepts of its life became. Of what avail such human life?

III

My father's cottage, set on a swell in the midst of a wide wheat farm, was unshaded and bleak, but my mother's smiling face gave evidence that her spirit was still unbroken, and when I saw my father bring to her a handful of wild roses, I was reassured. He had not lost the touch of gallant courtesy which he had brought with him from the East. "There's nothing prettier than wild roses in the wheat," he said.

In that hot little house I wrote my first story, a sketch descriptive of the life I had known as a boy. It was in truth only the amplification of a tale which my mother retold of an old neighbor in Iowa who, after many years of border life, went "back to York State" on a visit. "Mrs. Ripley" was not unlike a character in Mary Wilkins' stories and I wrote nearly two thousand words of her story one Sunday forenoon.

When I read it to my mother she said, "That's good. Go on and finish it."

This I did and sent it to *Harper's Weekly*. It brought me seventy dollars, the first substantial sum I had ever received for a manuscript, half of which I sent to my mother as co-author.

Sitting on the doorstep of this little Dakota cottage, I wrote "Color in the Wheat," a poem suggested by the actual waves of grain before me and my memory of the more luxuriant harvests on our Iowa farm.

> "Like liquid gold the wheat field lies,
> A marvel of yellow and green,
> That ripples and runs, that floats and flies,
> With the subtle shadows, the change—the sheen
> That plays in the golden hair of a girl.
> A cloud flies there—
> A ripple of amber—a flare
> Of light flows after. A swirl
> In the hollows, like the twinkling feet
> Of fairy waltzers, the colors run
> To the western sun
> Through the deeps of the ripening wheat.

> "I hear the reaper's far-off hum
> So faint and far, it seems the drone
> Of bee or beetle; seems to come
> From far-off fragrant fruity zone,
> A land of plenty, where
> Toward the sun, as hasting there,
> The colors run
> Before the wind's feet
> In the wheat.

> The wild hawk swoops to his prey in the deeps.
> The sunflower droops
> To the lazy wave; the wind sleeps—
> Then running in dazzling links and loops
> A marvel of shadow and shine,
> A glory of olive and amber and wine
> Runs the color in the wheat."

Notwithstanding the rigid economy of my mode of travel, I found myself without sufficient money to pay my way back to Boston, and to earn a few dollars I volunteered to work in the harvest field "provided I receive a boss's pay."

To this my father agreed and so on Monday morning following the writing of the poem, I returned to manual labor. Three years of literary life in "the Hub of the Universe" had robbed me of my strength. It was a test of my physical resiliency. My muscles were flabby and my hands soft, but I endured silently. The harvesting machine was a header which cut the grain and delivered it into huge wagon boxes. These carriers, three in number, kept me so busy on my stack that at the end of my first day I was barely able to crawl into the house for a bath and supper.

The literary value of this experience did not escape me, and in a letter to Kirkland a week later, I described my swollen hands, my chapped lips, and the cling of my dusty, sweaty shirt. "I am back right where I started from," I added ruefully.

"Fine!" he replied. "You are the first actual farmer in literature. Tolstoy is a make-believe. You are the real thing. Make the most of your experience. Note it all down. Leave out no essential."

This reference to Tolstoy was especially potent with me, for he was being pictured in the magazines in the act of holding a plow or seated on a shoemaker's bench, wearing an artistic smock and with nobly flying gray hair. Not being an aristocrat, my farming was painfully factual. Kirkland's line, "You are the first actual farmer in literature," stayed in my mind, and in my moments of rest I composed poems of the plains and jotted down suggestions for stories of farm life, more and more eager for my attic in Jamaica Plain in order that I might begin my career as a Western fictionist. The value of my experiences with the harvester increased with each day's labor and my correspondence with the author of "Zury" clarified my thinking.

The other workmen were puzzled by my efficiency. As a man from Boston, I was, naturally, a subject for jest. They respected my father, for he was the owner of seven hundred acres of land, but—I—well, I was a youth who had failed in the City.

Early in September I "resigned." Promising to come again next summer, I took the money which I had earned as boss stacker and set out for Boston, stopping for a day or two in the lovely Wisconsin valley in which I had spent my childhood, a country which seemed especially alluring after six weeks on the arid, treeless sod of Dakota.

Here, too, I gained material for stories. My ambition to be a novelist was fully aroused. "I am resolved to put my own region into literature in my own way," I said to Kirkland and when he introduced me to two young men who were starting a paper, I offered a poem!

IV

It was with a sense of relief, of satisfaction, and of antici-pated opportunity for work, that I climbed to the little attic room which was all that Dr. Cross could allot to me. "Stay as long as you like," he had said, and so with a powerful urge to record my new concept of the West, I set to work at my scarred little desk under my one narrow window, toiling hour after hour in such complete absorption that my sur-roundings did not count.

In a few weeks I had finished several short stories and a novelette and was ready to begin my bombardment of the magazines. My plan of battle was to "aim high and keep shooting" and to Gilder of the *Century* and Henry M. Alden of *Harper's* (high judges and advocates of local color in fiction) I sent the first of my almost illegible manuscripts. I had no typewriter (few authors made use of them) and no editor of to-day would read such a manuscript as "Mrs. Ripley's Trip" must have been. Alden declined this story but Foord of the *Weekly* accepted it. Gilder read and accepted another.

My visit to Burr Oak led to the writing of "A Branch Road," and my stop-over in West Salem gave me the theme for "Up the Coulée."

Having occasion recently to look through the bound volumes of several magazines published about 1885, at the time when I began to write of the middle West, I realized as never before the dense fog out of which my earliest verse and poems unexpectedly emerged. So far as the pages of the literary magazines of that year were concerned, Wisconsin, Minnesota, and Iowa did not exist. Not a picture, not a single story or poem, not even a reference to these states could I discover in ten thousand pages of print. Old World travel, New England fiction, New York historical essays, Civil War papers, articles on the Hudson River and the White Mountains were there, but nothing of the central West. England was depicted, and Palestine and Egypt, but not one word of the prairies of Illinois or the hills and lakes of Wisconsin could I find.

Why was this? The cause is simple. The Eastern readers of these magazines were not interested in descriptions of the monotonous mid-West. They were eager for the plains of Araby and the Vale of Cashmere, but the prairies of Iowa held no allurement. Cairo caused a deep stir in the reader's imagination, but Chicago was a bore. "Romance is in Europe, not in Wisconsin."

Nevertheless Edward Eggleston continued writing his stories of Indiana, and Riley was composing and successfully reciting his Hoosier poems. Joseph Kirkland had sent to the press one novel of pioneer days in central Illinois, and Edgar W. Howe of Missouri had actually found a publisher for his "Story of a Country Town." Alice French with her stories of Arkansas, I related to a Southern group.

The Pacific Coast, through the work of Bret Harte and Joaquin Miller, had been annexed to the literary world some ten years before, and the South, through the stories of Page, Harris, and Cable, had won space in the *Century, Harper's,* and *The Atlantic,* but my native state remained an unknown and unsought literary field. Nevertheless it was with tales of this drab and distant region that I bombarded the magazines, along with descriptive articles on farm life and poems of windy hills and waving grasses. I wonder that any editor took the trouble to read them, especially as they were all written in long hand on the cheapest paper.

But they did! Gilder of the *Century* and Alden of *Harper's* wrote me encouragingly and John Foord, editor of *Harper's Weekly,* took and paid for "Mrs. Riley's Trip," while other and lesser magazines accepted my sketches and poems. Here and there people spoke of me as a pioneer in the vaguely flat, repellent West. And this, in a sense, and without knowing it, I really was.

How did it come about? It came in accordance with the laws of perspective and a growth in comparative ideas. Four years in Boston had given me distance, standards, perception. Had I remained in the West I could never have given literary value to this material. This visit to the West marks the beginning of my fictional career.

What a winter that was for me! In the intervals of my teaching (every forenoon and often late at night), I wrought at my desk in the conviction that I had something to say which no one else had thought of saying. In this mood I wrote and rewrote, inspired by Howells, whose flexible yet always beautiful style I greatly admired. I had no wish to imitate him—my expression must be my own—but the care, the judgment, the taste which were so evident in every line that he published, held me to my resolution. "Nothing slipshod shall remain in my manuscript if I can weed it out," I said.

With a feeling that style should be a garment adjusted to the thought, and that my stories concerned that rugged folk, I kept my prose in their quality. My mood was dark and bitter, I must admit, and much of my writing during the next three years was austere. It was not all savage, however. Two or three sketches, like "Uncle Ethan's Speculation," were humorous and made successful readings in the programs which I occasionally gave to my classes.

Among my files I lately came across another of my little notebooks which bears the date 1888 and testifies that I spent a part of that summer lecturing at a New Hampshire summer school and here is a note which proves that my truth-telling mood held over: "*At Weirs.*—Such a collection of lean and hungry women. Such bare-bones of manners. Here is the American rural democracy, corresponding to the democracy of Boston Common. Here are women of no taste, no style—but of deep earnestness. They take their pleasures sadly."

Another record is a penciled poem preceded by the line, "Written at Mr. Howells' place."

This was at Watertown just beyond Belmont, the house and garden which he celebrated later in his novelette, "The Shadow of a Dream." He was away when I called but was expected soon, and as I lay out on the grass under a tall tree, I wrote a poem which later became "A Message to the Toiler" and expresses the reforming mood of the day:

> "Lying prone where a broad elm stands and sways
> I look with dreaming, troubled gaze
> To where beneath the far-off city's haze
> Worn men are toiling in the heat.
> O wind of the West, go greet for me
> These toilers in the city's deeps.
> Go teach them to be wild and free
> And chainless as the eagle keeps."

While I waited there in the shade, I could see through the open door, Mildred Howells, a little girl with hair in pigtails, working at her drawing, for she was even then determined to be an illustrator.

Howells came in soon after and as he led me through the fine old garden, tangled and weedy (it was a rented place), he said, "I can not bring myself to change it; it is so beautiful in its neglect." There was a hydraulic ram at the lower corner of the plot, and in speaking of it he said, "We always allude to its path as 'the walk along the ramparts.'"

This jocose remark remains with me while most of what we talked about is utterly gone. His talk was often deliciously humorous, but he seldom made a pun.

Another of my impressions in verse form is headed

The Isle of Shoals

Bare scarp of rock
Set like a share to plow the sea,
It lies, lava-like, naked
With crevices lit by gleam of splendid shells
And sheen of foam on glowing moss.
No tree against the cloudless sky appears,
No note of bird or farm-yard brute is heard,
Only the sun-bright sea's wild singing.
As white as snow the waters ramp
Across the polished granite capes.
Lost in mist the far horizon-line
Blends with the gray-blue of the sky.
I dream and shudder as I dream,
Of how the mighty thunder of the seas
Breaks in winter on these savage cliffs
Where now the fisher nods and sways
In warm clear light.

The remorseless mood in which I moved, even in New England, is shown by a third paragraph. I do not recall where it was written, but the heading is "A Working Man's Home."

"This means a small, bare, dingy room to sleep in. It means a table spread with a dirty red cloth, with aged napkins under each plate, a table swarming with flies and bare of wholesome food, with beans, sour bread, tough beef, and acidulous pies."

I dimly recall this as a description of an eating house, but that I saw other and lovelier places is indicated by this paragraph:

"In Kittery, Maine. The huge elms, the old houses, the sun-bright seas in vistas here and there, the apple trees, the green nooks, the quaint, familiar farmsteads so still and peaceful on this Sabbath day. . . . The Pepperel mansion is over two hundred years old. How lovely it all is in contrast to the hot Dakota plain."

My brother was with me, and it would seem that I was beginning to work on a play, the one I afterwards called "Under the Wheel" (my first published book or booklet), for I find in this same notebook jottings of scenes, characters, and situations. That I was groping in a misty world toward something high and stern and true, is made certain by incoherent scraps of dialogue and descriptions. It is all so long ago—so far away!

In order that my readers may understand some part of the generous and catholic spirit of Henry M. Alden at this time, I quote a letter written to me when I was feeling my way toward authorship. He says:

"I liked your story 'A Case of Embezzlement' very much, but you have not given it the care it deserves and which is necessary not only to its intrinsic excellence but also to its effective impression on your readers. It is partly because of this negligence on your part that the story is much too long. It is much easier to make a story of 14,000 words than to put the same structure within the limits of 9,000, and yet the limitations give better art and secures for the story twice the number of readers. . . . I have no faith in mere criticism. I never read a story in a critical mood, but I *feel* certain things and it is from this feeling that I am writing to you.

"I return the MS. and if you should revise it, I will gladly reconsider it."

Whether I took this criticism in the right spirit or not I am unable to state, but as I read it now I appreciate how much time this sympathetic letter cost an overworked editor.

I am certain that it was only one of many others of similar encouragement to other authors. Like Richard Watson Gilder, Alden was intent on developing the best that was in American writers. Essentially noble in every utterance, I gladly bear witness to the sympathetic hospitality of both these editors whose influence was second only to that of Howells; they welcomed every sincere attempt at native art.

V

My work at Brown's school continued and prospered to the point of providing enough money to take me to Dakota again in the summer of 1889, but everything conspired to keep me in the mood of a reformer. I wrote articles for the *Standard*, Henry George's New York paper, and held myself ready to speak on the "Single Tax" to any club or society willing to pay my carfare. In 1889 I wrote a single tax story, "Under the Lion's Paw," which *Harper's Weekly* published and which my friend, James A. Herne, read, now and again, with dramatic success. It is rather remarkable that I kept as clear of preaching in my stories as I mostly did, but this was due in a large measure to Howells, who had taught me to exemplify, not to preach.

My first play, "Under the Wheel," appeared in the *Arena* and was afterward published or printed, let us say, from these plates by the Barta Press, and the public was directed to address Garland Brothers for extra copies. We had a few hundred copies printed and I tried hard to give them away. To-day they are valuable as curiosities.

This was not the end of the theme, however, for I novelized it, and in the story which I called "Jason Edwards," I contrasted the tenement life of Boston with the settler's life in Boomtown, Dakota. That this was not an entirely foolish book is evident from the comment of William Stead in the English *Review of Reviews*. "I found in the July *Arena* a remarkable feature, a modern play by Hamlin Garland, a terribly realistic story, a grim representation of the way in which human beings are ground 'under the wheel' of incessant and useless toil."

It comforts me to recover these words of approval from my files, for as I became more of the artist and less of the preacher, I grew a little shy of bringing this work to mind. "Jason Edwards" long ago passed out of print and is of value only as an indication of the bitter and accusing mood of that day, a time of parlor socialists, single-taxers, militant populists, Ibsen dramas, and Tolstoyan encyclicals against greed, lust, and caste.

In all these revolutionary movements I shared to some degree. I advocated the stark realism of Ibsen's plays. I helped Herne to banish soliloquies and asides. I argued for "impressionism" as well as a layman could, and always, everywhere, I preached against special privilege and denounced the injustice of monopoly. In short, I was a very unpleasant person to meet. I wonder that any one invited me to dinner, but they did, and gradually I lost my eagerness for debate and in my less exacting moods I became almost conformable.

CHAPTER ELEVEN

WALT WHITMAN OLD AND POOR

I

ONE of the very first books for which I had asked at the Boston Public Library was Walt Whitman's "Leaves of Grass." I had heard much of this book in the West but had never set eyes upon it, and even here in Boston it was "double starred" on the list and issued only to serious students of literature. Heaven knows I was serious enough, and so at the age of twenty-five I began my acquaintance with "the poet of Democracy."

Of the tremendous vitality of his message I was at once aware. Formless as the book appeared, its deeply patriotic spirit, its wide sympathy with working men and women, and especially its faith in the destiny of "these States" exalted me. I caught some part of the writer's faith in American manhood and the part America was to play in the world's future history.

From "Leaves of Grass" I passed to "Specimen Days" which made him still more admirable to me. That he profoundly influenced my thinking I freely acknowledge. I reread De Tocqueville in the light of "Democratic Vistas," perceiving that the local-color novel had sociologic value in that it aided the readers of one part of our widely separated States to understand the problems of another. I began at once to say these things to my students at Brown's school and elsewhere.

127

I went further. I wrote to Walt (as he called himself) telling him how inspiring I found his prose and that I considered it the very best avenue of approach to his poetry. This was on November 24, 1886.

"MR. WALT WHITMAN: It is with profound sorrow that I read in the papers the news that you are again suffering from your old trouble. I trust it is not as serious as reported. My regard for you is so great that I am very sorry not to be able to buy more copies of your book and thus give a more substantial token of sympathy.

"I am an enthusiastic reader of your books, both volumes of which I have within reach of hand. I am everywhere in my talking and writing making your claims felt and shall continue to do so. I have demonstrated (what of course you know) that there is no veil, no impediment between your mind and your audience, when your writings are *voiced*. The formlessness is only seeming, not real. I have never read a page of your poetry or quoted a line that has not commanded admiration. The music is there and the grandeur of thought is there if the reader reads, guided by the sense and not by the external lining or paragraphing. Even my young pupils feel the thrill of the deep rolling music though the thought may be too profound for them to grasp.

"In a course of lectures before the Boston School of Oratory last summer I made a test of the matter. I do not think a single pupil held out against my arguments supplemented by readings from your works. The trouble is they get at your work through the daily press or through the defenders of Longfellow or Tennyson (whom it is supposed you utterly antagonize). When it is brought to them by one who appreciates and measurably understands your methods and ideals, I do not think there is any doubt of the favorable result. I have found much opposition, but it was mostly ignorant or misled.

"I am a young man of very ordinary attainments, and do not presume to do more than give you a glimpse of the temper of that public which would not do you wrong, deliberately, but who, by reason of the causes hinted above, fail to get at the transcendent power of 'Leaves of Grass.' If I have given you the impression that I believe in you and strive to interpret you, you will not feel that I have over-stepped the privilege of a pupil in the presence of a great teacher.

"The enclosed slip is a meager outline of a volume which I am writing and which I hope to get out this coming spring. As the motto page of this volume I have used a paragraph from your 'Collect.' While it is not strictly essential to the book, yet I should esteem it a favor if you would consent to its use. One sentence, 'In nothing is there more evolution than in the American mind,' I have also used in company with Spencer's great law of progress. It helped to decide the title, which is: 'The Evolution of American Thought;' an outline study of the leading phases of American literature, etc. In the latter part of the volume I have treated of the Age of Democracy and its thought, taking as foundation the splendid utterances of M. Taine upon the modern age. It is in this chapter that I place your work. I quote from you quite largely both in treating of your writings and in treating the general theme of present and future democratic ideals. I hope to be able to please you with my treatment of your great work. Besides this I am preparing special lectures upon the same subject. Have you any objections to the quotations which I find it necessary to use?

"In conclusion let me say that without any bias in your favor (rather the opposite from newspapers) your poems thrilled me, reversed many of my ideas, confirmed me in others, helped to make me what I am. I am a Border man, born in Wisconsin and raised on the prairie frontier. I am a disciple of Mr. Spencer and therefore strive at comparative methods of criticism. That your poems should thus convert me is to me a revelation of their power, especially when I can convince others in the same manner.

"And now, revered friend (for I feel you are a friend), think of me as one who radiates the principles of the modern age, and who will in his best manner (poor at best) strive to make his hearers and readers better aware of the 'Good Gray Poet' and his elemental lines.

"Your readers are increasing, and may you live to see the circle infinitely extended is my fervent hope. I do not expect a reply to this other than the signification whether I may quote you or not. I wish I might see and talk with you but that is not possible, except through your volumes."

This letter interested him and he replied, but it was not till long after that I learned how profoundly it had touched him. To him I was a "Boston professor" and a highly influential convert!

So far as I knew he had only one other public advocate of his books in all Boston. This was William Sloane Kennedy, a man of letters who acted as proof reader on the *Transcript*. Our common interest in Whitman drew us together and from him I learned that the poet was living in Camden, New Jersey, alone, broken in health and very poor. "He is confined to his room but enjoys meeting his friends. Go and see him if you are down that way."

II

This suggestion lay in my mind for two years before I found myself able to carry it out. Not till October, 1888, did I cross the river from Philadelphia in search of the poet whose presence had made Camden known throughout the world. The citizens from whom I inquired my way to Mickle Street directed me into a mean section of the town and when I came to the number designated, I could not believe that I had been rightly informed, so dim was the doorplate and so weather-worn the doorway. The street was ugly and narrow, and the house, a two-story frame structure, was such as a day laborer might have owned, and yet the poet's name was there.

In answer to my ring, a small gray man whom I guessed to be Whitman's attendant came clumping down the stairway and received my name impassively. "Wait here," he said, "I'll see if you can come up."

While he went back up the stairs, I studied the faded paper on the walls, and the worn carpet of the hall with growing astonishment. There was nothing to indicate that a poet of world-wide fame was living here. His sordid surroundings filled me with indignation.

From the landing above the man called down, "Walt will see you for a few minutes." He emphasized the brevity of my stay and warned me not to weary the old man.

On entering the door on the left I found myself in a fairly large, square chamber on the north front of the house, and in the center of it Whitman, standing by his armchair, with a broad white hat on his head, awaited me, a tall man clothed in gray, with a cloud of snowy hair and beard enveloping his face.

Without leaving his place he extended his hand and greeted me pleasantly in a voice rather high in key, mellow and cordial, inviting me to be seated. The grip of his hand was firm and vital.

He was dressed in a loosely fitting gray robe, and his linen shirt with rolling collar unbuttoned at the throat and his cuffs were all equally immaculate. I thought him one of the noblest figures I had ever seen. His head was magnificent in contour, and his profile clean-cut as a coin.

In contrast to his personal order and comeliness, the room was an incredible mess. Beside his chair rose a most amazing mound of manuscripts, old newspapers, and clippings, with many open books lying, face down, at the point where he had laid them aside.

The furnishings of the room were few and ugly. The bleak windows looked out upon a row of frame tenements whose angular roofs and rude chimneys formed a dreary landscape. It was a melancholy place of confinement for one who had roamed America's open roads and sung its sunlit vistas. No one had prepared me for this bitter revelation of the meager awards which "Leaves of Grass" had won for its author.

In spite of his surroundings, Whitman looked the hero of the poems, strong, self-poised, with a certain delicacy of action and speech. His face when turned toward me discovered a pleasant, searching glance. His mouth was hidden in his great beard, but his eyes were smiling and the lines on his brow were level. Nothing querulous showed in voice or word. His speech was nobly pure with nothing of the coarseness I had been led to expect. When he dropped into homely phrase or coined a word he did so with humorous intonation. It is because some of his interviewers failed to record his smile that so many misinterpretations of his conversation have been recorded. This use of the common phrase now and again lent additional charm to his speech.

He had no word of humor, however. He was grave without being low-spirited or grim, placidly serious in all that he said. He made no reference to his poverty or to his illness and nothing petulant or self-pitying came into his voice.

Once he rose in order to find some book which he wished to show me and I perceived that one side of his body was almost useless. He dragged one leg and he used but one arm. In spite of the confusion of his books and papers he seemed to know where to find what he wanted.

The attendant had said "a few minutes," but Walt was interested, I could see that, and so I stayed on with full realization of the value of every additional moment. We talked of his English friends, of his growing acceptance there, and I confidently predicted his acceptance in America. "I can sense a change in the attitude of critics in the last two years," I assured him, and he listened with an eagerness almost pathetic. "I hope you are right," he said.

He asked me about my work in Boston and seemed keenly interested in my praise of "Specimen Days." "I find it the best introduction to your poetry," I said. "I advise all my pupils to begin by reading it."

"That is very curious," he said musingly. "Most of my readers neglect my prose."

I went on to say, "Your descriptive passages have the magic of setting me in the midst of your landscape. I feel it and see it as you saw and sensed it. I even smell it!"

As I talked he studied me with dim, gray-blue eyes, as if marveling at my youth and fervor. He had laid aside his broad Quaker hat by this time and I thought the lines of his head the noblest I had ever known. His brow was like that of a serene and kindly philosopher and his sentences were well chosen and concise. He had no local peculiarity of accent or pronunciation, at least he left no singularity of speech in my memory. My recorded impressions of him were all in harmony with my preconceived notions of his nobility of spirit.

He spoke slowly, choosing the best word for the place with impressive care. There was no looseness or mumbling in his enunciation. Every word came forth clear-cut and musical. He had the effect of compressing sentences into single words, but with his noble voice and subtle inflection there was no excuse for failure to apprehend his thoughts.

"I am a good deal of a Quaker," he said, as if explaining to me his peculiarities of dress. "My ancestors were Quakers, and I delight to recall and to retain certain of their distinctive customs."

One of his "whims," as he called them, was to suffer in silence the sting of the various false reports about him. He would not authorize his friends to go into print to defend him. He reminded me of Grant in this regard. "I prefer to leave all that to time," he said. "Such things clear themselves up, or at worst they deceive only the unthinking whom your explanation would not reach."

Naturally I led the talk toward things literary, and being "moved by the spirit," as he smilingly confessed, he talked freely of his contemporaries and gave me full permission to quote him.

I told him that many good people considered him unduly severe on American literature in general and "certain of our poets in particular, Stedman and Gilder for example."

He became grave. "You refer to a report by a German

writer. I do not think Stedman was deceived, though many of his friends think I have the spirit to rasp him. It would have been ingratitude to have said such words even had I thought them, which I do not. I hold Stedman in high regard as a man of decided insight and culture. On personal grounds I owe him much. The traveler you mention either willfully or otherwise *twistified*," here he smiled, "what I said—if I said anything in his presence. I am beset with all kinds of visitors who go away thinking me fair game. It is one of the evils which men of any"—he hesitated again—"notoriety must bear patiently.

"As for American literature in general, I have insisted, as all my readers know, on the need of distinctive flavor in our poetry. There is an old Scotch word, Burns uses it occasionally, which expresses exactly what I mean—the word 'race.' A wild strawberry, a wild grape has the racy quality—this distinctive tang. Our poetry lacks *race*. Most of it might have been written in England or on the Continent. I myself like Cooper, Bryant, Emerson, and Whittier because they have this distinctive American quality."

This led me to bring up the work of George W. Cable, Joseph Kirkland, Joel Harris, Mary E. Wilkins, and others of my friends who were getting, it seemed to me, just that flavor he was demanding. "Their books are, in my judgment, forerunners of a powerful native literature."

After a pause he said, "It may be so, but I have not read many of them. Against some of them I *have* read I might bring a grave charge. They have a deplorable tendency toward the *outré*. I call their characters *delirium-tremen characters*. These writers seem not content with the normal man; they must take the exceptional, the diseased. They are not true, not American in the deeper sense at all. To illustrate, in a hunter's camp of twenty men there will always be some who are distorted, unusual, grotesque, but they are not typical of the camp. So in an 'army mess' there are always characters more or less abnormal, men who enjoy distorting their faces and cutting up antics. And yet in all my coming and going among the camps of the Civil War, I was everywhere struck with the decorum—a word I like to use—of the common soldier, his good manners, his quiet heroism, his generosity, even his good, real grammar. These are a few of the typical qualities of the American farmer and mechanic."

All this was said quietly but with deep earnestness, as if he were working the problem out while speaking. Then turning his glance on me he spoke with decision. "I say that the novel or drama claiming to depict American life is false if it deals mainly or largely with abnormal or grotesque characters. They should be used merely as foils."

This led me to say, "In the early stages of national literature it is natural to deal with the abnormal, the exceptional because it startles, claims the attention, so it may be that the novelists you speak of may be just in the preparatory stage and that they will pass on to something higher."

He fell into a profound muse, and at last said with deliberate precision as if making a concession which he had not hitherto directly stated, "I don't know but you are right. I can see that the novice would find the exceptional nearest his hand and most noticeable, and it may be that these books are preparatory to a new, indigenous fiction. The public itself, moreover, seems to demand and enjoy such work. It may be as you argue, that the writers and the public will grow toward a higher perception. At any rate I want to utter my protest against such work and to demand that the really heroic character of the common American be depicted in novel and drama."

I forgot his age, his sickness, his drab surroundings as I listened to his musical voice and lofty personal convictions. He appeared a grand and ageless spirit. His sublime faith in the average American was not that of a dreamer, cloistered and bookish; it was the judgment of one who knew the farmer, mechanic, cab driver, miner, street laborer, and roustabout from personal contacts.

"I guess I am aware of our political and literary fraudulencies," he said calmly, "but as things are going on in the States—our time—I am confident of results. I have no sympathy with current pessimistic notions of life, of government, of society."

This serene and buoyant optimism in the midst of old age, poverty, and physical pain filled me with admiration. It was majestic. It was another proof of the grand and simple faith of this indomitable soul who looked into the future with the unswerving gaze of an eagle. He was still of a mind to say, "I know the future will be well, for all that is, is well."

Seeing that my interview was nearing an end, I said, "May I carry from you a friendly message to these young novelists?"

"You may, with this advice and plea: Tell them to go among the common men, as one of them, never looking down upon them. Tell them to study their lives and find out and celebrate their splendid primitive honesty, patience, and what I like to call their heroism. When our novelists shall do that in addition to being true to their time, their art will be worthy all praise from me or any other who is insisting on native anti-class poems, novels, and plays.

"And finally I would say to the young writer, don't depict evil for its own sake. Don't let evil overshadow your books. Make it a foil as Shakespeare did. His evil is always a foil for purity. Somewhere in your play or novel let the sunlight in." Here he raised his superb head and in a grandly suggestive gesture of his arm made his point clear. "As in some vast foundry whose walls are lost in blackness, a scuttle far up in the roof lets the sun and the blue sky in."

As I rose to go I assured him that the circle of his admirers was swiftly widening, and that his influence on our literature was certain to deepen year by year.

"Burroughs tells me the same thing," he said, "and I hope you are both right."

He put on his hat, and rising painfully to his feet gave me his hand at parting. I understood the respect which this formality indicated and was proud of it.

As I went away down the street, my heart ached with sympathy and resentment. To think of this great poet, author of "Specimen Days" and "Democratic Vistas," a prisoner in that dreary, sunless, depressing room, shut off from even a glimpse of the sky or a green leaf, was tragic. He was only waiting, like a fearless watchman, ready for the summons of relief.

In a letter which I wrote immediately after, I said:

"It is a shame that this man who gave the best years of his life and the very blood of his heart for the Northern soldier, and who did more to relieve the horrors of our Civil War hospitals than any other man, an angel of mercy to nearly a hundred thousand sick and dying men, should now in his age and weakness be lacking a cheerful home and the comforts of air and sunshine."

In a review of "November Boughs" I ended by saying:

"The advocates of Whitman's case have demanded too much of the public; they have not taken into account as well as he the inertia of the average mind, whose thinking is necessarily along well-worn grooves, and can be but slowly and unwillingly turned aside. We insist now on the critics taking a new stand on the matter. Whitman is no longer a mystery; he is a serene, gentle, grand old man, living in Camden, who sends us what he thinks in his final volume, desiring readers and friends, amidst the democracy which he loves so well, his faith not shaken by all the buffetings, unkindnesses, and neglect which he has received. We should hasten to do him honor while he is with us. Praise too often builds monuments when it should buy bread; furnishes tombstones where it should warm houses. Royal praise for the hearing ear, I say, flowers of love for the throbbing sense of the living poet. I present my tribute, drop my bit of laurel into the still warm, firm hand of the victorious singer.

" 'Serene vast head with silver cloud of hair
    Lined on the purple dusk of death,
    A stern medallion velvet set—
    Old Norseman throned, not chained, upon thy chair,
    Thy grasp of hand, thy hearty breath
    Of greeting thrills me yet
    As when I faced thee there!
    Loving my plain as thou thy sea,
    Facing the East as thou the West,
    A handful of grasses I bring to thee—
    The prairie grasses I love the best;
    Type of the width and wealth of the plain,
    Strong of the rigor of wind and sleet,
    Fragrant with sunlight and cool with rain,
    I bring it and lay it low at thy feet
    Here by the shore of the gray salt main!'

"I have faith to believe that the circle of readers who feel as I do toward Whitman is constantly growing and will continue to grow as men come to know him. May he live to enjoy the ever increasing respect of the thinking people of his day."

My confident prophecy of wider acceptance was borne out in the dinner which his friends arranged for his seventieth birthday. For some reason not clear to me now, I was not only invited to attend the dinner, but was made one of the speakers along with Richard Watson Gilder and Julian Hawthorne, and when just before the speaking began, old Walt, riding in a wheeled chair, came grandly in, waving his hand to the guests who rose and applauded him, space was made for him almost beside me, so that I was able to watch the changing expressions of his happy face, for he *was* happy in this chorus of congratulation and praise. Not all his loyal friends were there, but many of them were, and others had sent messages. I do not recall seeing Burroughs, but it may be that he sat at the other end of the table. My clearest recollection is of a delightful colloquy between old Walt and Gilder. In his address Gilder spoke of the harmony of form and spirit in "Leaves of Grass," and said that he found the form always appropriate and often beautiful.

"No, no!" interrupted Walt incredulously, "you don't mean that?"

Gilder turned and smilingly said, "Yes, Walt, I mean just that. I find the form of your verse logical and peculiarly satisfying."

This praise for the structure of his verse was of especial value to Whitman, for it came from an editor whose interests were almost entirely esthetic. Although not a great poet himself, Gilder had taste, and as he went on quoting passages from "Leaves of Grass" in which the poet's thought found almost perfect expression, Whitman smiled in pensive pleasure, rejoicing in the confirmatory applause of his auditors.

In spite of his evident enjoyment of the dinner, he grew weary at last and his attendants reluctantly wheeled him away, waving his hat in farewell, while all the guests rose and cheered his exit. Many of us realized that we would never see him again.

Thereafter I received but three cards from him.

"Thanks for the *Transcript* notice. Have much to say and thanks but can not write. I am getting along comfortably (considering what might be) for the last ten days. I now am easier. Big volume with my writings complete ready in two weeks and shall send you a copy.

                                        "WALT WHITMAN."

"Y'r welcome letter received. I saw Baxter's ardent and noble notice and am very grateful. Am still cabin'd here in the sick room. Don't feel particularly sick, but the physical machine seems disabled and weakened almost to an extreme. Can hardly move across the room without assistance—fortunately retain good spirits. Fine, sunny weather here; give my best respects to Mrs. Moulton, to Chamberlin, and to all my Boston friends."

His name was signed in a firm, bold hand to these notes, and in the envelope with the second one was the following lines which had just appeared in the *Critic* and may be taken as his honest admission of defeat.

To the Year 1889

"Have I no weapon word for thee—some message brief and fierce?
Have I fought out and done indeed the battle? Is there no shot left,
For all thy affectations, lisps, scorns, manifold silliness?
Nor for myself—my own rebellious self in thee?

"Down, down, proud gorge!—though choking thee:
Thy bearded throat and high-borne forehead to the gutter:
Crouch low thy neck to eleemosynary gifts!"

He expected little of the new year—and he got little.

He lived a little longer, in constant bodily pain, as Traubel
has recorded, but with mind unimpaired to the last. I was
not able to attend his funeral, but several of my friends
described to me the impressive character of the assembly.
Many notables were in the company, and the newspapers
of New York and Philadelphia awoke to the fact that a
very great personage had been living obscurely and in poverty just over the river, but few of those who wrote of him
were aware of his dreary old age and confinement. No one
has revealed that home as I saw it, and no one but Traubel
(who dug into that pile of letters and clippings) knew
how widely distributed and how distinguished Walt's correspondents had been. To this bleak, bare little room, hundreds of tributes from the most authoritative authors and
critics in the Old World had come, to lie unanswered in
their dusty grave.

In my own case, I remained unaware of his interest in
me till Traubel's books appeared many years later. Considering myself but an obscure teacher and struggling young
writer, I had guarded myself from intruding upon a famous
poet who was old and sick. That he actually wished to see
me never entered my thought.

My own poverty prevented me from buying his books, and when he sent them to me autographed, I at once wrote of them in the *Transcript* which was my only way of paying for them.

* * * * *

As I write these lines forty years later I have before me the actual manuscript describing my visit, the yellowed pages on which Walt penciled his corrections and his comment, and from them rises an odor of camphor and other sick-room drugs which brings back with sorrowful vividness that drab and cluttered room, that heap of books and manuscripts, but also enables me to visualize the majestic head of the poet and to hear again his musical voice, reëxperiencing my sense of wonder at the unshaken serenity of his soul.

CHAPTER TWELVE

THE VERSE OF SIDNEY LANIER

I

ANOTHER of my literary enthusiasms during these early years in Boston was Sidney Lanier. As he died just before I went East I had no personal knowledge of him, but the impression his books made upon me was so vivid and so enduring that I considered him a near presence.

It chanced that I came at him through his volume of lectures on "The Science of English Verse" which appealed to me so forcibly that I hastened to secure his poems in order that I might test his theories by his practice. His verse confused me at first by its complexity, but it grew in music with each re-reading. It was almost as revolutionary as that of Whitman.

Eager for more knowledge of this singer, who had passed over my head, I read every accessible article by him or about him, every magazine note of his work, every obtainable comment, until at last I felt it my duty to let the world know (so far as I was able), the message which this poet, this thinker, had brought to me.

Surrounded by those to whom he sang in unavailing phrase (for New England is essentially without the inborn sense of song), I reasoned then as I do now that no common soul could so come to a fellow man unheralded and unknown, and exalt him and, in a way, transform him, as Lanier had exalted and transformed me.

144

I take this to be one of the supreme tests of a poet, to speak for another, a stranger, voicing his unuttered, and possibly his unutterable, thoughts and sympathies. As Lanier appealed to me as the ultra-modern poet, I at once set about letting others know how wise and sweet and fine he was. The South had not produced many poets then, and there was to me a pathetic, even tragic significance in his life, as there is in the life of Edgar Allan Poe, for his was just such another sad struggle within a harsh and bitter environment. He was of a kind with Keats and Shelley, a spiritual brother to Chatterton and Burns.

Although a poet of the South, Lanier's career was typical of the combat which every American artist had been forced to undergo from the earliest time up to my own day. It was not difficult for me to imagine what Macon must have been in 1860, nor how little there was to nurture and sustain Lanier after the war. It was a time of fierce sectionalism, and to a nature like his any race or class or sectional hatred was a torment. His father was a lawyer of French Huguenot ancestry, his mother of Scottish descent, a fine mixture.

After a merely rudimentary education in what he himself called "a farcical college" the war came, robbing him outright of four years of life, and fixing upon him a disease which made the few working days of his youth a piteous slow dying, reducing his artist life to the space of thirteen years. He was a beardless boy when he entered the Confederate Army, he was a broken and dispirited veteran when Lee surrendered to Grant—and yet, notwithstanding his pain and every other hindrance, the work which he did in the space of these few pain-filled years may be set against that of any Southern writer of his day or since. Certainly no artist ever followed an ideal more unswervingly in the midst of so many discouragements, and his story, to my mind, gives out a certain quiet sublimity. He had all that Poe lacked—patience, purity, constancy to a purpose, and perfect sanity.

In opening his volume of verse, I chanced upon "Sunrise" and was instantly and profoundly stirred by its freedom of form, its wealth of thought, its intricacy of metaphor, and its glorious music, and yet the subtleties of the metaphors, the changes in the rhythm, like the infinite, shimmering lights of a near-seen landscape, distracted me. I lost the general effect, though I knew myself to be in the presence of a true poet. I failed to grasp the full value of the poem at once, but its haunting rhythms took hold upon me so strongly that to this day it lives with me more closely than any other nature verse. Some of its lines I quote oftener than those of any other landscape poem.

This striving after something dimly seen and dimly felt I soon discovered arose from an overwhelming musical tendency, which made of Lanier first of all a singer, establishing the lyric quality of his writing as absolutely as it did that of Blake or Shelley. He was a musician in every moment of his life. His lines throbbed to the beat of an orchestra. His earliest passion was for music. As a child he learned to play the flute, piano, organ.

He was too intellectual, too masterful, too original, too sane, to be affected by Poe's morbid style. He belonged to the open air, the wide sky. From the very start, indeed, he united a sort of Saxon simplicity of diction with a wonderfully modern conception of verse form. He was lyric not as Poe was lyric, rather was he symphonic, and albeit so passionate, was never gloomy. His verses had the warmth

of daylight, never the depressing gloom of a haunted house
or a graveyard. Sadness was in them, but it was a brave
sadness:

> "O hunger, hunger, I will harness thee
> And make thee harrow all my spirit's 'glebe.'
> Of old the blind bard hero sang so sweet,
> He made a wolf to plow the land."

His love for archaic words was due to his intense study
of early English, but his verse form was the result of an
inborn musical genius and a love of modern science which
demanded freer, ampler, and subtler forms than conventional critics sanctioned. His poems were quaint only in
expression, in essence they were modern to the most astonishing degree. In depth of thought, in variety of rhythmic
flow, and, above all, in its brave outlook on life and nature,
his work is of a breadth with Whitman; it is cosmic in
appeal.

There was no decayed spot in Lanier's heart. His bodily
weakness seemed never to react in bitter verse; on the contrary, it produced a spiritual exaltation. In a poem called
"Opposition" he voices his philosophy:

> "Of fret, of dark, of thorn, of chill
> Complain no more, for these, O heart
> Direct the random of the will
> As rhymes direct the rage of art."

His verse is not all so serious. He could write dialect
easily and beautifully. The multiple forms of his verse were
born of the theory of evolution, for to his thinking poetry
and song are sister arts, daughters of one mother. "Poetry
is subject to the same laws of tempo as song. It *is* song,
measured by the ear and not by the eye," he said. "Silences

count precisely as in the musical score." His own verse did not "scan" in the conventional sense, but it conformed to musical measure like a page from a sonata.

"Whatever else his poetry may not be, it is perfect song," I said to my pupils. "It has a flexible, variant, vibrant quality which is well-nigh unapproached by any American poet."

Curious as it may seem to lovers of Lanier and Whitman, I found much in common between the "Marshes of Glynn" and Whitman's "Out of the Cradle Endlessly Rocking." Whitman was wilder, sterner, and more iconoclastic than Lanier, yet both were poets of cosmic sympathy. With singularly individual outlook on nature, each believed in uttering himself in characteristic fashion, each instinctively avoided conventional forms. I found no difficulty in loving and admiring them both. Whitman discarded verse, Lanier mastered it. Whitman said, "Rhymes are fetters." Lanier said, "We will make them bracelets of gold." Whitman said, "Ignore the old forms." Lanier said, "Let us build new forms from the old."

Both declared, "There is no war between science and poetry!" Whitman cried out, "Sail forth, O soul, steer for deep waters only. Are they not all the seas of God?" and Lanier wrote, "Poetry will never fail, nor science, nor the poetry of science. Till the end of time will deep call to deep, day utter speech unto day, and poets listen with eavesdropping ears to catch and sing to men some melodies from that sounding song rhetoric of the lights and the waters."

Thus Lanier, no less than Whitman, faced science with fearless eyes. He, too, was an evolutionist.

Diverse as were their methods, I felt that each was striving for a newer, freer form, a greater and broader poetic art. Each recognized that human nature was forever changing, that age-worn conceptions were forever giving way, and the bounds of art forever enlarging. The old was forever dying, the new forever being born, and they both taught that the song of the past could not be the song of the future. Just as surely as that the past cannot be relieved, just so surely as human life proceeds from the simple to the complex, just so surely must the forms of art expression of one age give way for others more complex, forever changing with the changing conditions of human life and the varying conceptions of the universe.

To Lanier as to Whitman, "every cubic inch of space was a miracle." The common did not exist. When closely scrutinized, the grain of sand was found to expand with the glory of that inexplicable entity we call force. He held:

> "The grace of God made manifest in curves—
> All riches, goods, and braveries never told
> Of earth, air, sun, and heaven, now I hold
> Your being in my being: I am ye—
> And ye myself."

Like Whitman, he appealed to me upon two great lines of feeling sympathy (altruism), unforced sympathy for men, and unbounded and spontaneous love for nature. These two passions rose above his love for mere beauty, above his archaic diction, above his love for music, making him cosmic at heart. His love of justice dominating the "Symphony," a poem without counterpart in our literature, made especial appeal to me at that time.

> "Look up the land, look down the land,
> The poor, the poor, the poor! they stand,
> Wedged by the pressing of trade's hand,
> Against an inward opening door,
> That trade's hand tightens evermore:

> They sigh a monstrous foul-air sigh,
> For the outside leagues of liberty,
> Where Art's sweet lark translates the sky
> Into a heavenly melody."

As a reformer I applauded these words, for they expressed so much of Henry George's self-sacrificing altruism. They had in them the essence of all reform, and the indictment which the poet goes on to bring against selfishness might well be quoted by the progressives of any age.

> "Does business mean die you, live I?
> Then 'trade is trade,' but sings a lie—
> 'Tis only war grown miserly.
> ... Alas, for the poor to have some part
> In yon sweet living lands of art,
> Makes problem not for head but heart."

Nothing seemed so monstrously unjust to him as the thought that the toilers of earth should only now and then catch through grimy windows fleeting glimpses of the wide landscapes of life.

Poverty not only pinches the flesh and callouses the hands, it sears and twists and callouses the soul. It herds men and women where only the brutal in their lives can spring up. It fixes them forever in a miasmatic atmosphere of greed, of crime, and it was this dwarfing, this distorting of humanity which appealed with such heart-wringing poignancy to the poet of "The Symphony." He lacked the large view, perhaps, which kept Whitman serene and calm, even while suffering both poverty and disease, the view which teaches that all things make toward some good though hidden end, but at his clearest Lanier rose above petulance and bitterness as in the conclusion of "The Symphony."

"Life, life! thou sea-fugue, writ from East to West.
Love! Love alone can pore
On thy dissolving score
Of harsh half-phrasings
Blotted ere writ,
And double erasings,
Of chords most fit.
Yea, love, sole music-master blest,
May read thy weltering palimpsest.
To follow time's dying melodie through,
And never to lose the old in the new,
And ever to solve the discords true,
Love alone can do.
And ever love hears the poor folks crying,
And ever love hears the women sighing.
And ever sweet knighthood's death-defying,
And ever wise childhood's deep implying
But never a trader's glozing and lying."

To him as a master musician, "Music was love in search of a word," and in all that he did he labored to supply a little more heart to an age which had too much head. He was American in the largest sense.

That he was an immense force in my life at this time, I gladly bear witness. He taught me freedom within law. His lines flowed down the printed page like rills of water rippling into whorls of rhyme, pleasantly, unexpectedly, and so easily as to be hardly more confining than prose.

There is no need to praise such work gingerly. It is beautiful, full of meaning, and supremely musical. It is unhackneyed in form and modern and high in its application. It is as certainly the voice of an individual soul as are the wild, sweet lyrics of William Blake. Because it was so individual, it appealed to me most powerfully. It spoiled my taste for quatrains, for jingle, for jogtrot. I perceived that large forms are necessary for large concepts; variant forms for varying themes.

No one can fully enjoy Lanier's verse who has not lain low in the grass of the plains or in the deep of a wood, abandoned to the wandering winds and the leaves, till the insects forget the intruder, and sylvan life with all its multitudinous stirrings and collocations proceeds, so intimately and so friendly, that the dreamer becomes a brother to the bird, a partner of the oak.

Lanier's exquisite natural sensibility seems to have been raised by his sufferings to an intensity that is well-nigh ecstatic. He was carried beyond the man who observes nature to the man who is at one with it. He did for me what Emerson theorized about. He made matter luminous, radiant, mysterious. He found a cousin in the cloud, a brother in the man-bodied tree, a friend in the sun. He was a far cry from Thoreau and his philosophic interest in ants and toads, which was also revolutionary in its time and in its own way.

Lanier's nature love had nothing in common with the medieval anthropomorphism that filled the water with nixies and the woods with fays. His was rather the scientist's conception which rises from the knowledge that as forms of force all organisms are akin. Evolutionary science runs all through his songs, aiding him to sing of space, of heat, and light, putting him in harmony with the deepest philosophies as well as with the highest religious teaching.

Standing by the marsh in the hush of sunset he watches the fowls adrift in the solemn air and his mind gains trust in the great "First Cause."

"As the marsh-hen secretly builds on the watery sod
Behold I will build me a nest in the greatness of God;
I will fly in the greatness of God as the marsh-hen flies
In the freedom that fills all the space 'twixt the marsh and the sky.
By so many roots as the marsh-grass sends in the sod
I will heartily lay me a hold on the greatness of God.
Oh, like to the greatness of God is the greatness within
The range of the marshes, the liberal marshes of Glynn."

This trust in the universal frame of things, this optimistic agnosticism, so to speak, became my own faith.

"Sunrise," which his biographer told me was written when he was too weak to lift food to his mouth, is one of the greatest poems of my reading. A hundred times as I sat at my desk in the broiling, toiling city, its opening lines came to me, expressing my own hunger for the green earth and the soaring sky. Closing my eyes to shut out the sight of hot bricks and the horrible lines of reverberating iron walls, I let the words repeat their magic:

"In my sleep I was fain of their fellowship, fain
Of the live-oak, the marsh and the main,
The little green leaves would not let me alone in my sleep.
Up breathed from the marshes a message of range and of sweep,
Interwoven with waftures of wild sea liberties drifting,
Came through the lapped leaves sifting,
Came to the gates of sleep."

It is not necessary to apologize for him, as many of our critics have done, feeling that he was too fine to be skipped. The work he did has raised him high among our men of letters, but the truth, beauty, and sympathy he suggested should place him among the prophets. As he says of the ideal poet I say of him, "He wholly lived his minstrelsy."

"His song was only living aloud,
His work a singing with his hand."

CHAPTER THIRTEEN

JOHN BURROUGHS, VINEYARDIST

I

ALTHOUGH I began to read John Burroughs in the late seventies, I can not be quite sure of our first meeting. I am inclined to think it was in 1889, for in my files I find a letter dated October, 1888, in which he addresses me formally as a stranger. Apparently I had just sent to him a note containing an account of a recent visit to Whitman in Camden, and some lines which this visit inspired:

"Serene vast head with silver cloud of hair
   Lined on the purple dusk of death,
   A stern medallion velvet set—"

For in response, he wrote: "I am glad you went to see Whitman (I presume it was your first visit). What a picture he presents! the like of which will not soon be seen again in this country—perhaps never seen. I think his the finest head that has appeared in modern times. Indeed I know nothing so fine in classical times in strength, grandeur, and simplicity.

"I am very glad to see rising men like you espousing Whitman's cause. I congratulate you. It is a battle for the young men to fight and to win. When I was younger and the odds were much greater than they are now, I took a hand, but I look upon the matter more philosophically now, and feel more inclined to let things take their own course, which means, I suppose, that I am growing old.

"I have just heard that Whitman is better—a marked improvement. We may have him another year. The summers are what pull him down.". . .

I was still living in Jamaica Plain at this time, and was called "Professor Garland," a title to which I had less right than a good banjo teacher, although I was lecturing each day on Browning, Shakespeare, Emerson, Lanier, and other of the great poets and novelists. Burroughs, like Whitman, believed me to be a much more important figure than I was, and if I did not undeceive him I hope it will be forgiven me. In truth I was only teaching in order that I might have time to write some stories of the West with which my brain was filled.

It could not have been long after this that I met Burroughs in New York, a brown-bearded man just beginning to show gray hairs—or so he seems to me as I strive to recall him. He was smaller than I and a little stooped, but he moved alertly and spoke with quiet authority on many subjects. I liked him at once and I think he found me worth consideration as an output of the prairie; anyhow, our correspondence continued. His letters were all in longhand and usually in faded ink as though he had let the bottle freeze—which (as I afterward came to know) was the fact.

For six years we met, infrequently, in New York City, never at Riverby, as he called his place at West Park, but in 1895, when I was about to go to West Point in pursuit of material for a "Life of Grant," I wrote him that I was coming to take a tramp with him and he replied:

"DEAR GARLAND: I am not tramping much nowadays—I am building a retreat on some wild land I have purchased, a big stone chimney I am building with my own hands. It is great fun."

On the day after Christmas, he wrote again:

"I hope you can come this way, and spend at least a day with me. I can not promise to keep you over night, matters in the kitchen are so uncertain, but we can have a pleasant day together and if things are at their worst we can take our dinner over in Whitman Land. [By this he meant Slabsides.] I have taken my dinner there every day for a week —except Xmas—and have relished it immensely. The chimney of my hermitage is done and we are putting on the slabs. Do come."

This letter is especially valuable to me, for it settles just when Slabsides was built, and his line "if things are at their worst" tells something of the disturbing conditions at home which made Slabsides a "refuge" in time of trouble.

It was no secret to me even then that his wife considered his writings a foolish waste of time. His skill as a vineyardist had her unqualified respect, but to knock off tieing grapes in order to put down some observation concerning a bird or chipmunk was ridiculously unproductive. Moreover, such actions provoked laughter on the part of the neighbors, one of whom is reported to have said, "Why people come around just to see old John Burroughs I can't understand."

It was in defense against such folk that he built Slabsides in the thick forest some two miles west of Riverby. It was a plain little frontier cabin, but in it he received Whitman, Muir, Roosevelt, and many other of his distinguished natureloving friends.

His associations were nearly all plain, very plain, American, and his daily walk lay quite outside "the dress-suit belt." In externals and in speech he was very much the rustic. Only when he put pen to paper did he manifest the authority, the precision of his mind and the wide reach of his reading. He was never witty and seldom humorous in conversation. His discourse was homely, mellow with country common sense, and penetrating with the wisdom of a natural philosopher who was also the scientific observer.

In speech he was almost the direct antithesis of Howells, for Howells spoke, as he wrote, with exquisite precision and with delicious humor. Although good friends, they were widely separated in their ways of life. Howells loved nature and birds not for their scientific interest but for their human association, while on his part Burroughs cared very little for fiction. Howells could not endure poor food or rude furniture. Burroughs was accustomed to cook his own meals. Both these men meant a great deal to me during those early years and I was able to share in some degree the enthusiasm of the naturalist without losing my interest in the fictionist. That they were both self-taught, and that their high place had been won by the magic of highly endowed personality, was to me profoundly significant and deeply encouraging.

Burroughs often talked of John Muir and his visit to Slabsides. "Muir is a great man, and a good man—and I like him," he explained, "but he is a wearisome companion. If you say 'two and two make four,' he is sure to retort, 'Aye, Johnny, but two and three make five. Now how is that, Johnny?' He always has something of his own to offer. He insists on holding the floor. He is interesting, but along about two in the morning he gets to be tedious. He talks well—much better than he writes—but there is a limit to my powers of endurance. I am exhausted when he leaves me."

Theodore Roosevelt was another bond of sympathy between Burroughs and myself, and always when we met we discussed him. "Roosevelt knows what he is talking about when he touches on birds and animals," Burroughs often said. Once after an expedition with Roosevelt in Virginia, he said to me gleefully, "I taught him one new bird and he taught me two!"

II

Burroughs, like myself, came of a long line of New England farmer folk. His grandsire cut his way across the timbered divide into the valley of the Pepacton in 1795. His farm was hewn from the mountainside nearly two thousand feet above tidewater and faced a range of still higher hills.

It was on these rugged ancestral acres that John spent his childhood and his early manhood, taking part in all the hand-and-foot, heart-breaking methods of husbandry which the time and the place made necessary. "It was a stern land, rocky, timbered, and hilly. A man's country and a man's climate. The summers were short and the winters long and bitter!" he once said to me.

"The homestead faced the sunrise and hence the most impressive objects in my landscape were the high hills across the valley to the East," peaks which must have seemed to him a lofty mountain chain. Back of the house stood "Old Clump," a wooded height, dark and forbidding at nightfall, but a source of firewood in winter and of maple sugar in the spring.

He was one of a numerous family—"mostly boys and girls," each member of which had definite duties to perform. It was necessary that all hands should be applied to the task of scraping a living off those stony slopes. Money was scarce and clothing hard to get, hence it follows that his schooling, as well as that of his brothers and sisters, was thin and scanty like the soil. In fact his education, aside from that which he acquired from reading and observation, was elementary.

However, all these limitations were typical of the time. He drove oxen, carried buckets of sap, hoed potatoes, swung the scythe, chopped wood and shoveled snow, sharing in all ways the varied tasks of a pioneer farmer's life in the forties. Only for a few weeks in the winter was he allowed to go to school—at first in a low stone building to the north, later in the small red house of the district to the south. And yet for some mysterious reason his boyish heart was filled with a growing desire to do something out in the great world, a world he glimpsed as he rode to Albany with his father on a load of wheat.

"I was a variant from the stock!" he once said. "How this difference between myself and my brothers arose I do not know."

It sprang from the fundamental mystery of personality. His divergence was due to that driving power we call "genius," the inexplicable urge which was at this very time filling the heart of Will Howells, a barefooted boy, a printer's son, standing at his case in a small Ohio town. No matter what John's brothers might say, he was determined to do something in the world beside milk cows and pitch manure.

This was not due to a hatred of work. John was a good worker; he shirked nothing on the farm, but he was not content to think of himself as merely the farmer; he longed for a larger field.

"There were not many openings for an ambitious youth in the valley at that time," he explained. "The only congenial employment open to me was that of teaching, and so, at seventeen, I left home to become the master of a school some thirty or forty miles away from Roxbury. For nearly ten years I earned my living in this way, now here, now there, and a precarious living it was. The wolf was almost always near at hand. If not precisely at the door, his voice could be heard in the dark of a winter midnight."

John's real education began when in his eighteenth year he took his first ride on the "steam cars" down to the almost mythical city of New York. In telling about this trip he made a point of his firm belief that the train always started so abruptly that it was necessary to safeguard one's hat. "The coaches were rude, the seats hard, and the cinders blew in on us, but it was a noble ride nevertheless—the first great event in my life."

It is highly significant to record that he spent almost his last dollar at a secondhand bookshop. "I was obliged to carry that bundle of books on my back as I walked the final twelve miles of my homeward journey. I did this on an empty stomach, every cent of my money having gone to pay my return railway fare."

As I learned the names of these books I wonder that his back was not broken, for they included among others St. Pierre's "Studies of Nature," Locke's "Essay on the Human Understanding," the works of Dr. Johnson, Spurzheim's "Phrenology," and the works of Thomas Dick! Certainly a most heroic load for a hungry lad on a mountain road.

Like many another receptive youth at this time, his first real inspiration came from a reading of Emerson, and yet, strange to say, he did this reading not in Kingston but in the little town of Buffalo Grove in northern Illinois, whereto he had adventured during his nineteenth summer, a romantic excursion quite in keeping with the westward urge of the day.

This glimpse of the West was important in other ways. It gave young Burroughs a concept of the prairie, and enabled him to forecast in some degree the marvelous possibilities of the Mississippi Valley. Just how he was able to break away from home I can not understand, for he often related the story of an uncle who kept his valise packed and ready under his bed for half a year, vowing each Saturday night that he would start west on Monday. "He never succeeded in leaving the valley, whereas I, a youngster (and engaged to be married), was able to do so, moved by an impulse to explore new fields."

Even in John's case it was but an excursion, for notwithstanding his success as a teacher, and in spite of the Buffalo Grove library and his new-made friends in Illinois, something drew him back to his native valley to renew the struggle to make a living. Perhaps this power was his love for Ursula North, but I like to imagine that he was drawn by something which no individual, no matter how attractive, could counteract or misdirect. Whatever the motive, whether homesickness, or a promise to Ursula, this much is certain, John returned to Roxbury and there worked on the farm till the day of his marriage which came just before his twenty-first birthday.

"Hardly more than a boy, with only my pay as a teacher or a farm laborer on which to maintain a household, my life problem was further complicated by a steadfast desire to write. In fact I had already begun to compose essays (somewhat in the manner of Emerson) on Expression,

Revolutions, Progress, and other grandly abstract subjects, papers which had little value except as practice for my pen and consolation for my hours of loneliness."

The years lying between 1857 and 1863 were years of struggle filled with poverty, doubt, and discouragement, almost with despair. "At the urging of my ambitious young wife, I tried to get into something more lucrative than teaching and failed. I read medicine—and gave it up. I tried to write acceptable articles—without success. Seemingly all I could do, except till the earth, was to teach and this inability to earn a respectable living disturbed my ambitious young wife, who resented the pity of her former classmates."

It was in this period of disheartenment that he wrote his noble poem "Waiting," which seems now to have been the expression of a subconscious conviction that somehow, some time, his own would come to him—"and yet these verses when printed had no perceptible effect on my fortunes. No one spoke of it. Nothing came of it."

June, 1863, was another notable month in his calendar, for it brought a meeting with Emerson on the parade ground at West Point, and also the reading of a book which changed his whole outlook on life. "I was teaching at the time in the little town of Highland Falls, a few miles below West Point, and it was in the library at the Academy that I chanced upon Audubon's monumental volume, 'The Birds of North America.' "

He had already reached Lowell and the *Atlantic Monthly* with an essay on "Expression," a piece of writing which seemed almost too good to be the work of a country school-teacher, nevertheless it had been accepted and was about to be published, although Burroughs himself perceived its imitative quality. "It was to rid myself of the Emerson style that I turned my attention to 'back-country' themes, themes which were native to me."

In the midst of this resolve to tramp the woods and fields he came upon the work of Audubon, a discovery of enormous importance in his development. "It was like bringing fire to tow. I was ripe for adventure. I was in a good bird country. How eagerly and joyously I took up the study. It turned my enthusiasm into a new channel. It gave my walks a new delight. It made me look upon every grove and wood as a new storehouse of possible treasure."

To his love of back-country habits and customs and people he now added a keen desire to know the birds and to write of them. In this way the John Burroughs whom the world was to honor came into being. He had entered upon his distinctive field of literature—for even in this he was always the writer first of all—the naturalist was secondary.

This was in the midst of the Civil War, however, and for a time he could make only desultory studies. Uneasy and distraught, he could not write on any subject but the war. He had a guilty sense of shirking and to a friend he wrote (just after the disastrous battle of Chickamauga), "I am thinking of enlisting. I want to do something. I am not content to stay here and teach school or farm.

"October found me in Washington on my way to enlist. I didn't know just what service I should enter upon, but I felt that I was getting nearer to the scene of conflict at least."

Here again fate led him in the right direction; he became a guard in the Treasury at Washington and he soon came into comradeship with Walt Whitman whose influence on him was immediate and fundamental. Furthermore, his confinement in the Treasury lent enchantment to his native landscape. "I saw its hills and streams through a haze of homesickness," he said, "a longing which put an aureole around every tree. At a desk in the Treasury in a sunless room, facing the blank side of a big iron door, I wrote 'Wake Robin' and other of my sketches."

In the cramping space and half-light of that gloomy place he dreamed of the radiant valley of the Pepacton, and heard the foxes bark around the dark summit of Old Clump. In imagination he saw the flights of birds along the Delaware. In the silence of his granite corridor he kept the clock of the seasons. Slowly, tenderly he began to write the pages which expressed his longings for the open air and the sun. Even when he spoke of this to me, long afterward, his voice took on retrospective tenderness. "I seized every opportunity to get into the woods. Every holiday, every Sunday found me wandering about the hills of Rock Creek. I was like a prisoner paroled for the day. That is how I came to miss hearing Lincoln on the occasion of his second inaugural. I was away in the woods making the most of my day off."

In spite of this keen delight in nature, notwithstanding his daily writing about birds and flowers and streams, his first book was controversial and not at all a treatise on outdoors; it was called "Whitman, Poet and Person." That this writing took precedence of "Wake Robin" was due to his love of Walt and his desire to defend him from the storm of denunciation which had followed the re-publication of "Leaves of Grass." John was a loyal friend and could not sit silent when the high priest of the Open Road was being maligned.

Emerson, Audubon, Whitman—these were the great teachers who each in his special way profoundly instructed the farmer from the Catskills, and of the three it is hard to say which one influenced him most. He was thirty years old at this time, a stocky, bright-eyed, brown-bearded man of quiet manner and rustic speech. The contrast between his conversational manner and his tone as a writer was singularly wide. He was acquiring a delightful style, especially in descriptive prose.

"For nearly ten years I made my home in Washington, breaking exile, however, by frequent returns to my native hills in summertime. In the course of my duties as Treasury guard, I went to England with a shipment of government bonds—a mission which enabled me to meet several Englishmen of letters and to make some valuable observations on English country life and landscape," but all the while his love for his native hills intensified. To a friend he wrote, "I feel like a fowl with no gravel in its gizzard. I am hungry for the earth—I could eat it like a horse," expressions which only a farmer could use or fully understand. At last, in the spring of 1873, he resigned his job in Washington and returned to the Hudson River Valley.

In the effort to satisfy his craving for the soil he purchased nine acres of land on the west bank of the Hudson, midway between Newburgh and Kingston, and there in the autumn of the same year of leaving Washington set about building his permanent home. "Having been appointed Federal Bank Examiner for the region roundabout I was able to combine love of the soil and my planting with a position which yielded me a living while my trees and vines were coming to fruitage."

His wanderings had ceased. He had found his home, a home which satisfied him. Within easy reach of the Roxbury homestead, in the midst of a wonderfully populous bird country, he began the work which was so evidently adapted to his hand. Busy and contented, he developed his vineyard and put forth book after book of intimate studies of flower, bird, and field. "Wake Robin," "Winter Sunshine," and "Pepacton" followed.

He remained essentially rural; there was nothing urban or suburban about him. He came to the city as a somewhat uneasy visitor, and while he enjoyed his friends, he found the sights and sounds wearisome and his visits were brief.

When my "Prairie Songs" came from the press I sent him a copy and was highly pleased when he wrote congratulating me on keeping nightingales and skylarks out of my verses. "I find your birds and insects mainly in their proper habitat and seasons," he said and that was conclusive for me. He did not doubt my "gulls in the blazing air of Dakota," but I think we had gone over that strange fact in conversation, following an article in the Boston papers in which I was criticized for putting gulls on a dry plain. "I didn't put 'em there," I said to him, "I found 'em there, millions of 'em catching grasshoppers in the early morning and resting on the alkali ponds at night. My theory is that these ponds are the last remaining traces of an inland sea to which these birds return from habit after a million years, guided by memory."

He made no objection to this. "Your guess is as good as mine," he said.

In August, 1894, he wrote me on several significant matters:

"I do not think I would care to come to Chicago to lecture, indeed I have never lectured, but have given a few talks to schools and girls' colleges. The thought of a formal lecture frightens me. I am now in the midst of my grape harvest—weather frightfully dry, and vines and fruit suffering much. No rain to go into the ground since June 12th. I have eighteen acres—last year I had forty tons of grapes and five tons of currants. This year the grape crop is much lighter. I grow currants, grapes, peaches, and pears, and I have made it pay.

"I must come at the soil in some way, and I find this sort of farming suits my taste well."

He then adds in answer to a question of mine:

"I do not remember that I have caught you tripping on the subject of nature unless it was in a story of yours called 'God's Ravens.' Do you not make the katydids sing in early summer in that piece? With us the katydids begin in the middle of August. I have noted the carping and unfriendly criticism of your volume of essays but always by obscure scribblers. The bark of these puppies is not worth noticing. You are on the right track *and do you stick to it.* Lucky is the man who excites opposition.

"I recently read a paper of yours on boy life in Iowa that pleased me very much—as it did my boy. I hope the *Midland Monthly* is a sure go, but I fear for it in these times. I know Brigham and like him. If you see him give him my love."

CHAPTER FOURTEEN

A DINNER WITH KIPLING

I

SOMEWHERE in 1890 or 1891 some books of short stories by a young man named Rudyard Kipling began to find their way into American print, some of them pirated, no doubt, and one afternoon as I was buying my evening paper at a Roxbury bookstand (my brother and I were then living on Moreland Street) I saw on the counter a little paper-bound volume called "Mine Own People." I bought it and that night I read it almost without leaving my chair. "Here is another local-color novelist," I said to my brother, "only in this book the color is East Indian."

There was something individual in the tang of this writing, something gay and vital, and a few days later I asked the newsdealer if he had any other books by this writer. No, he had not, but he could get me some. "You'd better lay in a supply," I remarked. "There is going to be a boom in his stock."

Knowing that I was something of a literary man, the dealer followed my advice, and for several months thereafter, whenever I entered his door, reproached me by calling attention to a pile of unsold copies of "Mine Own People" and "Tales from the Hills." I kept his courage up as best I could by repeating, "The boom is delayed but it will come."

My own faith in Kipling's boom was based upon reports

from New York and on the opinion of two of my friends on the Boston *Transcript*. Ultimately my prediction came true and the bookseller cleared out his shelf of paper copies and bought others in regular bindings. Kipling's stories came so fast in these pirated reprints that a bit of doggerel went the rounds, "When the Kiplings cease from Kipling and the critics are at rest." There was reason for this sudden flare of fame. The author's note was novel, his characters vividly seen, and his region romantic. Soon every one was reading and talking Kipling.

Howells told me something of his personality. "He is a brother-in-law of my young friend, Wolcott Balestier, who died recently," he said. "He is a young Englishman who began to write on a newspaper in India. He has established a home near his wife's family in Vermont and appears to have adopted America."

Beyond this I heard very little of Kipling, until some time in the spring of 1892, while living in New York City, I received a letter from him inviting me to dine with him. I was disposed to accept this invitation at once, but knowing that he was an Englishman and likely to insist on formal dress, I replied, "I should be delighted to come, but the truth must be told. I have no evening suit; in fact I have never worn one. If you will excuse an ordinary frock coat, I shall be only too glad to accept your kind invitation."

I have no copy of his reply, but it was something like this, "My dear sir, you may come in a buckskin shirt, if you like," an expression which he knew I would understand.

The night of the dinner happened to be rainy, and as I arrived at the place appointed ten minutes ahead of time, I decided to wait in the hall of the little hotel, which was on West Forty-sixth Street (as I recall it a very obscure hotel indeed), until my watch indicated exactly seven o'clock.

While standing thus absent-mindedly facing the street door, I became aware of a moon-faced, elderly man on the sidewalk peering up at the entrance as if to reassure himself of his destination. He wore a short, light-gray overcoat and a tall silk hat perched on the back of his head, and something in the shine of his glasses and in his broad, blank face made me think of Horace Greeley.

Suddenly I recognized him. "Why, it's Riley!" I exclaimed and hastened to open the door for him. "Yes, this is the place," I said, "come in."

He faced me with a perfectly blank visage, a look which he could assume at any time, and fixing me with a solemn gray eye, motioned over his shoulder with his thumb toward the interior of the hotel. "Dining here?"

I nodded.

"With Kipling?"

I nodded again.

His eyes lightened and a slow smile widened his mouth. "Now what do you suppose Kipling wants of two sich specimens of yaller-dent poetry as we are advertised to be?"

"I give it up, Riley, so far as I am concerned, but in your case I think his interest is justified."

Suddenly his tone changed to one of anxious pleading. Pointing a finger at me, he said, "Now see here, Garland, you've got to insure that I git back to the St. Denis Hotel. You know perfectly well that I cain't go for a walk around the block and come back to the hole I went out at." Then placing the tip of his finger just above his ear, he added, with a grin, "Nothing in my bump of location but mayonnaise dressing."

Chuckling with glee over this characterization of himself, I replied, "I'll see that you reach your hotel in safety, but it is time to go up." I started for the elevator.

"Wait a second," he called sharply. "Wait till I ad-just a hame strap."

Whilst I marveled over his meaning, he reached under his gray overcoat and pulled out a pin. Down dropped one of the tails of his evening coat about eight inches below his reefer. Without a particle of expression, yet watching the effect on me, he pulled another pin, and as the second tail dropped he mumbled a low-voiced explanation: "Couldn't find m' other coat. Must 'a' loaned it to a feller or left it in the street car, or something."

Shaking with silent laughter I finally managed to say, "If you'll take off your topcoat and fold it and carry it on your arm the Kiplings will never know how inadequate it is."

"Good idea!" said he but without enthusiasm, and with the makeshift garment on his arm he joined me in the elevator.

The Kiplings met us cordially if a bit apprehensively, and it soon appeared that we were the only guests and a strange pair we were. As we sat at their table in the general dining room, Mrs. Kipling occupied one end of the table and Kipling the other. Riley and Miss Balestier sat opposite me, and as I opened out my napkin I began to divine the situation. Kipling was interested in Riley and Garland as American representatives of the vernacular in verse and local color in fiction. We were interesting as specimens and I could not decide whether we should feel flattered or resentful. "If Riley can stand it, I can," was my conclusion.

Kipling, a short, dark-complexioned, alert young man nearing thirty, was Colonial in accent, quick-spoken and humorous. He was not at all English in manner, but his outlook was British.

For a time I gave my attention to my hostess, but with those immortal talkers going on at my left, I grew distraught, and at last Mrs. Kipling, sensing my predicament, gave up attempts to enlist my attention. Thereafter we all listened while Riley and his host exchanged quip for crank. It was delightful talk, but it was not till we three men retired to the small room which our host used for a study that he "cut loose." For half an hour his monologue was gorgeous with the color of the East. He dealt with cobras, typhoons, tropic heat, windless oceans, tiger-haunted jungles, and elephants, especially elephants. It was all sumptuous material and his descriptions were adequately representative. He spoke of elephants "muttering among themselves like wise old men." He told of the quiet, calculating malignity with which one vengeful old bull chewed a stalk of cane into a swab and wound it in the robe of his cruel, drunken keeper and jerked him under his feet. He described those which went mad and those which helped capture their wild fellows. In one story he pictured a vessel with a load of these great creatures becalmed under the torrid sun of the Indian Ocean, and how they had to be loaded alternate heads and tails to keep them from rocking the boat as they swayed uneasily in their chains. One of them died, and it was necessary to cut her to pieces and throw her overboard, a gruesome task whose details I will not record. In all that he told he created marvelous pictures, filling my mind with wonder of his experiences as well as with admiration of his powers of observation and description.

Nevertheless, eager as I was to have him go on, I was jealous for the honor of American literature. I wanted Riley to show what he could do. As we were about to rejoin the ladies, I said to Kipling in an aside, "Have you ever heard Riley recite his verse?"

"No," he replied, "but I wish I might."

"He is a wonder. Ask him to read a poem."

In response to this suggestion, Kipling said, "Riley, read us something," and Riley, without hesitation or apology, rose to his feet and stood for a moment with his eyeglasses in his fingers. Instantly his big blond face took on something quaint and tender, something Hoosier came into it as he began to voice "Nothin' to Say," that touching and wistful monologue in which a gentle old farmer replies to his daughter's remark, "Father, I'm going to be married, what have you to say?" with, "Nothin' to say, my daughter, nothin' at all to say." The poet followed this with "That Young 'Un," which is the story of the little son of the miller who knew what the bees said, what the birds sang, but could never quite tell "what the water is a-talkin' of." At the close of this exquisitely truthful and deeply moving poem in the vernacular, Kipling sprang to his feet and, pacing back and forth, said with unmistakable sincerity, "By the Lord, *that's* American literature!"

I thought so then and I think so still, although I realized at the time the marvelous skill with which Riley helped out the value of his words by voice and gesture.

In accordance with my promise, I guided Riley back to his hotel, and as we were walking along the street, he said in a musing tone, "Will you tell me just why you and I have been so honored by Kipling?"

"You can search me!" I replied in one of George Ade's graphic slang phrases, "but he knew what he was getting in my case, for I wrote in warning. I told him I was not fitted to enter the dress-coat zone."

"Well, dog the difference," said Riley with resignation, "we had a gorgeous evening."

So far as I know, Kipling had no regrets. He always asked for Riley when we met, and sent his greetings when he wrote. As for his own performance that night, I had only awed admiration. That we had been specially honored was evident, for some of the stories he told were never published, or at least I never saw them in print. All of them were new and for the most part in manuscript.

For some reason, the rights of which I never learned, Kipling found life in Vermont displeasing. Early in the nineties he removed his family to England and I saw no more of him for several years. Somehow he and Brattleboro did not rhyme and when I got a letter dated "Bateman's, Burwash Etchingham, Sussex, England," I had a feeling that he was more at home there than he could possibly be in America or even in India. He seemed quite as far from West Salem, Wisconsin, and Greenfield, Indiana, as he had been when writing from Bombay.

CHAPTER FIFTEEN

THE ARENA AND ITS RADICALS

I

In the summer of 1889 I made another trip into Iowa and Dakota and when I returned to Boston I was more embittered than before. All my old neighbors in Iowa and Dakota were in a despondent mood. Wheat was so cheap that farmers were selling at a loss. In Kansas and Nebraska beautiful corn was being burned for fuel. At ten cents per bushel it was cheaper than wood or coal.

The condition of the women in the homes I visited was especially moving, and the loneliness and the drudgery of their days led me to write a long short story which I called "A Prairie Heroine," wherein I delineated a farmer's hopeless wife. It was a savage and unrelenting picture, so starkly realistic that I had no thought of sending it to either Gilder or Alden. Knowing that it would distress them both, I looked about for an editor to whom such a manuscript might appeal.

Among the many other intellectual stirrings to which Boston was subject, I had noted the recent establishment of a monthly magazine called the *Arena*, a periodical of protest. Of its editor, Benjamin O. Flower, I knew nothing, but having read two or three numbers of his paper and finding it hospitable to articles on Free Silver, the Farmers'

Alliance, Spiritualism, and other controversial subjects, I ventured to mail "A Prairie Heroine" to his office which was in a handsome building on Copley Square.

My faith in his acceptance of the story was so weak, however, that I marked out certain of its openly polemic passages with intent to reduce its controversial content. On the first of May, 1890, a letter from Flower changed the world for me.

"I have just finished reading your story, 'A Prairie Heroine.' . . . If satisfactory to you I will send you a check for seventy-five dollars for this story. I notice you seem to suppress your thoughts in two or three instances, and have erased some lines from your story. In writing for the *Arena*, either stories or essays, I wish you always to feel yourself thoroughly free to express any opinions you desire or to send home any lessons which you feel should be impressed upon the people. I for one do not believe in mincing matters when we are dealing with great wrongs and evils of the day. . . . I do not wish you to feel in writing for the *Arena* at any time the slightest restraint."

This letter amazed me and heartened me. It not only put into my hand more money than I had up to that date received for any manuscript; it brought to me a new and loyal friend, for at his invitation I at once called upon him at his office. I was surprised to find him of my own age, a small, round-faced, smiling youth with black eyes and curling hair. He was a new sort of reformer, genial, laughing, tolerant. Nothing disturbed his good humor and no authority could awe him. I soon learned that he was already the center of a scattered yet related group of come-outers of all minds, moods, and opinions, whose pens were racing over paper composing declarations in defense of dearly beloved theories.

His desk overflowed with articles of protest from every State in the Union. His *Arena* was a dignified and fearless forum wherein every discontented citizen could be heard. It filled a need and was rapidly expanding in circulation and influence.

We were friends at sight. "Go on with your articles and stories of protest," he said. "Send them to me and I'll print them just as you write them."

His support was most comforting to me. It was all very fine for Gilder and other good friends to advise me against writing for controversial magazines, but as the *Century* and *Harper's* had taken only one or two of my stories, paying me less than the *Arena* was willing to allow for my most radical "preachments," I could not wait upon their judgment. With Flower backing me, I went my bleak road with more confidence in the future than I had hitherto achieved. I not only sold him several of my realistic stories, but an entire play. I wrote at his suggestion articles on the Single Tax, Free Trade, and other controversial subjects which brought me into fellowship with other critics of the social order.

It was at his request that I put together two of my novelettes and four of my short stories under the title, "Main-Travelled Roads," and brought them to his editors for publication as a book. The firm accepted these stories and brought them out in a small paper-bound volume in 1891. Laura Lee, a young artist of my acquaintance, drew the illustration for the cover, the picture of a stalwart young farmhand striding down the road, pitchfork on his shoulder, making his way to a threshing bee.

It may interest my readers to know that I posed for this figure and described the clothing I wore on the farm in order that it should be Western and truthful. We used to wear to our day's work our third-best frock coats and vests. We had no working smocks or blouses. When our Sunday suits became too shabby for Sunday wear, we wore them out in the field. In this illustration the exact character of my fiction is indicated. Whatever else my characters were they had nothing European about them.

The "katouse" which this little volume provoked was astounding. It saddened as well as irritated me. From the regions where I had expected most appreciation I received almost nothing but abuse. I was accused of disloyalty to the West. Certainly I was not helping the Western boom. Heat and cold and dirt and drudgery were all included in my book in what I considered proper proportions.

Up to this time writers on farm life had arranged the weather pleasingly. It was always lovely June and the hay-makers "tossed the fragrant clover" wearing jaunty, wide-rimmed hats, while the girls in dainty white gowns looked on from the shade of a stately tree. At frequent intervals the toilers gathered about the mossy well curb and sang "The Old Oaken Bucket." Corn-husking was equally social. Laughing lads and blushing lassies gathered in the barn of a moonlit October evening to husk the ears from garnered stalks and the finders of red ears won kisses from the maidens, just as in all Irish plays of the time the hero blacksmith, in a white silk shirt open at the throat, shod horses and sang songs for the villagers and such lords and ladies as happened to be passing the door. I am not exaggerating; such were the plays and stories descriptive of country life in the Old World and the New. All our rustic plays contained a male quartet, toilers who spent a great deal of time in the shade leaning on their hay forks and yodeling.

All this was delightful, but as a working farmer just returned from a sorrowful visit to old friends and neighbors in the West (who could hardly fetch a smile, much less a merry song), I could not for one moment falsify the life I had shared and the drudgery I had not yet completely escaped.

In order to present the realities of that life, I put in the storm as well as the sun. I included the mud and manure as well as the wild roses and the clover. Corn-husking and threshing went in for what they were, tests of skill and endurance, not as neighborhood frolics. To work all day in the dust at the tail of a straw stacker was no joke. To husk corn for ten hours on a mile-square field in a savage November wind, with your boots laden with icy slush and your fingers chapped and bleeding, does not make for song. Even haying meant streaming sweat and aching arms. However, the book was less austere than it appeared to the critic, but its proportionate mixture of work and play and sun and shadow rendered it repellent. It aroused wide comment, but few read it.

Howells came to my support and so did Chamberlin and other of my Eastern friends, and gradually the book made its way in the East, although its sale in the West remained small for many years. With no desire to provoke controversy, all this talk of "treachery to the West" was to me an amazement as well as an irritation.

Flower, of course, was delighted with this discussion and one day asked me if I could not write for him a serial novel based on the Farmers' Alliance, a prodigious uprising among the farmers, then at its height. I replied that I already had on my desk several chapters of a story dealing with farm life in Iowa and the Grange, an earlier agricultural organization, and that I could undoubtedly bring this narrative down to the present day.

"Just the thing!" he exclaimed, "but you'll want to make some new studies of the field. You should go to Kansas and study the Alliance leaders, also to Georgia. We will provide transportation for you—all you want."

This was in the spring of 1891 and marks the end of my quiet life as a teacher in Boston. The *Arena* put me on wheels. Filled with a desire to know every State in the Union, I bought a new valise, a notebook with an indelible pencil, and set forth. In those days railways gave transportation for "Advertising" and I made the most of my opportunity as a staff writer for a magazine. In less than two years I traveled thirty thousand miles, meeting all the leading advocates of revolt in the South and West.

First of all I went to Washington to write an article on "The Alliance Wedge in Congress," a title suggested by the fact that the members of this "bloc" chanced to have seats in the middle of the floor of the House of Representatives. For the first time in my life, I enjoyed a comfortable stay on Capitol Hill. Day by day I listened to the debates in Congress, an experience which made me impatient of those who forgot the husbandman toiling to produce wheat and corn and cotton at prices which left no margin for sickness and old age. I saw the homes of senators in suggestive contrast with lonely cabins on the Western plains. My companions were Jerry Simpson and his fellow reformers from Kansas, Nebraska, and Dakota.

From Washington I went to Des Moines as the capital of the State from which the "hero" of my story came, and while there I dined with the State senators at their boarding houses and saw them cheerily eating mashed potato and fried eggs with steel knives, debating meanwhile "Free Silver" and the tariff. One of these legistors was Fred Jewett, who in the early seventies led the singing school at the corner of our Iowa farm. At his invitation I sat beside him for an hour on the floor of the House. He was a genial and kindly man but not a logical lawmaker.

In Memphis, Atlanta, and Richmond, I met the chief Alliance orators of the South and studied the production of cotton plantations. Incidentally I visited negro churches for the first time and heard in their wild revivals the voices of the jungle. Their choruses, grand as Wagnerian preludes, delighted me and the panther-like screams of their women enlightened me. I began to know my country, but the more I knew of it the deeper my sense of weakness went. How could I even suggest in my novel the nation's widespread stir of protest? How could a nation so burdened with negro problems, bitter sectionalism, unassimilated immigration, and financial chaos survive? The vaster it grew the more complicated its problems became.

II

In all this travel in the middle West and South, I was increasingly aware that my education was incomplete so long as the Rocky Mountains and their varied industries were unknown to me, and when in 1892 Flower suggested that I go to Denver and Colorado Springs and talk with some friends of the *Arena* I was filled with ecstatic anticipation. In the High Country I would find beauty and romance. It was the fulfillment of a boyish dream of exploration.

If any of my critics wish to call this a confused, wavering, experimental period I shall not dispute their statement. I was a boy let loose to play. I could go where I wished and I particularly wished to go into every Western State and territory. I wanted to know as much about the Rocky Mountains as any other writer. Unfortunately I could not write and travel at the same time. The concentration which I had enjoyed in Boston for seven years now gave way to a period of casual composition, writing which was perilously journalistic in character.

Meanwhile I had succeeded in winning Richard Watson Gilder of the *Century*. In accepting a novelette, he wrote me a letter which was most helpful, for it not only revealed the heart of his editorial policy but was a wholesome lesson to me.

"I think if, without making the story too inartistically pointed, you could set in those ideas which you have expressed to me in your letter, it would dignify and make more useful the really very striking picture of life which you have presented. If you will do this and let me see the story again, I shall be greatly obliged to you.

"I must tell you what embarrasses me in stories of this sort. As you know, the newspaper press nowadays is vulgarizing. It not only expresses the vulgarity of the American masses but increases it—that is, to a large extent. Every decent man and woman, including many newspaper men, deprecates this condition of things. Now if we print too many stories which are full of the kind of language which should not be used, we seem to many persons to be continuing the work of vulgarization. On the other hand we value correct pictures of life—of even pretty common life—and the consequence is we are giving an undue proportion, possibly, of dialect fiction. People who are trying to bring up their children with refinement, and to keep their own and their children's language pure and clean, very naturally are jealous of the influence of a magazine—especially of the *Century Magazine*—in this respect.

"Here is really a predicament, and feeling that predicament, we at least think a dialect story—especially of this kind, where 'youp' is used for yes, for example, and where all sorts of vulgarisms occur—should very strongly recommend itself before being sent into almost every cultivated household in the United States! Had you thought of the matter in this connection? I am very far from wishing to go to an extreme in the other direction—lords and ladies— but I think we should not go to an extreme in this direction."

It was in the middle of this period of unrest, of vacillation between social reform and fictive art that I set out for Colorado to put myself in contact with a new, remote, and splendid region, the supplemental other half of my mid-West. My brain was like a sensitive film, ready to receive portraits of men and pictures of places.

I am a little vague as to the purpose of this trip, but I think Flower hoped that one of his Colorado correspondents might be induced to put money into the Arena Company. That I carried a note of introduction to Louis R. Ehrich of Colorado Springs is certain, for when I phoned him from the hotel he said, "Come at once to my house. Bring all your baggage and make your home with us."

In accepting this gracious hospitality I had my first taste of luxury. Mrs. Ehrich gave me a spacious room which looked out over the Garden of the Gods toward the snowy crest of Pike's Peak. Never had I occupied such a room with such an outlook. I felt like saying to my host and hostess, "You are acting under an illusion. I am neither a prince nor an editorial potentate. I am only a poor story writer from a Boston attic"—but I didn't. I calmly accepted their cordial ministrations and did my best to deserve them.

Ehrich, who was a member of a well-known merchant firm in New York City, had been ordered by his physicians to the high, clear air of Colorado Springs, and his home facing the mountains was new. He had four children, two boys and two girls, to whom he was a most understanding comrade, and I thoroughly enjoyed his joyous, friendly, carefree household. He made me feel, as never before, the civilizing power of money.

It chanced that while I was at his home, B. B. Fernow, our first chief forester, came to Colorado to make a tour of the Federal forests. I knew nothing of the mountains and had never heard of forestry as a science, and when, at Ehrich's suggestion, Fernow invited me to accompany him into the White River Plateau, I gladly accepted and for two enchanting weeks rode with him, making the acquaintance for the first time of the "high trails," whose life was to form so large a part of my later fiction. Enraptured with this glorious region, which lay two miles above the level of Boston, I rode through forests as beautiful and almost as commodious as those in which Shakespeare's lovers walked and wooed. No imagined mingling of mead and stream, no savannah of the poet could surpass the splendor and variety of the wilderness through which we camped. In its beauty I forgot all my social missions, all my sordid, savage years. I thought only of the poetry which this glorious park suggested.

Something of this exaltation I put into an article for *Harper's Weekly*, but this was only the beginning. Without doubt that experience in the saddle colored all my after work. It definitely marks my reaction from the drab life of the plain. There was something confident, joyous, graceful in this roofless land of the horseman, the miner, and the hunter. Furthermore I had no feeling of responsibility for its social conditions. It was all new, vigorous, manly.

As I came back into Colorado Springs, I saw men out-fitting for a prospecting trip into a new gold camp with the strange name of Cripple Creek, and Ehrich assured me that the discovery was authentic. "It lies just behind Pike's Peak and is one of the highest camps ever known. The mines are all ten thousand feet above sea level and some of them are a thousand feet higher yet. A tremendous rush is setting in."

This greatly excited me. I went down to a corral near one of the cheaper hotels and watched the men saddling and packing their horses and was mightily tempted to go with them. Had I not been under contract to the *Arena* I would certainly have become a gold-seeker. Reluctantly I turned away and took passage on a train just ready to slide down the slope. "I shall return," I said to Ehrich, "and when I do, I shall go to Cripple Creek."

"When you come, any time you come, make my house your home," he replied with a cordiality which I knew to be sincere.

III

On my return to Boston I found myself possessed of a new scale of values. From the Continental Divide I now saw New England as the small beginning of a huge west-ward-expanding nation, and "The Hub of the Universe" a local capital. In conversation with one of my literary friends I jocosely remarked, "I have seen peaks that reduce Mount Washington to a pimple," a piece of Western brag which some one sent to the *Transcript* and got me into trouble.

Flower, on the contrary, was glad of my lyrical Rocky Mountain enthusiasm. "I am not publishing a New England magazine," he said. "I love Boston as a home, but as an editor I am addressing the reformers of all America. You should now go on to the Coast. Your education is incomplete till you have a knowledge of California."

Meanwhile he was publishing my novel serially under the title, "A Spoil of Office," laboring loyally to extend my circle of influence.

The reader who is interested may now understand how my first long story chanced to deal with a political revolution, for the Alliance was at bottom a genuine uprising, as genuine as the Vendée. The book should have been as true and important as a novel by Charles Reade or William Dean Howells, but alas! it was not. In the writing of it I had remained too much the orator, too consistently the advocate. The book lacked artistry. Too much of it was written on the train. I hurried too fast and I included too much.

Furthermore, my hero, a radical congressman, and my heroine, a claimant for woman's suffrage, failed to hold the interest of my readers. They were worthy, but concerned with a cause which was then rather malodorous. Ida Wilbur was in advance of her time. As I look back on her, I see that she was a lovely forerunner of the well-dressed and wholly competent leaders who followed Susan Anthony's austere generation. I find her not altogether despicable. I knew her type as well as I did that of Bradley Talcott, but I failed to make her lovable.

One of the reviewers of this story said, "It begins magnificently but its end is pitiful." I resented this statement then, but I acknowledge its essential truth now. The controversial side of my book killed it. I included too many political arguments. My grandiose plan for a panoramic novel of agricultural unrest degenerated into a partisan plea for a stertorous People's Party. Nevertheless, there are many things in "A Spoil of Office" which I should like to preserve. It is history, even in its raw proselyting and some of it I still frankly uphold. It was a faithful picture and in registering my own bitter concepts I was undoubtedly representative of many thousands of common folk.

IV

The destruction of the People's Party and the failure of this novel, joined to my discovery of the "High Country," put an end to my political fiction. My reforming zeal narrowed its field. I gave more time to poetry. I listened to Gilder when he said, "You are too much the artist to be a preacher. Give us more stories in which the beauty of life appears." Encouraged by his praise, I sent him a novelette of Dakota called "Old Pap's Flaxen," which he not only accepted and paid for, but praised in a letter which turned me still further from economic pamphleteering. I decided to ease up on argument and give myself entirely to writing stories and poems of the mid-West.

I was not alone in this reaction from the ethic to the esthetic. Clemens was passing through the same phase. Howells, though still exemplifying the socialistic concept in his novels as well as in his essays, was each month less direct about its expression. The reform impulse was steadily waning in power with us all. "Looking Backward," like "Progress and Poverty," was a receding, fading banner, to which only a few referred.

The *Arena* struggled on for a few years and then died, and all its radical writers became silent or took up new themes and new war cries. Prosperity came back to the South and West, the Farmers' Alliance dwindled, and other problems claimed the attention of those to whom "Free Silver" had been a fanatical crusade.

What a bubbling, steaming, complaining period it was! And how little enduring literature it produced. The stories which live, the poems which we still quote, had nothing to do with the political unrest. It should not be so, but so it was.

CHAPTER SIXTEEN

STEPHEN CRANE

I

In July of 1891, I gave a series of lectures at Avon-by-the-Sea in a summer school managed by Mr. and Mrs. Alberti of New York. Among other of my addresses was one upon "The Local Novel," and I remember very distinctly the young reporter for the *Tribune* who came up to me after the lecture to ask for the loan of my notes.

He was slim, boyish, with sallow complexion, and light hair. His speech was singularly laconic. "My name is Crane," he said. "Stephen Crane," and later I was told that he had been a student in a school near by, but had left before graduating to become a newspaper writer in New York. As I recall it, his presence at Avon was due to the Albertis, who knew his family—anyhow, he was reporting for the assembly.

Although not particularly impressed with him in this short interview, the correctness of his report of my lecture next day surprised me. I recognized in it unusual precision of expression and set about establishing a more intimate relationship. We met occasionally thereafter to "pass ball," and to discuss the science of pitching, the various theories which accounted for "inshoots" and "outdrops," for he, like myself, had served as a pitcher and gloried in being able to confound the laws of astronomy by making a sphere alter its course in mid-air.

In the middle of my second week he turned up at my boarding house in a very dejected mood. "Well, I've got the bounce," he said with a sour twist of his mouth. "The *Tribune* doesn't need me any more."

Not taking him seriously, I laughingly said, "They're making a mistake."

"That's what I told them," he answered. "But you see I made a report of a labor parade the other day, which slipped in over the managing editor's fence. When he read it in print he sent for me, made a little speech, and let me out."

"I should like to see that report," I remarked.

Thereupon he took from his pocket a clipping from the *Tribune* and handed it to me. It was very short, but it was closely studied and quite merciless in its realism. It depicted that political parade of tailors, house painters, and other indoor workers exactly as they appeared—a pale-faced, weak-kneed, splay-footed lot, the slaves of a triumphant civilization, wearing their chains submissively, working in the dark for careless masters, voting for privilege, seemingly without the slightest comprehension of their own supine cowardice; but it was Crane's ironical comment, his corrosive and bitter reflection upon their servility, and especially their habit of marching with banners at the chariot wheels of their conquerors, which made his article so offensive to the party in power.

Handing the article back to him I asked, "What did you expect from your journal—a medal?"

He smiled again in bitter reflection. "I guess I didn't stop to consider that. I was so hot at the sight of those poor, mis-shapen fools shouting for monopoly that I gave no thought to its effect upon my own fortunes. I don't know that it would have made much difference if I had. I wanted to say those things anyway."

He went away a few days after this, and I forgot all about him till in the winter of 1892 when I met his friends, Mr. and Mrs. Alberti, with whom he kept in touch in New York City.

My brother Franklin was playing at this time in Herne's famous New England play, "Shore Acres," and I, busied on some unimportant book, was "baching it" with him in a small apartment, when there came to us through the mail a yellow, paper-bound volume called "Maggie, a Girl of the Streets." The author's name was given as "Johnstone Smith," and across the cover in exquisite upright script were these words: "The reader of this book must inevitably be shocked, but let him keep on till the end, for in it the writer has put something which is important."

The first sentence of the story had not only singular comprehension and precision, it threw over its sordid scene a somber light in which the author's tiny actors took on grandiose significance. "A very small boy stood on a heap of gravel for the honor of Rum Alley. He was throwing stones at howling urchins who were crowding madly about the heap and pelting him. His infantile countenance was livid with fury. His small body was writhing in the delivery of great crimson oaths. His features wore the look of a tiny insane demon."

In another paragraph the bully appears. "Down the avenue came boastfully sauntering a lad of sixteen years, although the chronic sneer of an ideal manhood sat already upon his lips. His hat was tipped with an air of challenge over his eyes. Between his teeth a cigar stump tilted at the angle of defiance. He walked with a certain swing of the shoulders that appalled the timid." This was Pete.

Such were the principal male characters. Maggie was the sister of one, the victim of the other, and the heroine of the book. On her fell all the tragedy, all the disgrace of a life in the East Side slums. Frail flower of the muck, she went early to her decay and death.

It was a bitter story, but it interested me keenly. I secured Crane's address from Mrs. Alberti and wrote at once to him, accusing him of being the author of the book. I gave my own address and asked him to come and see me. Soon afterward he came to our little apartment and confessed his authorship of the book.

" 'Maggie,' " he said, "has been only privately half published and therefore remains entirely unsold." (A sample copy of this edition of "Maggie" sold recently for over two thousand dollars, illustrating once again the unpredictable trend of literary taste.

He was living at this time with a group of artists or art students ("Indians," he called them), in an old building on East Twenty-third Street. According to his acridly humorous description of their doings, they all slept on the floor, dined off buns and sardines, and painted on towels or wrapping paper for lack of canvas. He complained of the noise and confusion of these "savages, all dreaming blood-red dreams of fame."

He was distressingly pale and thin at this time, and appeared depressed, but no sooner had he filled his "crop" with the meat and coffee which my brother served, than he gave out an entirely different expression. He chortled and sang as he strolled about the room, comically like a well-fed hen, and for an hour or two talked freely and well, always with precision and original tang.

He interested me more than he did my brother, and although his change of mood was very flattering to Franklin's skill as a cook, he never offered to assist in washing the dishes. I did not ascribe this to laziness; on the contrary, he always appeared to my brother and me as one remote from the practical business of living. We were amused rather than irritated by his helplessness. He never mentioned his kin and I assumed that he was estranged from them.

One day late in March he arrived, reeking as usual with stale cigarette smoke, with a roll of manuscript in the side pocket of his long, shabby gray ulster.

"What have you there?" I asked, pointing accusingly at his conspicuous burden. "It looks like poetry."

He smiled sheepishly. "It is."

"Your own?"

"Yes."

"Let me see it!" I commanded, much amused by his guilty expression. Handing the roll to me with a boyish gesture, he turned away with pretended indifference, to my brother. Upon unrolling the manuscript, I found it to be a sheaf of poems written in blue ink upon single sheets of legal cap paper, each poem without blot or correction, almost without punctuation, all beautifully legible, exact and orderly in arrangement. They were as easy to read as print and as I rapidly ran through them, I was astounded by their power. I could not believe that they were the work of the pale, laconic youth before me. They were at once quaintly humorous and audacious, unrhymed and almost without rhythm, but the figures employed with masterly brevity were colossal. They suggested some of the French translations of Japanese verses, at other times they carried the sting and compression of Emily Dickinson's verse and the savage philosophy of Olive Shriner, and yet they were not imitative.

"Have you any more?" I asked after I had come to the end of the roll.

"I have four or five up here," he replied, pointing toward his temple, "all in a little row," he quaintly added. "That's the way they come—in little rows, all ready to be put down on paper. I wrote nine yesterday. I wanted to write some more last night but those 'Indians' wouldn't let me do it. They howled so loud over the other lines that they nearly cracked my ears. You see we all live in the same box," he explained with sour candor, "and I've no place to write except in the general squabble. They think my verses are funny. They make a circus of me."

I was greatly interested in his statement that the verses were composed in his mind all ready to be drawn off. "Do you mean to say that these lines are arranged in your head, complete in every detail?"

"Yes, I could do one right now."

"Very well. Take a seat at my desk and do one for me." Thereupon with my pen he wrote steadily, composedly, without a moment's hesitation, one of his most powerful poems. It flowed from his pen like oil, but when I examined it, I found it not only without blot or erasure, but perfectly correct in punctuation. I can not be sure of the poem but I think it was the one which begins:

God fashioned the ship of the world carefully

and goes on to tell how "a wrong called," God turned His head and this ship without rudder slipped down the ways, and as a result has ever since wandered helplessly, going foolish journeys, doubling on its track, aimlessly drifting through the universe.

It appealed to me with enormous force at the moment. Coming from this hungry, seedy boy, written in my commonplace little study on a sunlit winter morning without premeditation—so he said—it wrought upon me with magical power. I understood a part of the incredulity of "Those Indians" who could not take their fellow "Indian" seriously. He declared that it had never been on paper before and that he had not consciously arranged its words in his mind. He just knew in a general way that it was there to be drawn off.

After he went away I read the poems aloud to my brother, pausing to exclaim over their ironic humor, their brevity, their originality of phrases. "What has the fellow been reading? If they are wholly the work of this unaccountable boy, America has produced another genius as singular as Poe," I concluded.

I confess that I took these lines very seriously. I hastened to show them to my most scholarly friends in order to detect the source of their inspiration. They remained original. I could not say that Crane had imitated any other writer.

He continued for some weeks to "precipitate" others but in diminishing flow. I recall that he came into Herne's dressing room at the theater one night to tell me that he had drawn off the very last one. "That place in my brain is empty," he said, but the poem he showed me was not a cull—it was tremendous in its effect on Herne as well as on me.

Later, much later, he wrote to say that he had gained the power to "turn the poetic spout on or off," but my interest in his verse was momentarily weakened by another and still more amazing demonstration of his subconscious endowment. One day he turned up just in time for luncheon with another roll of manuscript, a roll so large that it filled one of the capacious pockets of his ulster. "What have you there," I demanded, "more lines?"

"No, it is a tale," he said with that queer, self-derisive smile which was often on his lips at this time.

"Let me see it," I said, knowing well that he had brought it for that purpose.

He handed it over to me with seeming reluctance, and while he went out to watch my brother getting lunch I took my first glance at the manuscript of "The Red Badge of Courage," which had, however, no name at this time. The first sentence fairly took me captive. It described a vast army in camp on one side of a river, confronting with its thousands of eyes a similar monster on the opposite bank. The finality which lay in every word, the epic breadth of vision, the splendor of the pictures presented—all indicated a most powerful and original imagination as well as a mature mastery of literary form.

Each page presented pictures like those of a great poem, and I experienced the thrill of the editor who has fallen unexpectedly upon a work of genius. It was as if the youth in some mysterious way had secured the coöperation of a spirit, the spirit of an officer in the Civil War. How else could one account for the boy's knowledge of war?

I spoke of this and in his succinct, self-derisive way, he candidly confessed that all his knowledge of battle had been gained on the football field! "The psychology is the same. The opposite team is an enemy tribe!"

At the table, while he applied himself with single-hearted joy to my brother's steak, I brooded over his case, and looking across at him, sallow, yellow-fingered, small, and ugly, I was unable to relate him in the slightest degree to the marvelous manuscript which he had placed in my hands. True, his talk was vivid, but it was disjointed and quaint rather than copious or composed.

Upon returning to my little study I said to him very seriously, "Crane, I daren't tell you how much I value this thing —at least not now. But wait! Here's only part of the manuscript. Where's the rest of it?"

Again he grinned, sourly, with a characteristic droop of his head. "In hock."

"To whom?"

"Typewriter."

"How much do you owe him or her?"

"Fifteen dollars."

Plainly this was no joking matter to him, but my brother and I were much amused by his tragic tone. At last I said, "I'll loan you the fifteen dollars if you'll bring me the remainder of the manuscript to-morrow."

"I'll do it," he said as if he were joining me in some heroic enterprise, and away he went in high spirits.

He was as good as his word, and when I had read the entire story I set to work to let my editorial friends know of this youngster. I mailed two of his completed sketches to B. O. Flower of the *Arena,* asking him to be as generous as he could, "for the author is hungry"; and I suggested to Crane that he call upon Irving Bacheller, who was then running the Bacheller Syndicate, and say to him that I had advised Crane to make certain studies of East Side life in New York City and that I hoped the Syndicate would commission the writing of them.

Crane seemed grateful for the little I was able to do, but was not at all confident of earning a living with his pen.

I remember talking with him about "the bread lines," which regularly formed each night at certain bakeries which gave away their stale bread, and at my suggestion he went down one winter's evening, joined one of these lines, and made a study which he afterwards called "The Men in the Storm," a fine sketch which syndicated, I believe, along with others of somewhat similar character. And yet in spite of my aid and these promising activities, he remained almost as needy as ever. Thin and seedy, he still slept on the floor —according to his own story, smoking incessantly and writing in any possible corner.

One day when he was particularly depressed I said to him, "You'll be rich and famous in a year or two. Successful authors always look back with a smile on their hard times."

"You may be right," he replied soberly, "but it's no joke now. I'd trade my entire future for twenty-three dollars in cash."

Without claiming too much for my powers as a fortune teller, I could not believe that this boy would long remain obscure. He had too much to give the reading world. His style was too individual, his imagination too powerful, to fail of winning the applause of those who count originality among the most desired qualities of American literature. Some of his phrases were to me quite inevitable for their condensation and clarity.

He had a genius for phrases. For example: in speaking of a truck driver he said, "In him grew a majestic contempt for those strings of street cars that followed him like *intent bugs*." As for Maggie, "To her the world was composed of hardships and insults." Of the mother, "It seems that the world had treated this woman very badly and she took a deep revenge upon such portions of it as came within her reach. She broke furniture as if she were at last getting her rights."

Of course I am aware that the character of these books did not make for popularity, but I was sure that the marvelous English which this boy had somehow acquired would compensate for his street loafers, birds of the night, beggars, saloon keepers, drunken tenement dwellers, and the like.

"Your future is secure. A man who can write 'The Red Badge of Courage' can not be forever a lodger in a bare studio."

He replied, "That may be, but if I had some money to buy a new suit of clothes I'd feel my grip tighten on the future."

"You'll laugh at all this—we all go through it."

"It is ridiculous, but it doesn't make me laugh," he replied smilelessly.

In the *Arena* for June, 1893, I reviewed a novel by Bourget and "Maggie" under the caption, "An Ambitious French Novel and a Modest American Story." So far as I knew this was the earliest review of Crane's first book. In this notice I made use of these words: "It is a story which deals with vice and poverty and crime, but does so not out of curiosity —not out of salaciousness, but because of a distinct art impulse to utter in truthful phrase a certain rebellious cry. It is the voice of the slums. The young author, Stephen Crane, is a native of New York City and has grown up in the very scenes he has described. His book is the most truthful and the most unhackneyed story of the slums I have ever read—fragment though it is. It has no conventional phrases. It gives the dialect of the people as I have never before seen it written, crisp, direct, terse. It is another locality finding voice. Mr. Crane is but twenty-one years of age."

II

Shortly before I left for the West he called to tell me that he had shown his verses to Mr. John D. Barry and that Mr. Barry had "fired them off to Copeland & Day."

"I am sorry—I was on the point of interesting a New York publisher in them."

The poems appeared soon after in a form which too strongly emphasized their singularities. With the best intention in the world, Messrs. Copeland & Day gave a leading to the critics who quite generally took the "Black Riders" as a cue for laughter.

I saw nothing of him during 1894, but in May of that year he wrote me from Chicago a letter in which he mentions the poem he read to Herne and me:

"I have not written you because there has been little to tell of late. I am plodding along on the *Press* in a quiet and effective way. We now eat with charming regularity at least two times per day. I am content and am writing another novel which is a bird. That poem, 'The Reformer,' which I showed you in behind Daly's Theater, was lost somehow, so I don't think we can ever send it to the *Arena*. I can't remember a line of it.

"I saw 'Hannele.' Its reason for being is back somewhere in the Middle Ages, but as an irresponsible, artistic achievement, it's great. I sat and glowed and shivered.

"When anything happens, I'll keep you informed. I'm getting lots of free advertising. Everything is coming along nicely now. I have got the poetic spout so that I can turn it on or off. I wrote a Decoration Day thing for the *Press* which aroused them to enthusiasm. They said in about a minute, though, that I was firing over the heads of the soldiers. I am going to see your brother soon. Don't forget to return to New York soon, for all the struggling talent miss you. Yours as ever."

His next letter was from 143 East 23d St., Nov. 15:

"So much of my row with the world has to be silence and endurance that sometimes I wear the appearance of having forgotten my best friends, those to whom I am indebted for everything. As a matter of fact, I have just crawled out of the fifty-third ditch into which I have been cast and I now feel that I can write you a letter that won't make you ill. McClure was a Beast about the war novel and that has been the thing that put me in one of the ditches. He kept it for six months until I was nearly mad. Oh, yes, he was going to use it, but finally I took it to Bachellers. They use it in January in a shortened form. I have just completed a New York book that leaves 'Maggie' at the post. It is my best thing. Since you are not here, I am going to see if Mr. Howells will not read it. I am still working for the *Press*."

Another note written at 111 West 33d Street, City, Wednesday P.M., begins abruptly:

"I have not been up to see you because of various strange conditions—notably, my toes are coming through one shoe and I have not been going out into society as much as I might. I hope you have heard about the 'Uncut Leaves Affair.' I tried to get tickets up to you, but I couldn't succeed. I mail you last Sunday's *Press*. I've moved now—live in a flat. People can come to see me now. They come in shoals, and say I am a great writer. Counting five that are sold, four that are unsold, and six that are mapped out, I have fifteen short stories in my head and out of it. They'll make a book. The *Press* people pied some of 'Maggie,' as you will note."

Another note from the Lantern Club, New York City, July 17, 1895, refers to his book of poems:

"I have lost your address and so for certainty's sake send this to the *Arena*. I am just returned from my wanderings in Mexico. Have you seen 'The Black Riders'? I dedicated them to you, but I am not sure that I should have done it without your permission. Do you care? I am getting along better—a little better—than when I last saw you. I work for the Bachellers."

Thus it appears that in spite of the booming of friends and the talk of critics he had not achieved even comfort. His letter was written at the old place in Twenty-third Street.

The serial publication of "The Red Badge of Courage" brought him an admirer in the person of Ripley Hitchcock of Appleton's, who made him an offer for the book at "customary royalty." He accepted, glad of the chance. This helped him somewhat, but as royalties are only paid annually and as the book sold very slowly, he continued to suffer need.

At this point his affairs took a sudden turn upward. He became the figure I had hoped to see him become two years before. Some English critics wrote in highest praise of "The Red Badge," and the book became a critical bone of contention between military objectors and literary enthusiasts. Crane was accepted as a man of genius.

Some time in the summer of 1896 he called at my New York hotel and, not finding me, left the following note:

"Just heard you were in town. I want you to dine to-night with me at the Lantern Club, sure! Roosevelt expects to be there. He wants to meet you. Don't fail. I will call here at six, again."

He also left a book, "George's Mother," in which he had made this characteristic inscription, "To Hamlin Garland of the great honest West, from Stephen Crane of the false East."

This dinner at the Lantern Club was important in several ways. I do not recall meeting Roosevelt, but Irving Bacheller was there and we had much talk about Crane and other matters. The club met in a very old building, in its loft, as I recall it, on Williams Street and the walls of the dining room were covered with the autographs of so many distinguished writers that I hesitated to add mine. It was a bit of the Colonial New York which had perilously survived, I say perilously, because it gave way soon after to a modern building, and remains but a pleasant memory to the older newspaper men of to-day.

I saw Crane several times during his troubles with the New York police, and while I sympathized with him in his loyalty to a woman whom he considered had been unjustly accused of soliciting, his stubborn resolve to go on the stand in her defense was quixotic. Roosevelt discussed the case with me and said, "I tried to save Crane from press comment, but as he insisted on testifying, I could only let the law take its course."

The papers stated that Crane's rooms had been raided and that an opium layout had been discovered. Altogether it was a miserable time for him. The shady side of his bohemian life was turned to the light.

Meeting him in McClure's office one day, I said to him very earnestly, "Crane, why don't you cut loose from your associations here? Go to your brother's farm in Sullivan County and get back your tone. You don't look well. Settle down to the writing of a single big book up there, and take your time to do it."

Impulsively thrusting out his hand to me, he said, "I'll do it." Alas! He did not. He took a commission to go to Greece and report a war. On his return from Greece he went to Cuba.

Long afterward Louis Senger, one of his companions on this mission, wrote to me, conveying the information that just before they went to Cuba Crane told him to write to me in case anything happened to him down there.

"There was no particular message for you, but if you do not already know it, I believe he wished me to assure you that the appreciation shown for his early work by yourself and Mr. Howells was the first of that particular success which he so much craved. I read your article in the *Post* and liked it much, but Crane's force was entirely in himself, I think, and entirely natural. I'm sure I do not know why he should have showed me so much of his work, and God knows I must have hurt him. I read 'Maggie' from chapter to chapter in a house over on the far East Side, where he lived with a crowd of irresponsibles. I brought Lawson, who is my cousin, and Crane together and we were the first to read his 'Lines.' One day he told me he was going to write a war story and later he showed me some chapters of the 'Red Badge.' 'I deliberately started in to do a pot-boiler,' he told me then; 'something that would take the boarding-school element—you know the kind. Well, I got interested in the thing in spite of myself, and I couldn't, I couldn't! I *had* to do it my own way.' This was the first and only time I ever knew Crane's courage to falter in the least, and this was after five years of it, and he was writing then on the paper the meat came home in.

"I saw him only once after the Cuban affair. He was sick and joked mirthlessly that they had not got him yet. You know that he was essentially a soldier. He would have elected to die in battle rather than wait for the slower death of which I believe he had a prophetic knowledge.

"He spoke of you often, and always with a sense of blame for himself lest you should think him ungrateful. He was never that."

After the Cuban war, Crane married and went to England, where he lived till he was ordered into Germany for his health. I have only one letter from him while he was in England, and in that he told me nothing of himself. It was all about a new writer he had discovered, a certain Joseph Conrad. "Get his 'Nigger of the Narcissus,' " he wrote. "It is a crackerjack. Conrad knows your work. You should meet him when you come to England."

It was more than twenty years later when I met Conrad in Bishopsbourne and talked of "The Nigger" and of Crane. "A wealthy admirer turned over to the Cranes a great, half-ruined manor house not far from here," said Conrad, "and Stephen kept open house there. The place was so filled with his semi-bohemian associates in London that I seldom went there—I didn't enjoy his crowd, but I liked him and valued his work. I went over to see him when he was brought to Dover on his way to the Black Forest. He wore a beard and was greatly emaciated. The moment I looked into his eyes I knew that he was bound for a long voyage —and that I should not see him again. He died soon after in Bavaria."

In an article written soon after Crane's death, I said:

"He was too brilliant, too fickle, too erratic to last. He could not go on doing stories like 'The Red Badge of Courage.' The weakness of such highly individual work lies in its success by surprise. The words which astonish, the phrases which excite wonder and admiration, come eventually to seem tricky. They lose force with repetition and come at last to be distasteful. 'The Red Badge of Courage' was marvelous, but manifestly Crane could not go on repeating a surprise. When he wrote in conventional phrase his power diminished. If he continued to write of slum life, he repeated himself. It seems now that he was destined from the first to be a present-day Poe, a singular and daring soul, irresponsible as the wind. We called him a genius, for he had that quality which we can not easily measure or define.

"His mind was more largely subconscious in its workings than that of any man of my acquaintance. He did not understand his own processes or resources. When he put pen to paper he found marvelous words, images, sentences, pictures already formed in his brain, to be drawn off and fixed on paper. His pen was 'a spout,' as he himself says. The farther he got from his own field, his inborn tendency, the weaker he became. Such a man can not afford to enter the dusty public thoroughfare. His genius is of the lonely wood, the solitary shadowland.

"To send him to report actual warfare was a mistake. His genius lay in depicting the battles which never saw the light of day, and upon which no eyes but his own had ever gazed. He was a strange, willful, irresponsible boy, one that will not soon be forgotten out of American literature."

I see no reason to change this estimate of him.

CHAPTER SEVENTEEN

THE POET OF THE SIERRAS

I

WHEN a lad of fifteen or sixteen—that is to say, in 1875 or 1876—I chanced to read a poem called "Kit Carson's Ride" which appealed so strongly to my imagination that I seized upon it for use as a public declamation. It dealt with heroic characters and depicted in tumultuous rhythms a prairie fire and a race for life on the plains of Texas. It was romantic and high colored, but it had in it a quality which no one but a Western man could employ. It represented the direct opposite of the world to which Emerson and Longfellow belonged. It had something of the magical West in it—horsemen, buffalo, and red men. It was as new in subject as it was swift and free of movement, and the author's name, Joaquin Miller, suggested Spanish or Mexican origin. Its opening lines were a picture. Carson is speaking:

"We lay low in the grass on the broad, plain levels,
Old Revels and I and my stolen brown bride;
'Forty full miles if a foot to ride!
Forty full miles if a foot, and the devils
Of red Comanches are hot on the track
When once they strike it. Let the sun go down
Soon, very soon,' muttered bearded old Revels
As he peered at the sun, lying low on his back,

> Holding fast to his lasso.—Then he jerked at his steed
> And he sprang to his feet, and glanced swiftly around,
> Then dropped as if shot with his ear to the ground,
> Then again to his feet, and to me, to my bride,
> While his eyes were like flame, his face like a shroud,
> His form like a king, his beard like a cloud,
> And his voice loud and shrill as both trumpet and reed,—
> 'Pull, pull in your lassoes and bridle to steed,
> And speed you if ever for life you would speed,
> Aye, ride for your lives, for your lives you must ride
> For the plain is aflame, the prairie on fire,
> And the feet of wild horses hard flying before
> I hear like a sea breaking high on the shore,
> While the buffalo come like a surge of the sea,
> Driven far by the flame driving fast on us three
> As a hurricane comes crushing palms in his ire.' "

Faulty as these opening lines now seem they had force and fire and novelty in 1875—and the rush of the rhythm carried through to the end.

I recited this poem with great success at the Burr Oak schoolhouse one winter night, and at the close of it a neighbor who had recently returned from western Nebraska came up to say "that poet, whoever he is, has drawn a true picture of the plains. I've seen the buffalo just like that and a prairie fire."

From that time on I read every available line of Joaquin Miller's writing. He did not destroy for me the poetry of New England; he supplemented it by presenting in verse certain phases of the wild West, as Bret Harte with his prose tales and dialect verses was presenting the gold-seekers.

In my Boston studies of the local-color novel and the vernacular in verse, I came to a careful study of Miller, grouping him with Harte. I made him one of the leaders in a new and most significant Coast literature. In point of time as well as in the spirit and color of his work he was a pioneer, as Walt Whitman somewhat cautiously admitted.

Admiring Miller's verse at its best I was less outspoken when dealing with his plays, his descriptive articles, and his short stories. How could a man be at his best while skittering from Oregon to England, from England to Italy, and from New York to Nicaragua? I never knew where to look for him or what next he would attempt.

He built a log cabin in Washington and abandoned it. He wrote travel sketches and poems for weekly magazines from New Orleans, and his books appeared under various publishers' imprints in hopelessly ugly form, and yet through all his blunders and wanderings he persisted as a picturesque and powerful personality. He was said to be part Mexican, and that he had been a filibuster in Nicaragua, a horse thief in California, and an Indian fighter in Oregon. Others considered him a *poseur*, a make-believe miner, and a stage cowboy. Gilder said to me, "While in London Miller wore jack-boots, a Mexican serape, a broad-brim hat, and long hair like a scout. Similarly attired, he called on me at the *Century Magazine*, all for the advertising which resulted," and in saying these things he put Joaquin aside as of no account.

Notwithstanding all this, I continued to quote his poems in my lectures with the remark, "I can forgive a poet many things who can write such lines as these:"

CROSSING THE PLAINS

A tale half told and hardly understood;
The talk of savage men that chanced to meet,
That leaned on long, quaint rifles in the wood,
That looked in fellow faces, spoke discreet
And low, as half in doubt and in defeat

Of hope. A tale it was of lands of gold
That lay toward the west. Wild winged and fleet
It spread among the swift Missouri's bold
Unbridled men, and reached to where Ohio rolled.

Then long chained lines of yoked and patient steers.
Then long vast trains that pointed to the west—
Beyond the savage West. The hopes and fears
Of blunt untutored men that hardly guessed
Their course. The brave and silent women, dressed
In homely spun attire. Then boys in bands.
The cheery babes, that laughed at all, and blest
The doubting hearts with laughing lifted hands.
What exodus for far untraversed lands!

The plains! The shouting drivers at the wheel.
The crash of leather whips. The crush and roll
Of wheels. The jar of grinding steel,
And then at last the whole vast line
That seemed to stretch and stream away
Toward the west, as if with one control.
Then hope loomed fair, and home lay far behind.
Before, the boundless plain and fiercest of their kind.

Then dust arose—a long vast line
Like smoke from out the riven earth!
The wheels went groaning by.
The thousand feet in harness and in yoke
They tore the ways of ashen alkali.
The desert winds blew sudden, swift and dry.
The dust! It sat upon and filled the train.
It seemed to fret and fill the very sky.
Lo! Dust upon the beasts, the tent, the plain—
And dust alas, on breasts that rose not up again.

*   *   *

They stood at last, the decimated few
Beside a land of running streams, and they—

They pushed aside the boughs, and peering through
Beheld afar the cool refreshing bay.
Then some did curse, and some bend hand to pray.
And some looked back upon the desert, wide
And desolate in death, and all that day
They mourned. But one, with nothing left
Beside a dog to love, crept down among the ferns and died.

Eager as I was to know more of him I had no expectation of ever seeing him, for no one seemed to know where he lived, although some of his later poems indicated that he had retired to a home on the hills near San Francisco, defeated and embittered by his contact with New York and London. The only persons I knew who could tell me anything about his personal history were frankly contemptuous of him. "He is a mountebank," Stedman said with gentle authority. "I've no use for a poet who turns up at a reception looking like a scout or a gambler from a Rocky Mountain mining camp."

"But he can write."

"Yes, he can write. He's done a few fine things, but he writes too much."

This I was obliged to admit, but my interest persisted, and when in the autumn of 1892 I found myself booked for a tour of California, I promised myself a call on the "Poet of the Sierras" if he could be found.

A hundred times on my journey across the continent I quoted him. His lines upon the plains and mountains rose again and again to my lips, so apt were his descriptions, so comprehensive his moods. From the time the train struck out upon the green slope which leads to the Rocky Mountains till I saw "St. Helens in her sea of wood" and watched the "terrible heights of Hood" rising to the clouds like a tower of rose and violet marble, I found in "Songs of the Sierras" the fullest description of this mighty land whose peaks and cañons demanded new rhythms and new figures of speech.

At the foot of Mount Shasta I understood his line, "sit where the cool white rivers run," and I measured at last the depth and tenderness of his apostrophe to the Sierras, "eternal tents of snow that flash o'er battlements of mountains." "They stand, a lifted line of snowy isles!" he sings at another place. No wonder Lord Houghton pencilled on his copy of the "Songs" the words, "pictures! pictures!"

At my earliest opportunity I asked my San Francisco friends about him. "I want to know the man who can put these mountains into songs. He can't be altogether fraudulent. Great streams do not rise from desert sands."

"He lives in Oakland," they said, and so early one morning I took the ferry across the bay with the entire day before me. It was well that I did this, for no one could tell me where he lived. In the directory I found this modest inscription:

C. H. MILLER, Fruit Grower,
Residence on the Heights.

A characterization which made me think of rugged John Burroughs in his vineyard on the Hudson. I inquired for the Heights and how to get there. Everybody had heard of Miller, but nobody seemed to know where to find him. One young man said, "It's a long walk up in the hills. I was up there with a party of young people once, but it was in the night and a hard climb, and I don't remember much about the road."

The druggist asked me if I were going up to interview him, which made me understand something of the poet's reason for getting so far away.

Another man said, "Yes, I know Miller. He's a rough old fellow—wears boots." This was all that he could tell me of the poet.

Taking a horse car which, I was told, ran within two miles of his house, I started toward the mountains. At the end of the line I got my bearings and set out along a rising road, bordered with eucalyptus trees whose shining blue-green leaves intermingled with the beautiful feathery frond-age of the Australian acacia. As the road began to climb, the city sank slowly into deepening distance. The walking was not unpleasant, but the hills (faint green and dotted with brush) grew steeper. It was midwinter but the air was still and soft and springlike.

The road was lonely and I had no guide to the house, but I trusted to the lines wherein the poet had said:

"... Be my reward
Some little place to pitch my tent;
Some tree or vine
Where I may sit above the sea
And drink the wind as drinking wine."

I knew that I had not reached the altitude which he would seek; there was not enough of sea and sky within my sweep of vision.

After an hour's walk I came upon a little log hut which I recognized from illustrations of it. It was one of four or five little cottages standing in a row on the hillside amid a carefully terraced and abundantly watered fruit farm. They were minute, hardly more, architecturally, than Dakota

claim shanties. Roses were in bloom though it was Christmas week and small olive and orange trees, trout ponds,
beds of flowers, and a team plowing in the background,
gave evidence of care and taste.

Oakland lay below flattened and remote, while afar in
the haze of the western sun, across the bay (where ferry-
boats were shuttling to and fro), San Francisco rose upon
its hills, and out on the placid ocean far beyond, ships poised
and waited, with shining sails, indecisive and hesitating. It
was exactly the spot which a poet would settle upon, a place
of wide range and pure air, aloof yet not out of reach of
the city, which is, after all, civilization as it exists to-day.

At the door of one of the little houses, the poet's mother,
a wholesome, pleasing German type, met me. "My son is
not at home," she said, "but he will come soon. Make
yourself comfortable in his cottage till he comes."

I had not long to wait. While walking about the garden
I saw a man coming up the hill. I recognized him at once.
He wore a large soft hat, and carried his coat upon his arm.

As he approached, his head reminded me of Whitman,
though his expression was sterner, less patriarchal. He eyed
me grimly as a possible interviewer.

His hair was getting gray and his beard was long. There
was nothing absurd in his dress, nothing unusual save a
certain simplicity and freedom from conventional linen. As
he greeted me in offhand Western fashion, I looked into
his quiet blue-gray eyes and liked him. He impressed me
as a man of strength and marked individuality.

When I told him my name, his face lighted up. He seized
me by the hand. "Boy! I'm glad to see you. Come in."

Holding me by the hand he half led, half dragged me
into "the abbey" which was plainly his workshop. The walls

were covered with autographed letters, newspaper scraps, clippings from magazines, and prints of the faces of his friends and correspondents.

Among these were relics of his former life in the woods and mountains. A Mexican saddle hung in the corner, bear skins and wolf skins covered the chairs and lay upon the floor. The room was a camp, the camp of a man of letters, reminding me of Burroughs' bark study.

We were soon in the thick of talk. He refused, however, to discuss Miller. He wanted to hear of other things. He would not allow me to bring up questions concerning his verse, but talked freely of his little ranch, and his plans for growing fruit. Little by little, however, he opened his deeper self to me. "I believe there should be more of individual freedom in living. Most families live too close together, therefore in place of one large house I built four small ones. In one my mother lives and keeps house. There we all eat. In this cabin I sleep and write—the third is for my brother and the fourth for my guests. I believe in the open air. My doors are never shut. I live practically without fire the year round, a thing quite possible on this protected slope where the sun always falls.

"I took this piece of land when it was nothing but barren hillside, incredibly sterile. With the work of my own hands I led the water down from the cañon. I terraced the hill-sides, built stone walls, hollowed out trout ponds, and planted orchards of olives and walnut trees. I have a mile of roses," he ended with smiling pride.

He told me that his habit was to drive away at his writing all the forenoon, and to work with the man to whom he had given part of his plow land in payment for his assistance about the orchard. He had some such philosophy as that expressed by Tolstoy in walking behind his Russian harrow.

Inevitably we fell to talking of the red people whom we had both known and he told me of some of his experiences as a warrior, now on the side of the reds, now on the side of the whites. "I was but a lad," he explained. "I ran away from my father's home in Oregon and came down to California in the hope of winning gold enough to relieve the necessities of my mother." He paused as with a fear that he was becoming too serious or too intimate and said with a smile, "Do you know, when I was living among the Indians I learned how to make rain."

"Did you indeed?" I exclaimed incredulously.

"Yes, one of the old medicine men taught me the secret. I'll show you." Here he rose and placed a chair fronting the open door. "Now you sit here and keep your eyes on the sky, while I make a medicine song."

Taking the seat as directed I smilingly awaited his hocus-pocus, whatever it might be. There was not a cloud in the sky, and the path before the door was dusty. While I looked and listened I heard him moving about and chanting some monotonous humming song of incantation—and then, suddenly, I thought I heard the sound of rain on the roof. It sounded exactly like a gentle shower, and a moment later I saw, or fancied I saw, gray lines of rain falling athwart the open door. I imagined I saw the heavy drops send up little puffs of dust. The rain increased to a roar.

Joaquin appeared before me. "What do you think of that?" he inquired triumphantly. "My medicine heap strong."

"Wonderful!" I exclaimed as I looked into his laughing eyes, "but what were you doing over there in the corner?"

His smile deepened. "Oh, I was just turning on the

water." Then abandoning all pretence he exclaimed, "I brought that water all the way down from the cañon. I laid part of the pipe with my own hands, and on the long hot days of autumn when all the hillside is burned and brown with the sun, I can turn the spigot and sit in my own individual shower."

Was not this the creation of a poet?

We ate supper in the tentlike dining room of his mother's cottage, a simple meal which he served quietly, talking on about the great new world of liberty and equality which he declared was sure to come.

After the meal we walked out to see his Italian chestnuts and his olives, and in this stroll I saw more of his mile of roses. His remarkable water system enabled him to have springs and fountains at most unexpected places. He took a boyish delight in showing each of them to me.

Returning to the cabin, he gave me a bear skin to keep off the chill, and as we discussed art and literature and altruistic living, the shadows fell over the distant city and the light fled from the sea. The longer I studied him, the more elemental and admirable he became, and yet I saw how easily he could be misunderstood and caricatured.

He had no books about him, not even his own. He had ink and paper and manuscripts, but no library. "I have little need of books. I read a great deal in the way of current literature, but my time is mainly given to creative work or to my orchard."

The room in which we sat had the simplicity of a tent, and yet it was unmistakably the home of a powerful and original genius. The names and pictures upon the wall, together with autographed letters from all over England and America, showed his wide fame and the catholicity of his friendship.

Consenting at last to talk about himself, he told me a part of his life, sketching it in outline. He laughed at the recollection of the wild stories which still passed current with the uninformed. He looked grave when I said, "Why don't you let somebody straighten out the distortion which irresponsible paragraphers have twisted into your life?"

"Time will straighten it all out," he said at last slowly. "My brother is in possession of the facts. He may tell the truth some day."

He spoke of his work without egotism and yet with an unaffected freedom which has probably been mistaken for egotism. He constantly reminded me of Whitman. His voice was gentle and unaffected in tone, and his diction very pleasing by reason of its spontaneity and aptness.

His most striking peculiarities were those associated with the trail and the elemental life he had lived beneath the sky.

"I love the traditions of the woods and mountains," he said abruptly with a sweep of his hand about the room, which was filled with mementos of the wilderness. "I was born in the forest of Indiana and as a child I made the overland journey through the Rockies to the Coast. My boyhood was spent in Oregon, my youth in California. I have always lived close down to the earth."

He execrated certain aspects of our civilization. "I hate and fear your dark and terrible cities."

There was pathos as well as poetry in his description of his attempt to found a new community on the hillside. He told me that his doors were never locked and seldom shut, and the proof of it was in his attempt to close the door on my behalf. It was warped so strongly to an open position that it refused obstinately to shut out the air which seized upon me with disturbing vigor.

He glowed with delight as he described the owls which came at night to perch on a pole he had placed for them before his open door.

"There they sit," he said, "and perch and peer and marvel at the man stretched on his bed within. I suppose they wonder why any creature should go to bed in the finest part of the day."

He knew all the birds of the region, and took me into the orchard to show me a minute lizard which a butcher bird had impaled on a thorn, and afterward he showed me the cantenas made of bear skin in which he had carried gold dust in the days when he rode pony express. His talk of pioneer days was quiet and dignified and very graphic. He spoke interestingly of his Chinese laborers and told me several pathetic stories of them.

As night came on he talked of high things, of Christ and His teaching, of death and the spirit. He impressed me as a man of natural refinement, one who had done a great deal of original thinking. His ideals of life, expressed in his latest verses, were of lofty significance, concerned with the progress of humanity, the laws of God to man and the laws of nature to man.

It was a moving experience to find this man high on the Oakland hills expressing the same sense of human brotherhood which had produced "Progress and Poverty," "News from Nowhere," and "A Hazard of New Fortunes," a conviction which had sent Father Huntington and Father McGlynn out among the miners and into the slums.

He was at work on a metrical "Life of Christ," some parts of which he read to me, very musical and lofty verse. He also showed me the manuscript of a prose romance which he called "The City Beautiful."

This manuscript so moved me that I asked permission to take it back with me. "It may be that Flower can use it or some part of it in the *Arena*. Also I'll see if I can't find a publisher for it in book form."

This offer almost brought the tears to his eyes, for he confessed that he had no hope of its ever being published. "There is not story enough to it, and it deals with an imaginary city, a city of my dreams. It is not like Bellamy, but it undoubtedly is of the same spirit."

He read me one magnificent passage describing the roar of a lion in a cavern, as he was about to attack a man and a woman, poised on a huge granite block, which was the pedestal of a figure in armor. It was this passage, I suspect, that led to my taking the manuscript away with me.

II

At last I rose to go. As I stood at the door, the lights of the city bloomed out of the vague masses which lay below and Miller joined me in admiration of that splendid garden of golden and sapphire lights. Neither of us spoke. It was too beautiful for words, and yet both of us knew that under that veil of mist, beneath that starry sparkle of lights, human wretchedness and sin and vice lay. Must it always be so?

We went down the hill together. Watchdogs barked at us as we passed, but they only threw into more impressive relief the peace and beauty and springlike silence of the night.

The poet talked on with an undercurrent of deep emotion, telling me how much he wished to get people of sincerity and fraternal feeling to come and live with him there on his hillside slope.

"My belief is that if Christ were to return to this earth, He would not live in a great house in the roar of a city, attended by servants; it would be impossible for Him. He would live on the soil, would serve Himself or be served by those who loved Him. He would live simply, without greed or envy or reproach, and His action, if taken for example, would reform our whole society.

"The one positive law of God to man is this: 'In the sweat of thy face shalt thou eat bread.' All other laws are negative merely. If this law were absolutely carried out, all inequality, all grinding toil, all the hurry and bitterness and insecurity of life here on earth would vanish."

I can only recall the main idea. I can not reproduce the lofty diction nor express the solemn earnestness of his manner which was somewhat in the way of Tolstoy. It was, in fact, the Christ idea as expressed in his everyday life. With great clearness and with the majesty of simple truth he taught that it was time to consider the daily life of Him who plucked the standing wheat for his noonday meal. "It is time to make action conform to creed. Christ was not a money changer. He believed in justice. He was a commoner."

The totality of impression made upon me by this mountaineer was very strong, and when I gripped his hand in parting, it was with that vague sense of loss which I often feel when I take leave of those who are brothers and sisters in the deep currents of common thought and common action.

I walked off down the hill seeing in an abstracted way the splendors of the lighted city below, and smelling the buoyant, warm air that swept softly down the mountainside as if gentle and weary of its long journey across the Eastern deserts.

My mind was filled with ideas called up by this man at whom the world smiles, one whom I called the most interesting, if not the most important, figure on the Pacific Coast.

I followed him in fancy as he stalked up the trail wrapped in his bear skin, going back to his garden on the heights, and I wished the message he had uttered might reach the heart of every murderous city, of every insanely selfish business man in this America of ours.

He impressed me as being greater than his poems, and even more contradictory. I knew of no poet who had sung of the mountains and the plains with the same strength and sincerity of passion, and with the same native and noble music. Whitman had this estimate of him, and in my record that night I said:

"Throwing out all imitation, all Byronic romance, all effectism, Miller remains our very greatest singer of the mountains and of the race of overland pioneers. Of his life beyond what he told me I know little. Certainly in our talk he impressed me as a man of striking individuality, high social ideals, and tender sympathies."

Much of his finer nature and many of his ideals he had put into the romance which he called "The City Beautiful," and for which I undertook to find a publisher. The following letter, which I fortunately preserved, bears witness to the arrangement and also hints at the ultimate publication of it by Stone & Kimball a year or two later. I do not recall whether Flower published any part of it in the *Arena* or not. Certainly I accepted no pay, and this letter will be a surprise to those who regard Miller as a kind of spurious wild West desperado.

"MY DEAR GARLAND: Your fine, strong letter has sent out rays of light like a rising sun, and we are all glad, so glad you found the thing worth reading. I like loyalty! How many would have forgotten a promise to look after the MS.! But here you are, not only reading but commending the matter. Bravo, Garland!

"Now my first idea on reading your letter was to ask you to cut it (the manuscript) down and build it up and work it all over to suit you, and then share the good we might do, the glory and the few shekels which it might bring unto me. But Miss Coolbrith—who is so wise and good—advises that I ask you to cut out whatever your fine sense detects as touching on Mr. Bellamy's ground and do all that you think ought to be done and then, if you can dispose of the MS. to the *Arena* or elsewhere, to pay yourself first for your work and worry and then remit me. So I ask you to do this. Of course I am to have the property in the manuscript *after* it goes through the magazine and then, by your help and advice, make it up for a book.

"Yes, I can see where it is too long—so slash away on it, please. Keep the pages and all parts which you cut out, so far as you conveniently can.

"I am tenacious, however, about adhering to the idea that all shall toil; also that God or Nature shall elect—Potentates. Also I am anxious to show that old age is beautiful and that death is not to be dreaded. So the things that lead up to or illustrate these truths should not be cut off. At the same time, my dear boy, I gladly confide the entire matter to you, certain that you can put it in much better form than I. Mother is well and all send you love. Yours,

"JOAQUIN MILLER.

"Oakland, Feb. 17, 1893."

CHAPTER EIGHTEEN

IN RILEY'S COUNTRY

I

IN the years following upon my meeting with James Whitcomb Riley in Boston, his fame and fortune greatly prospered and his Indiana publishers gained in substance. He was the most popular poet of the day and his royalties were said to be prodigious—this was before Eddie Guest, Walt Mason, and other syndicated rhymesters had emerged from high school. Riley was the most distinguished citizen of his State, and his fellow citizens recognized it and were glad to pay him honor. Lecture committees and magazine publishers competed for his time, and at last Sam McClure, whose little orange-colored magazine had thickened into obvious prosperity, commissioned me to go into Riley's country, search him out, and engage him in a "Real Conversation." I had already recorded such a talk with Eugene Field.

Accepting this pleasant task, I took passage for Indianapolis and the New Dennison Hotel, which was the place from which all Riley's letters came.

He was not in his rooms, however, and on inquiry at the office of his publishers, I learned that he was spending the summer at Greenfield (some thirty miles away) in the family homestead which his royalties had recently purchased, and there I found him, on the porch in the middle of a glorious midsummer afternoon in 1893 "loafing between two books and two lecture seasons" as he complacently explained on greeting me, and nothing could be farther from Joaquin Miller's heights than this scene.

The Homestead, a white, two-story frame building, standing with its side to the street, had a spacious garden at the back, but was built close upon the highway in the fashion of the "airly days," when as pioneers the Rileys took comfort in seeing their neighbors pass. It was not unlike my own Wisconsin home and hardly more luxurious.

"Yes, I am living here," he replied to my question; "that is to say, I ply spasmodically back and forth betwixt here and Indianapolis. I've bought the old place and shall make it my home."

After a few moments of talk, he invited me upstairs to his "study," a plain chamber with few books and no desk. His tone indicated an appreciation of the room's surprising bareness as he said, "This is about as sumptuous a study as I ever get. Live most of my time in a Pullman car or a hotel room, and you know, yourself, just about how blamed luxurious an ordinary hotel room is."

Although living so simply he confessed to me, somewhat shamefacedly (yet with boyish pride), that his royalties that year were greater than those of any other American poet except Longfellow. In addition to the income from his books, he was in constant demand as a reader. Altogether he was entitled to be proud and happy.

As I took a chair, I spoke of our meeting at Kipling's table.

He grinned. "Great story-teller, Kipling! I specially liked his tales of animals. Remember that story about the elephant who chewed a stalk of sugar cane into a swab and wound it in the cloak of the drunken keeper when he couldn't reach him any other way and dragged him under his feet?"

"I do, and I have a suspicion that Kipling was 'drawing the 'long bow' for the benefit of a couple of simple-minded Western farmers who had never seen an elephant except in a circus."

"Waive the difference for genius," responded Riley with a comic gleam in his eyes. "He made a gorgeous story of it." After a moment's pause he added, "Aside from his great gifts I like Kipling. I like him because he is interested in the common man. Consider his 'Three Soldiers.' He had the good fortune to get started in the right direction early and he's kept busy right along. A man who is great has no time for anything else." He stated this and other opinions with a quaint aptness of phrase which I am unable to adequately report. Had I taken it down in shorthand I would have missed the expression of his face.

Having just come from the Fair at Chicago, I spoke of the lack of native quality in the work of our own painters and of the significance of the Norwegian and French canvases which were so vividly true to the lands from which they came. "All the work of our own artists is reminiscent of visits to Holland, France, Spain, or some other country. They go hunting themes in foreign lands," I ended with some bitterness.

"They do," Riley agreed, "and thereby ignore the best material in the world, material just out of God's hand, beautiful subjects lying around:

> " 'Thick as clods in the fields and lanes,
> Er these 'ere little hoptoads when it rains.' "

A little later, as we were discussing the value of a college education for American poets, I remarked, "If you'd had four or five years of Latin you'd be writing classic odes or translations in the manner of our dull and scholarly Eastern poets."

With a roguish glance and with one corner of his mouth puckered up he dropped into the Hoosier vernacular: "I don't take no credit fer m' ignerunce. Jest born that-a-way." Then with characteristic shift to earnestness, he added, "My work did itself. I'm only the 'willer' through which the whistle comes."

When I praised his fidelity to farm life, he surprised me by saying, "My father was a lawyer. All the knowledge of farm life I have I picked up right here in this old town. Of course Greenfield was nothing but a farmer's village in those days, and as father owned a farm just on the edge of it, he used to work us boys into service at certain times of the year. We went loathfully, at least I did, but I got a hold on farm life in some way, all ways in fact. I might not have made use of the facts if I had been closer to 'em."

"There is something in that," I agreed. "The actual all-the-year-round drudgery of a farm does not lead to poetry—not at the time. Toil is a good thing in the abstract or in retrospect or when you can regulate the amount of it. You had just enough of it, just the right kind of an experience, that is evident. You put it into poetry."

He smiled again, a slow, wide smile. "Sometimes a country boy gives me a round turn by criticizing me on my farm poems. For instance one youngster came steppin' up to me. 'You never lived on a farm,' he says. 'Why not?' said I. 'Well,' he says, 'a turkey cock gobbles but he don't

kyouck as your poetry says he does.' He had me right there!
'It's the turkey hen that kyoucks.' 'Well, you'll never hear
another turkey cock of mine kyouckin',' I said to the boy.

"However I generally hit on the right symbols. I get the
frost fairly on the pumpkin and the fodder rightly in the
shock. I see the old axe they split the pumpkins with, and
I get the smell of the cornstalks and the cattle in such wise
that they bring up the whole picture in the mind of my
reader. I don't know how I do it. It ain't me. I was a
failure at school in everything, except reading in public. I
liked to recite poetry. I don't remember when I didn't
declaim. I took natively to anything theatric. History I
disliked as writing with no juice, and so I am not particularly well stocked with dates and events of the past. To
please my father, I tried to read law with him, but didn't
seem to get anywhere. Forgot as diligently as I read. So
far as school equipment was concerned, I was, at eighteen,
an advertised idiot, and my health was bad, very bad—bad
as I was!"

His grin came back as he said this, and I understood something of the kind of "bad boy" that delicate youngster was.

"A doctor here in Greenfield advised me to travel, but
how could I travel without money? It was just at this critical
time that a patent medicine man who needed a painter came
along. I argued, 'This man is a doctor, and if I must travel,
better travel with a man who can look after my health.' He
had a nice team and some good-looking young fellows with
him, so I plucked up courage to ask if I mightn't go along
and paint his signs for him." Here the memory of his triumphant mood overcame him, and he solemnly added, "I
rode out of town behind those horses without saying good-by
to any one.

"This experience on the road put an idea into my head, a business idea for a wonder, and the next year I went into partnership with a man in Anderson, Indiana. We formed an advertising troupe called the Graphic Company, a troupe of four or five young fellows, all musicians. We used to ride into town, capture the crowd with our music, and paint signs for the merchants. One of our fellows could whistle like a mockingbird, another sang like an angel, a third played the banjo, whilst I *scuffled* with the violin and guitar."

Here again he grinned. "Our only dissipation was haberdashery. We dressed loud. You could hear our clothes at an incalculable distance. We had an idea that it helped business."

It is only now and again by referring to my notes that I can even faintly suggest the humor of Riley's phraseology and the charm of his smile as he relived that summer's experiences.

He played all the parts. At times his words were flawlessly exact and musical, but for the most part he took on the tone and diction of his characters. "One day whilst we were in a small town somewhere with a big crowd watching us in breathless admiration, one of our fellows said, 'Jim, let me introduce you as "the blind sign painter." ' So just for the mischief of it, I assumed a crazy look in my eyes and pretended to feel my way. The boys led me carefully to the ladder and handed me my brush and paints and I set to work. It was great fun. I heard the crowd discussing me as I worked. 'That feller ain't blind!' 'Yes, he is. Didn't you see him fall over his paint?' "

Moved by a powerful dramatic impulse, Riley rose and reënacted the scene almost as skillfully as James A. Herne would have done it. His helpless pawing of the air and his blank look were almost perfect reproductions of a blind man's action. No wonder the villagers were deceived.

Resuming his seat he said, "Now, that is all there was to that blind sign-painter yarn. I forgot about it the next day, but the story keeps goin'. They say I played the part all summer."

This was in character. It was Western and democratic. It couldn't have happened in Boston.

"I was always looking for verses that were *natural* enough to speak. As a child I always flinched at false rhymes and inverted clauses. I was always trying to write of the people I knew, and especially I wanted to write verse that I could read just as if it were being spoken for the first time."

This struck me as a very illuminating statement, for it explained the words and movement of his own best poems. I valued him because he did *not* write like Lowell or Walt Whitman. He then told me how he got into newspaper work.

"When I got back from one of my trips with the Graphic Company, young Will Crean, who heard that I could write, took it for granted that I would be a valuable man in his advertising department. I was. I inaugurated at once a very successful feature of doggerel advertising. I wrote reams and miles of this stuff. I had written a lot of what I called poetry, all quite different from the doggerel I have just mentioned, and when I found something that pleased my friends I'd send it off to some magazine. It all came back quite promptly by return mail. Still, I believed in it.

"I had a friend on another paper who was always laughing at my pretensions as a poet and so, just to show him that I could write poetry as good as any that he praised, I concocted a poem in imitation of Edgar Allan Poe. With no idea of doing more than trap my critic into praise of something local, I sent this poem which I called 'Leonainie' to a neighboring paper and when it appeared I attacked it myself in my own paper, thus throwing my hypercritical friend off his guard.

"I had no idea the rhyme would pass outside of the State exchanges, but it did. It went all over the country as the discovery of an unpublished poem of Poe's and I was appalled. First of all my own paper fired me because I permitted a rival to have the benefit of the discovery, and then when I tried to say that I had written the poem myself not one of my friends would believe me. They said I was trying to attract attention. The hoax which began as a raid on a hypercritical friend ended in being one of the most unpleasant experiences of my life. I was denounced as a plagiarist and a presumptuous egotist.

"It was just at this dark time, just when I didn't know which way to turn, friends all dropping away, that a letter came from Judge Martindale of the *Indianapolis Journal,* inviting me to go on his staff with a regular salary. That letter helped to put me on my feet, and not long after this, Longfellow wrote me a lovely letter concerning some verses which I had sent to him for judgment. He said, 'The verses show true poetic faculty and insight,' and his verdict gave me courage and confidence in my work."

"When did you begin your dialect verses?"

He mused a moment. "After I went on the *Journal.* I was a sort of free lance, could write anything I felt like writing, and so I began a series of poems which I printed as if they came from a farmer down in Boone County, commenting upon them editorially as they appeared in my column. Some of my readers, who thought I was making fun of the old man, sent in protests. Others wrote in praise of them. The series was so well received that I thought I would make a book of them. I argued that it couldn't break me, so I printed a thousand copies of that little parchment-covered volume you spoke about."

This little first book of Riley's is now worth several hundred dollars—"a rare item" the collectors call it.

"Did it sell?"

"It did. It bothered me so to mail the copies ordered that I got Bowen & Merrill to take the job off my hands. Since then I haven't had any financial worries."

"That little book was a new note in American song," I interjected. "You gave the farmer's point of view. Whittier wrote *of* the farmer, you *represented* the farmer."

"Yes, but people shouldn't get all twisted up on these poems, the way they do. I've written dialect in two ways, first as a writer bringing to bear all the art he possesses to represent the way some *other* fellow *speaks* and second as a Hoosier farmer might *write*. Old Benjamin F. Johnson was supposed to have written the poems for the paper. They represent his way of writing, while the others are my interpretation of his speech. In either case it's the other fellow doin' it. I'm not trying to present people as they ought to think and speak. In other words, I'm not editing nature human or physical.

> "Tell of the things jest like they was,
> They don't need no excuse.
> Don't tech 'em up as the poets does
> Till they're all too fine fer use."

I don't believe in dressin' up nature. Nature is good enough fer God and it's good enough fer me."

We fell to discussing the caricaturist, the man who, as Riley put it, infers that "because a man is out o' plumb in his language, he must be askew in his morals. Now old Benjamin looks queer, I will admit. His clothes don't fit him. He's bent and awkward, but that don't prevent him from havin' a fine head and deep and tender eyes, and a soul a man can recommend." Here was that vein of mysticism, lying deep in the comedian, rising to the light. "I tell you the crude man is generally moral. Nature has jest let go his hand. She's jest been leadin' him through the green leaves and the daisies.

> "My religion is to jest
> Do by all my level best
> Feeling God'll do the rest.
> Fact is, fur 's I can see
> The Good Bein' makin' me
> 'll make me what I'd orto be."

I am leaving this interview on the homely plane of that bare room in that village home. It was all absorbingly interesting to me then and it has a certain mellow charm to me now.

II

We had been talking for a long time, when Riley suggested that we go down and have a glimpse of the town. In taking a last look about the room I remarked, "You don't read much out here."

He turned another quizzical look on me. "I'm *afraid* to read much—anywhere, I'm so blamed imitative, and besides I've no place to keep books. Have to write my own things wherever I can catch time and opportunity."

"If you had a room full of books you might not get so many people into your poems," I replied, and while we were still at the head of the stairs, I spoke of his father whom I had met and found sympathetic on certain reform measures I was interested in. "Your family is Irish, isn't it?"

"Yes and no. Father's characteristics are Irish, but he was born a Pennsylvania Dutchman and spoke the German dialect before he did English. It has been held that the name Riley comes from 'Ryland,' but there's an O'Reilly theory over which I muse pleasantly."

I give this almost precisely as Riley gave it to me. Although greatly mystified at the time, I did not investigate further. I had a suspicion that he was having his joke with me.

When we reached the sidewalk, I said, "Well, now, where is the Ole Swimmin' Hole?"

His face lighted up boyishly. "Right down here on the Brandywine."

"Let's go and find it."

To this he agreed, and we took our way down the street leading eastward. Soon we were outside the village and walking a dusty country road. Locusts quavered in the iron-weeds and were answered by others high in the dreaming trees. Large yellow and black butterflies flapped from flower to flower. The gentle wind came over the orchards and corn fields laden with the rich odors of groves and gardens. It was all familiar, homely, hot, and commonplace, most unpromising material for the poet, a region without hills, rocks, or rills. It was a long way from "The Wayside Inn" of Longfellow or the pickerel pond of Whittier—and yet Riley had translated it into poetry! In that his genius was made manifest.

Half a mile beyond the town the road took a gentle dip toward a creek which was almost hidden among the sun-parched weeds along its banks.   Riley paused in some uncertainty.   "I haven't been to the Ole Swimmin' Hole in sixteen years, but I remember we used to cross the field just about here.   Used to go through the grass—all except the feller with a busted toenail—he had to go round."

He pointed gleefully at the print of bare, graceful feet in the dust and quoted from the poem:

> "We could tell by the dent of the heel and the sole
> There was lots of fun on hand at the Ole Swimmin' Hole."

Looking out over the landscape quivering with heat, I was reminded of another Riley poem, one of his best, and I asked him to tell it to me.   This he did, reciting it with exquisite sense of rhythm and a delightful quality of tone.

> "The air and the sun and the shadows
>   Were wedded and made as one;
> And the wind ran over the meadows
>   As little children run;
> And the wind flowed over the meadows,
>   And along the willowy way
> The river ran, with its ripples shod
>   With the sunshine of the day.
> Oh, the winds poured over the meadows
>   In a tide of eddies and calms,
> And the bared brow felt the touch of it
>   As a sweetheart's tender palms.
> And up through the rifted treetops
>   That signaled the wayward breeze,
> I saw the hulk of the hawk becalmed
>   Far out on the azure seas."

As he chanted this I felt once more the magic of the poet who was able to transmute a commonplace landscape into song.

After climbing several fences we came upon some boys

just putting on their clothing after a swim in the pool in the
shade of the leaning sycamores. Some of them ran off in
alarm on seeing us, not knowing that we had for them a
tender and reminiscent sympathy.

Stately green thorn trees flung their fernlike foliage across
the gray and white boles of buttonwoods, lending a touch of
beauty to the scene, but the creek, alas! was only a thread
and the pool so shallow that not even the smallest boy was
afraid of getting in over his head. It was all rather melancholy to Riley, and when, at last, we turned back toward the
turnpike he again quoted a line which had in it a bit of
protest:

> " . . . where
> The blame cars now passes there."

The old red mill which he describes in another poem was
farther on down the stream and I did not see it, but it was
easy to imagine how simple it all was. The whole country
was level, monotonous, fertile. As the Dutch painters had
glorified Holland, so Riley had transfigured Indiana.

When we reached the town again the people were seated
in their back yards eating watermelons and the sun was
declining toward the west. We passed by the low court-
house in which Captain Riley, the poet's father, had prac-
ticed law for fifty years. The captain lived near by in an
odd-looking house of brick, its turret showing above the
trees. We met him on the walk, a small man with a shrewd
and kindly smile, whose attitude toward his famous son was
a blend of toleration and wonder. He refused to be drawn
into a discussion of Jim's work or the place he held in the
world, but was plainly proud of him.

On the main street groups of men were loafing or sitting

in quiet discussion of the weather, the crops, and the latest political news. They were all of humble rank and condition of life, but they all greeted the poet with offhand heartiness. "Hello, Jim," they called, and to one and all he replied in kind. They liked him and were glad of his success. In truth he was their minstrel. He had sprung from this soil as Burns rose from Mauchline and Ayr. No mysterious chasm lay between these men and the poet. He had simply caught up and carried to higher power the qualities they possessed.

Back at the house with his gentle and self-contained sisters, we sat at tea while he poured forth a steady stream of characteristic prose and verse filled with figures of speech so quaintly humorous that I ached to make note of them but could not, and so—they are only dim memories to-day.

I took my way to the train, mentally paying tribute to the genius which could so miraculously transmute a flat and commonplace landscape into a region of poesy.

III

In the years that followed, I saw Riley less often, but I kept in touch with him by letter. After he gave up his lecture tours I met him only when I chanced to visit Indianapolis. He had established himself in a Lockerby Street house which belonged to a friend with whom he had lived for many years as a member of the family. He had never married and it was whispered that the wife of this friend had been his sweetheart of the olden time, a sweetheart whom he never quite won. Of the truth of this I have no proof.

I called upon him at this house in his latter days after he had suffered a slight stroke, and was introduced by him to the lady in question who was then a widow, a tall, thin, gray-haired woman, silent, bent, and sad, out of whose eyes something remotely tragic shone. Whatever grace or bloom she had once possessed was gone, but in her glance was a quality which neither age nor toil could utterly destroy.

It was a singular place in which to find a poet, any other kind of poet, for the furniture, the pictures, the hangings were all of the graceless sort with which I was familiar in the homes of my New England aunts. This housekeeper, like those I had known most intimately, had no notion that colors could fight. Comfort was there and a kind of hominess, but nothing harmonious or pleasing in line.

A friend of mine explained this situation by saying, "Riley is like a cat that has found a comfortable corner and does not care to leave it for another that is reported to be better."

The last time I saw him he was very feeble, but his waggish mind played round a great many subjects just as of old, but alas! a veil had fallen between us. I cannot tell exactly why we could not reëstablish our old relationship, but we could not do so, much as we both desired it. We gazed at each other as through a haze. We clasped hands as in a mist. We said tender and fraternal things at parting, all to no cheerful end. I went away filled with sadness.

Perhaps that barrier arose from the lies which were on our lips, for I knew that the shadow of death was upon him, even as I pretended to find him much improved, and he knew that I was lying (like his other friends) to sustain him in his fight. They all loved him, these citizens of his native State. They refused to believe that his work was done and were all for heaping honors upon him even to the last, and when one day he went away into shadow they paid him such tribute as few poets in any land ever gain. He was not only "The Hoosier Poet"; he was the embodiment of the humor, the

self-centered philosophy, and the homely neighborliness of
the mid-West.

"I can not say, I will not say,
He is dead. He is just—away!"

CHAPTER NINETEEN

EUGENE FIELD

I

To many readers in 1893 the most interesting citizen in all Chicago was Eugene Field, journalist and poet, who filled a column called "Sharps and Flats" in the *Daily News*. Coarse and hard as much of his writing was, Field had won distinction by a series of poems about children. "Little Boy Blue" and "Wynken, Blinken, and Nod" had presented the mystical world of babyhood and thousands of parents were grateful for them. Their author was one of the features of the city, and his house on Fullerton Avenue (on the North Side) swarmed with visitors. He was in frequent demand as a dinner guest and was on terms of intimacy with many of the best known business men in the central West.

He had been on the *News* less than ten years, but in those years he had made his column an institution. It was only a string of jocose references to his distinguished friends, combined with translations from Horace, pithy comment on public affairs and original rhymes, but it was held together by a singular personal quality. He was a renowned jester, an unscrupulous wag, and the clubs were filled with stories of his pranks in Denver and St. Louis as well as in Chicago, and his paragraphs were read by hundreds of thousands every day. The mere mention of his name provoked a smile.

No friend, however eminent, was quite sure of escaping

the touch of his humor, but there was no malice in any of his skits; they were just by way of making copy and having fun with his acquaintances at the same time. He pretended to classical scholarship and made many references to "the Amen Corner" of one of the big bookstores wherein he was accustomed to place such of us as he thought eligible. From day to day he quoted remarks as coming from Melville Stone, Dr. Frank Gunsaulus, Franklin Head, and others of his "lay brothers." At times he commented on public events or reviewed a book or a play. In short, he was the first of "the columnists."

The *Detroit Free Press*, the *Burlington Hawkeye*, and the *Danbury News* had maintained their funny men who wrote occasional humorous sketches, but Field was the first man to conduct a daily column of verse and personal comment, which was essentially bookish if not literary, and *McClure's Magazine*, realizing that here was another character with wide appeal, commissioned me to visit Field and to write another "real conversation" concerning his home and work. To this I readily agreed, for Eugene and I had already become something more than acquaintances, and I was certain he would lend himself to the task.

From my article which appeared in the magazine, August, 1893, I here quote some passages which have the advantage of being written on the spot and at the time.

"One afternoon, quite recently, I sat in the attic study of one of the most interesting homes in Chicago, a home that is a museum of old books, rare bindings, Indian relics, dramatic souvenirs, and bric-a-brac—all in indescribable confusion, yet each with a history. It was a beautiful June day and the window looked out upon a lawn shaded by large trees. It was a part of Chicago which the visitor seldom sees, green and restful and dignified, with the lake not far away to the east.

"My host was a tall, thin-haired man of New England type. His face was of the Scotch mold, rugged, smoothly shaven, and generally very solemn—suspiciously solemn—in expression. His infrequent smile curled his wide, expressive mouth in fantastic grimaces which did not affect the steady gravity of his blue-gray eyes. He was stripped to his shirt sleeves and sat with his feet on a small stand, chewing reflectively on a cigar as he talked. His voice was deep-toned but rather dry in quality."

Such was Eugene Field as I saw him, essentially Yankee in face, form, and habit—as characteristically American in his way as Joaquin Miller and Whitcomb Riley were in their ways. His was also a type of wide significance. Yankee as he appeared, he was in truth a native of St. Louis. "My parents were from Vermont," he began, "and from my seventh to my nineteenth year I lived in Amherst, Massachusetts. When I was about nine years old, my father sent my brother and me to the old homestead where our mother lived. We stayed there seven months. My love for New England dates from that visit. I tell you, Garland, a boy's got to have a layer of country experience somewhere in him. Sooner or later a man rots if he lives too far away from the grass and the trees.

"I remember, when I was about thirteen, a Vermont cousin said she'd give us a real Christmas tree, so Roswell and I went down into a neighboring swamp and dug up a little pine about as tall as ourselves and planted it in a tub. On Christmas night, just when we were dancing around the decorated tree, grandma looked in at us. 'Will this popery never cease!' she exclaimed and out she flounced. New England was not strong on Christmas in those days. We planted that tree at the corner of Sunset Avenue and Amity Street and it's there now, a magnificent tree. Some time when I am East, I am going up there with my brother and put a tablet on that tree—'*Pause, busy traveler, pause, and give a thought to the happy days of two Western boys who lived in old New England; and make resolve to render the boyhood near you happier and brighter.*'"

Something fine and tender came into his face and voice at this moment, something quite different from the spirit of his journalism.

"My first piece of writing was a sermon," he went on to say. "I was nine years old at the time and being much chagrined to find I had no middle name like the rest of the boys, I took the name of Phillips, being a great admirer of Wendell Phillips, and my sermon was signed E. P. Field. After my father died, I left Amherst and returned to the West—to Knox College and later attended the State University at Columbia, Missouri. Columbia was an old slave-owning town, but I liked it. I've got a streak of Southern feeling in me. I am by nature an aristocrat. I am a Horace, looking for a Mæcenas. I have mighty little in common with the wealthy, but wealth in the abstract pleases me."

With ruminative pleasure, smiling faintly, he said: "At twenty-one I came into an inheritance of sixty thousand dollars and immediately set out for Europe, taking a young fellow of about my own age with me. I had a lovely time." He paused and a slow smile widened his mouth. "Just think of it! A boy of twenty-one without father and mother—and sixty thousand dollars! I just swatted the money around. When it gave out I came back to St. Louis and went to work on a daily paper. I *had* to go to work, I was busted.

I soon got to be city editor, but I didn't like the routine of it. I liked to joke with people. I wanted my fun as I went along."

When I asked about his first work in verse, he brought his foot down to the floor with a bang. "There! I'm glad you said *verse*. Don't call my stuff poetry! I never do. From St. Louis I went to Kansas City as managing editor of the *Times*, then to the Denver *Tribune*, where I stayed till '83, at which time Melville Stone asked me to come to Chicago and work on the *News*.

"My column was at once established. I told Stone that, as I intended to write a good deal about music, 'Sharps and Flats' seemed an appropriate title for it."

I spoke of his war on sham culture and this roused him, a deeper note came into his voice. "I hate a sham or a fraud—not so much a fraud, for a fraud very often means brains, but a sham makes me mad clear through."

"Some people say you've hurt Chicago art."

"I hope I have—so far as its bogus art is concerned. I've consistently jumped on the crowd of faddists but I've never willingly done a real man or woman an injury."

"I've had offers to go East, but I'm not going to accept them. Why should I? I'm in my element right here. They haven't any element in New York. They have literary atmosphere, but I don't want 'literary atmosphere.' I want to be in an *element*, something in which I can tumble around and yell without falling in a fit for lack of breath. I'm a newspaper man, I don't claim to be anything else. I never put a very high estimate on my work. That it is popular is due to the fact that my sympathies and those of the public happen to run on parallel lines just now. Not much of it will live."

Although agreeing with this estimate, I deprecated it by saying, "I think you underestimate some of your work. Your reminiscent boy-life poems and your songs of children are American and moving and will last."

A little farther along in our talk he said, "I hate logarithms. I like Speculative Astronomy. I am, naturally, a lover of romance. The present doesn't interest me—at least not taken as it is. I like it after some of you realists get through with it, but I don't care to deal with raw material myself. I like the archaic."

"Yes," I replied, "Time helps you there. Time is a romancer; he haloes the fact, but we veritists find the present fact haloed by significance."

He mused on this. "Yes, Time helps. My boyhood comes back to me, all of it sweet and fine somehow. I've forgotten the unpleasant things. I remember only the best of it. I like children. I like young men. I like the buoyancy of youth, and grass and trees. It's a God's pity that every child can't have a taste of country life some time."

When I spoke of the broadening effect which his knowledge of East and West had upon his work, he dryly remarked, "And it's also a big disadvantage. When I go East Stedman calls me a typical Westerner, and out here they call me a Yankee."

Here I declared my faith in the West and especially in Chicago. "The city is swarming with artists and writers from all over the world. We have entered a new era. You are only forty-three. Your best work is before you."

"Yes, my serious work has just begun. I am a man of slow development. I know my faults now and my weaknesses. I'm getting myself in hand. I'm going to write a sentimental life of Horace. Scholars know mighty little about Horace, but what I don't know I'll make up. I'll write such a life as he must have lived, the life we all live when boys."

On this curiously exotic note our conversation ended. For a Chicago journalist to be writing a life of Horace in the attic of a suburban cottage seemed to me quite as illogical as the action of Joaquin Miller composing a metrical life of Christ in his little shack on Oakland Heights. The West was producing interesting characters if not great writers.

II

Field was naturally hospitable, and in my later visits I usually found his house swarming with visitors, some of them casual callers, related to him by reason of a common love for junk; others were merely his commonplace neighbors toward whom he was kindly disposed.

He had many acquaintances among actors and actresses and they often ran out on Sunday. I recall meeting Francis Wilson there, also E. S. Willard, Bram Stoker, and Robert Edeson. Eugene had a calmly assured air in entertaining his most distinguished guests, but I think they liked him all the better for his confident poise. He was not a flatterer and he was not a lady's man. There was nothing gallant about him. On the contrary, I have heard him speak with blunt candor to women who bored him with their adorations.

That he was greater as a personality than as an author, all his friends admit. His books have mostly faded out—only his child poems remain. Very few remember what he wrote, but his sayings and especially his odd doings still linger in the minds of those who knew him and liked him. His fame hardly survived his own generation, but those who worked beside him in editorial offices still continue to relate stories which make of him an almost incredible character. Of such reminiscences a permanent volume might be made, one something like that which immortalizes Theodore Hook, the famous practical joker of England.

One of the meetings which I recall as peculiarly typical of him happened on the street one day toward the end of the World's Fair. He was wearing a very long, faded plaid ulster with deep side pockets, and as he neared me he deliberately barred my progress. Looking down upon me with grim and solemn dignity, he thrust his right hand into a pocket and said, "Look!" I looked, and saw him lift a long brass candlestick into the light. Dropping this, he reached into his left-hand pocket and displayed another similar piece. Then without changing a line in his face he said, and his voice boomed with exultation, "Brother Garland, you see before you a man who lately had ten dollars."

With that he passed on.

Another story which I heard told in his presence and to which he offered no rebuttal concerned an order for a new rug which Mrs. Field gave him one morning as he was starting downtown. "Now, Eugene," she said, "you go to Mr. Black of Marshall Field's carpet department and ask for a rug which I have ordered set aside for me. Here are eighty dollars. Pay for it and have it sent home at once."

Without a word of any sort, Eugene took the money and went away to his desk in the city.

That afternoon along about half-past five o'clock his wife saw him enter the door with two enormous flat boxes under his arm. With shining face he jubilantly called, "Julia, what do you suppose I've got here?"

With instant apprehension, Mrs. Field replied, "I don't know. Something worthless, I presume."

Paying no heed to her dismay, Field joyously went on,

"When I reached the office this morning, I found a note from old Joe Cotton, the actor, telling me that he had with him that collection of Lunar Moths that I've long coveted. I hurried over to his hotel to see them. He offered to sell the collection to me for a hundred dollars. I told him that I had only eighty dollars, and do you know, he let me have that wonderful collection for just what I had in my pocket!"

III

When in 1886 Howells engaged to write a regular series of articles for *Harper's Magazine* he suggested a department to be called "The Editor's Study." He had written "The Modern Instance" and "Silas Lapham" and was in the fullness of his powers. It was well that this was so, for his first article, an essay, on fiction, started a war between writers which raged with deadly fury for eight years.

"I broke so many lances in the war between Romanticism and Realism," he declared long afterward, "that my floor was strewn with embattled splinters. The study was the scene of such constant offense that I had no time for defense."

It was at the very beginning of this war that I came to know him, and very naturally I became his partisan, and shook a pen in his support. It was in truth a most astonishingly bitter war, quite as bitter as any sectarian conflict of recent years. In it Howells not only sustained the labors and responsibilities of critical leadership; he pursued the dangerous task of exemplifying his doctrines by writing them into fiction. As a critic his method was twofold. While delineating the faults of certain revered British novelists, he illustrated his points by reference to the work of certain French, Spanish, and Russian authors whom he loved. In his quiet and essentially humorous fashion, he was a prodigious irri-tation. He went so far as to say quite calmly that Walter Scott was long-winded, and that Thackeray fondled his char-acters or shoved them about with the toe of his boot. He made game of the heroic romance and referred to its char-acters as survivals of the knights of medieval minstrels. He praised the American short story for its fidelity to life and to the vernacular of the day. He called upon the writers of plays to be equally faithful to native conditions and to refine their art by the study of good models.

He made fun of the romantic situations in the historic novel where the hero in the nick of time comes rushing to the rescue of the maiden and his whirling sword presents a "wall of steel" to his foes. He questioned the truth of heroic love and said, in effect, women love men for what they are, not for what they do. That the notion of romantic service to win a maiden by running down a flight of stairs or carrying her on one arm, while holding a dozen would-be abductors at bay with the other, was medieval, drawn from Spenser's "Faërie Queene," and other chivalric sources, unconvincing to grown-up present-day minds. He pointed out that saving the heroine from a runaway horse was only the modern equivalent.

I am not trying to reproduce his arguments. I can only suggest the humorous comment which he made from time to time and which was more effective perhaps than Whitman's thunderous assaults on themes of war and caste. It filled the literary world on both sides of the Atlantic. Although a war of ink it was bitter, and it was important in the developing art and literature of the nation.

In writing a review of Howells' "Hazard of New For-tunes" I condensed the theory into two paragraphs.

"It is an interesting comparison, putting this book over against the old-time studies of cities, where the houses were always askew, their doors battered and sagging, blinds squeaking in the blast and cellars full of spooks. Cities filled with caricatures only. Streams of men with one leg, blind, long-nosed, or bow-legged—bloodless and grotesque peculiarities, doing duty as characters and walking through the somber half-light of ramshackle, perilous, and endless streets. A nightmare city, with people arranged in symmetrical groups of good and bad, the city of the humorist and satirist, but not the reality.

"It is not so much the question of 'greatness' of art as *difference*. The aim of the modern novelist is to be true first of all, and effective afterward, seeking truth and leaving effect to take care of itself. Dickens and Scott were the great masters of their time; they met the needs of their time, but they are not to be taken as models, nor are we to attempt to assume their point of view. We couldn't, if we would, and the true artist wouldn't, if he could. Art, to be living art, must change with the changing conditions of society, and to direct the writers of a new age to live by the works and methods of the older age would result in stultification and failure. The artist of to-day should have but one law—to be true to himself and his time, absolutely regardless of any other man in the universe. As Tolstoy has said: 'The first law of art is that the artist love his subject, and then study how best to express that love.' That is the whole of realism. Because, leaving effectism out of sight and being true to self, the modern artist will find that he loves realities that are near him."

From time to time during this controversial period, I published in various magazines, other essays dealing with fiction, painting, and the drama. Supporting in my crude way some of Howells' contentions, I sustained some hard blows in return. Nevertheless several editors welcomed these diatribes, among them Walter Page, who was conducting the *Forum*. Page was a Southerner, a tall, loose-jointed, pleasant-voiced Carolinian of about my own age, a decided comeouter in respect to the political faith in which he had been reared, and a disturber of those who lived in the traditions of an aristocratic literature. With little interest in his political heresies, I took comfort in his support of my theories concerning fiction and the drama.

He reveled in my fury, assuring me with glee that one of my articles had brought forth nearly a thousand editorial comments, commendatory and otherwise. Most of the editors disagreed with me, but that did not "alarm" him or me. He was editing a polemic periodical whose lifeblood was controversy whilst I was advancing—or thought I was advancing—American literature.

Page deserves honor also for being one of the first of the Southerners to confront the future. In a book called "The Southerner" he bluntly asserted that, facing the past, mourning over "the Lost Cause" was worse than futile. Much of this book, which was autobiographic, he expressed to me in vivid phrase at our many meetings. "I have no use for the professional Southerner," he once said. "The man for whom the clock of history stopped in April, 1865, is a drag on the wheels of progress. The South should be studied, as New England and the West are being studied, with an eye to its realities, and I am with you in your demand for truth in literature and art."

IV

Eugene Field's share in this serio-comic phase of our warfare is set forth by Charles Dennis in his book, "Eugene Field's Creative Years." Dennis, who was editor of the *Chicago News* at the time that Field was carrying on his "Sharps and Flats," devotes a chapter to a local skirmish.

"Field was a convinced adherent of the romantic school of writers and an outspoken opponent of the realists of his day," he writes, "and was particularly fond of exchanging cudgel strokes with his friend, Hamlin Garland, during the summer of the World's Fair, a controversy that developed many points of humor."

Field began it by declaring that he stood with Mrs. Mary Hartwell Catherwood in defense of romance. He mourned over me as a young and impressionable author who had fallen under the baleful influence of William Dean Howells. "Howells loves Garland, he confesses that he is responsible for Garland as he exists to-day. When he took Garland up, Garland was a mere boy hustling around the streets of Boston with his trousers fringed with burdock. Having created Garland it is Mr. Howells' duty to protect him. So we bid the romanticists to 'watch out.'"

To this warning I replied in a letter which Field published wherein I called attention to the comical situation. "It certainly is a curious sight. The lords and ladies of romance appear to be making a last desperate stand in the home of Milwaukee beer and Chicago pork, but the baleful influence of Mr. Howells seeks them out even there and makes life miserable for them. Realism or veritism (or Americanism, at bottom these words mean practically the same thing) is on the increase. We are in the minority, we admit, but we're a minority that grows. We are likely to be a majority soon, because, and this is the most terrifying fact of all, realism or Americanism pays. Even Mr. Howells contrives to live on fifteen thousand dollars per year, and it is this sorrowful revelation which casts a gloom over Chicago romanticism, judging from the tone of your plaintive pipe. Only at rare intervals do I get a glimpse into the sad court where you romanticists sit upon the ground and wail the death of kings."

A few days later a letter from Mrs. Catherwood appeared in Field's column. "I, too, had my laugh at your impalement of Mr. Hamlin Garland and myself," she wrote, "and I did not intend to lift either lance or embroidery needle in defense, but Mr. Garland brings me up in spite of myself as he has brought me up before." She then went on to plead with wistful intensity for the aristocratic in literature, instancing La Salle as a hero worth any writer's admiring skill. "If Mr. Garland would look at these great men of the past he would see the same human soul struggling with human problems that one sees to-day. . . . Is looking at the beautiful side of life insincerity? What is sincerer or more truthful than love and gratitude?"

To this plea, Field appended this comment, "We approve of everything the lady says—everything except that passage at the beginning of her letter where she speaks of 'Mr. Garland's big, sympathetic heart.' This is an admission which we shall not make. In dealing with Garland and his piratical crew we propose to concede nothing. They are worse than iconoclasts, they are but one remove this side of anarchists. In his lucid moments Garland has confessed that he would burn up all fairy tales and ghost stories—just think of that! Do you suppose that any person bent upon such a purpose could, by any freak of nature, be possessed of 'a big, sympathetic heart'?

"When Garland made his appearance in Chicago early last summer we began to scent trouble. He tried to make us believe that he came simply as one crying in the wilderness; that he was merely the forerunner of one, the latchets of whose shoes he was not worthy to unloose. He alluded, of course, to William Dean Howells, the Mohammed of the realistic religion, skilled in all those wiles which proselyte, but prepared to exterminate where all his sugared sophistries fail.

"Garland opened out headquarters in Dearborn Street, a locality long sacred to the uses of insurance agents, epic poets, mortgage brokers, and idealistic novelists. This was what he termed 'carrying the war into Africa,' and he had not been there ten days before he ran afoul of the queen of Western romanticism, Mrs. Mary Hartwell Catherwood. In his dire emergency, Garland sent a piteous message to his lord and master. Mr. Howells answered the call with his presence. Having created Garland, it was his duty to protect him. Mr. Howells admits this. Nobody can, metaphorically speaking, dispossess Garland of an eye or an ear or a tooth without receiving from Mr. Howells an intimation, at least, of his disapproval. This has been given to us in confidence by Mr. Howells, so again we bid the romanticists 'watch out.' Particularly does it behoove the queen of Western romanticism to be on her guard, to fortify herself in her stanch castle at Hoopestown and have that enchanted sword, Bon Temps, always within reach."

As I read these comments, the whole absurd alignment comes back to me. I see the gentle "Queen of Hoopestown" and her retainers arrayed against me. The reader should know that one of the subordinate activities of the World's Fair in Chicago in 1893 was a series of Literary and Esthetic Congresses and it was at one of these conventions (which Gilder honored with his presence) that I spoke in opposition to Mrs. Catherwood, and also in a measure, to Alice French, whose work I admired. She was essentially on my side, but like many other prosperous town dwellers, was of the opinion that I had over-emphasized the dirt and toil and loneliness of the farmer's life.

In my earnestness I fear I was not a gallant debater, for I remember saying to her, "What do you know of the farm realities I describe? You are the daughter of the banker in the county town riding up our lane in a covered buggy. You look across the barbed-wire fence and you see two young men binding grain on a Marsh harvester. 'How picturesque,' you say. 'How poetic!' But I happen to be one of those binding the grain. I have been at it for ten hours. I have bound my half of eight acres of oats. My muscles are aching with fatigue. My fingers are worn to the quick and my wrists are full of briars. I know Western farm life. No one can tell me anything about it. I have been stung by hail, and smothered in dust behind the harrow. I have spaded manure in the rain and husked corn in November's mud and snow. I have risen at dawn month after month to milk cows and curry horses, and I have stood at the tail-end of a straw carrier till I was black as a negro and half blind with sweat. You city folk can't criticize my stories of farm life—I've lived them."

All this appears inexcusably violent, but I had suffered so much criticism from sentimental critics that I was savage. Gilder, gentle, tolerant, and chivalrous, tried to smooth away

all disagreement, but when the next speaker attacked Howells, I again took the floor.

"American literature can not be built up out of romantic
tales of medieval France," I declared, "and stories of country life will be false if they deal only with June sunshine,
roses, and strawberries. We must put in the dust, the mud,
and the snow in their proper proportions. We must base our
fiction on reality."

All of this was grist for Field's mill. He enjoyed the row
and continued to comment on it from time to time.

He died soon after the World's Fair, and his life of
Horace was never written. Extravagant claims were made
for him at the time. He represents a phase of Chicago journalism, a journalism which Henry Fuller knew and despised,
and his writing belonged to a city which was at once rowdy
and pretentious—a mercantile metropolis which was trying
to be literary. He is important because of the representative
character of his work. He wrote many poems which he himself called doggerel, but his poems of childhood, especially
those which dealt with the loss of a babe, were deeply and
genuinely felt, for he had suffered from the death of a little
son. It was from this source that all his best verses sprang.
We all know the pathos of forgotten toys, and few of us
failed of response to the wistful note of "the toy soldier."

'Gene Field is a tradition in the newspaper offices of the
Loop, and only the best of him is remembered by those of us
who knew him in those simpler days of an aspiring city.

V

Much of my argument for Veritism can be found in a little
volume (now happily forgotten) which Stone & Kimball

published for me in 1894 under the sufficiently provocative title, "Crumbling Idols." It was a tiny tome, exquisitely printed and bound, not at all a dangerous-looking object on a library table, but it had in it the seeds of discord, as the following letter from Thomas Sergeant Perry, my most scholarly friend, clearly indicates. Perry, a friend of Howells, was a literary critic and historian whose opinion I valued.

"Dear Garland: Only a day or two ago I got hold of yr. 'Crumbling Idols'—to be sure, in spite of yr. book, they are not yet dust—and have just finished reading it. I must say in self-defense that I have been abroad for more than three years and tho I came back last July, I have been but 6 weeks in town and able to get hold of bks.

"What I want to say is, I have greatly enjoyed reading yr. little volume and I think you have said many very true and necessary things. I wouldn't go bail for all yr. remarks, and I doubt if now you wd. confine yrself to repeating all of them. But I don't care to fall out with you or anyone about those, what I can say is that you have written a good book for wh. you deserve many thanks. I think you see the direction in which literature is moving, and you see it with hopefulness. That is a good thing.

"I might go on, but I should repeat the same approval, or, if I were to take up the differences of opinion, I should talk abt. trifles. I suppose that in fact no two human beings ever received just the same impression from the multiplication table; they certainly have never done so from the alphabet.

"If it's not too much trouble, let me know what you have found to do of late, and if you ever come to this obsolete town, let me see you."

As I take up this small volume after thirty-six years have wrought their changes in me as well as in the world I inhabit,

I find it logical for the most part and singularly prophetic. Taking for my motto Whitman's line, "All that the past was not the future will be," I dedicated the book "To the men and women of America who have the courage to be artists" and added this verse:

> "To love the truth in an age of lies
> To hold fast art when hunger cries,
> To sing love's song in spite of hate
> Keeping his heart inviolate—
> These are the artist's victories."

In my preface, I assured my reader that I did not assume to speak for any one but myself. "The power of this writing to destroy or build depends upon its reasonableness. It is intended to weaken the hold of conventionalism upon the youthful artist. It aims also to be constructive by its statement and insistent re-statement, that American art to be enduring and worthy must be original and creative, not imitative.

"My contention is not against the artists of the past, but against literary fetichism. I believe in the living, not the dead. I do not advocate an exchange of masters, but a freedom from masters. I defend the right of the modern to create in the image of life and not in the image of any master, living or dead."

How young all that sounds to me at seventy, and yet it had in it the breath of life. That it struck a responsive chord in thousands of readers is still evident, for occasionally, even now, some gray-haired man or woman comes up to me to speak a word of praise for that small volume which was appropriately decorated with golden cornstalks on a green ground. There was something heraldic in those designs which had never been used before (so Herbert Stone, my publisher, assured me) and were a sign of my derivation as well as symbol of my faith.

As I am sometimes accused of giving precedent and lending aid to our present-day school of pornographic fiction, I think it only fair to quote another paragraph from this booklet, from the chapter called "New Fields": "This literature will not deal with crime and abnormalities, nor with diseased persons. It will deal, I believe, with the wholesome love of honest men for honest women and with the heroism of labor." And again, "If the past celebrated lust and greed and love of power, the future will celebrate continence and humility and altruism. Measured by our standard, the writers of 'The Restoration' were artificial in manner and vile in thought. They smell always of the bawdy house and their dramas sicken us with the odor of filth through which their writers reeled the night before."

At another point in describing the veritist, I said, "He aims to hasten the age of beauty and peace. He is tired of war and diseased sexualism. Life is to be depicted, not love life. Sexual attractions and perplexities do not form life but only part of life. Ibsen, I repeat, is a realist in his choice of subject. He treats of ideas, emotions, and situations new to the drama, and deals with them in a new way," and to this I added, "Illicit love is the most hackneyed theme in the world."

What I was contending for was a fiction not based upon libertinism or animalism. Originality would be gained by leaving them out. The writers who interested me were those who were not dependent upon the use of sexual license. A vital national literature did not lie in that direction.

Howells and Whitman each in his own way supported me in the contention that the average man is a decent and orderly person and that the most original modern novels and plays were those which departed from age-old million times repeated sexual themes. As an evolutionist I rested in the conviction that order and decency must prevail in life. "Between the slime at the bottom and the scum at the top, rolls the great river of national life," wrote Taine in dealing with England's most licentious age, and in my small way I was insisting that American literature should keep below the scum and above the mud, for by doing so it would be in harmony with a new land of active and wholesome life.

In all this I was re-stating Emerson, of course, but my words had some power of their own. The book raised an acrid dust of controversy, and drew the fire of the classicists (for the moment) from Howells, but it won for me the support of certain undesirable radicals who confused freedom with license and forced me to repeat my articles of faith. "The most original American writer is he who finds new themes in the everyday life of the average citizen. Themes of lust and war, as Whitman has said, are worn out and tawdry. *All that the past was not, the future will be.* If the past was bond, the future will be free. If the past ignored and trampled upon women, the future will place them side by side with men. All that the past was not, the future will be. The question is not one of repetition but of difference."

The book ended on a high plane, "Of such cycles is the history of art. Rebellious youth breaks from the grim hand of the past and toils, in his own way, till (grown old) *he, too, becomes oppressor in his turn* and death again liberates those whose keen nostrils breathe anew the air of heaven as if the centuries were but clock-ticks.

"What fear ye, artist to whom life smells so sweet? Accept the challenge cheerfully as those before you have done.

What you win you must fight for as of old, and remember: life and death both contend for you. Idols crumble and fall, but the skies lift their unmoved arch of blue, the earth sends forth its rhythmic pulse of green, and in the blood of youth there comes again, as of old, the wonder-working fever of rebellious art."

As I write these words, in 1930, it is only fair to underscore the line in which I foretold, at thirty-four, that I, in my turn, would surely come to be conservative, a barrier to be overleaped. I commend this cautious forecast to those of our present-day writers who feel that in them the ages have culminated and that nothing superior can conceivably arise.

CHAPTER TWENTY

HENRY B. FULLER

I

My belief in Chicago as a future literary center deepened with the growth of its World's Fair. At various times during the building of "The White City" I came into contact with Franklin Head, Melville Stone, Charles L. Hutchinson, and many others of its promoters, men with decided literary or artistic sympathies, and at the Press Club I met Brand Whitlock, Will Payne, Opie Read, George Ade, and other young newspaper men who were celebrating its glories, and it was inevitable that I, catching the spirit of its boom, should decide to abandon my home in Boston and ally myself with the writers of Chicago. It was in this glow of confidence that I signed over to Francis Schulte, an aspiring young publisher, two of my books, "Prairie Folks" and "A Member of the Third House." I believed that the Columbian exposition marked the turning of the literary tide from East to West. I argued that the City by the Lakes was the logical publishing center, the most economical place for printing and distributing books to the middle West. "Geographically it is the hub of the nation, as Boston is the hub of New England."

As I look back on it now, I can see that it was only a big country trade center containing less than a million people, an ugly, smoky, muddy town built largely of wood and without a single beautiful structure. Its great men were sons of villagers, its university had only a few mean buildings.

The university at this time was just beginning, and Chicago's one great hotel was the Auditorium. The Art Institute was a small building on the unkempt lake front. Miles of the streets were lined with smoke-blackened wooden houses, set high as if to avoid spring floods. In rainy times the downtown pavements were deep with a slimy mixture of mud and soot. Its street cars ran by cable on north and south avenues, and its numerous railway stations were all dark and noisy, and yet under its cloud of smoke, a band of devoted idealists were toiling to make a city which should be the antithesis of the dreadful actual Chicago. The White City became an inspiration to the Central West.

Most of these city planners were young, although I thought of them with high respect as of an older generation. All of them were of native stock, New York and New England by derivation, a fine body of men, powerful, clean-minded, and unitedly determined to make their city the wonder of the world. Daniel Burnham and John Root were its chief architects. Burnham, a big man, big in every way, was largely responsible for the classic beauty of the palaces which housed the exposition.

Lorado Taft, a sculptor and a writer on art, was another of the esthetic prophets whose faith helped me to remove from Massachusetts to Illinois. He was a tall, black-bearded young son of Illinois, whose five years in Paris had given him comparative ideas without robbing him of a loyal faith in his native State. His belief in the coming greatness of its capital was inspiring. With an important commission for sculpture in the decoration of the exposition buildings, he had bravely established a studio "in the Loop." He also lectured on painting and contributed frequent articles to the *News*.

From the state university at Urbana, he had gone to Paris at an impressionable age, and had naturally developed an adoration for Grecian art, whereas with respect to painting he was inclined to celebrate the plein-air school. Inevitably he and I fell to argument concerning New World sculpture. He upheld the classic forms whilst I argued that Greek ideas had no place in our land. "Our sculpture, like our poetry and painting, should be our own. I don't know exactly what its form should be, but as other nations have modeled in conformity with their daily life, so should we. Why not model our own hewers, diggers, athletes, and warriors? Why drag into our life concepts which are alien to our climate, our customs, and our physique?"

He withstood my assaults smilingly, insisting that coats and trousers, as sculptural material, were comical. "Our land is already peppered with cast-iron soldiers in badly fitting belted jackets and baggy pantaloons. I've made some of these effigies myself, I'm ashamed to say, and such sculpture may be 'significant' but it isn't beautiful. Sculpture should not illustrate life; it should only symbolize it."

There was truth in this, but I still held out that whatever we did must be characteristic. "We should not feebly imitate. There must be forms of our life suitable for sculpture. Our pioneers, our red hunters, our horsemen should furnish something to start with. We fictionists are doing work that belongs to the New World, you sculptors and architects must ultimately do the same. Take these exposition buildings, for example. They are for the most part imitations in wood and plaster of Greek temples, beautiful in themselves but wholly unrelated to America."

Taft admitted this. "They *are* derivative, but they have immense cultural effect—that has been proven. Isn't it better to have a beautiful example of classic art than a bungled attempt at what you would call original art?"

"No, it is better to bungle than to slavishly imitate. We learn by trying."

In some such discussion we spent many hours of his valuable time. I wonder that he didn't lose patience and show me to the door. In truth he was nothing like as conservative as he talked. Sensitive to the forms and faces which surrounded him, his Old World conventions were already giving way. Wild animals did not attract him, neither did the cowboy or the Sioux warrior, but certain types of workers took the place of French peasants. In modeling the female figures for his fountains, "The Great Lakes," he drew upon the women about him, making it, as Brander Matthews said, "entirely American as well as beautiful."

Taft was a careful student of painting as well as sculpture, and as a lecturer after the World's Fair, carried to hundreds of raw Western towns their first concept of beauty. No one man did more to instruct the mid-West in the fundamentals of painting and sculpture. He wrote well, wisely, and wittily, but not as wisely and wittily as he spoke. As an authority in his field he fitted in well with literary groups and aided in all that concerned the higher life of the city.

II

The finest of all the Chicago writers of that day was Henry B. Fuller, who had won high praise with two books of European travel, "The Chevalier of Pensieri Vani" and "The Châtelaie de la Trinité," romances as far from Eugene Field's column and George Ade's stories in slang as any works by an American author could possibly be. In him the mid-West owned a stylist of continental rank and quality, but few knew it. I didn't know it—then. Deep in a fight for "Veritism" I had little patience with Fuller's leisurely romances of Europe, and hence, during my first year in Chicago, he and I walked our separate ways, "He havin' his opinion of me and me havin' my opinion of him." To him I was a rude anarch of the prairie, preaching a subversive social and literary creed, whereas he, to my thinking, was a literary trifler who despised his native town and wasted valuable time dreaming of French châteaux and Italian castles.

As a recent adoptive citizen of Chicago, I resented this hypercritical attitude of a native son. Without the sense to perceive that Fuller's fine art was precisely what the city most needed as a counterpoise to its tasteless journalism, I went about saying that an aspiring use of local color was of more value than a derivative romance no matter how exquisite.

"We must have fiction as new in design as our skyscrapers," I repeated, and then quite unexpectedly Fuller took me at my word and published a novel which had the definition of a steel tower wherein all of the characters were connected in one way or another with the newest of our architectural monstrosities. He called his novel "The Cliff Dwellers," and I, recognizing that he had beaten the realists at their own game, at once wrote to him acknowledging the art as well as the truth of the book, a letter which drew from him a reply so characteristic and so intellectually arrogant, that it should be read at this point.

"My dear sir" (he began with cool aloofness), "I have to thank you for yours of the 17th in regard to 'The Cliff Dwellers.' The book is to be taken really as a sort of wrist exercise" (observe the implication of this) "preparatory, perhaps, to something better in the future. At the same time, I have no fixed literary creed; on the other hand I experience now and then a disposition not to use the same model too many times running. I am equally indebted to Mr. Howells and Mr. Boyeson, as well as yourself, for a generous welcome." (Here he felt that he had gone too far in compliance and checked himself, adding a contemptuous qualification) "There are a good many ways to skin a cat, and the realistic way, I dare say, is as good a way as any.

"I shall take pleasure in meeting you here next month. Yours very truly, H. B. FULLER."

In this fashion we began an acquaintance which was to ripen into friendship. He wore at this time a full brown beard and carried himself with fastidious grace, a small, alert gentleman who resented the mental and physical bad smells and the raucous noises of his native town. He studied me at our first meeting with bright eyes aslant as if only half liking my appearance, whilst I felt in him something puzzling and remote. He was reported to be more European than mid-Western, a man of independent means who had traveled widely in Italy and France. That he was the best informed man of all my acquaintances in Chicago was evident, although he made no direct display of his acquirements. He said little and his sentences were short, precisely controlled, and pertinent. He had little patience with fuzzy pretentiousness. Intellectually arrogant but never bitter, he worked away on the book to which he had alluded and when it came out a year later I found in it a mellower quality than I had hitherto perceived in him.

Masterly in the precision of its phrase, its characterizations, and its humor, "With the Procession," in my judgment, ranks with Howells' "A Modern Instance" and "Silas Lapham." Cosmopolitan in its technique, it made all other stories of Chicago seem raw and crude.

Here was a novelist after my own rules! Choosing a local subject, he brought to bear upon it a literary technique which could be matched only by the best French or English masters.

I am writing this paragraph thirty-five years after the publication of the book, and at the close of a fifth reading of it, and I still consider it a delightful historical document. Social Chicago of the nineties lies in these pages, more perfectly preserved than in any other story then or since. It is a transcript of life as Fuller saw it and lived it. It has humor, understanding, and a nipping irony. The author not only knew his material; he had shared it. Born in Chicago when it was a small town, just before the Civil War, he had grown up with it, and in this story he had put much that was family history and something that was intimately autobiographic; how much I have never been able to define.

Like myself, he had little to do with the journalists of the city, but "With the Procession" brought him many new admirers, among them several artists in whom he found something congenial. We often met in the studios of Lorado Taft, Ralph Clarkson, Bessie Potter, Charles Francis Browne, and Herman MacNeil. If my readers wish to know how these groups appeared to Fuller, they will find that concept in "Under the Skylights," for there he depicted our artist colony with quiet humor and authority. We are all there, reflected in his shrewd and laughing eyes. He liked us, but he measured us and weighed us. He was at once cosmopolite American.

Some of us knew that Fuller had what the old town needed, comparative concepts of art and life, but for the average citizen Eugene Field remained the city's "big" character. His work—that of a newspaper jokesmith—was congenial, while Fuller, who saw the city from the standpoint of a cultivated Old World traveler, was an irritation. At a time when writers from Madison and Peoria were awed by the palaces, jewels, and servants of the newly rich, Fuller turned on them the light of his educated, critical glance. He knew "Mrs. Bates" and "Malvina Woode-Shedd." They had been friends of his father. He knew that Malvina, despite her mansion with its "period" rooms and "old masters," was only the wholesome daughter of a neighbor who assumed the airs of a duchess in public but sang in private the songs of her girlhood, finding comfort in the little old-fashioned chamber she had built above the gorgeous gold and brocade of her "Looey Kans" drawing-room. To my "Rose of Dutcher's Coulée," Mrs. Bates was an awe-inspiring aristocrat, but to Fuller she was just Susan Wood, whom he had known as a girl in his Sunday school class during the Civil War.

This true and entirely sympathetic treatment was appreciated only by a few. Those who wished to think of these manufacturers from Racine, these grain merchants from Des Moines, these bankers from Akron as romantic aristocrats, dukes and earls of commerce, were not interested in Fuller's humorous estimate of them. He wrote as a philosopher, not as a local journalist. In his stories were no scandals, elopements, or melodramatic business battles, and in consequence his fine work counted for little with his sensation-loving fellow citizens. He came and went unnoticed by any one except the very small group to which I belonged.

Furthermore, he stood aside from all the upbuilding artistic schemes which Taft and I glowingly promoted. He refused to claim more for our community than it possessed, and he continued his merciless criticisms of its pretensions and its boasting. He admitted, but grudgingly, the progress which all the others of us insisted upon acclaiming.

This attitude I came to understand and to share, but I was always a year or two behind him. I remained the hopeful boomer, the vibrant promoter of "Western Art and Western literature" as late as 1898, at a time when he, more aloof, more critical than ever, would not spare any mid-West writing or painting because it was indigenous. In "Under the Skylights" he made game of me and my boyish plans for "advancing Western Art."

Perverse as he was—and he could be incredibly perverse—we all welcomed him as a guest and his merry "ha-ha" was often heard in the circles wherein he felt most at ease, but it would not do to count upon him. If he thought we were involving him too deeply, he failed to turn up, or, if he came, his stay was brief. Silently, velvet-footed as a cat, he stole away, vanishing into the mystery from whence he came. None of us had ever been inside his home. We understood that he had a room in his mother's house on the South Side, but he could not be reached by telephone, and no one presumed to call upon him. Sometimes he disappeared for weeks altogether and no questioning when he reappeared afforded any clue to his whereabouts. He never entertained us and no one knew whether this was due to poverty, shyness, or an inherited "nearness." Whatever the cause, no one resented his economy.

He was withal a "Puritan." He did not drink or smoke or swear and, like Howells, he used slang only with quotation marks. He was essentially New England and often alluded to his ancestor, the Reverend Samuel Fuller of early Colonial history.

In spite of his affectation of indifference, his sympathies were wide and his interest in his friends sincere. There was nothing shadowy about his alert figure and all-seeing eyes, and his knowledge of his home town was kept up by the most minute and constant study. He knew the boundaries of every park, and the size and character of every addition. He spent many days wandering through the ugly West Side parks or surveying raw suburban developments, a small, lonely figure walking swiftly but eccentrically along weed-grown avenues. He ate at all kinds of places, usually in such cheap and noisy restaurants as happened to be convenient. Fastidious in the highest degree as a writer and critic, he cared very little apparently for nicety of surroundings or service, but this may have been from the need of saving his money. That he had no adequate returns from his books we all knew, but of his patrimony we had no definite knowledge.

We discussed his peculiarities endlessly, but loved him all the more because of them. He was "Henry B." among us. His oddity, his perversity delighted us. We sometimes laid bets as to whether or not he would turn up at an important studio dinner or tea. With all our group he remained a mystery, a familiar presence but a mystery nevertheless. Harriet and Lucy Monroe, who had known him for years, and Irving and Allen Pond, with whom he was most intimate, could tell us little about his family life. He occasionally spoke of his mother to me, but alluded to his youth only in general terms, and I carefully refrained from asking questions. The only time I saw him in his family relation was after his mother's death. Although not definitely invited, I went to the funeral service in the family home, and he seemed touched by my consideration. The Fuller house was a spacious, old-fashioned place, plainly the home of transplanted New Englanders, without grace but dignified and comfortable.

The death of his mother threw upon Henry the management of the estate which (we learned from an occasional remark) included a number of tenement houses and small shops. This property became a burden. He ceased to write and became plumber, furnace man, janitor, and agent, and in these employments lost something of the joyous irresponsibility which had delighted us. He had periods of depression in which he admitted that he could not attend to roofing and carpenter work and make books, but something of that quality we call "New England conscientiousness" kept him to his job. I considered him an unpaid drudge, but he never admitted this. He dressed like a man who could afford only the plainest and most durable apparel. When he went to the theater or opera he sat in cheap seats, and the only luncheon of his providing I recall is one given in honor of Howells when he came to Chicago to lecture, but he was punctilious and generous about wedding presents, and at Christmas time remembered all his friends. Certain things he would not do, that was known to us all. He would not spend money carelessly. He carried himself like a man with a fixed income within which he must keep.

He had a fine, resonant voice and could have been successful as a lecturer, but he refused all invitations to speak, whether because of his small stature or because of characteristic perversity, none of us could tell. That he could speak competently and with charm he proved by giving a talk on Goldoni at Anna Morgan's dramatic studio as introductory to her production of "The Fan." This address was a delight. Its precision, its humor, its knowledge made it valuable as a piece of literature, and as I listened I imagined it in print in some magazine. But in this I failed to reckon on the author. He spoke from notes penciled on small sheets of paper, and these, as fast as he used them, he rolled into pellets and threw upon the floor. I felt like calling out, "Here! Stop that!" but I didn't. I sat still and watched a delightful essay disperse in a flock of minute paper wads upon the floor! That was Fuller at his best—and worst.

The Maeterlinck craze gave him another opportunity for satire, and in a book called "The Puppet Booth" he had fun with symbolism, but he did no more work of the weight and quality of "With the Procession." He hadn't the time, but he continued to influence us all by his laconic comment. He was always lucidly brief. He represented the Old World and the future in much that he said, and in "Under the Skylights" he depicted our artist colony not as a European would have done but as a fellow craftsman. He was never bitter in his criticism, but he saw things in something like their proper places and proportions. One by one I attained his positions until at last we were in substantial agreement, although I never quite took on his hopeless philosophy.

It is probable that my wife and I knew as much concerning his peculiarities and perversities as any one outside his own family, for he often visited us in the country, and for three summers occupied our flat in New York City. His visits to the country were short, for to him the song of the robin was a "yelp" and the voice of the katydid a "drone." He detested rural noises and complained that he could not sleep after the birds began their "tumult." He carried wads of cotton batting with which to defend his ears against the cackle of hens and the crowing of roosters. He didn't mind the clatter of a milk wagon or the roar of elevated trains, for they were the natural sounds of the morning, but the "infernal din" of springtime frogs and birds drove him distracted.

He loved cities. He knew every street in New York as

well as Chicago. He inspected every new building and while with us made tireless daily explorations of Manhattan. One day would be spent in the negro quarter, the next would see him wandering along the waterside of Brooklyn. On the third day he would set out for Staten Island. Plans for new avenues and new bridges absorbed him. As self-appointed supervisor of parks, he studied their needs from week to week with most meticulous care. He was well qualified to understand architecture, for he had studied it all his life and had detailed knowledge of its examples in Europe, but the place in which he was most completely at home was a library. He drove his eyes almost blind by incessant reading.

All his spare time was spent with print, and he remembered what he read. This made him impatient of careless blunderers like myself. His statements were clear-cut, exact and lucid, while mine were blurred and only partly true. Once as I came upon him in the Newberry Library, I said, "What are you reading now?" Taking off his glasses to wipe his tired eyes, he replied, "I've been posting up on the relative size and gun power of the various navies."

This was characteristic of him. If anything interested him, he straightway went to the library and informed himself upon it in all its details. In the case I have mentioned he had no intention of writing about European navies; he merely wished to know exactly how many and what size guns the various fleets carried. He knew the history of Florence, but so he did that of Savannah and Charleston. His interest was catholic in its scope. Once when he came to visit us in West Salem, the County Fair flared forth a block or two below us. Fuller seized upon the opportunity. Early on the first morning he started out precisely as if he were touring Genoa and spent all the forenoon gravely surveying fat hogs, panting sheep, and prize cows, and in the afternoon, with equal care, he passed upon the "spatterwork," the preserves and other housewifely exhibits in "Domestic Hall." At the end of the day he knew more about the show than any other visitor, and ten times as much as I. We laughed at him (and with him) over this painstaking interest, for he saw the humor of it, but as I was busy at my desk he felt that he should improve the hour, "and besides the Fair is there to be studied," he added.

I must not end this early portrait characterization (he will come into my story many times) without repeating my statement that he was a most desired guest at all our feasts. He could be, and he usually was, delightfully gay and wittily candid, and we never left him out. He was indispensable to every party or project and when he appeared a shout would go up, "Here comes Henry B.," and then in the midst of the evening it often happened that some one would say, "Where is Henry B.?" only to find that he had slipped away, back to the obscure lodging house in which he lived.

CHAPTER TWENTY-ONE

THE *CHAP-BOOK* AND ITS WRITERS

I

ANOTHER of the city's vital esthetic forces was young Herbert Stone, son of my friend Melville Stone of the Associated Press. While still a senior at Harvard, Herbert had secured from me the right to bring out a new edition of "Main-Travelled Roads" along with "Prairie Songs," a companion volume of verse, and late in 1893, these books appeared in such style of print and binding as no books in all America had won.

Up to this time publishers had given little thought to the finer points of print and binding. All the commercial editions were without adornment and most of them were bad. Stone & Kimball, with the rashness of youth, set out to make books which should be at once tasteful and serviceable. Herbert had studied printing in England and in Germany. He had a feeling for type; proof reading was less important, and he was essentially the artist in matters relating to decorative design. He printed my books on hand-made paper, and bound them in green with three cornstalks in thick gold on both sides. Furthermore he brought out a special numbered edition on larger paper, bound in white buckram, at ten dollars per set!

Amazed and uplifted by the silk and gold in which my Cinderella children were clothed, I thought well of myself and of them, till our returns began to come in; then my confident glow faded into gray. The public would not buy my books even when clothed in beauty. Stone & Kimball lost money on them although they sold the numbered edition. I got very little royalty from any of my books.

Herbert was not only in advance of his time as a publisher of books; he was a pioneer in the little-magazine field. So far as I knew, his *Chap-Book* was the first magazinelet to be published in America. It was minute in form and exquisitely printed on special paper. It strove for quality. It was suave in tone, intellectually urbane and catholic in its comment on books and men—in all ways metropolitan. It brought to us the writings of George Bernard Shaw, Israel Zangwill, Max Beerbohm, Gilbert Parker, William Archer, and many others, and its designs and illustrations by Aubrey Beardsley, Bradley, and similar radicals added to the generosity of its appeal. It proclaimed neatness, order, wit, and beauty. In short, it was a cosmopolitan guest in a city of farmers' sons once removed.

Each issue contained a series of short editorials written by Stone in combination with Harrison Rhodes, another of Herbert's classmates, and it is safe to say that no such comment had ever been printed in Chicago. It was the direct antithesis of Eugene Field's column and supplemented the messages which Shaw and Beardsley, each in his way, were sending out from London. Its circulation was limited, but its zone of influence was wide—too wide to be exactly defined. It heralded a new day in American authorship.

No one was in greater need of its preachment than I, and when Herbert said, paternally, "You started right, Mr. Garland, but you've gone wrong," I listened meekly. He went on: "You're a bit of the preacher where you should be only the artist. The *Arena* was all very well once, but you need a different kind of publishing now. You must write for the *Chap-Book* and forget your 'cause.'"

He was right. My reforming zeal had led me astray. I put aside economics and gave myself up unreservedly to my work as literary historian. I not only sold Stone & Kimball the rights to "Crumbling Idols," my book of essays on art, but I contracted to let them have the Wisconsin novel on which I was at work. In doing this I felt that I was not only gaining a different audience, an audience of beauty lovers, but that I was helping to build up the esthetic side of Chicago.

Herbert found the city deplorably lacking in poets. Stupendous as the dreams of its builders were they had failed to inspire or develop song writers. Miss Harriet Monroe was almost alone in her brave attempt at interpretation, and she, at this time, was highly classical in form. Her official ode, heard at the opening of the exposition, had made her the chief versifier of the region, but her poems were too formal to win wide acceptance in the midst of the whoop and halloo of journalistic literature. She and Eugene Field represented opposite poles of poetic interpretation and the *Chap-Book* was not sympathetic with her designs.

I did not meet her at this time, but I saw her often, a serious young girl with a fine profile. Later her sister, Lucy, became assistant editor of the *Chap-Book* and we often met at the office.

Alas! Herbert and his *Chap-Book* were too fine for Chicago. One by one his idealistic enterprises failed. The *Chap-Book* fell first. Then a difference of opinion led to the purchase of the book-publishing firm by Kimball, who took it to New York, leaving Stone with nothing but a magazine called *The House Beautiful*. The West was not yet ready for a literary booklet of the high quality which the *Chap-Book* possessed. Copies of it now are so rare as to command a curio price.

Herbert went down in the *Lusitania* and Harrison Rhodes recently joined him on the far side of the sky. They were a brave pair and I think of them with a smile for their gallant attempt, and a pang of regret for their untimely passing.

II

Among the writers who won distinction during the Fair was George Ade, whose column called "Stories of the Street and of the Town" was a series of sketches quietly humorous, keenly observed, and admirably written. These sketches, illustrated by outline drawings signed "McCutcheon," interested me and upon inquiry I learned that Ade and McCutcheon were two young Hoosiers, graduates of the same university, who had only recently come to town. Both were tall, slender, pale, and rather serious—as became humorists. They hunted in pairs and I occasionally met them at Field's home. I liked them both. Ade was singularly laconic, but McCutcheon was almost entirely wordless. The work they did was so characteristic and so delightful that I called Mr. Howell's attention to it, and for many years he read Ade's books and often praised him in private as well as in public. "His work is native to the soil and without a particle of imitation of any one," he once said to me.

Each day something characteristic of Chicago life appeared over Ade's signature. He had the faculty of seeing comedy in the doings of ordinary people, and employed current slang as no one else had done, and when Stone &

Kimball brought out a volume of his stories under the title "Artie" which was the name of the principal character, it was instantly successful. "Fables in Slang" continued to be his chief work and are in their way historical, just as Edward Townsend's "Chimmie Fadden" is of New York's East Side.

On the *Post*, another humorist, Peter Finley Dunne, was recording the opinions of "Mr. Dooley," an Irish philosopher who commented with racy wisdom on all subjects which interested him. His shrewdness and humor soon won for him a national reputation. From a chair in his saloon on Halsted Street, he addressed his remarks to his friend, Hinnesey, who was always "seein' b' the pa-apers" that this or that man or woman was pretending to be thus or so. The dialect was phonographically correct, but the structure of the sentences and the wisdom of the satire were characteristic of Peter Dunne.

I seldom met Dunne in Chicago and only twice after he left Chicago, once at the White House where we were both luncheon guests of President Roosevelt, and once at the office of *Collier's Weekly,* with which he became associated. He had the somber temperament of the Celt. I felt in him a sadness of outlook, a fatalistic philosophy which was curiously at variance with his writing. He was very serious in his talks with me, perhaps because he felt something depressing in me. We discussed weighty things most weightily. He was the satirist and Ade the humorist, and while successful, neither of them quite lived up to the promise of their early performances, but then few of us do.

Ade wrote a successful play and retired to a farm in Indiana. He once said to me (this was before automobiles had overrun the earth), "I want to own a farm with a herd of Percheron colts galloping over it." Whether or not the tractor destroyed his dream, I do not know, but I fear it did. I have heard nothing recently of his horses. The last time I saw him he was walking with a cane, but announced that he was setting out for a trip around the world.

III

Field's direct opposite at this time was Hobart Chatfield Chatfield-Taylor, who was reported by society editors to be the glass of fashion and the mold of form. He was considered the shining leader of the city's "Four Hundred," but I knew of him as one who had valiantly tried to establish a weekly paper, with Slason Thompson as editor, which was intended to be an outlet for Western writers.

To me he was, like Fuller, a wholly illogical product of this smoky town. Believing that we had little in common except our faith in the value of the World's Fair, I made no effort to meet him. At this stage of my career, rich men were under suspicion as enemies of society. That some of them were well meaning I reluctantly admitted, but that their ways ran counter to my social theories was evident hence I avoided them. Franklin Head and Melville Stone were exceptions. They were rich but not corruptingly so, and I made excuses in their cases and ate their dinners remorselessly. Later I came to know and highly esteem Hobart, who was in truth a scholarly and serious writer. His study of Molière in a book called "Fame's Pathway" especially delighted me. It was at once colorful and true.

IV

Among other aspiring authors hack-writing on newspapers, while dreaming of New York and London, was a genial, heavy-set young man named George Barr McCutcheon, a quiet and rather inconspicuous guest of the Little Room, who decided to leave local material to George Ade and devote himself to Old World romance. One day the manuscript of a story called "Beverly of Graustark," a romantic love story of a mythical kingdom in Europe, came to Herbert Stone. Stone saw its value at once and published it. Its success was instant and started McCutcheon on a long and highly prosperous career as the historian of imaginary kings and queens. The scenes and characters of his books were in no way suggested by their author, the plump, rather uninteresting man I met at the club. He had never been abroad and knew little of America, but he had the faculty of imagining princesses in terms of Cook and Brown counties, and this was precisely the kind of fiction most Americans understood and loved. His novels sold enormously and soon he was able to visit (in princely state) the countries he had so alluringly described without seeing them.

If royalties are a measure of merit, McCutcheon's books must have high rank, for they sold in hundreds of thousands. He, too, could have had herds of Percherons had he wanted them, but he did not. He contented himself with high-powered automobiles, a home in New York, and suites in palatial London hotels, remaining throughout all this luxury the same genial, slow-spoken, loyal Hoosier we had known on Michigan Avenue. None of us ever grudged George his fortune, for his work was good, wholesome entertainment, of more real value, perhaps, than the laborious attempts at social history which so many others of us were making.

Several of his Hoosier neighbors were specializing in similar romance. Something in the level lands of Indiana appeared to foster a fanciful fiction. Charles Major, a young

lawyer in a small town, became famous as the author of
"When Knighthood Was in Flower" and Maurice Thompson wrote "Alice of Old Vincennes," a most unexpected
efflorescence of romance in the backwoods of Indiana. That
they appealed to many thousands of readers in city and country was evident, and as they were all heroic in action and
chivalric in spirit, no one could complain of them. McCutcheon, Meredith Nicholson, and Major all wrote of what
interested them. Bored by their surroundings they took flight
into lands so remote that the flat prairies and flimsy towns of
their daily walk were forgotten—for the moment.

What an amazing outbreak of sentimental imagining these
books subtend! They met a need. They satisfied a hunger,
and while I resented them and scoffed at them then, I now
see that they were a natural reaction from dusty roads and
weedy fence corners, just as to-day millions seek relief in
jazzy music and illicit love affairs. Only a few are content
with wholesome life, even when expressed in the best literary
form.

CHAPTER TWENTY-TWO

INSPIRATIONAL PILGRIMAGES

I

THE building of "the White City," as many editors had foretold, brought to Chicago a numerous colony of painters, sculptors, and architects, some of whom had declared their intention of making it their permanent home. But as the glow of the exposition faded, only a handful lingered on and the city fell back into something like its former drabness of business enterprise, with little to offer the artist. Among those who remained were Hermon MacNeill and Edward Kemeys, both sculptors, Charles Francis Browne, a painter of landscapes, and Ralph Clarkson, a portrait painter—all of whom became my friends.

MacNeill and Browne were "Yankees," the one lean and keen, the other plump and easy-going. Neither of them had ever been west of the Mississippi River, and both were eager to see the red people; and so in the summer of 1895, two years after the fall of "the White City," I agreed to conduct them to Colorado and Arizona in search of "Wild West" material. To them, Manitou, Cripple Creek, and Creede were only names, vague but alluring. "Very well, we'll make them realities," I said; and late in June we set forth.

What a summer that was to us! Our first stop was in Colorado Springs, where two years before I had found many suggestions for stories. From here we staged into Cripple

284

Creek, then at the height of its fame as a mining camp, and for a week we absorbed its life and scenery like sponges. One of the men whom MacNeill modeled, a young cowboy and miner (beautiful as a black panther), suggested the hero of my novel, "The Eagle's Heart"; and a group of cowboys contesting for a prize suggested a chapter in another novel called "Hesper." And then while MacNeill was making a sketch of one of these men, I rode off into the Currant Creek Country in search of a round-up, an experience which enriched another chapter in "The Eagle's Heart."

At an altitude of about 8,000 feet, I came out upon the floor of a grassy valley with crested buttes standing about like fortresses. The lower hills were delicately modeled, with curves delicious as the cheeks of peaches. Behind me the Pike's Peak range lifted to the sky gray with rain.

At 7,000 feet I came upon a finer, wider basin, speckled with cattle. Here my guide had a cabin, and I stayed all night with him and his partner. The cattle were range cattle, wild and fierce, especially the bulls—great, lithe, tiger-bodied fellows with white heads and wide horns, a cross between Hereford thoroughbreds and Texas long-horns. I saw one or two of the few remaining longhorns mounting the hills with the ease of deer and that night I slept in the midst of coyotes and wild cattle, hearing—when awake —the bawl of restless bulls and bleat of calves.

The next morning I planned to take the trail alone, with a little diagram to guide me. As I went out to get my horse, the cattle began to sniff and bellow, and to gallop toward me. One immense bull seemed particularly out of sorts with men. A heavy fence stood between us and for this I was grateful; but my horse, unfortunately, was on the same side of the fence as the bull. With a big rock in one hand and my bridle in the other, I climbed the fence. The bull stopped to paw the sod, and while he was thus occupied, I ran in and slipped the bridle on my horse. The moment I was mounted I became invisible. The six-legged animal the cattle knew; it was the two-legged animal they feared and hated.

Climbing painfully up a slippery trail in a heavy rain, I crossed a high park, and plunged down a trail in a cañon, very steep and blind in places. A little stream singing along uttered the only sound. Overhead the sky was gray, and the cañon's sides were like walls of jagged masonry.

As I entered Wilson Creek Valley I came upon the round-up. The outfit consisted of three covered wagons, four tents, eighty saddle horses, three cooks, and about twenty riders, all in command of a "cow boss," or "captain," who took me in charge and showed me every possible courtesy.

The bunch was on one side of the creek and the corral on the other. The corral was a high, strong fence, constructed of pine logs set between stakes. All around me the speckled hills rose, the cattle bellowed and moaned, the calves bleated, the ropers uttered wild cries.

I went to the fence and peered over. One of the ropers was just noosing a beautiful calf. With a deft fling, he caught it by the hind legs, the horse swung about quickly, and the angry calf was dragged across the yard. A stalwart young herder seized it by the left side and threw it to the ground. The herder called "Open Box," which was the brand to which the calf belonged. From a smoking fire near by a man brought a rudely shaped branding tool and pressed it upon the calf's palpitating, glossy side. Smoke arose; the poor beast gave a wild outcry as the cruel iron scarred his hide. The smell of burning flesh and the unconscious brutality of the process disgusted me; yet there was something fine in the action of these expert and powerful men, and in the intelligent work of the horses. After the poor brutes were thrown, each horse sat back upon the rope and held it taut until the signal came for release.

After the calves sprang up they ran a little sidewise, as if afraid the burning scars might touch something. I asked the boss whether some other mode of marking might not be used. "I don't know of none," he replied.

When the branding was over, the camp began to move. The next round-up lay over a formidable ridge, and as I rode with the troop behind the boss, I saw a characteristic scene. Toiling up the terrible grade, one horse on the cook's wagon gave out, and four of the cowboys hitched their lariats to the pole and jerked the wagon up the gulch "like a bat out o' hell," as one man graphically put it.

As we rose, the snow-covered mountains came into view again, and far to the northwest, Pike's Peak lifted, a rosy moon with silver bands. All about were tumbled granite ridges and glorious grassy swells, and just at sunset we wound down into a wide, deliciously green valley where no mark of man was set, save in the trail. In the center of the basin a drove of cattle was feeding. Beyond, swift riders were pushing before them a herd of saddle horses. Below, out of a deep defile, a platoon of other riders came forward to meet us. It was all beautiful, unworn, impressive.

The horsemen drew up under a row of cottonwood trees and awaited our approach. The wagon stopped amid shouts. The cook tumbled out. The horsemen flung saddles from tired ponies. Others, with ready lariats, galloped away for logs of dry wood. Hammers were heard driving stakes. The tents rose, the stove clattered into place, and in ten minutes the water was on the fire for coffee. In all this I saw the movement, the activity, and the orderliness of a cavalry camp.

They were rough, iron-sided fellows—mainly Missourians, and mostly less than thirty years of age. They wore rough business overalls and colored shirts, quite generally gray with dirt and sweat. Their boots were short and very high-heeled, and their wide hats and "slickers" were the only uniform articles of dress.

As we were eating breakfast the next morning, everybody feeling damp and stiff in the joints, we heard the dull throbbing of hoofs, and down the valley came the horse wrangler, shouting, troop of horses rushing wildly before him.

The wrangler rounded the drove toward the tents, whence issued the riders, lariats in hand. The horses were all bronchos, small, alert, flat-limbed, wild-eyed, and tricky, and had to be caught with the rope. The men surrounded them, herding them into a compact squad. The riders advanced into the herd one by one, with coiled ropes ready, and noosed and pulled out their best horses, for the ride was to be hard. At last all were secured, the riders swung into the saddles and dashed away with that singular, swift-gliding, sidewise gallop so characteristic of these men and their ponies, off for some seven hours of the hardest riding in a blinding fog and a thick-falling rain.

No one who has not actually ridden in the drive on this range can understand its full rigor. All about were hills built of granite, clothed in places with a light soil and with grass; in others the bulbous ledges lay clear to the air, and were wet with rain. Up and down the hills the half-wild cattle feed like goats, and on a wet morning they are all on the hills or upper parks. To find them and to drive them means hard riding on any day, but to find and drive them on such a morning was well-nigh appalling; and yet these reckless young daredevils vanished in the rain, singing and shouting.

For a couple of hours the bunching place was silent, the rain dropped from the rim of my hat and ran down my slicker. The creek roared sleepily, but sullenly, below. I rode up a hill to see if I could discover any of the riders, but the great curling masses of wool-like fog hid everything from me. I came suddenly upon a half dozen cattle in the mist—they rushed away, snuffling like elk, the stones rattling behind them.

I returned to the valley and waited. In a short time I heard a trample and the clatter of hoofs, and over a shingly ridge came a herd of cattle, bawling, snorting, and behind them, riding like mad, a couple of herders. They came down the bank with a rush, the horses coasting on their haunches, loosened stones grinding and clattering behind them, their riders sat calm and easeful in the tumult.

One by one the other hands came in out of the wild, gray obscurity, and soon a herd of a thousand excited animals circled and fought in compact mass. At the west the herd began to move toward the corral and the camp, wading streams, plunging into gulches, and rising tumultuously over ridges. The jocular, boyish voices of the herders rang out. The blur of their yellow slickers came to the eye through the rain with a glow like dull flame. There was in the scene something fine and strong and manly.

In my notebook I set this paragraph:

"These hardy horses and these powerful and reckless men are a product of these hills as truly as the cattle. It is not a lonely life—it does not appear to be a very high sort of civilization and it will give way before the plow. It makes men hard and coarse; and yet it carries with it something native and wholesome. It has retreated from the plains to the mountain valleys—from the mountain valleys it has sought final refuge on the mountaintops, where grain and fruit will not grow. At an altitude twice as high as the peaks of the Alleghanies, these cattlemen have fixed their ranges. Whether the settler or the miner will dislodge them from these rigorous and rugged altitudes, remains to be seen."

II

On my return to Cripple Creek I became acquainted with a superb type of free miner, a handsome Irishman who suggested one of the chief characters in "Hesper." I do not mean that he is literally described there, but he started me on my characterization of "Matt Kelly." He was a man of forty, handsome, picturesque of phrase, and humorous of outlook.

Leaving MacNeill to complete his sketches, Browne and I took the narrow-gauge train down to the Royal Gorge which we traversed from end to end on foot in order to sense its majesty to the full. At my request Browne painted it at one of its most impressive points, leaving out the railway bridge, for I wished the cañon to look as it did in the days of the explorers. (This sketch hangs on my study wall to-day, but the genial artist has passed to the arcanum of his mystic faith.)

From this tremendous gorge we rode over Marshall Pass into Ouray which sat among its mile-high cliffs like a town in the Andes. For several days, in almost breathless enthusiasm, alternately swearing and praying, Browne sweated in the effort to record the grandeur of the cliffs which rose on every side, gorgeous with snow and grass and cloud. "It's inhuman—it can't be done," he protested. "I am not a painter of mountains—I am a man of meadows."

We climbed the Grizzly Bear Trail (which figures in "Her Mountain Lover") and spent the day with a miner who read the magazines and was familiar with my work, a surprising kind of miner. We spent the night in Marshall Basin, another mining camp surrounded by snowy peaks, a camp from which the ore descended in buckets on high, far-stretched wires (now all silent, all vanished!), and met a gorgeous, glorious dawn.

After a week in this region we went on to Silverton; and there in a rough boarding house I met the woman who suggested "The Widow Delaney," and an old miner who helped me to describe "Sherman Bidwell." He invited us to visit his mine, but was in doubt about Browne. "It's a pretty hard climb," he said. "My cabin is over twelve thousand feet above sea level. Your painter friend may wilt on the way."

Browne was willing to chance it and so we spent two days with this old prospector who was a poet as well as a miner. At sunset, Browne, with a sketch box on his knee, breathing hard, groaning in awe and ecstasy, tried to snatch some of the glory which haloed the peaks rising in endless waves against the western sky. "I must do something with it," he muttered. "I can't let it go by without trying for it."

From here we slid down to the Southern Ute Agency where MacNeill joined us, eager to model red men; and there among Chief Charley's people we soaked ourselves in the sunshine and silence of the noons, and absorbed the moonlit, song-filled mystery of the nights. Chicago was a forgotten tumult, a smudge on the edge of a distant, far-down lake.

This land of the Utes was as new to me as to my Eastern companions. Never before had I come in contact with the Mexican influence. Here I wrote "The Ute Lover," a poem which later appeared in the *Century Magazine*, and several sketches of the life about the agency.

The trader at the agency spoke Ute, a very rare accomplishment, and with his aid I made a list of its most elemental words, words like sky, sun, water, horse, and man. I sat every day in his wareroom, watching his Ute customers and listening to his banter with the women. Something Oriental was in their speech, a wistful, childish whine which the trader could exactly reproduce. I watched the issue of rations, and wandered about the camp, while Browne sketched for me characteristic customs and costumes. Nearly all the young men wore white robes drawn to their eyes, a habit which lent them the remoteness of Arabs; and as I listened to the singing of the dancers around the fire, I found in the voices of the women something Oriental, something resembling the Persian music. Each night I went to sleep to the sound of a lover's flute wailing above the solemn rush of the river.

From Ignacio we descended to the ancient city of Santa Fé, to the still more ancient pueblos of Isleta and Zuñi; but as we were on our way to the Snake Dance at Walpi (which promised to be the most exciting and valuable of all our experiences), we dared not linger.

I knew something of this incredible ceremony, this survival of prehistoric religion among the strangest people in all America, for I had read several accounts of it, but

Browne felt himself to be in danger of falling off the western edge of the world. He was dazed by the primitive conditions he now encountered.

At Winslow we hired horses, three wretched nags, and set out for Keams Cañon, some fifty miles away, where a trader's village offered shelter. Neither of my companions had ever ridden a horse, but they pluckily climbed to their saddles. As we entered the sand dunes, the heat became terrific and it soon became apparent that our mounts were perilously weak. My horse was capable of only a slow walk and the others were little better.

We reached "La Rue Wash," our first watering place, about noon, and Browne, groaning with pain, fell from his saddle and lay out on the sand under a cottonwood tree, and MacNeill, though lighter and more athletic, was glad to dismount.

On the opposite side of the shallow stream bed, some freighters with two four-horse wagons were camped. One of the drivers, a young Navajo, came down to the edge of the brook and said, "Mebbe so you better cross. Velly soon heap rain."

Although the sky showed nothing of the storm he predicted, I had confidence in outdoor weather prophets, and as we could rest just as well on the other side of the wash, I urged my companions to mount and ride across.

The boss of the freighting outfit was a young Englishman, who professed to despise the "bloody Navajos," but admitted that they were wise when it came to weather signs. "If Carlo says rain, rain it will!"

Carlo was right. In less than an hour, rain was falling in torrents and a wall of water six feet deep was rolling down that sandy wash. The transformation of our world from sun to shadow was astounding. Cold, hungry, and wet, we crouched under the axle of one of the wagons and waited for the cloudburst to cease.

Our first chance for shelter was at "Mormon Ranch," some ten or fifteen miles ahead; and the march which had seemed so simple while the sun was shining, now appeared almost impossible, for our horses, chilled and hungry, were like wooden horses.

The storm passed as suddenly as it came, and mounting our dejected steeds we started up the trail which followed the valley. For an hour or two our ponies splashed and sprawled in the greasy mud, barely keeping ahead of the freight wagons. Toward sunset the Navajo suggested camping and as Browne was "all in," I asked permission to remain with the outfit. This the English boss readily gave, and while our animals picked at the sparse grass, MacNeill and I gathered greasewood for a fire.

It was a desolate situation for the Navajo boy, but he showed no irritation or dismay. With a shovel he skimmed away the wet ground under his wagon, and on the dry, warm earth spread his blanket. We followed his example although we had only saddle blankets to cover us.

While we were drinking the coffee which the trader hospitably offered us, a man on a pony and leading a burro came up. I had seen his like before. He was not precisely a mounted hobo but was closely related to the family. He called himself a prospector, and a pick and shovel on his pack were arguments in his favor. It will not do for me to slur the little man, for he offered me a place on his rubber blanket and a piece of his tarpaulin to shelter me from the wind.

None of us slept much and when the moon came out with

flaming brilliance about three in the morning, I arose, caught and saddled my horse, and rode away on up the trail in search of the Mormon ranch.

That ride I shall never forget. At times I passed the huts of sleeping Navajos, with packs of wolfish dogs snarling at my horse's heels, and as the sun rose, tall, dark men with gay sashes around their waists and bands of red or green about their hair appeared. Once I passed a flock of sheep and goats driven by a boy singing a wild refrain. Women appeared at the doors of their low conical huts and began their work, weaving at rude looms suspended from cedars, or cooking over minute fires. It was like a morning in Arabia or Palestine.

At about nine I came to the ranch, two small red stone houses and a corral built on a low ridge near a spring. Its keeper, a Mormon who hadn't even one wife, was about to eat his breakfast, and at his invitation I joined him most gratefully.

MacNeill and Browne came along at noon, and we decided to send our horses back with a Navajo and hire the Mormon to drive us the remaining part of the way. This we did, reaching the pueblo at sunset.

Walpi is a high mesa rising out of the plain like an enormous battleship; and as we approached it we came upon a group of government ethnologists camped near its base. The man in charge was Dr. Walter Fewkes and with him was a youth named Hodge who invited us to lodge with him; but as my artist companions wished to live in the midst of the Hopi, we went up the steep trail and found lodging in the home of Heli, a comely Hopi woman, whose children spoke English, and who did their piteous best to make us comfortable.

III

For a week or more we slept on the dirt floor of Heli's house, ate her bread and eggs and bacon, absorbing the prehistoric forms of life which this sky-born habitation presented. The nine-day ceremony of the Snake Dance was in progress. Each morning the priests went forth to gather the serpents in each quarter of the earth, and each night we watched them come in, weary, serious, silent, each with a buckskin bag heavy with snakes.

We stood above the underground ceremonial chamber, listening to the throbbing songs, many of whose words were unknown to the singers themselves, feeling ourselves back in the dawn of human history—and then at last came the sacred dance, which is in essence a prayer for rain.

In order to witness this ritual, ranchers and storekeepers had driven in over the desert and Navajos had assembled from their near-by hogans. Sponsored by Dr. Fewkes, I kept close to the elbow of the snake priests, seeing and hearing everything, understanding some of the ritual by reason of his explanations.

I saw the painted priests of the cult snatch rattlesnakes from a bag and take them in their mouths. I saw these serpents bite the cheeks of the devotees. I saw the snakes writhing in a great heap at my feet. I stood like a man in a dream. I ceased to hear a sound. The dancers circled the plaza in silence, two and two, the one holding the serpent in his lips, the other teasing it with a feather. It was all so far-reaching, so deep-sounding in human experiences that I forgot every other fact in the world. I heard nothing, felt nothing—I only saw.

Now came the girls to fling a shower of sacred corn meal over the squirming heap. Then, swift, undulating, lithe, the priests bending over that mass one by one filled their hands with snakes and then holding them aloft like banners, plunged down the steep sides of the mesa, dutifully returning these sacred messengers of the gods to their homes in the rocks of the plain. From the edge of the cliff I could see them speeding away, swift as antelope, north, east, south, west. I saw them halt and kneel to pray as they released their captives, who were now to carry to the gods of the underworld the thanks of the people for rains past and a petition for rains to come.

The close of this astounding ceremony left me mentally and physically benumbed, so elementally savage and serious was it. Its effect was hypnotic. For an hour I had been in the world which these people inhabit. I had never been so carried out of myself, and I set to work at once to record what I had seen, not as a scientist but as a writer of stories, a singer of songs.

One of the observers of this ceremony was a tall, lean, brown man who said his name was Prudden and that his home was in New York. We became friends at once and when he found that I expected to go on to the Grand Cañon of the Colorado, he said, "Why not go with me? I am on my way."

The immediate result of this summer was an article on the Snake Dance which *Harper's Weekly* used some time during the autumn; but the deeper impressions came later in stories of the Hopi, Ute, and Navajo peoples. Later still I used the glory of the Uncompahgre Mountains in "Her

Mountain Lover," but deeper yet and vaguer, all my later work was influenced by the concepts and emotions of this inspirational outing.

MacNeill was almost equally benefited. The work he did at Cripple Creek and Ignacio helped him to win the Roman Academy Scholarship, which in turn made him one of the leading sculptors in America—and when in 1927 I helped elect him to the American Academy, I took some credit in his education.

IV

All through the nineties, with Chicago as a center, I continued to make tours of the South and East as a lecturer, but in summer I sought the high solitudes of Colorado, Montana, Wyoming, and New Mexico, eager to reënjoy their glories; and always I carried a pocket notebook in which I set down, on the spot or at close of the day, impressionistic studies of hill and stream, and shorthand records of the characters I had met.

For the most part my paths were solitary. I was never content until I had climbed above the wagon track. My favorite camping places were just below the timber line, at about eleven thousand feet. Sometimes I had a prospector for companion, sometimes a forest ranger, never a hunter, for I carried no gun and had no desire to fish.

These records made and dated on the spot have an authenticity which I could not have given them a week or even a day later. In these small books are the moods of the moments, the veritable seeds of fact from which many of my stories subsequently grew.

People often ask, "Do you take your stories out of real life?" This chapter is intended to explain my answer: "No, but I get the *suggestion* from life." I see a face or I hear a word or phrase which sets my imagination going. For example, in Cripple Creek I saw a handsome gambler sitting on his high lookout chair, silently yet alertly watching his gaming tables. A few days later I stopped for luncheon at a small Colorado hotel whose clerk was a serious, brown-eyed girl. I did not speak to either the gambler or the girl, but out of these two glimpses came "Mart Haney's Mate."

At another time, in riding through a magnificent forest straight toward the soaring snow-white dome of an Oregon mountain, I got the notion of a story which I called "The Man at the Gate of the Mountains," a story which Edward Bok printed with a fine illustration of its chief scene.

In 1897, on the Fourth of July, my brother and I mingled with the Sioux in "The White Man's Big Sunday" at Standing Rock Agency, North Dakota, and later messed with the soldiers during a Cheyenne "outbreak" at Lame Deer. From these studies, although I made no literal use of my notes, many of my stories took form. I had the advantage of being Western born. I knew the men and women of the mountains, for they had been my neighbors in Iowa and Dakota.

It is true that I skittered from State to State, but I carried with me a point of view which gave, I believe, a certain cohesion to my work. That my fiction is essentially historical, I must contend, for it arose out of a careful study of real people and real conditions. My stories might have been better stories, that I will admit, but they are never falsifications of life and character. They are based on studies in the field such as I have depicted.

What gorgeous, glorious scenes are outlined in these fragmentary records! In them are camps beside icy tarns close under towering granite cliffs along whose narrow ledges the wild sheep clambered. Trails are there, purple bands running through arches of aspens whose milk-white branches are hung with leaves beautiful as burnished golden coins. Some of these pages bring back days in silent forests where the snows fell through the pines with silken rustle, and awe-filled nights on the desert when I lay with soft winds curling the sands at my feet. As I turn the leaves, I hear again the sound of Navajo song and the throb of the painted drum.

My artist friends all declare these notes to be true impressions of color, sketches such as an artist might make; and so I think they are. That is why they have the power to awaken the mood which moved their penciling. Had I been a poet I might have fused all these momentary exaltations into one great song, although I suspect that even Whitman would have catalogued them, as I am tempted even now to do, relying on the cumulative effect of such grouping.

Many of these notes were set down while poised upon a rocky peak or as I sat my horse at a turn in the mountain trail; but others, written beside the camp fire, are more coherent and complete. In them are intellectual snapshots of half-breed interpreters, grave red chieftains, grim old cattlemen, and the lovely daughters of bent and querulous mothers in lonely ranch houses. They picture of miners, prospectors, Navajo teamsters, stage drivers, and scores of other forms and faces of interest to me at the time, some of which are to be found in my stories, but many are still awaiting use, preserved as if in amber.

As I read I find myself moved to fill in the lines, to restore so far as I can the physical sunshine and shadow as well as the mental exaltations which are only suggested.

In many cases the fictional reason for their presence has vanished. They are only half-formed ideas for stories, poems, plays—suggestions which came to nothing. I can not quite bring my hand to destroy these records—it would be like destroying some part of myself, and yet I doubt if they will ever find their way into print.

CHAPTER TWENTY-THREE

THE STORY OF ULYSSES GRANT

I

In December, 1895, after two years' absence, I returned to New York and for several weeks rejoiced in a renewal of valued friendships. I lunched with Howells and Burroughs and met Gilder at his club. Alden I saw at his office. Herne welcomed me at his home on Harlem Heights and I had tea with Kate Douglas Wiggin, Ruth McEnery Stuart, and other of my women friends. I was a guest at The Players and also at The Salmagundi Club, courtesies which made my stay unusually pleasant. I was not a member of any club at this time.

Outwardly the city was vastly cleaner than Chicago and I rejoiced in its sunshine and freedom from soft-coal smoke. It had fewer skyscrapers than Chicago and appeared more foreign in its population, more Jewish. Rightly or wrongly I recorded the fact that Eastern writers were in militant groups. "They know one another, but have few good words for one another. The struggle for place is sharper than in Chicago, where something of the get-together spirit of the boom town still lingers."

Without realizing just what caused this rancor of criticism, I recognized that it existed. It was, in truth, the expression of a city arrived. New York was each day less of a town on the edge of culture and more of a center of national forces. Critics snarled at the conditions, with no care as to their effect on the fortunes of real-estate speculators. It was not a question of encouraging growth. Each editor knew that he was right and that most of the others were wrong, and that all critical comment outside Manhattan was negligible.

There was less "nursing of genius" each year. When it had no first-class writers, New York had proclaimed the merits of second-rate men as loudly as any; but now that she was drawing to herself the best in the nation, she was beginning to question the merits of those who did not happen to be of the dominant school or group at the top.

One of the men at the club who was most valiantly working in the new spirit was Hopkinson Smith, who was in truth three men in one. As F. H. Smith, he was a civil engineer and built lighthouses on the New England coast. As F. Hopkinson Smith he painted water colors and made drawings of picturesque bits of New York, and as Hopkinson Smith he wrote novels of Baltimore and Washington Square and short stories of Virginia and Maryland. His Colonel Carter—"Cyahtah of Cyahtahsville"—was one of the earliest of the humorous yet sympathetic studies of the ex-Confederate soldiers who prided themselves on being unreconstructed.

Smith was one of the happiest men of my acquaintance. He enjoyed his work. He was a delightful companion, and I, a struggling author ten years younger than he, regarded him with admiration, with full admission of his skill. Everything he did succeeded. His water colors sold. His stories were in demand, and his lighthouses not only withstood the pounding of the waves, but gave him material for a successful novel, and in addition he was highly popular as a platform reader and lecturer.

Among my notes I find this:

"I spent last evening with Grinnell, the student of red men. I was profoundly pleased by the modesty of his manner and the candor of his statement. It is almost impossible to imagine that he has been as closely in touch with the plains Indians as his work would indicate. He is a handsome, well-cared-for bachelor of forty-eight or so, alert and brown and sinewy. His curious sidewise glance is searching and humorous. His knowledge of the Pawnees, Cheyennes, and Blackfeet is authoritative. He never goes beyond his experience. There is no display of what he knows and he is eager to do justice."

Another note was on Thanksgiving Day:

"A cold gray sky over leafless trees and a dull light upon the earth. After two months in the city I am feeling the bad effects of it in my weak muscles, and seeing it in the increased pallor of my face. This is no place for me. I need the outdoor life. I must have a horse and a chance to get out where the sky can be seen. The city palls. I have lost much of my power of absorption. I no longer 'see things.' The vast and varied panorama of the streets makes no impression on me. I come and go, busy with my dreams of the wild country. The bricks, mortar, moving masses of men do not poignantly interest me."

II

Among the men of ideas with whom I worked during the early nineties and who must be reckoned with in any history of the times, was S. S. McClure, a young Irishman who had made his way from Illinois to Boston and New York, and whose nimble mind had shaped a newspaper syndicate of growing importance. McClure was a man of ideas—no one who met him failed to grant that—and one of his notions was the application of the coöperative idea to journalism. He argued that if a large number of journals would agree to pay a small sum for the use of a serial to be published at the same time at stated intervals, he could furnish them with the most popular literature of the day.

The plan prospered. McClure's Syndicate in 1892 had become an exceedingly well-known institution and Sam McClure an equally well-known character. He was a small, blue-eyed, quick-spoken man, dynamic of soul and bursting with schemes. He always walked like a man in a hurry, and his thoughts often outran his tongue, mobile as that organ was. He amused some people by his boyish enthusiasms, his sudden changes of plan, and his extravagance of statement, but notwithstanding all these peculiarities he was a force to be reckoned with.

From the ground of his syndicate success, he began to shape a monthly magazine which should be as topical as a weekly. "I have no time for leisurely repositories of scholarly articles and stories for the few," he said. "My magazine will be a monthly newspaper." And so in 1891 he established *McClure's Magazine*, a thin, little periodical with yellow covers whose table of contents was made up partly of his syndicated articles and partly from new material, a singular and apparently hopeless venture.

One day as I was visiting him in his office, a loft on Lafayette Place, he suddenly turned to me and said: "Garland, come in with us. Turn in some manuscript against stock in our concern. We'll make you rich."

At this time he had as editor John Phillips, another mid-Westerner, and at the head of his "Art Department" was an artist named Jaccacci, but their united capital was only a few thousand dollars.

"Come in with us," repeated McClure, "and we'll make you rich. We can't afford to pay you what you ought to have, but we'll pay part and give you stock in the magazine for the rest. We're going to build this into the biggest, livest periodical in the country and we'll make you one of the best known writers in America."

It was really fine of McClure. He wanted me to share in his prosperity, but John Phillips, while sanguine, was less ready to guarantee success. He was the balance wheel of the engine, and I (being of no vision at all) could not see on the news stands any room for another magazine, especially not for a magazine made up of reprints. I thanked McClure for his offer and agreed to write for him, but declined to surrender the moderately sure income of my pen for that of a bundle of stock in a most audacious enterprise.

I was wrong and he was right. In two years he and Phillips had made *McClure's* a national success, first by publishing serial novels by popular English novelists, and then by bringing out a "Life of Lincoln" by a young woman named Ida Tarbell. This piece of work was suggested, I suspect, by a series of "Human Documents" which McClure had been running. "I want the real Lincoln," he said, and made it easy for Miss Tarbell to travel anywhere she felt impelled to go in search of authentic records. She trailed the Lincoln family from Virginia into Kentucky and out across Ohio to Illinois. She collected letters, court records, ambrotypes, prints, and any other material which could in any degree humanize her story and make it more authoritative.

I doubt if McClure cared very much about its literary style; he was concerned with making his magazine known as a bold and enterprising truth dispenser. I must not do him an injustice. He admired Miss Tarbell's work, but it was an admiration based on its array of new and interesting data rather than upon its finish. He was essentially the journalist. Miss Tarbell's "Life of Lincoln" was in the nature of a "scoop."

Phillips, slower to move and much more logical in method, smiled at some of his partner's enthusiasms, but accepted others and made them practicable. Together they made a powerful team. They changed the quality of American magazines as Hearst was changing the tone and make-up of newspapers. Soon other periodicals were approximating McClure's idea of a monthly newspaper. He made each issue up to date or as near to it as the public would allow, and put the price low. He tried it at ten cents, then fifteen, and it prospered. It found a place on the news stand and I was a prophet discredited.

One day in January, 1896, as I was talking with McClure at his new office on East Twenty-fifth Street, he said, "Garland, I want you to write a life of Grant to follow Miss Tarbell's 'Lincoln.' We'll allow you a monthly salary and all your expenses in search of materials, and a royalty on the book when it comes out."

I was not altogether surprised, for I had once said to him that a life of Grant was the one history I could afford to write; but I asked for a day or two to think it over. I had just published "Rose of Dutcher's Coulée," a novel of Wisconsin, and had in hand a series of short stories of Colorado. To undertake a life of Grant would mean at least two years of hard work upon facts, and I wondered if historical research might not dry up my fictional enthusiasms altogether. . . . Was this to be the end of my story writing?

The consideration which finally led me to undertake the work was the fact that Grant was essentially the pioneer. All his early life was spent on the border. Furthermore he was my father's commander and my boyhood's hero. His fine Scotch name had rung in my youthful ear like a deep-toned bell. Two of the finest words in my childhood memory were Grant and Lincoln. What noble names they were! One Scotch, the other English. "I will undertake the task at once," I said to McClure, "but I must do it in my own way. I want to do a new kind of biography."

The concept which I had in mind was substantially this:

"As no man can at any time foresee his future, I shall picture Grant as he lived from year to year with no prevision of his ultimate fame. I shall tell his epic story as it unrolled, never once saying 'no one would have supposed'—or 'who would have imagined that this man, busily hauling wood into St. Louis, would in three years . . . etc.'—for to do so would be to give away every climax. Such a method leads to false emphasis. Grant was in despair in 1856. He saw no way out and I shall treat of him, at every stage of his career, as if he were the chief character in a novel. I shall present the facts in their chronological order, following my hero from one climax to another."

I remember outlining my concept to Howells and receiving his approval of it; but McClure was not convinced. He wanted each installment to be successful in itself, not as a step in a dramatic progress. Nevertheless I succeeded measurably, for correspondents asked, "Why did you end your chapter with Grant so hopeless?" McClure saw this as a criticism, whereas to me it was precisely the compliment I most valued. I had succeeded in making Ulysses Grant so real that these readers forgot his later triumphs and shared his hopeless days in the home of Harry Boggs in 1859, just as they would have done in life.

Naturally I sought the aid of the Grant family. Mrs. Grant, a plain little woman, gave me several interviews and told me much of her early life on the Gravois when Lieutenant Grant used to ride over from Jefferson Barracks to visit her; but I got most help from his son, Ulysses, Jr., who was living on a noble farm in Putnam County, New York. First of all he aided me in visualizing the general, for he said, "I am of the same height as my father, with the same coloring of hair and eyes, and I am said to possess the same voice and manner of speaking."

It chanced that Ulysses Grant, Jr. and I were of the same weight and height and as I did not consider myself a small man, I began to understand why General Grant was "a little fellow" to Lincoln and of "medium size" to most people. He was a powerful man physically and capable of prolonged endurance of hunger and fatigue.

One of the most astonishing things Ulysses, Jr. said was this:

"My father was a singularly gentle and kindly man. He never spoke harshly to me in his life, and only once reproved me sternly. He was always low-voiced even when expressing anger. I was present in the White House when one of the officers whom he had dismissed for cause came in to plead for reinstatement. My father was writing. For a long time he endured the man's pleading which was almost hysterical. At last he raised his eyes and looked the officer in the face; then without a word, waved his lifted pen back and forth in a negative sign, and resumed writing. The man rushed from the room and out of the office. I never knew my father to exhibit greater anger than this."

As I entered upon my search for biographical material, I found myself acting as judge and jury in weighing the mass of confused testimony. On the one hand I discounted the testimony of those whose political prejudices led to a belittling of the general, and on the other made allowance for the loyalty of his friends. But this fact stood out: the closer I got to his fireside in camp as well as at home, the plainer, simpler, and more admirable he became.

Another point on which all agreed was his astounding memory. Over and over again, men and women who had met him in youth and again long years afterward, related precisely the same experience. "Grant knew me at once and called me by name." He never forgot a name or a face, and similarly he never forgot a kindness. No matter how humble the individual he remembered and rewarded him. He was the most democratic of commanders. He detested parade, glitter, pomp, but he was a disciplinarian. He was reticent and singularly clean-lipped. He never swore, never told coarse stories and he would not permit others to tell them in his presence. He never raised his voice even in command. He was generous in allowing others their full share of honor.

His enemies repeated stories of his drinking, of his poverty, but none of them made charge against his honesty, his magnanimity, or his essential justice. They called him an "accident," a "blunderer," "a weak executive," and "a bad judge of men"; but they admitted that he was "a kindly, nice man." Some of these allegations offset others. How could a "decayed West Point captain" command "the influence of the great"? How could an "accident" grow against circum-

stance? One man, one of his bitterest enemies, after raging
against him all one afternoon, ended by saying to me, "With
all that, he was a nice, friendly man."

I soon found that most of the stories discreditable to him
arose from the pen of a reporter sent out by an opposition
newspaper after his nomination as candidate for the Presi-
dency. I learned at once that he had never worked in a
tannery, and that the nearest he came to it was driving a
horse for a bark mill. His father did not own a tannery in
Galena; it was a leather store, and Captain Grant's work
was that of clerk and bookkeeper.

There was nothing complicated in his life. The closer I
got to his actual character the simpler it became. The dreadful complications were all in the minds of his enemies, who
saw him from the outside. Whatever he did was straightforward, plain, unadorned, with no subtleties. The machina-
tions of which he was accused by those who did not know
him are comical. He was "plain as an old stove," one of his
under officers said of him; and so he was until his subconscious military genius came into play. "He wrought best
when pushed hardest," said one of his generals. Another
said, "He grew with circumstance." To me his life was more
essentially epic than Lincoln's and the deeper I dug into his
records the keener my interest became. To go, in less than
four years, from a little leather store in a small Western
town to the command of a million men, is one of the most
astounding flights in all history—and stranger still, he
remained the same considerate, unassuming neighbor he had
been at the beginning. He grew with circumstances, but he
kept his head, his poise through it all. "He is a quiet little
fellow," said Lincoln; "the only way I can tell he is around is
by the way he keeps things moving."

In my search of local records which would give me the facts of Grant's youth, I went to Georgetown, Ohio, St. Louis, Sackett Harbor, and Detroit. For his early war record I dug up local newspapers in Springfield and Galena, and called upon the men who were associated with him at Vicksburg and Chattanooga.

One of the most memorable of all my interviews was that I had with General Longstreet, his classmate at West Point, and one of the most formidable of his antagonists during the war. I found him living in the outskirts of Gainesville, Georgia, and when my guide pointed out a small frame house and said, "General Longstreet lives there," I was amazed. It was as humble as the home of a day laborer, and I could not relate the farmer, somber, gray who met me at the door with the Commander of whom Grant wrote with affection and respect as a great soldier and a man of high character. He said in his "Memoirs": "I considered him one of the ablest military leaders of the South." Longstreet had been one of the first to renew his allegiance to the Union and he had done all he could to rebuild the South in terms of peace, to the result that he had been almost completely ostracized by his own people. Now here he was, earning a scant living as a Georgia fruit grower.

He was a tall old man, slightly stooping and partly deaf, but a noble figure withal. In the talk which followed, he conveyed to me in spite of his bare and ugly surroundings the epic sweep of his own life, and testified to the greatness of Grant. Few men understood Grant better than he. "I knew him," he said authoritatively. "He was a noble citizen and a great soldier. Nothing is gained for Lee by belittling Grant.

"I live alone in these two rooms," he explained; "the

other end of my house is rented to a workman and his wife. The woman helps me in my housekeeping." He said this quietly, but to me it was an incredible situation. I walked away with a sense of wonder that so great a change could come in the fortunes of a citizen once so renowned. I had found other officers of both armies living obscurely but none so drearily as this great Southerner. The sight of his gaunt figure moving about his little shack gave me an appalling sense of change. "Haste is imperative," I wrote, "for the chief actors of the war are dying." Even as I copied out my notes some of the most valuable of my witnesses died. Before the book was completed, scores of others dropped away.

III

I returned to New York just in time to attend a receiver's sale of the books of Stone & Kimball. They had dissolved partnership in Chicago a year or two before, and Kimball after a year or two in New York had failed; and as he had several of my books in his list, I was on hand to see what was to be done. I found the handsome offices dismantled, the furniture in disorder, and the officer (a consequential little German) bustling about seeing that the goods were properly marked. Buyers from department stores and second-hand bookshops were assembling like birds of prey—unclean, sardonic, pitiless.

Kimball, who alluded to himself as "the corpse," kept up a show of cheerful youth, alluding to Stedman, Woodberry, and others of his authors as "chief mourners," which in truth we were. Stedman was especially disgusted. Alert attorneys were there to protect the interests of other and more important creditors than those who had written the novels and edited the poems, and several clerks looked forlornly on while intending purchasers elbowed through the rooms and thumbed the books which had been set aside in lots of five and ten cents per volume. For the most part the buyers were too ignorant to know the names of the writers. They were there to buy books at three cents if they could. It was not a cheerful scene.

Stedman said to me, "If we could but contrive to put our publishers' insouciance at auction, we should all be paid in full."

Through it all, Kimball tranquilly smoked his pipe, but I suspect it was only a gesture. The passing of his firm could not have been a small thing even to him. To me it was a calamity. It left my best books without a publisher.

IV

On October 6th, I was present at a meeting which I recognized at the time to be of historic significance: it was the ratification in Cooper Union of Henry George's nomination for mayor of New York City, an exciting convention of excited men. When the doors were opened the delegates and their friends came pouring in with thunderous trampling, their faces tense with emotion. In five minutes the hall was filled to the walls, and as I looked out over it, I caught a momentary sense of its larger meaning. Here sat four thousand men ready to take whatever odium might attach to their endorsement of a radical mayor. Their pale foreheads denoted indoor labor. They believed in George and were ready to meet martyrdom for "the Cause." They stamped and called, impatient for their advocate, and when he appeared they rose to meet him like a wave, with tossing arms and waving hats.

George, whom I had known so long, was visibly moved, wrought to higher tension than ever before. While the roar of cheers went on, he walked back and forth on the platform, alert, lionlike, somber, the calmness of strength under restraint. His action was tensely dramatic. He knew that to control that audience he must control himself, and on his face was the look of one who surveys wide horizons. I had seen this look on his face before, but never with such loftily impersonal lines. Mingled with his sense of power was the mood which comes to a man weakened by age and pain. He was twenty years older than when I had last heard him on this same platform. His hair was thin and gray and his eyes dim. His face was deeply lined—only his noble profile remained unchanged.

When he spoke, it was (as of old) with such simple directness that men forgot the quality of his voice and thought only of his message. Such a speech was never heard before on a mayoralty platform. In a few words he lifted the campaign to a height from which the toiling millions of every nation could be seen. He spoke in behalf of the landless and disinherited of every clime. It was not a question of votes but of abstract justice. He spoke as one who recognized that death could not be far away, and I sensed in his face and voice a premonition that this was not only his last campaign but a hopeless issue.

A few weeks later, just at the close of his campaign which had developed into an almost hysterical social war, his heart gave out. He fell in harness, stricken on the platform, and died in a near-by hotel, and his going lent a tragic close to the race he had so reluctantly entered upon.

He had come to be something more than an economic

prophet. He was my friend. I had a liking as well as a deep respect for him, and he found in me, I think, something more than a disciple. He often invited me to his house. I sat at his table among his sons and daughters, finding them delightful companions. His home was finely typical of the New World, informal yet essentially dignified. Naturally his circle was doctrinaire, especially of a Sunday when reformers from all over the world dropped in to see him. Once when I had taken Howells to one of these gatherings, he pleased me by saying as we came away, "What a noble head George has, and such almost Christlike patience with his critics, and his disciples." These visitors were intellectual but not always gracious. Many of them were cranks of such dynamic power that they would not give ear to the voices of others or discuss other phases of life.

I went to see his body at the Union Square Hotel in which he died. He made a noble sculpture.

> "His presence was so waxen still,
> He seemed to listen in his house of clay,
> Holding his breath by force of will.
> He was so Saxon fair! The ease
> Of that still presence, with the soul away
> Was like to ancient Socrates."

His sons asked me to head the committee of arrangements for the funeral and I willingly lent myself to this task; but I could not have arranged its details had not another friend, John Brisben Walker, come to my aid with all his office force. We were overwhelmed by public interest.

The funeral, solemn but triumphant, was a noble, spontaneous tribute to one who had given his life for the good of others. No one doubted his devotion and self-sacrifice. The night parade was profoundly impressive. Miles of people stood with uncovered heads to see his body pass. It was a revelation of the respect which this fearless advocate had ultimately won.

"It is well," Howells said. "He died at his work and at his best."

CHAPTER TWENTY-FOUR

EDWARD MACDOWELL

I

WHEN my little book, "Crumbling Idols," was published in the spring of 1894, I was still living on Elm Street, Chicago, not far from the lake, and among my neighbors was a musical critic by the name of Armstrong, a delightful young Southerner. One day in the autumn of that year he came to me to say that he had just been calling on Edward MacDowell at the Auditorium Hotel and that MacDowell had expressed a wish to meet me. "He has been reading your 'Crumbling Idols' and wants to talk with you."

This surprised and delighted me, for MacDowell had been a shining figure ever since I first heard him play in the Boston Music Hall in 1888, but I had never had any expectation of meeting him.

Among my few extravagances in 1884 and 1885 (while beginning my literary career) was an occasional attendance upon the Boston Symphony concerts in Music Hall. For the privilege of leaning against the wall, one paid fifty cents, but dollars were dollars in those days and fifty cents looked very large to me. By going early and joining a throng of waiting women and music students, I could have found a seat in the top gallery, but I usually took my music standing, in a side aisle.

It was in the autumn of 1888 that we music lovers were

pleasantly excited by the news that Edward MacDowell, a young composer who had won great fame abroad, had returned to America and that he would appear with the orchestra, playing one of his own concertos. Naturally, as one pledged to advance art of whatever sort, I at once purchased a ticket and was in my place to applaud the artist when he appeared.

It was on a Friday afternoon. The hall was crowded with musicians, music lovers, and students eager to see and hear this conquering young American, whose fame had preceded him by several years, and when he came on, shy, smiling, nobly handsome, I added my bit to the thunder of applause. He was our first great creative musician, and we welcomed him with joy, applauding his youth and his handsome face as well as his skill.

With what Celtic fire he played! and how superbly triumphant he appeared to me, a seedy youth leaning against the wall to rest my weary legs. To me he was a prince of the world, a triumphant aristocrat to whom all honor and wealth and happiness had come.

Thereafter I followed his career in Boston and New York, learning with pleasure that he had settled in New England and that he was at work upon native themes, but in all these years I had never come in contact with any one who knew him till William Armstrong came for me, and as I followed him down the broad halls of the Auditorium Hotel, I could not quite bridge the gulf which lay between that shining youth in Boston Music Hall and the composer on whom I was about to call.

As we neared the door of his room, the sound of a piano played with masterly skill proclaimed the great musician at work. Armstrong's timid knock silenced the player, and a moment later a small woman smilingly presented herself. It was Mrs. MacDowell, and after a word of greeting, she turned and called, "Edward, here is Hamlin Garland, whose book you liked so much."

Edward who had retreated behind the piano now came forward to meet me, shyly, boyishly, sliding one hand along the edge of the piano as a child runs a palm along a banister to relieve its embarrassment. To my eyes he was a glorious young prince. His scintillant, laughing blue eyes, his abundant brown hair, his graceful mustaches, but beyond all his ready smile and jocund voice delighted me, and when he told me that he had been reading my "Crumbling Idols," and that its plea had been an inspiration to him, I was quite overwhelmed with surprise and pleasure.

There was something akin in our blood and our upbringing. We were both a balanced mixture of Scotch, English, and Irish ancestry, and we were of the same age. Furthermore he was a modern in music as I was a modern in fiction, and he knew and loved Howells.

"My problems as a composer are precisely those you have delineated in your essays," he said. "I am working toward a music which shall be American in the creative sense. Our music thus far is mainly a scholarly re-statement of Old World themes. In other words, it is derived from Germany, as all my earlier pieces were," he added with a chuckle. "I shall probably play one of them this evening."

Knowing that he was preparing for his concert, I did not stay long, but we parted with a promise to meet again and thresh the question out.

In the years which followed I heard much of him, for he was one of the most alert minds of his profession, and when he was called to Columbia University to head its music department, I rejoiced. He was not merely the musician, he was alive to all the arts. His summers were spent in Peterboro, his New Hampshire home, composing his noble music, whilst I was trailing for material in Montana, New Mexico, or Colorado. We met only in the city, in winter. As often as I could I sought him out.

One such evening, which I recall most vividly, was at his home in New York in 1896, just after my return from a long vacation in Colorado and New Mexico. He was at work on an Indian theme and had on his piano a volume of Alice Fletcher's versions of Omaha songs. Naturally we spoke of them. After playing one or two he asked me what I thought of them.

"They suggest red Indian themes," I replied, "but they are Sankeyized. That isn't the way they sound as I listen to them in a tepee or while sitting around a camp fire. They have been robbed of their Stone Age fire and rhythmic force. I've been hearing Navajo and Ute songs this summer."

"Can't you sing some of them?" asked Mrs. MacDowell.

"No," I confessed. "They are very difficult to catch. They seem to me to be on a different scale from ours. If I had a drum and was seated in the light of a lodge, I might feel my way into the spirit of them."

She seized upon this. "I'll turn down the lights," she said, "and for a tom-tom, here is a tambourine."

Caught in my own trap, I took the tambourine and after some preliminary howling and humming, succeeded in touching once or twice on something like the savage strains I carried in my subconscious memory. Ending on the deep humming chant so characteristic of all red Indian music, I said, "That's the best I can do, and it's only a hint of the real thing. I assure you they are not tame."

MacDowell gave the manuscript on his piano a flip and said, "You make these things seem like milk and water."

I then spoke of the hooting and the yelping with which the Navajo men begin their songs, an imitation of owls and coyotes, and explained that they appeared to be singing for the fun of it, like a group of college boys. "Some of the Ute love songs, however, are plaintively beautiful. I was especially moved by hearing a Navajo boy singing a high, clear strain at dawn as he drove his flock out into the valley. I especially wish you could have heard that. It would make a magnificent theme for a composition."

"I'd like to hear it, but I fear you are confusing the beauty of the landscape with the song of the herder. You would expect me to put into music things which belong to painting or to poetry."

"But couldn't you put *just that* into your composition? Wouldn't your own emotional reaction to what you heard and saw pass into your music?"

"It might."

"Why not go West with me next year and see what would happen?"

He looked at his wife and smiled rather wistfully. "I'd like to do that but it is a long way to go, and besides I'm afraid I couldn't stand the food and the beds. I'm not used to roughing it. You admit the food is bad?"

"Dreadful, but we could take our own outfit."

Half promising to consider it, he turned to another phase of the problem. "I do not believe in 'lifting' a Navajo theme and furbishing it into some kind of a musical composition. That is not American music. Our problem is not so simple as all that." After a pause he went on, "it is a question of personality. If a composer is sincerely American at heart, his music will be American. Almost any hack composer can imitate the Persian, Chinese, or any other racial music, but the spirit of it is not caught. The weakness of our music is in its borrowing. I began by imitating the German composers. I am now on the way to being myself and as I am myself I will be Celtic-American rather than German-American or Afro-American. A national music can not be founded on the songs of reds or blacks."

If I could report those hours of talk, I could make a very real contribution to the discussion which is still going on as to the direction American music should take. I could not follow him in his argument, and with some of it I was not in agreement, but it was couched in austerely idealistic phrase. He held his art high. He wished it to be a sister art to literature and not a poor relation called in to amuse the other sisters while they feasted.

He admitted that in music, as in all our other arts, we have been subject to waves of Old World influence, mainly from Germany, but the French and Italian had furnished some of our "inspiration," and when I said "we are at our weakest in musical art," he agreed but saw no way of strengthening it except to educate our talented young musicians.

"That is my notion concerning the Columbia Music Department. If I can develop one good composer in five years, I shall feel justified in the expenditure of time and money."

"What a dependent situation we are in, not only with respect to music but as to all the arts! Our painters have imitated first this school and then that. Our sculptors are confused between Greek austerity and French flamboyancy. Our fiction has been English and now is being 'influenced' by Russian and French novelists and critics, and our drama is about to be Ibsenized. Will there ever come a time when we can stand on our own pins and utter ourselves in our own way?"

Something like this I said—a gloomy note which I had not allowed myself to put into "Crumbling Idols," but Mac-Dowell only laughed, "Yes, we are still provincial, but in time we'll grow up, as you said in your little book."

"I said it then, but I'm not too sure about it now. At best it will take a long time to develop a native art. How long will it take you to raise a crop of American composers? How much welcome would an American opera get in our Teutonic opera house? Every symphony conductor is a German."

Mrs. MacDowell urged that these conductors had welcomed Edward, to which he responded, "But I was educated in Germany, and my music had the Teutonic flavor."

"Just now Italy is flooding us with immigrants. Most of them come in the spring and go back in the autumn. Suppose they stay. Suppose they become as numerous as the Germans, and suppose, as some people argue, they are to bring their musical geniuses with them, how does that help? We will have Italian masters instead of German masters, that's all. Can't we grow up? Must we forever remain *doppel gängers?*—fake doubles of Old World artists? These are the questions which lie at the bottom of my little book. I meant no disrespect of the masters, but I opposed and still oppose the imitation. I believe in a national art. No outsider can express our essential character, our national spirit."

"That's just the point," interrupted MacDowell. "Have we a national spirit? Aren't we still in the cultural stage? I'm afraid we are not yet grown up. Borrowing is to be our business for a long time, I suspect. Some day, when you and I are old, there'll be an American School of Music, as well as of fiction. We'll have composers as cultured, as American in their work as Howells is in his."

In spite of his gay confidence I went away with a deepened sense of America's weakness in music as in the other creative arts. Only by looking back ten years could I discern any progress.

Just to show Edward's quickness of retort and his humor, I add this story which he used to tell against himself. He was giving a concert for a fashionable girls' school not far from the city one afternoon and as he came off the stage into the dressing room during an intermission he passed an elderly man reading a newspaper. He did not recognize in Edward the piano player to whom he had been listening, and looking over his glasses he said: "Well, that noise was too much for me. I had to get out."

"You did quite right," replied MacDowell. "I am sick of the man's accursed clatter myself."

CHAPTER TWENTY-FIVE

BARRIE AND I MEET ROOSEVELT

I

THE autumn of 1896 found me back in New York, and is made notable by the establishment of several most valuable friendships. Among my files, I find a letter from James M. Barrie, whose work as novelist and dramatist had already made him one of the best beloved of all the English writers of that day.

"Dear Mr. Garland: I thank you most heartily for your book" (this was "Rose of Dutcher's Coulée") "which only reached me this week. It is certainly the best novel I have read for a long time, and I expect when Mason" (one of the characters in the story) "publishes his novel he will find himself forestalled. Rose herself is the triumph of the book, very subtle and fresh. That is a beautiful scene where they find the old father in grief. I am coming to America in a few days and you give me a keen desire to see Chicago, which had seemed too far afield for me. If possible we shall go now. In any case I hope to meet you."

The meeting which he was kind enough to desire took place in October at a luncheon given in his honor in the private dining room of The Players, a luncheon which was made still more memorable by the friendly greeting of young Theodore Roosevelt, Commissioner of Police, who was there out of interest in Barrie. Our host, if my memory is not at

326

fault, was young Kimball, of the firm of Stone & Kimball, and among the ten or twelve guests was a dark-eyed, black-haired Canadian hunter, artist, and story writer whom Kimball introduced to us all as "Wolf Thompson." I had heard of him as an illustrator through Edward Kemeys, the Chicago wild-animal sculptor, who greatly admired Thompson's drawings; but I had never before met him. He was the most picturesque guest at the table, and held a larger share of the attention than Barrie, a shy, small man who seemed to find in me a pleasant shadow, probably because he felt somewhat acquainted with me. After lunch we drew together on a sofa at one side of the room and held a brief but very agreeable dialogue. I welcomed this opportunity, for I had read nearly every page of his writing, and rejoiced in his amazing success. He began by saying, "We are just off the boat and at the Holland House. My wife, who read your story coming over, would like to meet you."

As we talked we discovered many mutual friends and common interests, and so interested was I that I forgot his part in the luncheon until in the midst of our conversation our host announced that Ernest Seton Thompson, in response to a request, would tell a wolf story.

This interested Barrie mildly but he refused to do anything himself. He shrank from observation and would not rise. Some of the guests resented his reserve and his failure to make a speech and privately called him "a cold fish"—others thought him offish; but I understood him better. He was merely shy.

Calling upon him the next day at his hotel, I met his wife, a vivacious and attractive young actress of whom I knew little. He again spoke of Chicago, but I do not think he got there. He was accompanied on this New York visit by Robertson of the *Bookman,* but neither of them remained long in the city.

One day soon after this, Brander Matthews invited me to a luncheon which he was giving in honor of Theodore Roosevelt, who was reported to be resigning his position as Police Commissioner. My seat mate was Owen Wister, whom I had never before met but whose writings had given me pleasure. I found him a self-contained young man, not unlike Roosevelt in physical bulk, a sturdy, broad-shouldered individual with a peculiarly firm clip of mouth. I took satisfaction in his manly vigor and his genial personality. He and Roosevelt would have made the luncheon illustrious, but Howells gave it dignity and significance.

Roosevelt, who was about to go to Washington as Assistant Secretary of the Navy, was overflowing with his stories of experiences as Commissioner of Police. He was humorous, yet showed at times the deepest earnestness. He entered upon a gay and delightfully comic description of "my cops," as he called his policemen. He dominated the table, for we were all glad to listen. He had the power of making us see what he had seen. His stories of the foreign peoples and their street ceremonies especially interested Howells, who repeatedly urged him to go on. "You must put these impressions into writing before they are overlaid by your Washington experiences," he said. "They are of great value as history."

Roosevelt became serious. "I have no time to write."

"We will be content with a record such as you have given us to-day. All you need is a stenographer," Howells replied. "Get it down in essentials and refine it afterwards."

I had very little talk with Roosevelt at this luncheon, but apparently something was said about an exchange of autographed books, for in my files I find a note from him which is an acknowledgment of a note from me. In this note I recall joining Howells in urging, "You should at once make record of your experiences." I think also that I expressed a regret that he was about to resign his position in New York, for he hints at some such statement on my part. This is, I believe, the first letter I received from him.

"You are very good. Instead of 'The Winning of the West,' will you let me give you the book I am proudest of?— 'The Wilderness Hunter.' In return, 'Prairie Folks' or 'Prairie Songs' would be more than welcome. You cannot have enjoyed that lunch half as much as I did. I shall at once look up 'The Cliff Dwellers,' Henry Fuller's novel. Next week I shall be away, but the week after I shall be back here, and if you can come around to the office, I will do everything I can to put you in contact with the police machinery. Perhaps the best way would be for you to make a tour with me some night around the precincts."

That he had more than a casual eye on me was made still more evident when I received another note from him asking me to lunch with him at a bakery restaurant not far from his office. He explained "I have only a short hour off duty and must go to the nearest place."

On arrival at the café I found that he had three other guests, William Chanler (a big-game hunter), Jacob Riis, the social worker, and Stephen Crane. Crane, whom I had not seen for a year or more, appeared thin, sad, and sallow, and his teeth and finger tips were yellowed by the incessant smoking of cigarettes. Riis, a newspaper man who had achieved distinction by his sympathetic work among the East Side poor, was a Dane, a short, unimpressive individual, but he, too, enjoyed Roosevelt's regard.

Hardly had I taken my seat at Roosevelt's left, when he turned to me and said, "Your story of that fight at the brewery is capital. I like your Steve Nagel. He is like the men I used to know in Dakota."

This commendation surprised and pleased me, for I knew something of his Western sketches and of his interest in all things American. To have him recall the name of a character in one of my short stories was highly flattering. I told him that my first knowledge of him was drawn from a news note to the effect that he had purchased a piece of wild-animal sculpture by my Chicago friend, Edward Kemeys. "And just to show how things work out," I added, "it was Kemeys who first drew my attention to Seton Thompson's masterly drawing of wolves. We are all members of a small informal association, lovers of the West and the open air."

This appeared to please him. "I like to be known in that connection," he said.

He talked African hunting grounds with Chanler, and the need of East Side parks with Riis. I liked Riis, but he said nothing memorable, and Crane sat in silence, speaking only in reply to questions. He looked like a man in trouble.

During the meal Roosevelt invited me to return to his headquarters. "I am trying some of my 'cops' to-day. You can sit on the bench and help me court-martial some of them," he jovially remarked. This invitation I promptly accepted, curious to see him in action as commissioner.

His associates were Alton B. Parker and Colonel Fred Grant, neither of whom he held in very high respect. He was the whole board so far as jurisdiction went, and it so happened that he was judge and jury on this date—a just and kindly court, as I can testify.

All the cases which came up that day involved the investigation of delinquencies on the part of his roundsmen. Neglect of duty, drunkenness, and sleeping on post were some of the charges, and, while little time was taken in any one case, the essential facts were quickly discovered by Roosevelt's swift, relentless questioning.

One judgment I vividly recall, for I influenced the verdict. The delinquent cop was a tall, good-looking, fair-haired youth, unmistakably a farmer's son. He approached the bar of justice with a mixture of shame and timidity which won my sympathy; and as he stood looking up at us I whispered to the commissioner, "Why, that is Lemuel Barker from Willoughby Pastures!"

Roosevelt had read his Howells. He recalled the chief character in "The Minister's Charge." "By George, so it is! He is charged with sleeping on post. What shall I do with him?"

"Go easy on him. Give him another chance."

"I'll do it." Leaning over his desk, he said very gravely but kindly, "Officer, you were found sleeping on your beat. What have you to say?"

"Nothing, Mr. Commissioner, except that I had been up with a sick friend for several nights and was worn out."

"Have you ever been here before?"

"No, sir."

Roosevelt opened a big book and studied a page. "Your record is good. I don't want to dishearten a loyal officer. Remember that your duty as an officer comes first. Don't let this happen again. Return to duty."

Tears came to the fine eyes of the young man as he said, "Thank you, Mr. Commissioner."

Others who came up did not fare so well. Sharply, sternly Roosevelt disciplined them, fining some, suspending others.

To him these men were soldiers in a civic army and derelictions in duty were something more than negligences. They were offenses against the city.

It was in the effort to raise the character of the service that he made frequent rounds of the city at night, observing his men on their rounds, studying them at hours when they were disposed to forget discipline. At the close of his hour on the bench he again suggested that I join him on such a night tour of the East Side. I accepted and a day or two later entered his office at about ten o'clock at night.

Jacob Riis was there when I arrived, and at eleven, Roosevelt, who was dressed in a rough, dark suit, pulled a soft hat low down over his spectacles and led the way into the street.

The night was fairly dark and our path a devious one, winding in and out of the East Side tenement districts which were strange and highly exciting to me, but to Riis, whose life had been largely spent in this region, the region was commonplace. It was a little like accompanying Grant on his rounds at Vicksburg.

Once the commissioner accosted a loitering roundsman. "What are you doing here? Resume your beat!"

"Who the hell are you?"

"I'm Commissioner Roosevelt," was the curt reply, and the officer stiffened into an attitude of alert attention.

Roosevelt went on: "I've been watching you for ten minutes. You're loafing. Get back to work or I'll put another man in your place."

Roosevelt's enemies called this "playing to the gallery," but he explained: "How else can I know what the men are doing? This is the only way to test their service. Catch 'em alone on their job."

My liking as well as my admiration for Roosevelt deepened. At intervals we talked of Stephen Crane, Owen Wister, Howells, Brander Matthews, and others of the friends we held in common. He showed the keenest interest in all far-Western subjects, and while he criticized my economic notions, he liked my stories and was greatly interested when I told him that I was setting out to write a life of Grant.

This led him to characterize Colonel Fred Grant with one of his acidulous phrases. He called him "a worthy citizen but a fathead"; and of Parker he was almost equally outspoken, "well meaning but inefficient"—and so indeed he was when measured against Roosevelt's vital, unresting, swiftly moving personality. They were like a team of horses in which one animal does all the pulling or pushing, while the others lag or ride the pole.

This evening with Roosevelt increased my knowledge of him, and my liking. He was most friendly, outspoken, and unassuming. Thereafter we met as friends and fellow enthusiasts for the West and Western literature. I was careful not to impose myself upon him when he was busy, and I wrote him only when I had something to say; but he was always (apparently) glad to see me and certainly was instant in the courtesy of his replies.

Like many other of his friends, I hated to see him leave the high office he filled so admirably in New York City for a subordinate position in the Navy Department in Washington, but some of those who knew him better than I said, "Don't you worry; he is not the kind of man to play a subordinate part—not for very long."

Crane and I met only once thereafter, in the office of *McClure's Magazine,* and this meeting was not entirely free from restraint. I still regarded him as a boy and lectured him—I hope with affection—on his way of life, urging him to cut loose from those who kept him from doing his best work. This was uncalled for, some will say, but I remembered the days when my brother had fed him; and if I erred it was on the side of desiring to be of further service to him. He resented my lecture then, but in later years spoke of me with almost filial regard, indicating that I had been right in my reproof.

His complexion and the cloudiness of his eyes led me to say to his friends, "His will be a short life." I also felt that there was no growth in the sort of genius he displayed. I could not see him developing as Owen Wister and Booth Tarkington were developing. His genius was not of that kind. It was not based on study or conscious observation. It arose from a subconscious endowment of amazing power, but this endowment could not be replenished. My study of the subconscious mind led me to the belief that he would fail as a reporter, and that his work would lose in value as he mixed with other writers and consciously strove to record events—just as his little store of verse failed of replenishment after it had run out upon his page.

It was at about this time that I was made a member of The Players. I think Brander Matthews proposed me and Gilder, Stedman, and other of my good friends who had known Edwin Booth vouched for me. My election to this club changed the City for me. I felt at home in New York for the first time. I found myself in association with vigorous young leaders in all the arts. Thereafter I was never lonely in New York.

CHAPTER TWENTY-SIX

OLD EDITORS AND NEW MAGAZINES

I

AMONG the men who most interested me and with whom I had most to do in the early nineties was Richard Watson Gilder, editor of the *Century Magazine,* a slender, dark, low-voiced, thoughtful man who was one of the busiest citizens in New York. He not only read and edited enormous masses of manuscript—and in those days much of it *was* manuscript —he acted as a director on many altruistic boards and presided at various civic meetings, almost on demand. I never saw him at leisure, for even when lunching he and his associate, Robert Underwood Johnston, appeared to be transacting business.

He always left the office with a bag crammed with stories by aspiring writers like myself, which he read on the train or at home. His editorial enthusiasm never faltered. He lived in the constant hope of discovering genius in every mail. He was kindly and tactful, and met his authors with a cheerful word and a quizzical smile. He never monologued, as Alden and Stedman were accustomed to do, but on the platform he was entirely at ease. Although a true poet in feeling he found time to write only an occasional verse, scholarly, thoughtful rather than lyrical. Beauty was his watchword. He realized more clearly than any other of my advisers of that time the ugliness of American life and the crudeness of our art. With but limited powers of expression with the pen he preached the need of literary grace with persistency and quiet power.

His home on East Eleventh Street was a meeting place for music lovers, poets, painters, and other esthetic folk whose interests were congenial. It was a plain brick house with the usual double parlor and a little garden at the rear. In this long room on the first floor, he received his literary and musical friends. He took pleasure in maintaining a meeting place for interesting folk of all kinds. The passing English critic, the Southern novelist, the Boston painter spending a few days in town, could usually be found there. If you were a regular guest you might even bring a friend along without a formal invitation.

Howells, kindly as he was, never encouraged such parties, but Stedman did. He, too, enjoyed being host. His salon, however, was almost entirely poetic, while Gilder enjoyed the presence of social reformers—if of the right temper—and musicians were always welcome at his door. Like Howells, he tempted his guests to talk and often went so far as to have one or two "address the meeting" on some ethical or esthetic subject. Good music was often heard in these rooms.

In breakfasting at the club, I frequently sat with Stedman. His home was out of the city, but he usually came to town for the winter. He was growing gray and his face was often worn and sad. He complained continually of overwork and often spoke of a pain in the back of his head, keeping his hand pressed against it as if to relieve the ache; but he seemed to *enjoy* the thought of his serious condition. "It is my heart," he said; "I expect to fall dead some day."

Unlike Gilder, he spoke openly of his troubles, of his

sickness and of his discontent with his home. He characterized his work on the Stock Exchange as "mere gambling."
His manner impressed me as that of a poet driven to imperil
his life in every way in the war of business—yet enjoying it.
Sprightly, airy, not too refined, a boy with the boys, he
refused to grow old. There was something birdlike in his
alertness, and in the brightness of his fine eyes.

He had a house in Lawrence Park some fifteen miles north
of the city and I sometimes went out there of a Sunday. It
was a large, plain frame cottage filled with books and paintings, the accumulation of many years. The walls of his
library were stocked with volumes of poetry from all lands
and all ages, for his work was largely that of editor. He was
an authority on verse writers, especially those of America,
and he had compiled the best known anthology of New
World poets.

In his study he was wholly admirable. I forgot his work
as stockbroker and his stories at the club, and honored him as
a scholarly and charming man of letters as he sat behind his
desk surrounded by treasured portraits, manuscripts, and letters. He knew almost every distinguished writer in England
and America, by correspondence at least, and his judgments,
on the whole, were sound. There was nothing malicious or
bitter in his criticism. Like Gilder and Howells he desired to
be helpful and was especially hospitable to young poets.
Perhaps, like Howells, he sometimes took promise for
achievement, but our verse writers needed just such an advocate at this time. That a man so fine, so learned in letters as
he should be forced to descend into Wall Street and fight for
money with which to keep the roof above his books and
manuscripts, was sadly disconcerting.

Notwithstanding his aphasia, his memory for poetry was

amazing. He could quote, and did quote, long passages from all the poets and essayists he most admired, a faculty which Howells did not possess, or if he possessed never used. He seldom quoted anything and never to make display of his reading, which was wide and thoughtful. He belonged to the modern type of literary man who has no need to illustrate his point by quoting from another author or from another language.

Stedman was naturally much beloved by Southern writers, for he had been generous in his estimate of their work. In "The Poets of America," he had given adequate space to Timrod, Haynes, Lanier, Poe, and other men whom other Northern critics had minimized; and he had been quick to praise James Lane Allen, Thomas Nelson Page, George W. Cable, and others of the younger Southern novelists. His influence was altogether helpful to authorship. To me, he was one of the saving graces of New York. Like Gilder and Howells, he stood for plain living and high thinking quite as distinctly as Emerson and Lowell had done in their time, and he held an even clearer notion of what American literature and art should become.

With a similar high standard of workmanship, Henry M. Alden was editing *Harper's Magazine*. His office, which was two flights up a circular iron stairway, was a queer little box of a room hardly larger than a closet, a den wherein he had wrought for nearly fifty years. Just large enough for a battered desk and an extra chair for a caller, its window frame almost touched the elevated road, and when a train passed its rattling thunder made conversation difficult. Nevertheless the inhabitant of this dusty closet was a power for good in American literature, a kindly dragon, so low-voiced that I missed something of his monologue even when the street was quiet. For all his gentleness and remoteness he was a shrewd and practical trader when it came to dealing with an author, a curious blend of the mystic and the Yankee. With well-defined notions of what fiction should be, he let his writers know very firmly that he was editing a work with one another often asked, "Is this the kind of magazine to suit himself, and authors in discussing their thing Alden would like?"

When at leisure he was inclined to philosophize along certain lines of a foggy transcendentalism; and once when I went out to visit him in his New Jersey home, he took me to his study after dinner, and there talked and talked and talked, smoking cigar after cigar whilst I forced myself to listen, gripping the arms of my chair and leaning forward from time to time. As near as I could understand it, he was discoursing on the mystery and the beneficence of death; but I hardly understood two connected sentences of that four-hour monologue. I comprehended the words, but the argument was a mist, a bleak obscurity. I did my best to look alive and deceived him by saying, "I see it!" "Quite so," and the like, pinching myself now and again to keep awake.

It was a torturing session, and I was never more relieved in my life than when along about one o'clock he paused and remarked, with a kindly beam in his eye, "Whenever you feel like retiring—" This was my opportunity. Springing instantly to my feet I assured him that I felt very much like it; and so he showed me to my room. As he said good night, I vowed never to put myself into his hands in that way again.

It was a cruel punishment, one which I am perfectly sure he had no intention of inflicting. Later I came to know that he was only trying on me the spoken version of a book on which he was at work and which he afterwards published, the result of his musings on the Great Mystery.

As an author he was of subordinate rank. His writing was dignified and weighty but without special distinction. Sitting in judgment as he did on the manuscripts of all the writers of his time, he failed to compose a book of any permanent value. Whether he was a great editor or not is debatable, but there can be no doubt as to his effect on the young writers of that day. His kindliness, his sympathy, and the nobility of his taste profoundly aided in the development of a characteristic American fiction. Like Gilder, he was receptive to the vernacular whenever it was truthfully and artistically employed; but he never edited down to his readers. He bought what appealed to him and not the kind of stuff which the millions were supposed to want.

II

Meanwhile another editorial group was coming into power, led by Sam McClure and Edward Bok, men who believed in reaching the millions. With them John S. Phillips and Walter Page were associated. Bok, the most successful of them all, lived in Philadelphia, and I was often an overnight guest at his house. It was the fashion in New York to sneer at Bok's *Home Journal,* and professional jesters like James L. Ford made sport of its "Heart-to-Heart Talks" and culinary departments; but this was a very superficial view of the magazine. Bok had a well-defined policy; he employed the best writers and paid them well. His *Journal* carried household hints, but it also included excellent fiction (some of mine) and stood editorially for the highest ideals in social and political life. It catered to an enormous list of readers, and remained essentially aspiring. Bok and McClure, like Lorimer of the *Post,* had the will and the skill to represent the American mind. The invasion from the south of Europe had not yet colored their periodicals.

Sam McClure represented the conquering side of the editors' guild. He was all for making a magazine popular, and James L. Ford or some other wicked paragrapher reported McClure as demanding of a noted author that he make his life of Christ "a little more snappy." This may have been a wheeze, but the spirit of the new editor was in this jest. As manager of popular periodicals he regarded magazines like *Scribner's, The Century,* and the *Atlantic Monthly* with good-natured contempt. They were journals for the few—his was for the many. Striving for wider "circulation" and knowing that for every added hundred thousand readers, advertising rates could be advanced, the businessman consulted the wishes of the average reader—or the reader below the average.

Under this plan, literature became an aid to trade and magazines turned into advertising bulletins. Subscribers counted for less and less, it was the news-stand sale which mattered; and in the end the price of such periodicals fell below the cost of their raw paper. The advertisers paid the bill but passed it on to the buyer of their goods. In this scheme the money set aside for manuscripts was but a small item of the annual budget and the prices paid for strongly popular material became astounding. Authors received four or five times the sums they had hitherto enjoyed.

Naturally the editors of such magazines studied the appetites of the millions and not the tastes of the cultivated few. They justified themselves—whenever they attempted justification—by saying, "We are teaching the myriads to read. We are reaching the sons and daughters of peasants who never read before"; and there was truth in this statement. But the fact remains, editing became more and more a process of purveying, and writing more and more of an appeal to shopgirls, tired business men, and others who demanded easy and exciting reading.

Whether Gilder and Alden saw the end of their reign before it came, I cannot say, but I think they did. They lasted well on toward 1900, maintaining themselves and their magazines side by side with the onrushing stream of "flat magazines" supported by a diminishing list of subscribers, men and women of adult intelligence whose tastes were for the carefully considered page, content to get their news from other periodicals.

As a lover of literature I leaned to the side of Gilder and Alden, but I sold most of my stories to Bok and McClure. Corrupted without realizing it, I pretended to scorn the tempter. One day McClure turned on me. "Garland, you're on the wrong track. You despise journalism, but the journalist is the man who wins. Now you can write, but you write of people and subjects that only a few care about. Why not take subjects which interest everybody? You would then stand a double chance of winning. Drop your literary pose and come in with us. Use your skill on topics of the day, or stories of big personalities, and you'll make a place for yourself, as Miss Tarbell and William Allen White have done."

He was right. I knew he was right, but I refused to go over to his side. I temporized. I did a few things along his line, but held on to my hope of creating something of permanent value. I had the wish to be a kind of social historian and in the end fell, inevitably, between two stools. I failed as a reporter, and only half succeeded as a novelist.

What I am saying is this: Gilder and his associate, Robert Underwood Johnson, of the *The Century,* stood for the aristocratic in literature. Along with Stedman, Howells, Alden, Burlingame, and in less degree Walter Page, they supported the true magazine, while McClure, Lorimer, and Bok representing the popular or journalistic side led the all-conquering host which in later years loaded the news stands with gaily colored pyramids of snappy stories and easy-going comment. In the end the "yellow journal" and the "tabloid daily" circulated in billions.

If you are charitable and philosophic you may say, "literature was thus carried down and spread out among the masses"; but to many of us this "literature" has the appearance of a commercial exploitation of humankind.

In the beginning these popular editors were so high in mind, so genial and so persausive, that they won me to their plans before I realized my danger. Page, Bok, Doubleday, Phillips, Lorimer, and McClure appeared so genuinely interested in me that it was hard not to write to their order, especially as I was poor and could only now and again finish a story which Alden or Gilder considered worthy of their approval. Therefore I found myself writing three-part romances for *The Home Journal,* essays on Ibsen, Impressionism, and other controversial subjects for *The Forum,* biographical studies for *McClure's,* and stories of the mountain West for Lorimer's *Post.* I claim no alibi. If I am less guilty than other writers, it is only because I had less ability. My journalistic efforts were too feeble, too half-hearted to be of much service. I wrote for *McClure's,* but I continued to visit *The Century's* literary salon!

II

Among the few journalists who interested me at this time was Irving Bacheller, who had established a syndicate somewhat on McClure's lines; and in one of my days of depression I went to see him concerning a series of articles which he had suggested.

I found him in an office on the north side of a building in midtown. He was a large, blond young man of gentle speech and slow motions, frank, kindly, but curiously absentminded. I recall that as I entered he was sitting at his desk, gazing out of the window at a blank and ugly wall, evidently dreaming of something beside business, for the glance which he turned upon me was that of a man returning from a far place.

I liked his face and voice, and as we talked I learned that our lives were singularly similar. Born of a New England family in the North Country, he had come to New York as I had gone to Boston. He knew my people as I knew his. We had studied the same schoolbooks and held in memory the same songs and poems. He had drifted into journalism to earn a living whilst I had boiled my pot by teaching and lecturing. My stories of boy life on the prairie had interested him, and he had in mind an arrangement whereby he could be sure of a series of stories and sketches of the Wisconsin pioneers.

As he talked I marveled at his ability to sustain himself in the journalistic world—so much of the dreamer and poet he appeared. McClure belonged to the hustle of the New York newspaper office, but Irving Bacheller did not, although he had occupied an editorial chair in the office of the *World*. His mind dwelt upon the North Country and he was even then beginning a book which was to outsell all of its contemporaries and take him permanently out of journalistic life. He had begun to write "Eben Holden," but this I did not know, and I went away wondering if his syndicate could possibly make its way in opposition to that of McClure. The reader will find this blue-eyed, low-voiced dreamer coming again and again into this story, for we became friends of a type which only a close community of origin and interest can maintain.

CHAPTER TWENTY-SEVEN

THE VANISHING LEGION

I

DURING all of these months, while meeting Roosevelt, Barrie, and other Eastern and Southern writers, I was at work gathering the material for my serial "Life of Grant." Part of the spring I spent in Washington and part of it in St. Louis. I had already visited Vicksburg, the Wilderness, Chattanooga, and other of the great commander's battle-fields and the mythic Grant, the silent, grim, remorseless Grant, has disappeared and a low-voiced, modest, kindly citizen had taken his place. Even those who spoke of his weakness for drink, which was most in evidence at the time of his deepest discouragement, declared that he was never the roysterer. His native dignity was never lost.

The woman in whose St. Louis house he roomed while trying to find work as a surveyor, spoke of his essential kindliness and the correctness of his speech. He was the strangest warrior in history. Gentle as he was, hating war and avoiding its parade whenever possible, he could never-theless order a charge in the spirit of the patriot who looks over and beyond the blood of the battlefield to the end for which the battle is fought.

As I talked with his veterans in their homes or offices, I found it difficult to imagine them in the high command to which they referred. I think they had come to marvel at it

346

themselves. The era of which they dreamed was rushing into oblivion. To many of them, those who had been called from the farm or the factory to serve under Grant, and who were now walking a humdrum round as country lawyers or city merchants, the voice of the bugle, the thunder of the cannon, and the rattle of musketry came faintly, as part of an epic interlude, a phantasmic period in their personal career.

They could not express this feeling in words, but their eyes dimmed with emotion as they recounted these, their heroic hours. Some, like Longstreet, resembled aged captive eagles brooding over remembered flight across seas and over cliffs. Others were naïvely boastful. That I was marching in the rear ranks of a disappearing army was evident. I began to understand the early blunders, defeats, and blind campaigning of our democratic armies. Our volunteers were not warriors, and their leaders, for the most part, knew nothing of military strategy. Those who had received a West Point training had never commanded a thousand men. At the opening of the war, Grant himself, a humble ex-captain, with no opportunity to test his training, aspired to be only a regimental commander.

All this is not in criticism but an explanation. Our genius was for pioneering, for settlement, for subduing the soil, not for the conquering of cities and the destruction of men. It explains Grant and Longstreet, who made war because it was their duty, not because it was their delight, although in after life they both looked back upon certain phases of it with illogical wistfulness. After all, it was an epic and they had lived it.

For two years I lived among these dying giants, absorbing their concepts, trying to organize their confused memories, and even as I worked at their records, they died! With appalling swiftness they disappeared. Invaluable witnesses, generals like Franklin, Wright, and Buckner dropped out of the lines, and those of humbler rank, Grant's intimate coworkers and relatives, unnoticed, almost unrecorded, had gone over to the silent host. My work had begun not a moment too soon. In truth it had not begun soon enough, for many of Grant's most intimate associates had been "mustered out" before I began my study. However, I persisted, traveling thousands of miles to talk with some one who really knew him.

I am fully aware of the danger of trusting to the words of friends and relatives, in arriving at a judgment of Grant's character, but I am equally certain that the biographies made up from reports of his political and military enemies are false and quite worthless. They defeat themselves, for in belittling Grant they belittle the opposition leaders whom they seek to aggrandize. Lee and Longstreet saw this, and checked their subordinates in the midst of their contemptuous references to their great antagonist. If this Union is worth anything, Grant, who under Lincoln saved it, should rank above the man who used all his great gifts to destroy it. Sentimental acclaim for the leader of a lost cause does not appeal to me so long as I believe the maintenance of the Union to have been on the side of progress—a part of the natural evolution of a great nation.

General Grant's son Ulysses, upon receiving a copy of my book, wrote me a letter of such tactful, modest, candid comment that I am moved to quote from it. I liked this son. I had talked with him freely and he had frankly replied. I saw no reason why his testimony should not go in to offset the political slandering of the local press. As the lawyers say, he is a competent witness.

"I received your 'Grant.' I have read the book because I felt too much interested to put the reading off, but will read it again when my mind is at ease. My friend Purrington, who was anxious about your book while it was coming out in the magazine, has spoken twice about it in terms that would please you. I quote from his last letter which I still have in pocket: 'extraordinary performance of great interest, and fuller of merits than faults.'

"I hope in your next edition you will erase all credit to me for supplying you with photos. It seems to make me sponsor, in some small degree, for your performance and I deserve no credit in that direction whatever; while if I had had any authority over your work there are a few statements and expressions of opinion which I would have altered (if possible). You are responsible for the results of your studies and for the deductions therefrom. You have striven (successfully) to produce a great work without prejudice to any one, and I would be sorry to see that any one thought you were biased by an acquaintance with me."

II

My pursuit of the "Vanishing Legion" of the Civil War had another advantage: it brought me into touch with several of the most eminent of Southern novelists. I had not counted upon this, but one by one the chief writers of the South crossed my path.

While in Richmond, I called on Ellen Glasgow, the author of "The Descendant," and was surprised to find her a girl of only twenty-three, tall and fair, with a childlike roundness of cheeks and chin, but her mind was very far from being childish. As a student of Herbert Spencer and Charles Darwin she displayed an alarming candor of statement. She frankly confessed that she didn't like happy people. "Happy people irritate me," she said with a smile. She showed me a volume of her poems all dealing with the dignity of despair, the splendor of hell, and the stern decrees of fate—many of them succinct and powerful of diction, and I set down this comment, "The order of her progress seems reversed. She is beginning with the bitterness of age. She is likely to be a marked personality in Southern literature. Her work will not be pleasant, but it will be original and powerful."

Among others of those I met in this way was Ruth McEnery Stuart of New Orleans. Mrs. Stuart belonged to "the new school" of Dixie novelists, writers who had begun to study the life around them. She had reached the point of describing the negro in a direct and understanding way, picturing him and his women as she saw them on her lawn and in her kitchen, amusing in their primitive disregard of marriage customs and the laws of property, and by their barbaric notions of medicine and religion. Her negroes were jocose critics of one another, kindly and tolerant, but retaining their childlike notions of life. All this was new and valuable.

Later she made her home in New York and I often saw her there, finding her a delightful hostess. She told stories with artistic plan and precision, with a chuckle in her voice and a comic light in her gray eyes. I often said in speaking of her, "She's a good fellow," meaning that she met me like a genial, refined man with humorous outlook. She could make a joke and take a joke. She often made fun of herself, which was rare among women then and is not common now, although I hear self-derisive feminine comment more often to-day than yesterday.

Mrs. Stuart's work was not great, but it was significant of a change of attitude, a change which was more powerfully expressed by Joel Chandler Harris, whose "Uncle Remus" stories had made him famous. He also saw the "hill billy" in perspective, as Hopkinson Smith perceived the old Virginia planter in relation to New York, whereas Page of Virginia still lingered in the romantic haze of the Old South, presenting stately ladies and cavalier gentlemen against the walls of mansions, a fiction which Walter Page bluntly criticized in his autobiographical book, "The Southerner."

On one of my Southern tours I called upon Joel Harris at his desk in the *Atlanta Constitution*—an amusing experience. He was sitting in his shirt sleeves, quite like a country editor, in a cluttered, ugly, and noisy office. He was not prepossessing in appearance and plainly showed that he was aware of it. He was short, red-haired, and ungainly, but his face was interesting and his eyes attractive.

He cleared a chair for me and for an hour we sat amid the ruck and clatter of his office, discussing our many mutual friends and listing the makers of Southern literature. He talked easily and well, but was inclined to let me take the lead, which I did by asking questions.

He had few illusions about the South. He saw it somewhat as I did, a region without mental stir, unkempt and unenterprising. "But it is changing for the better," he said, "not as rapidly as I should like to see it, but it is on its way toward a more modern way of thinking."

He told me that he was of mountain stock and that he had earned his own living from boyhood. "My life has been somewhat like your own," he said, "only you've kept clear of newspaper work."

I surprised him by speaking in praise of his stories of the mountaineers. "I like them better than your 'Uncle Remus' books." I spoke especially of "At Teague Poteet's" and "Trouble on Lost Mountain." He knew the negro's soul better than any of his contemporaries, but he also knew the men and women of the mountains. He saw the aristocratic South from the angle of a poor white farmer. He was not bitter, but he was bluntly critical of "the old régime."

I asked him if he ever came to New York, and he smiled as he answered, "No, I stay right here summer and winter."

I suspect that he knew what was in my mind. I was thinking of his failure to appear in New York at a dinner in which he was listed as a guest of honor. "He got as far as Baltimore," the story ran, "and turned back, unable to face the bright lights of Broadway and the speeches that awaited him." I suspect he dreaded the remark, "Is *that* Joel Chandler Harris? Well, I didn't know he was short and fat and red-haired." Something of the same distaste for public appearance caused Howells to decline all invitations to preside at dinners or to lecture. A public speaker is more likely to be criticized on his figure than on his facts.

George W. Cable, although an unimpressive little man, was an intrepid lecturer notwithstanding. His slimness and his high-keyed, soft-toned voice were proper to his material. In some strange way he and Mark Twain were induced to appear together on the platform, and two more divergent types I never saw side by side. My first sight of them was in a Boston hall, where to a huge audience they gave a program of readings under the management of Major Pond. Mark, by contrast with Cable, appeared to be six feet in height and for many years I thought of him as a tall, thin man. Not until I met him in his own home some ten years later did I find him to be of about my own height. Stedman and Gilder were undersize, but Charles Dudley Warner, like Edward Eggleston, was large, self-contained, and handsome. To know that one is sizable, good looking, and well dressed helps one to self-possession as a speaker and lends an air of authority to one's words. Cable was natively of great dignity and seriousness, but his small frame and soft voice made him appear weaker than he was.

One of the most distinguished women writers of this time, Mary N. Murfree (Charles Egbert Craddock), I never met, but I am moved to mention her by way of contrast to Joel Chandler Harris. They both wrote stories of the Allegheny Mountain folk, but their methods were almost directly opposed. Miss Murfree's mountains were gloomy and glorious and awful and her folk of similar romantic character. She saw them from the outside, whereas Harris, who was born among them and knew them as neighbors, discarded all theatrical coloring. He characterized them as his people. They were not types; they were individuals. He recorded their homely humor, their prejudices, and their everyday tribulations. Naturally the highly colored romances of Miss Murfree won the applause of the many, but Harris was content with the support of the few, and his stories have the value of social history as well as good fiction.

John Fox, Jr., saw the mountaineers as an outsider, but reported them in "Hell for Sartin Creek" with something like the humorous precision and brevity which characterized Harris' "Teague Poteet." Although a Kentuckian, Fox was often in New York and Chicago. His joyous spirit, his liking for good clothes and gay company, his popularity as a diner-out put him as far from Harris' way of life as a man could possibly be, and yet their short stories were akin. He did not imitate Harris, but he studied the same people and presented them with much the same precision.

We met only occasionally, but I always enjoyed a chat with him. He talked crisply, clearly, and always had a good story to tell. He read his stories from the platform and read them extremely well. He was most successful in suggesting the mountaineer, almost as successful as Riley was in depicting the Hoosier, and was in great demand. He died comparatively young, but left a considerable list of stories which can not be neglected in a study of the literature of the mountain South.

III

When I returned to Washington in January, 1898, I found Roosevelt established there as Assistant Secretary of the Navy—at least they called him the assistant. Whatever John D. Long thought of him, he was chief of the office. In truth he was "it"—the vitalizing force of the department. To this I can testify, for he at once made me free of his office. "Come in any time," he said, "and see the wheels go round."

Naturally I seized upon the opportunity. It amused and flattered me to be treated as a privileged guest and with no favor to ask I was a welcome caller, I am sure. Roosevelt gave me a seat near his private desk and while we talked he continued his routine, receiving reports and signing papers, exactly as he had said he would. I saw the wheels go round.

Nevertheless I expressed my regret that he had given up his commissionership. "That was a big job."

He smiled with a characteristic twist of his lips and said with humorous inflection, "*This* is a big job, if our navy is ever to count for anything;" and as I heard him outline plans for an increase of gun power and order more frequent target practice, I perceived that he meant that it should amount to something.

It was through him that I met Lodge of Massachusetts, and I suspect that an invitation to dine at the senator's house came at Roosevelt's suggestion. I had never met Lodge, but I had often heard him speak in the Senate and admired his method. He had the calm grace of an intellectual aristocrat. He knew what senatorial dignity meant, and was a very able politician and parliamentarian, as some of his blustering colleagues sooner or later discovered.

"He is a writer as well as a scholar and owns one of the finest private libraries in Washington," said Roosevelt, and as I entered it that night, it added to the high respect in which I held its owner. It was a working library. It suggested the historian and the essayist. It was spacious, reposeful, with chairs and mellow lights inviting reading, a refuge from the tumults of business and of politics. The senator was a conservative but by no means a reactionary.

The guests that night were few: Brooks Adams, Theodore Roosevelt, and myself. The talk at the table was brilliant, but my memory fails to record it. I recall only the heckling to which I was subjected after dinner while we were seated before the library fire. Roosevelt set them going. After explaining that I had enjoyed an exceptional opportunity to study the West and South, he began to draw me out for the benefit of Lodge and Adams, whom he called "you Easterners," ranking himself with me as a Westerner. "I am of the short-grass country, Garland of the blue-joint prairie."

While they listened to me (I don't know why), I told them what the West was complaining about. I described the actual life of the average farmer. At Roosevelt's repeated urging I spoke freely. He applauded me—"Garland knows the farmers," he said. I asked them how they could expect tillers of rented farms two thousand miles from a seaport to take an active interest in shipping or the building up of a navy. "Theoretically they are patriotic, but their interests are not those of New York or Boston."

Adams then took the floor and opened a world-war possibility. He had a theory that the equatorial zone of the earth was "a furnace into which, for a million years, the weaker races of the world have been crowded." In the north temperate zones men came to greatest power as warriors as well as food producers. "Nothing worth while ever came out of the equatorial belt," he asserted, and just what its bearings on our discussion were he did not say; but I recall that in all his positions he was the unrelenting theorist, the hopeless scholar, an autocrat ridden by a remorseless theory.

Roosevelt appeared to enjoy this exquisitely phrased diatribe against God and civilization. No doubt he had heard something like it from Adams before, but if he had not, he was too soundly the optimist to be disturbed by it. He did not openly smile, but he turned a humorous look on me now and again as if to warn me not to take the savage philosopher too seriously. "It's all a literary pose," he appeared to convey.

IV

One of the most notable men with whom I talked concerning Grant was John Hay, who lived in what seemed to me, at the time, a noble mansion across the square from the White House. He was a small man, dapper in dress and cultivated in speech, in no way suggesting the son of an Illinois pioneer, but he was admittedly very able both as diplomat and statesman. He wore a full gray beard and, though diminutive, was a man of marked dignity.

He received me genially and related some pleasing incidents of Grant whom he saw many times during the war and afterward. He admired the General and attacked some of the misconceptions concerning him. He was distinctly literary in his speech and his analysis of the General was delightful. At the end of an hour's talk he said, "I must go up to the Army and Navy Club. Perhaps you'll walk along with me."

Naturally I was glad of the opportunity, and as we walked along he confided his great regret that he had never been able to follow out his ambition to be a writer. He spoke of his share in the Lincoln biography, and asked me if I had seen Nicolay. He remarked rather ruefully "more people knew of my 'Pike County Ballads' than of my work as historian." We talked of Howells and I was glad to have him speak so warmly of his work. Altogether I remember the man of letters, rather than Secretary Hay, statesman and diplomat.

His suggestion that I see Nicolay, his fellow historian, led me to seek him out. I found him living in a modest brick house just back of the Congressional Library, surrounded by books. He was a tall, plain man, the direct opposite of Hay, a countryman in tone and manner, but scholarly in his rough-hewn way. He had little to tell me of Grant, however, and made upon me the impression of a man forgotten, one who had been given a tremendous opportunity in his Lincoln history and had failed to make the most of it. His writing was, like himself, plain, matter-of-fact, and rather dull.

It must have been this very afternoon that I carried out a long-cherished plan to visit the home of Edward Eggleston, which was not far away. Eggleston was almost a tradition in my boyhood home.

In the autumn of 1871, when I was eleven years of age, my father brought back from the county town one day a copy of a little monthly magazine called *Hearth and Home*, which had in it the beginning of a story which marks an epoch in American fiction as it marked an epoch in my own literary life. This story was "The Hoosier Schoolmaster."

Up to this time, I had believed that literature was concerned with something afar off, and romantic. All the stories I had read concerned themselves either with Indians and trappers in the far West, or with dukes and duchesses in Eastern ancestral castles. "The Hoosier Schoolmaster" was my first realization that stories could be written of people very like my father's friends and neighbors. I had the feeling that if I should mount my pony and ride away to the east, I might conceivably pass the door of "Old Man Mean's" cabin, and the schoolhouse in which "Ralph Hartsook" was a teacher or catch a glimpse of "little Sharkie" coming down the road to school. That this story was vital is evident, for the magazine was, each month, a bone of contention between my sister and myself. In the years which followed I read every new book which came from the pen of Edward Eggleston, but with no expectation of ever meeting him. Now here he was, only a few blocks away.

I found him a big, hearty man, gray of hair, leonine of

head, and ruddy of complexion. His laugh was frank and his manner cordial. He, too, gave me some valuable reminiscences concerning Grant.

Unlike Grant he was a tremendous talker, but a talker who had something to say. So well stored was his mind that a word sufficed to set in motion the vast fund of his learning. To any one who was himself eager to talk, Eggleston would have been a bore, but to me he was delightful. I was entirely content to set him going.

In my copy of "The Hoosier Schoolmaster," a copy of the first edition (with all of its atrocious illustrations) he wrote the following lines in lovely handwriting:

"This book was published in *Hearth and Home* in October, November, and December of 1871 and in book form, December 15. It sold about ten thousand copies the first six months and about ten thousand in each of the two following half years. It was pirated and sold in England in an edition of ten thousand copies, and has since been reprinted there with no profit to the author. Madame Blanc rendered it into French for the *Revue de Deux Mondes*. It was published in book covers in French, German, and Danish and perhaps other tongues. This copy has all the original crudities, exuberances, and violations of artistic canons that have helped to give the book itself now beyond a hundred thousand in the United States.

"These facts are set down here for my good friend, Mr. Hamlin Garland, with the sincere regards of

"EDWARD EGGLESTON."

We then fell quite naturally into a discussion of "The Hoosier Schoolmaster" whose inception was of interest to me historically. He told me that it was written after he left the ministry and while he was editing *Hearth and Home* in Chicago. "It was written to fill space in the magazine," he admitted with humorous inflection. "I had no idea of its appeal to my readers. As it went on, my interest in it grew with theirs. I was born in Vevay, Indiana, and grew to manhood there, but only part of my literary material relates to that period of my life. 'The Mystery of Metropolisville' is based upon my life in southern Minnesota, where I went for my health. In those days Minnesota was supposed to be a place of healing airs and waters—a place to which Eastern doctors sent their hopeless cases. . . . All my writing was done after I left the backwoods and most of it after I came to New York. I realized that I was not giving my material the best form, but my intent was right. I wanted to do what the Dutch painters did, paint the homely and grotesque men and women I knew, with artistic truth. I was breaking new ground. It was an attempt at the right thing."

There was something in him which reminded me of my mother's people, the McClintocks. His upright figure, broad shoulders, and hearty laugh were all akin to my own kind. His judgments were cultivated, kindly, and just.

During the last six months of my stay in Washington I met him frequently at the Cosmos Club, where he was a notable figure. His flowing gray beard, his shapely head, and his graceful bearing distinguished him in any company. Usually he was the center of a group of listeners. Immensely learned in early American history and customs, he loved to talk and did talk endlessly on these especial subjects. I recall his statement of the curious folklore which surrounded the early practice of medicine. "Doctors pulverized dried toads and various other grewsome objects in order to cure various obscure diseases, and certain Virginia farmers opposed the coming in of the iron plow because they believed it would 'poison the land.' "

The effect of Eggleston's work on American fiction can not be overestimated. And yet there was a time when Indiana did not honor him. I am not sure but that his pictures of backwoods life are still held, by many people, to be caricatures, and yet at a dinner to Booth Tarkington at the Lotos Club some years ago when I said in my speech, "Edward Eggleston is the father of us all," Tarkington heartily applauded and called out, "You are entirely right."

Undoubtedly Eggleston was a pioneer in the work of depicting the early life of Indiana, Illinois, and Minnesota. He deserves to be honored for these attempts. In spite of their defects his books are bits of authentic border history.

At a time when New England was being exploited by Harriet Beecher Stowe, Oliver Wendell Holmes, Rose Terry Cooke, Thomas Bailey Aldrich, and William Dean Howells, this circuit rider of Indiana had the perception and sufficient skill to put certain phases of the middle West into fiction. Rude and crude as they appear to us of to-day, they were brave beginnings and deserve honor. Edward Eggleston is a noble pioneer in our Western fiction.

I never saw him again, but he remains a handsome and gracious figure in my memory of Washington life.

v

Another of the powerful and picturesque figures resident in Washington at this time was Major J. W. Powell, head of the Ethnologic Bureau, whose "literary evenings" were a feature of life in the capital. He had been a military engineer under Grant in the siege of Vicksburg, and after the war led an exploration of the Grand Cañon of the

Colorado. I met him as a student of the red men and honored him as one of the heroes of a deeply significant national era.

It was in his home that I renewed acquaintance with Dr. Edward Everett Hale, whom I had not seen for ten years. He was sadly aged, but greeted me bluffly with cordial, booming voice. He had come to Washington, it appeared, as chaplain of the Senate. He wore a wide Western hat on his shock of gray hair and was a noticeable figure as he walked about the capital.

He developed a curious notion of my reasons for leaving Boston. Speaking to Powell, he said: "By our lack of sympathy we drove this man Garland out of Boston at a time when we needed young writers. The Boston of my youth would have welcomed him."

To this I replied, "No, no, Dr. Hale! The people of Boston were kinder than I deserved."

He refused to listen and I heard him repeat this statement to others. I suppose he held dimly in his mind my first call upon him wherein I voiced a complaint against the library. Then, too, as one of the old Bostonians, he resented the invasion of the city by the Irish and Italians. To him the city was in decay—certainly it was no longer the chief literary center of the nation.

Powell, small, bearded, one-armed, interested me very keenly, although it was difficult to imagine him leading that desperate attempt to navigate the waters of the Grand Cañon. One day a few years later, as I was passing down the street, I encountered him, gray and feeble, shuffling along on the arm of a colored attendant. He responded to my greeting with pathetic vagueness and said, "I know you and I ought to recall your name but I can't. I've lost my memory."

He had suffered a stroke and was only the shell of what he had been. At about the same time my Uncle William, a hunter and mighty axeman, was stricken in the same way; and it was with these two men in mind that I wrote the following poem, called "The Stricken Pioneer"—intending it to be a tribute to these men and all their kind:

> In him behold the story of our best
> The chronicle of riflemen behind the plow.
> His the life of those who knew
> No barrier but the sunset in their quest.
> On his bent head and grizzled hair
> Is set the sign of those who show
> New cunning to the wolf, who chase
> The mother panther to her lair
> And strike the lion from the mountains' face.
>
> And when he dies—as soon he must—
> A magic word goes with him to the grave.
> Above his dust
> Set these plain words: "He was a brave."
> He faced the desert winds unscared
> And met the savage stark alone.
> Our velvet way his steel prepared,
> He died without a curse or moan.
>
> Then bury him not here in city soil
> Where car-wheels grind and factories spill
> Their acrid smoke on those who toil:
> Bear him far away—to some high hill
> That overlooks the mighty stream
> Whose thousand miles of pathway through the corn
> Blazons his progress. There let him dream
> And wait his resurrection morn!

CHAPTER TWENTY-EIGHT

WASHINGTON AS A MEETING PLACE

I

WHILE the number of distinctly literary personalities in Washington was small, there were many men of other interests commanding notice, for they represented every corner of the nation and all departments of scientific research. For example, as I was leaving the library one afternoon, I met one of Major Powell's ethnological assistants, a young redman named Peter la Flesch, sauntering across the capitol grounds with a white girl, a very pretty girl, to whom he introduced me, and in the course of our conversation I learned that Alice Fletcher, compiler of Omaha songs, was at home and wanted to see me.

There was no trace of his tribe in La Flesch's speech; on the contrary his diction was notably succinct, definite, and clear, and as I walked away I thought, "Here is the subject for an American romance. Think of that man with his tepee derivation and his savage psychological inheritance, married to a white woman. What a chance for some novelist to discover deep-seated antipathies!"

I met him again the following evening in the home of his patron saint, Alice Fletcher, and came to fuller knowledge of him. His dignity and self-restraint were entirely admirable. He spoke at the right moment and always to the purpose, and when Miss Fletcher sang some of the plaintive songs she had collected, he skilfully accompanied her on the flute.

The combination of instruments was melodious but presented in most cases only a sweetened dilution of the native songs as I had heard them sung. As MacDowell had pointed out, the process of transposing them to the conventional scale and adapting them for the piano, necessarily dimmed their fire and slowed their speed. Nevertheless I enjoyed them, even in their conventionalized form. The love songs were especially effective but the war songs were curiously mild. Heard in the light of a council fire or from a tepee, to the accompaniment of booming tom-toms, they were of entirely different effect. Even the love songs seemed weak and poor by contrast with those I had heard at dawn across a mountain lake or at dusk along a willow-fringed river in Montana.

Among the few writers who actually made their homes in Washington was James Lane Allen, and in my diary I find this record of him:

"He is big and blond, six feet and more in height, muscular and deep-chested. He looks like a serious-minded young physician. His voice is soft and his words well chosen. Under his softness, however, lies a very rigid and well-developed theory of fictional art. He can become sharply argumentative and sternly dogmatic on occasion. There is something of the schoolmaster in the precision of his statement and in the multiplicity of his theories, and yet (for all his dogmatism) I like him, and in so far as he is trying to catch and preserve the vanishing phases of Kentucky life, he has my heartiest support. He and John Fox are the leading representatives of Kentucky literature, although Fox is Northern in most of his relationships."

Allen moved to a New York apartment some years later and in calling on him there I was surprised and amused by the gentility of his surroundings. The ladylike character of his ornate desk was especially incongruous. No signs of labor, no sawdust or chips appeared in his literary workshop. His study might have been the tea room of a delicate, beauty-loving spinster, so precise, so correct, and so delicately colored were its furnishings. I could not imagine a tall man working at that little spindle-legged desk and yet he assured me, with pride, that he did all his writing thereon.

None of the authors resident in Washington at this time was more exotic than Charles Warren Stoddard, a Californian, whose "South Sea Idyls" had won him wide recognition, and who bitterly complained of the cold and damp of the city and of his overheated apartment. He was a fine-featured, gray-haired man of sixty, distinguished in manner and graceful of phrase. He was withal a writer of power and imagination, tender and wistful at times, dreaming of his beloved islands. He could not make his home in Washington although as Professor of Literature he was lecturing three times a week at a Catholic University. Bitterly resenting it as a grind, he said, "I do it only because I *must* pay my board."

Against his study walls stood rows of autographed books, while shells from the South Seas, braided mats, embroidered cloths, and grotesque images hung or lay about him. Mingled with these primitive objects were ivory figures of Christ, sadly painted Madonnas, and other emblems of his faith. How much these symbols meant to him I could not discover, but they did not lighten his gloom. He suggested an aged lion muttering behind his bars, patient but breaking forth now and again in growls of pain. He was a sensitive soul, too much the poet to grapple with a hard and pushing Eastern world. He remembered the South Seas as a blessed haven from which he should never have flown.

He had many distinguished friends. Howells liked him and so did Henry and Brooks Adams, who often entertained him. He had lived in San Francisco and had known Bret Harte, Joaquin Miller, and Robert Louis Stevenson and talked of them most delightfully. His English was delicately precise and he told a story well. I recall one narrative which resembled Thoreau's account of the battle of the ants in his chip pile.

"One day while sitting at my desk on which a fly of some notable sort stood impaled on a tall pin for closer study, I saw an ant, plainly a scout, come wandering across the table. At the foot of the pin, which was to him the bole of an enormously tall palm, he paused and stared up at the huge monster perched at its top. He touched the pin as if to test its bark. He appeared to cogitate, looking up it as if calculating the climb. At last he disappeared. Soon he returned, leading a squad of his fellows. Guiding them to the foot of the towering pole, he said: 'Here it is, fellows, see for yourselves.' They conferred, calculated, and at last one of them, a daring soul, agreed to make the dangerous ascent."

Stoddard had forgotten his aches and worries. His eyes had brightened, his voice had deepened. He became dramatic. When he spoke of the enormous height of the pin, he looked upward as if from the place of the ant. "What a magnificent piece of daring! It was as if I had volunteered to climb a pole two hundred feet high to dismember an elephant."

I listened with intent interest as Stoddard described the ultimate triumph of that ant, displaying the imagination of a poet and the humor of a philosopher.

He had something to give which I relished and I went several times to see him, but my last meeting with him was at the home of Henry Adams, where John La Farge, another South Sea enthusiast, was a guest and where the talk was wholly exotic.

My first view of La Farge remains a vivid picture. As he came creeping down the stairs I thought of Richard Mansfield's character, "Baron Chevrial." His make-up and his action were quite the same. He walked like an old and suffering man and his scanty black hair, dark skin, and huge eyeglasses suggested something sinister, almost satanic. He appeared a kind of Mephistopheles grown suddenly old, whereas in truth he was kindly, retiring, gentle, almost reverential in tone, a highly cultivated artist and a citizen of outspoken loyalty.

He was suffering, he told us, from lead poisoning, his third attack, and had been laid up for months. "My visit to Washington has done me good," he said, and Adams replied, "I am proud to be your host and physician."

He had heard of me through Howells and knew something of my insistence upon "Americanism in Art" and at once said, "On the whole I agree with you. The older I grow," here he addressed the group, "the more certain I am that we of the New World must do things in our own way."

He was a fluent talker, quiet, with a delicate fancy, and as he, like Stoddard and Adams, was a great traveler, the conversation mainly sailed the South Seas, touching at Hawaii, Fiji, Japan, China, and Cambodia with equal ease. Only as they reached the Nile did Stoddard fall behind.

Adams was a strange man. Relentless in judgment, he had a timid glance. It appeared to me that he was much less savage than his brother. He remained kindly, hospitable, and charming. As I left Washington soon after this dinner, I never saw him again.

At my hotel, for several days, Susan B. Anthony was a much admired figure. She had been a warning and an inspiration in the public life of women for forty years and we had met (as fellow cranks) on various platforms. She was a handsome old woman, with a strong, fine face, not precisely masculine yet with too much strength in it to be that of an ordinary grandmother. Her eyes were introspective. She appeared at times to be looking out through peepholes in a mask. Her face was expressionless, but she was not dead or even dozing. She was very much alive.

II

At the Cosmos Club I walked among swarms of specialists, men who knew all about bugs, earthquakes, electric machines, Hottentots, and air currents, a singular company, each man walking his narrow way exact and dryly cautious. I found it exceedingly difficult to develop with them any general conversational theme. Literature as I understood it and imagination as they understood it, were out of place in their world. That we who paint and model and write are equally one-sided I readily concede, but we have many enthusiasms, rages, and revolts, which these scientists have not. They pursue a cold, undeviating course whereas writers are forced to be sympathetic with other interests. It was this catholicity of interest which made Theodore Roosevelt so astounding.

There was in him a love for all of the fine arts—except music. I do not think he cared much for music.

When he learned that I was about to start for the Klondike by way of the Overland Trail, he invited me to have a farewell dinner at his house.

He was living alone at this time, for Mrs. Roosevelt and the children were still at Sagamore Hill, and the only other guest was a son of Senator Lodge, a fine lad of twenty-one.

As he introduced us he said, "Cabot, this man is about to hit the Overland Trail for the Yukon River, and by George! I wish I were going with him. I'd be inclined to do it if it were not for the possibility of a Spanish War."

"Our differences will never lead to actual war," I declared, but he was equally certain that the break would come and come soon; then, as we drew up to the table, he beamed at me and said, "To think I have again at my table a man who knows the difference between an aparejo and a parfleche!"—and for an hour our talk was almost entirely of Colorado trails and Montana valleys, to which young Lodge listened with rapt attention, expressing now and then his hope of some time seeing the High Country in my company.

Roosevelt asked me about my Grant history and this led to my saying, "I have been for two years among the vanishing legion. It is appalling to count the number of Grant's soldiers, subordinates, and opponents who have dropped away in two years. This work should have been done ten years ago."

We then returned to the discussion of a possible war with Spain, and I asked, "Will it not be mainly a naval war?"

"Yes, the navy would play a big part in it."

"I begin to see why you resigned your position in New York. You are in a strategic position here."

He smiled. "I am not a swivel-chair officer. If war comes I'll go in as a field officer of some sort."

That night I made this record of him:

"I dined to-day with Theodore Roosevelt, the present Assistant Secretary of the Navy, a man who is likely to be much in the public eye during his lifetime. A man of great energy, of good impulses, and undoubted ability. A passionate lover of the wild country and of the plains life. He is strong physically, full of talk, always interesting, ofttimes vividly so. He is not unlike Kipling in physical frame, strong-necked, square-headed, and deep-chested. He is a man of powerful prejudices and intense dislikes, but manly and just in his impulses."

CHAPTER TWENTY-NINE

ANOTHER ADVENTUROUS INTERLUDE

As the end of my history approached, I began to think with elation of "hitting the trail" for the Klondike. I had secured all the information which the Canadian Government offered—I had taken a journey to Ottawa to talk with Clifford Sifton, Minister of the Interior, and with Dawson, the National Geographer, in order to glean any more recent reports which might be floating about the capital.

Dawson smiled when I asked for the latest and most accurate maps of the Telegraph Trail. "We have no such maps. No one has been through that trail, not even the Indians, for they know only such part of it as lies within their own hunting grounds. No one knows the course of the rivers—except in a general way. However, we are sending out a crew to blaze the trail. If you will wait till they get through and report, we'll know more about it."

"I can't wait," I replied. "I want to start as soon as there is grass for my horses—and I have arranged to meet my partner in Ashcroft on the first of May."

This partner, Babcock, was a singular character, an old playmate who had ridden the Iowa prairies with me twenty-eight years before, a man of about my own age. He had been living for some years in a small town on Puget Sound, but was acquainted with a wide range. Beginning as a student of theology, he had by some mysterious sequence of mental changes become a fearless trailer in the mountains of Washington and Oregon, and was wildly eager to take this overland route to the gold fields. He was too poor to pay his own way and had welcomed my offer to take him in with me, waiting impatiently for my final instructions.

At this point I must make note of two rather significant happenings in my literary career. On my return from Ottawa I stopped for a few days in New York and called to say good-by to Howells. In my talk of "the last great trail to the American wilderness," I laid before him one of the maps which Dawson had given me and said, "At this point I go in, and at this point I come out, over a thousand miles of unknown country;" and as I said this, Howells looked at me in wonder. In his glance I saw my action reflected as a dangerous as well as a foolish project. I had a vision of myself, a minute insect, crawling over icy mountains, swimming dangerous rivers, and wandering in trackless forests. Suppose I broke an ankle? Suppose I fell sick in that wilderness?

These possibilities led me to consider the making of some sort of record of my career up to this time; and immediately after my return to Washington, I dictated to a most expert typist a rough chronicle of two migrating families, the Garlands and the McClintocks, under the title, "The Life of Grant McLane," a manuscript which later became the basis of "A Son of the Middle Border." "If I don't get through, or fail to return," I said to Richard Burton, "this manuscript will present certain phases of my life on the Western border."

Up to this time my records had been irregular and often undated, but now, feeling the need of a daily jotting, I bought a small diary and so began a series which reaches to this present hour, a shelf of journals upon whose entries I now depend for an accurate report of my impressions and moods for nearly thirty-two years. As I look at that first little faded, ragged little volume, I experience a sense of security. I feel under my feet the reef of solid fact. I can smell the camp-fire smoke, and hear again the rush of glacial streams. The steady drum of raindrops sounds upon my tent, and I *know* that journey was not a dream.

According to this record, I left West Salem April 19, 1898, for British Columbia with intent to lead a pack train over the Telegraph Trail from Ashcroft to the Skeena River, and from the Skeena Forks across a still wilder trail to the third fork of the Stikine River. Burton Babcock had agreed to meet me at Ashcroft. He was a veritable gold seeker, whereas I was merely seeking adventure and a more advanced schooling in the art of the trailer.

For several years I had been going to the Rockies, but they were no longer wild enough to suit me; I wished to explore the primitive. Believing this to be the last opportunity to share in a westward march in any degree comparable to that which my ancestors had made across the Allegheny Mountains, I turned my history over to my publisher and set forth into the North.

Babcock met me as agreed and with an outfit of five pack ponies and two saddle horses we started up the valley of the Fraser. At Fraser we purchased an additional pack animal and entered upon the long and almost forgotten Telegraph Trail. For seventy-eight days we rode through mud and rain in endless forests. We were eaten by insects and worn down by the toil of the trail. High in the mountains we got beyond any definite blazing. Traveling alone we found our way across the tundra of the alpine meadows by "the lay of the land."

It was not a dangerous journey, but it was not the pleasant outing I had visioned. It rained almost every day in the Skeena Valley. We camped in the rain, cooked in the rain, saddled in the rain, and rode in the rain, while the wet willows sloshed millions of tons of water upon us. I got my schooling in trailing, but it was not precisely exhilarating.

To express our mood I can not do better than quote a short verse which I wrote on my saddle, condensing in a few lines the spirit of our journey.

RELENTLESS NATURE

> She laid her rivers to snare us,
> She set her snows to chill,
> Her clouds had the cunning of vultures,
> Her plants were charged to kill.
> The glooms of her forests benumbed us,
> On the slime of her ledges we sprawled—
> But we set our feet to the northward,
> And crawled and crawled and crawled!
> We defied her, and cursed her, and shouted:
> "To hell with your rain and your snow.
> Our minds we have set on a journey,
> And despite of your anger we go!"

After nearly eighty days of this wearisome and melancholy progress, we came down with other bands of gold seekers to the Third Fork of the Stikine River, thin, ragged, and hungry, too late in the season to cross the divide between the Stikine and the Hotalinqua, as we had planned to do.

After resting at Glenora, a Hudson Bay trading post, I decided that to raft down the Yukon so late in the year would be to "freeze in" somewhere on its shores, and when news of my mother's illness reached me I turned my outfit over to my partner, reserving only my horse, Ladrone, a beautiful saddler, Arabian in his markings and intelligence. He had saved my life several times on the trail and to leave him in that desolate country to starve or freeze (as all the other horses must surely do) would have been criminally ungrateful, and when the last Hudson Bay steamer arrived, I purchased a place for him as well as for myself. "You carried me over a thousand miles of dangerous trail, now you shall go with me in state," I said to him as we started for the coast with intent to catch a steamer for Seattle.

While waiting at Wrangell in glorious golden autumn sunshine, I caught the news of a new gold rush from Skagway into the Atlin Lake country, and at once resolved to take a hand in it. It seemed necessary to complete my education. Leaving my horse in pasture, I sailed for Skagway on a small boat densely crowded with excited prospectors.

Outfitting again in Skagway, I crossed the infamous White Pass, a grim and grievous way, and took passage on a scow sailing from Lake Bennett to Tagish Water. From here we portaged over to Atlin Lake. From Atlin City (a group of tents) I prospected the neighboring streams for two weeks and finally located a placer claim on a creek. Late in September I turned my mine over to my partner, an Englishman, and I left for the coast—and home.

From Lake Bennett I walked thirty-five miles over a high pass through fog and rain and down to Dyea harbor in less than ten hours—one of the most exhausting days I ever endured. During the last two hours of this journey I waded an icy stream a dozen times, my legs so numb with cold and weariness that I could scarcely feel the ground beneath my feet. At ten o'clock I reached a hotel, a fire, and some hot soup!

Early the next day I caught a steamer for Wrangell, where I picked up my faithful horse and went on to Seattle. Loading Ladrone in a box car with a supply of hay and water, I set out over the range on the Northern Pacific Railway, leaving him to follow. At Missoula I waited for him to overtake me. He was well and resigned. At Livingstone and Bismarck and also St. Paul I waited for him, and at last we arrived together at West Salem, Wisconsin.

I had been gone a little over five months. I had no gold to show and to bring my horse out with me had cost over a thousand dollars; but I was rich in knowledge. I had served a severe apprenticeship. "No one can tell me anything about riding the trail," I said to my friends. "I am now a master trailer."

I put this into some lines:

What have I gained by the toil of the trail?
I know and know well.
I have broadened my hand to the cinch and the axe,
I have laid my flesh to the rain;
As hunter and trailer and guide
I have touched the most primitive wildness again.
I have threaded the wood with the wild deer's stealth,
No eagle is freer than I;
No mountain can thwart me, no torrent appall,
I defy the stern sky.
So long as I live these joys will remain;
I have touched the most primitive wildness again.

Three days after my return, while helping my father build a fence to form a pasture for my horse, I was approached by a neighbor, who handed me a package from the post office. It was a copy of my story of General Grant, the first copy I had seen. I opened it and glanced through it, my father waiting impatiently meanwhile; then putting it on the top of a post I returned to my spade. I had no sense of importance in either fiction or biography at the moment.

In the same mail came a letter from John Phillips saying, "I have read the bundle of Klondike poems you sent us and I like them so well that I intend to print several pages of them in an early number of *McClure's Magazine*."

This letter gave me pleasure, for these lines had been written while in the saddle, or at the camp fire surrounded by clouds of mosquitos. "Whatever else they lack," I had written Phillips, "they are direct reactions from the environment they claim to depict."

These few months had done more. They had cut me off from all historical research. "Henceforth I am the novelist," was my definite resolution. I set to work next day on a story which I had begun at Livingstone while waiting for my faithful pony to arrive, a story which began under the title, "The Eagle's Heart."

CHAPTER THIRTY

JOAQUIN MILLER IN CHICAGO

I

CHICAGO, gay with flags and filled with cheering crowds, was celebrating the close of the war with Spain when I returned to it in October. As I listened to the marching bands and heard the comment of the crowd, I was aware of my complete detachment from its emotion. "It was only a little war," Roosevelt had said, and it had come and gone whilst I was in the wilderness concerned with trails, rocks, and rivers. Santiago, San Juan Hill, and Manila Bay meant nothing to me except as they involved the fame of certain of my friends. Going straight to my desk in Elm Street, I resumed work upon "The Eagle's Heart," which I had begun while traveling through Montana and Dakota.

On meeting Lorado Taft and Henry Fuller, I found them almost as unaffected by the war as I; but Stephen Crane, Richard Harding Davis, and many other of my New York friends had won distinction as war correspondents. Some of them had taken on grandeur by their service, but Crane, it appeared, had made a failure of it. He was not a reporter. He wrote of his own reactions to events and not of the events themselves. Furthermore, he had met with certain physical mishaps which had prevented him from reaching the war front. Although he made the most of his own psychology in the situation I found it all rather comical in outcome.

Shortly after my return to my desk in Mrs. Watter's home on Elm Street, Joaquin Miller sought me out. He, too, had taken part in the Klondike rush. He had carried a pack over the Chilkoot Pass and rafted down to Dawson, where he had shared a miner's cabin. He had come East under contract to lecture on the vaudeville stage. "Garland," he said earnestly, "you must look after me while I'm in Chicago. I can take care of myself in the mountains or in the woods. I'm at home on the back of a cayuse, but this town scares me. Any minute a trolley car is liable to ramp around a corner and jump on me."

"All right," I replied. "I'll look after you every afternoon. How long are you going to stay?"

"Two weeks or more. My durn contract calls for two addresses each day."

He had changed greatly in seven years. With his long hair now very gray and his flowing beard he suggested Tolstoy, but his dress was picturesquely Western. He wore a broad-brimmed hat, a long black frock coat, dark trousers, and cowboy boots; and his overcoat, a superb wolf-skin garment which came nearly to his ankles, carried a double row of oblong yellow buttons each about the size of my thumb. Upon closer examination these turned out to be nuggets of gold.

"See here!" I said. "You're not going about Chicago with these nuggets on your coat?"

"Oh, yes," he replied, and thrusting his hand into his pocket displayed a fist-full of other smaller nuggets. "No one will think they are real."

There was some truth in that, for I would not have known their value; and we started out to lunch with two of his friends.

The reader must remember that Miller was not only a dramatist and poet, he was the son of a typical overland pioneer, and a lifelong adventurer. As a lad of ten he had crossed the plains to Oregon with his father and mother. He had lived with the California Indians. He had acted as scout, horse herd, and miner. He had camped with Walker, the famed filibuster, in Nicaragua. He had ridden pony express in the Sierras, the most strenuous and dangerous occupation of those strenuous and dangerous days, and he was just returned from the Klondike. In him the wearing of a broad hat, jack-boots, and long hair was not an affectation; it was a habit of dress persisting from his days on the far border.

His trust in me arose from the fact that I not only knew the horse and the mountain trail but was Western born— a neighbor. His reliance upon me touched me and amused me. He followed me with the meekness of a country lad, waiting for me to lead him across the street and trusting me to locate the restaurant in which we were to meet two of his friends.

He told me of them. "P. B. Weare," he said, "has done more to destroy the wild fowl and wild animals of the middle West than any other man I know. For years he was a merchant in fur and game. John J. Healey is the man who put the first steamboat on the Yukon. He is the Kit Carson of the Northwest."

We made a remarkable group at the table. Healey was a small, quiet, graceful man of sixty with wide and varied experiences in the wilderness, while Weare, a slightly younger man, was a bald, alert, keen-eyed business man. That he possessed a vein of poetry was evident, for almost immediately he said, "My house is in the middle of a piece of virgin prairie. I don't allow any one to touch a weed or flower on it. If you come out you'll find all the blooms and grasses natural to the season."

The restaurant was crowded and as all my companions were low-voiced it was not easy for me to follow their talk; but I permitted no word to escape me. It was like reliving the scenes of an epic. Healey and Joaquin had faced the cold winds, barren peaks, and tumultuous rivers of Alaska. They had been hungry, on the trail, weary to numbness, and many times in danger of death by beast and savage. They knew every phase of mountain life, yet here they sat quite unnoticed in a commonplace Chicago restaurant. Something tremendously moving went with their low, unhurried reminiscences.

At the close of our meal, Healey, who was a man of substance, asked the waiter for the bill, but Joaquin interposed. "No, no, John, this is on me."

"Nothing of the kind," retorted Healey, as he rose and took from his trousers pocket a roll of bills.

Joaquin also rose and reaching back under the tail of his long coat said in level, deadly monotone, "Sit down, or I'll kill you—right where you stand!"

Healey laughed and dropped back into his chair. "All right, Joaquin. It's your ante. Go ahead."

It was a fine piece of play-acting, but it was a revealing glimpse of the old Indian fighter, the man who had ridden pony express in the mountains of Idaho, some forty years before. It amused me greatly, as I suppose Joaquin intended it to do, but he gave no sign of humor and made no reference to it afterward.

In accordance with my promise, I met him every day and guided him about the city which deeply interested him. He had not seen it or any of the large cities for many years, and his poetic quality and his prophetic earnestness so won me that I led him to the Fine Arts Building and introduced him to Taft, Clarkson, and other of my artist friends.

He was deeply impressed with this building and spoke of "the elegance, the gayety, and the refinement" of its studio floor. "This puts soul into Chicago," he said.

Taft, attracted by the poet's noble head, asked him to sit for a portrait bust. To this, Miller readily consented.

I then suggested that he should allow Clarkson to do a painting of him at the same time. "All right," he said pleasantly. "Whatever the gentle Garland commands shall be done."

All this will surprise those of my readers who have imagined an entirely different Joaquin Miller, but such was the man I knew. He soon won the respect of Taft and Clarkson, and as I sat near him during each sitting, he talked on many subjects with such precision and such quiet dignity that we were all delighted with him. He was the seer at times, passionately mystical, uttering great concepts with biblical simplicity and precision.

He gave voice to the most beautiful fancies concerning trees and flowers, but was capable of strong words when they seemed called for. He was a mixture of mountaineer, storyteller, and poet, as his dress indicated. With his broad hat laid aside, he presented a profile which resembled Whitman's and his full face suggested Tolstoy. On social themes he spoke like a prophet.

He wore boots because he had always done so and because they had associations with the West he loved; and his gallantry in the presence of women was of the same tradition. "What do you do besides looking pretty?" he asked one of my writer friends. He stroked the hair of another as if she were a child. She *was* a child to him, and in his eyes shone a remote look as though dreaming of a far time in a far country.

He said things which might be called rustic, but which were always accompanied by a look or gesture which put a comedy touch upon them. When John Vance Cheney, an old friend, invited him to dinner and added, "I'll come and get you if you want me to," he exclaimed, "Will ye now! That'll be dog-gone nice of you."

After the second sitting he glanced at Clarkson's sketch and remarked quizzically, "I see you're digging the old man out of the shadow."

To Henry Fuller he remarked, while looking at the bust Taft had made, "That is a great head. It ought to do good work, if it hasn't done so already"—and a whimsical tone came into his voice.

He talked of his life in London—of Whistler, Rossetti, and Swinburne. He told the famous story of his call on Swinburne with a well-known writer who claimed to be a friend of Swinburne.

"We sent up our names as 'Joaquin Miller the American poet, and friend.' The irascible old poet sent back word, 'Bring the American poet up and tell the friend to go to hell!'

"Whistler was the light of London when I was there," he said, and later he added, "He was used to sheriffs, there was always one around his studio. . . . There is only one thing more vulgar than boasting of your high birth and that is boasting of your low birth. I was born in Indiana. My father's people were Kentuckians, of Scotch descent, but my mother was of Pennsylvania-German family. Father was a good deal of a Quaker—he never fired a gun in his life. He was a school-teacher and people called him 'Squire.' I was about eight when he decided to go to the Coast over the Oregon Trail. This was in 1851. . . . Grant was stationed near our home in Oregon. He was a good, clean man. I went fishing with him once. He remembered this long after when I met him in the White House at a big reception to a visiting nobleman. He and the duke were standing to receive a crowd of people. As I came up he said, 'I remember you. You put worms on my fish-hook in Oregon.'

"I do all my writing in bed," he said in answer to some question by Clarkson. "I don't want 'the literary stoop.' I leave that to the Yankees. Time has squat heavily on my shoulders and bent 'em a little—but I won't acknowledge even that."

He carried himself with simple dignity, and his silken shirt, golden necktie, and frock coat became him well. Although not lacking in humor he was essentially serious. One story which he told with comical intent bore upon the enormous numbers of salmon which used to make their way up the rivers to spawn. "Father had to build a fence to keep them off the pasture grass," he said, and pretended great surprise when we doubted his word. He described in splendid phrase his run through the White Horse Rapids on his way to Dawson, filling the passage with mystery and drama.

He told us of his life in Washington City and of the log cabin he had built out near Rock Creek. "I made that my home for four years, but I was away much of the time. I didn't like it there. Congressmen and their silly wives wore me out. They all came to Washington as the great men in little towns, and their women, raw, silly, curious, had nothing better to do than to seek out Joaquin Miller, 'the man who lived in a tree.' They made life miserable for me and I fled."

"It must be almost as bad in Oakland," I said.

"It is. I shall go down to posterity as one of the vainest men who ever lived, by reason of the cameras leveled at me. They come to my home in throngs; they get mother on their side—she is so kind and easily managed—and when I appear their guns are all set for me. *Snap! Bang!* I am taken every time I turn a corner."

The third sitting was especially merry. As I guided the old mountaineer along the street he hummed a song. At the elevator he bantered the boy whom he called "Robin." "Careful, Robin, don't take us through the roof!" He alluded to Taft as "the Lord of Mud," and said to Clarkson, "I *have* known painters who were at once clever and good looking." He kept us laughing with similar remarks which were all the more amusing coming from such a venerable face and figure. He was a compound of Tolstoy and Walt Whitman.

His head was magnificent, but he wore his long mustaches waxed and pointed, insisting that Taft should so represent them. "They are significant," he said; and so indeed they were. They denoted that curious mingling of dandy, sage, and poet—which he was.

These two weeks' association with him increased my liking and my admiration. We talked incessantly of red men, the plains, the Oregon Trail, gold mining, Walker of Nicaragua; and while we talked we both forgot the smoky, tumultuous town. There was something tremendous in the contrasts and oppositions he suggested. He typified our far Western literary life with all its interwoven glories, grandeurs, and crudities. He was at once mystic and miner, sage and mountaineer. He had no vanity about his work. He knew that it was a hodge-podge; and when I said, "Joaquin, your poems need editing, ruthless blue-penciling," he smiled and said, "All right, Youth, go ahead and do it."

He was never bitter or unkind in any comment, and my only dislike of him was in his over-gallant attitude toward women. That softness was unworthy of him. In most ways he was of large stature, with an epic outdoor quality. Without knowing enough about it to say so definitely, I felt that his susceptibility to women had wrecked many of his grand plans. With them he was incurably Byronic in gesture, and yet he was a tender, loyal, and obedient son. He loved and cherished his mother throughout her long life. He was a great character, far greater than his writing—and some of his writing is nobly great. I was sorry when he took my hand in parting.

I never saw him again, but last year I went by motor up the long road to "The Heights," to pay tribute to his memory. I hardly knew the place. A forest had sprung up where his orchards had been. The pipes of his fountain were rusted and broken. His tiny "cathedral"—tinier than I had remembered it—was closed, but in his mother's cabin a caretaker showed me a few dusty, faded, pathetic reminders of him, a kind of scrapheap which I know he would have destroyed if he could, but on a stone post outside the door a bronze tablet testifies to the regard in which California holds this most illustrious of its poets.

CHAPTER THIRTY-ONE

ANOTHER WINTER IN NEW YORK

I

WHILE Joaquin Miller was still lecturing in the vicinity of Chicago, Israel Zangwill (whom we had all come to know through his "Children of the Ghetto" and more intimately by his essays in *The Chap-Book*) came to town and set everybody talking of him and his novels. No recent visitor had so deeply stirred Western literary circles. His wit, his humor, and his brilliancy of comment quite won the reporters, and long accounts of him filled the daily press. Naturally the Jews of the city took an exuberant pride in him— their modern Disraeli.

At his request I called for him one afternoon at the home of one of his Jewish friends on the South Side and piloted him down to the Fine Arts Building, a most distinguished progress, for he insisted on walking and was almost as noticeable as Joaquin Miller, albeit in a different way. Dozens of people recognized him as we paced the boulevard, but he, with a brain swimming in seas of new impressions, appeared unconscious of the smiles and comments of admirers. He was filled with wonder of the city. "Think of it!" he exclaimed, "this place was a happy hunting ground only half a century ago! Extraordinary!"

His cushion of thick, black, curly hair was topped by a soft rag of a hat, so small that it fantastically emphasized his large and very plain face. I considered him one of the ugliest men I had ever seen, but, like Disraeli's, it was an interesting ugliness, relieved by pleasant brown eyes and an expression of kindliness and alert good humor. His walk was an irregular and uncertain shuffle, always out of step and bumping occasionally into me. His feet never once got into rhythm with mine, but he kept up a steady stream of self-derisive and witty comment which compensated for the irritation of his awkwardness.

He personified literary London as Joaquin Miller represented the Sierras. He was entirely urban. He talked precisely like his essays in *The Chap-Book,* wittily, fluently on all sorts of literary subjects and I had nothing to do but applaud and keep him from being destroyed by callous coachmen and truck drivers.

In due course we reached haven at the Press Club, where he had promised to meet several local writers—among them Opie Read and Will Payne. He was especially pleased with Opie, who represented something typically Southern. "He is the spirit of Kentucky and Arkansas," I explained afterward.

At five I took Zangwill to the "Little Room" where he met Taft, Clarkson, and others of its members. All were impressed with his detailed knowledge of studio life in Paris, and with the workers of modern literature. He knew every phase of London and his lecture on the drama which took place in Music Hall that night was like one of his essays, adroit and humorous. When I went in back to congratulate him, he met me with a self-derisive smile. "What do you suppose I did?" he demanded. "I forgot to remove my goloshes. I lectured in them!" This so amused and embarrassed him that he hardly heard our praise of his address.

For several days I saw much of him. In the midst of

racial adulators, intellectual beggars, and persistent journalists, he found me (so he said) a consolation and my study a refuge. At his insistence I attended one formal dinner and sat beside him, the only Gentile in the midst of several hundred of his Jewish admirers, who must have wondered at my presence. At his request I aided him in meeting certain leading citizens who interested him, and at my suggestion he also sat for Taft, who made a rapid sketch of him, a remarkably good likeness.

And through it all he impressed us as a kindly, self-cultured, highly individualized dreamer, rapt and swift-thoughted. Shambling of foot, he had an amazingly self-contained, powerful, and ready brain. His front face had something spiritual and fine in it, but his profile, like that of Savonarola, was old—centuries old, sorrowfully old, and quaintly ugly.

His mind darted about in bewilderingly unexpected ways. He replied to all questions with instant reaction, never repeating himself, and when he paused, as he sometimes did for an instant, a roguish glint came into his eyes and then— out bubbled the unexpected phrase! His witty replies sometimes made his questioner appear foolish, but there was no malice in his fun.

When about to leave for New York he said, "You must come to London. You have many friends over there now. They'll find you as American as Joaquin Miller, though in a different fashion."

This brought up the question of English dress and English dinner customs. "You forget that I am just an old trailer. I have no high hat and no evening suit."

"Neither has Bernard Shaw. He goes everywhere in tweeds—but then he is Shaw—you must have the proper uniform. As soon as you arrive I'll introduce you to my tailor and in a few days you'll be clothed to meet nobility."

I protested, "We of the mid-West consider the swallow-tail coat undemocratic."

"You are all wrong there. It is the most democratic of garments. When you are encased in correct evening dress you will be indistinguishable from an earl or—a waiter."

There was force in this, but I went on with the threadbare statement, "It isn't so much the swallow-tail coat as the high hat and all that goes with it—and besides, I can't afford it."

"You're wrong again. A good suit will last ten years and they never go out of fashion, and you can wear any kind of studs and ties you like."

Outwardly firm, I was inwardly weakening, for on several recent dates I had found myself shut out from literary meetings of great interest just for lack of appropriate apparel. To go to London as Joaquin Miller had done, wearing a sombrero and jack-boots, would be to imitate an outworn audacity. "You're right," I admitted. "The time has come to abandon my mid-Western prejudices against dress suits. My frontier prejudices must give way—even if I don't go to London."

The story of my Klondike experiences was still unsold, and with this and other literary business in hand, I now planned another invasion of New York. Chicago publishing had failed me again. Stone & Kimball had dissolved partnership and my books were without a printer. My only sources of income were the magazines, supplemented by an occasional lecture or reading, and the only market for my manuscript was Manhattan Island. Theoretically Chicago should have been an increasingly important literary center. Actually it had lost ground. *The Chap-Book* had failed, and Way

& Williams another ambitious firm of book publishers, had given up the struggle. The city had no literary or artistic club other than our informal Little Room, which met in Ralph Clarkson's studio on Friday afternoons. The outlook was disheartening. While not as pessimistic as Fuller, I admitted a partial defeat.

Nevertheless, as I set about the packing of my trunk, I experienced more strongly than ever before a distaste for pulling up stakes. "Soon I shall be among those who are content to move in a groove," I wrote. "Perhaps I am wrong. It may be that I would suffer if I were to stay six months in any one place. For seven years I have been on the go. What my state of mind would be after a year's continuous life under the same roof, it is impossible to tell. This tendency is something to be reckoned with in my dream of becoming a family man."

II

One of the first of my New York friends to greet me was Brander Matthews, who heartened me greatly by praising my "Life of Grant" which he had just reviewed for the *Book Buyer*, and my first evening was spent with Howells, who was eager to hear all about the Klondike Trail. "Of course you will make a book of it," he said.

"I'm going to try," I replied.

My mood was not exultant, as the following entry shows: "From my anchorite cell on East Twenty-fifth Street I look out on the gray skies which roof New York and am not cheerful. . . . Last night I finished reading for McClure the manuscript novel of an unknown Indiana novelist, the glorification of a small town, very sweet and fine, the best of its kind. Booth Tarkington is the name of the author—

possibly a pen name. No one knows him. McClure should publish the story serially."

On returning the manuscript, "The Gentleman from Indiana," I seized the opportunity to say, "Why not print an American serial? It may be that your people are getting a little tired of your English romances."

John Phillips, the editor, assured me that they intended to use the story. "Sam has wired the author to come on. He lives in Indianapolis. We regard this story as a good one on which to base a change of policy."

While still in McClure's office, Stephen Crane came in. I had not seen him for a year and he looked yellow and dingy and the fingers of his right hand were soaked with nicotine. He had just returned from Havana and his speech was full of odd turns of thought as he told of his experiences. He appeared physically delicate, less vigorous than when I saw him first and I recorded my impression:

"He was carelessly dressed and used an English accent on some of his words. He was not overwhelmed with joy at sight of me, and his gaze was less frank than at our last meeting. His attitude toward me has changed. He is not a man of long life."

I set this down as it was written at the time, for it gives my precise impression of Crane. Since our last meeting he had become mixed up with several unsavory episodes, affairs which he knew I viewed with disgust. I really liked the boy and was saddened by his evident deterioration. It was long afterward that I learned how deeply he valued my friendship.

My Christmas started with a melancholy breakfast in a ratty place near by, and I spent the entire day in my room rereading the autobiographical chronicles which I had so hurriedly dictated in the Congressional Library just before leaving for the Klondike. I became so interested in the possibilities of the manuscript that I read right on to the end, and registered my impression: "It is very crude and must be rewritten, but it seems to me, to-night, that if I could tell the story precisely as it unrolled, it would make an interesting book," but I added, "I am too young to write an autobiography. One doesn't do such books at thirty-eight."

"Frederick Remington was at the club to-day in one of his most cantankerous moods. After complimenting me on taking the long trail to the Klondike, he said, 'From all I hear, you are a master trailer. No one can teach you anything about running a pack train!' From this he ran off into a long, confused monologue in which he repeated again and again: 'You mustn't criticize the army in its relation to the Indians— military men best friends of Indian. You mustn't criticize the army. Army's all right!' He is never fluent even when at his best, and on this occasion he was at his worst—truculent and hesitant. Bryanites and Injuns were all sons of dogs together. He evidently had me confused with those who argue that army officers should not control the reservations. 'You know the West,' he admitted. 'You were born out there—but you mustn't abuse the army!' Seeing that he was in no mood to listen to me, I made no reply and slipped away at the earliest moment.

"I don't like him or his illustrations. His red men and trappers are all drawn from one model. All his trappers have close-set eyes and bushy beards, and his red men are savages without being graceful. He does not see the Western men and Indians as I see them. With all these reservations in my mind, I can not be chummy with him even when he is in genial mood. I admire certain aspects of his work. He is a man of power but has very little poetry in his writing or illustrations. I don't see how he does so much work."

Zangwill having written me that he was staying with Daniel Guggenheim, I called on him there, finding him in a vast guest chamber littered with manuscript and clothing, a comical mess, through which he scuffled, kicking aside shoes and shirts in absent-minded fury of haste. "I am going to call on a painter friend of mine, Louis Loeb. Come along with me and then take me to see Howells as you promised to do."

This I did and it was a most interesting experience for me, as it undoubtedly was for them. Both were keen observers and each studied the other with frank curiosity. Howells was serious, almost sad in effect and modest almost to the point of humbleness in his claims or lack of claims. "I am of a past fashion," he said in effect.

Zangwill, less freakish than with me, addressed Howells with high respect, breaking out now and again with a quaint phrase which brought a chuckle from his host. Both men apparently enjoyed the meeting. On the way out Zangwill was unusually silent, as if pondering something. At last he said, "Howells' humility is surprising. I have never known a man so eminent to be so modest. It is amazing!"

On January 8th, I went up to dine with the Hernes, at whose home I felt welcome at any time. Our talk was all of their new play, "Griffith Davenport," which was in rehearsal at this time. I could not tell him so, but I was less interested in this play than in any of his others, mainly for the reason that it was based on a book by another writer.

He asked me to come in and see the rehearsal and this I did the following night, a most exhausting experience. Richard Burton went with me and sat through one act and fled. To listen to Herne's endless repetition of lines and business was destructive. I marveled at his patience and endurance and in the end came away limp as a rag. My brain echoed for hours with his hammering drill. For me it was all a waste of time. I served no purpose. I could not tell him what I really thought, which was that the last act was feeble and inconclusive and that it ought to be entirely reconstructed. That he would not do this was certain, for he was too deeply enmeshed with the facts of the novel, the "Unofficial Patriot," which Helen Gardner had written as a piece of family history.

On my return to the club, I found a letter from Henry James, inviting me to visit him at Rye whenever I came to England. This invitation moved me and gratified me. To have this remote and subtle critic like my work was marvelous. He was more alien to my world than any other American writer. For fifteen years I had read him, with no hope of gaining his interest. His judgment was as much the "judgment of posterity" as that of any English novelist—not excepting Thomas Hardy. I wrote him that his letter had found me considering a summer in England and that nothing would give me greater pleasure than a visit to him.

In lunching with Brander Matthews, one of my most congenial companions, I discussed James' letter and the cost of a summer in England. "You should go," he said. "You should know London and Paris—nothing else matters, but before you go I want you to know more of Columbia University and to meet its president, Nicholas Murray Butler."

At the close of our meal he took me to call on Butler, whom he called "Murray," a handsome and vigorous man of about my own age, cordial, humorous, and ready of speech. I liked him, notwithstanding the fact that he had been responsible for much of Edward MacDowell's worries. As a modern college president, he believed in being practical and demanded that all departments should be useful to a large number of students, and the university which gave off an air of newness, roominess, and solidity, represented him. I felt in it his abounding energy and practical scholarship.

The possibility of going to England gave me a great deal of thought, and when one of my editorial friends spoke of Piccadilly as familiarly as he named Fifth Avenue, I plied him with questions concerning prices at hotels and lodging houses, and the cost of steamship tickets. It was to me a much more serious adventure than my five thousand mile trip into British Columbia and Alaska. Could I afford it?

This question was answered in an unexpected way. Among my fellow members at The Players was the publisher, George Brett, head of Macmillan, an American of about my own age, a slender, dark-complexioned man who never spoke except when he had something to say. We often met at lunch and on one or more occasions he had spoken to me of my work. "I know the West," he said one day. "I spent a year or two out there on a ranch. Your books mean more to me by reason of that experience."

It was his habit to eat his luncheon at the long central table, and afterward to retire to a particular leather couch in a particular corner of the sitting room and there smoke a pipe or cigar in meditative seclusion. Now and again I joined him on the couch, although I did not smoke. Early in January, on the fourteenth (to be exactly historic), as we were sitting together in this way, he suddenly said, "You were involved in that Stone & Kimball failure, weren't you?"

"I was, and in several other somewhat similar failures in Boston and Chicago. I am a Jonah."

He smoked for a moment in silence, then asked, "Why don't you put all your eggs in one basket and let me carry

them for you? I'll take over and republish your Stone &
Kimball books, provided you will agree to write for me a
story based on your recent Klondike experiences and a book
depicting your life as a boy on the Western plains. I will
advance you five hundred dollars against royalty on each of
the three old books and fifteen hundred against the other
two." He rose. "Think it over and let me know, soon," he
added and walked away leaving me in a daze.

For an hour I sat there going over all the implications
which this proposition presented. First of all I was
astounded to have such an offer from a man of Brett's known
acumen. He was held to be one of the ablest and least sentimental of all our publishers and I had never before sus-
picioned in him such confidence in my books. His way of
speech was coldly level, laconic, unhesitating. He had not
said, "I believe in you and I like what you are doing." He
had made an offer which spoke in dollars.

For the second time in my life I attained a slight sense of
security in the future. Recognizing the solidity and high
standing of his house, I knew that whatever he promised
would be carried out. Even at that time he was acknowledged to be one of the soundest men in the publishing world,
and on the strength of his offer, I began to plan improve-
ments on my West Salem homestead and to dream of buying
a certain farm which my father coveted, a forecast of prosperity which was emphasized that very day by a check from
Doubleday & McClure in payment of royalty earned by my
little book, "The Spirit of Sweetwater."

Having disposed of my unhatched chickens in this way, I
considered my obligations. "First of all, 'Rose of Dutcher's
Coulée' must be entirely remade, for it is full of irritating
errors. Then the Klondike story must be finished at once.

Third, 'Boy Life on the Prairie,' though partly written, must be reshaped and enlarged. The other books will only require proof-reading!"

To Zangwill I said, "From a period of hesitation and stagnation, I am called upon to plunge into a winter of most strenuous labor. All this work must be done before I can even consider a trip to London."

One of the first to be told of my good fortune was, of course, my elder brother, Howells. For the first time in my life I succeeded in luring him to lunch with me. He came into The Players in almost youthful health and spirits, clear-eyed and alert, and we had an hour or two of talk, delightfully witty and sympathetic on his part.

He was particularly pleased to think that "Main-Travelled Roads" was about to pass into safe hands. "It never pays to take the promise of high royalty from a poor firm rather than the actuality of lower rates from a reliable one," he said, and at the close of the conference asked me to lunch at his apartment. "Mrs. Howells wants to see you," he said. "She will rejoice in your good fortune and will advise you about steamships and London hotels."

"January 20. Just as I was dressing to go to Howells' home, John Burroughs came in, looking hale and hearty, bringing a suggestion of wintry landscapes and open fires. We had an hour's talk on all kinds of literary subjects. He was interested in what I told him of Zangwill and agreed to come to the club to-morrow and meet him. My luncheon at Howells' home was delightful, a revealing glimpse into the great novelist's intimate life. He is one of the most considerate husbands in the world and while his daughter frankly worships him, they are on terms of humorous literary companionship. As a family they all live on a very high plane, the plane of those widely read and widely traveled. For some reason which is obscure to me, Mrs. Howells likes me. Howells told me that she would see me when she would see no other visitor. She expressed pleasure when I told her of the new edition of 'Main-Travelled Roads,' which she praised again in terms I could not fully credit—although I took pleasure in hearing her say them. She also gave me detailed advice as to the location of my stateroom and how to avoid seasickness."

At noon the next day the contracts came from Macmillan's. I signed them at the club and turned them over to Brett, who pocketed them with hardly a change of countenance, merely saying, "I trust you are going to work on the books at once."

My record reads:

"The deed is done! I am committed to Macmillan's. I now have a real publisher. The Arena Company was of vital service to me at the first but it failed. Then I went to Schulte of Chicago and he got into trouble and quit. I joined Stone & Kimball in their attempt to build up a high-class publishing house in the mid-West. As a result they, too, fell into bankruptcy. We shall soon see whether Macmillan's can stand the shock of taking on such a Jonah as I appear to be."

That not even I could check their prosperous career is evident.

III

In the midst of my period of absorbed labor on the books for Macmillan's, I received a note from Howells saying, "Come in. I want to talk to you."

The matter which he wished to discuss with me was of

distinct historical significance. He said, "Last year the Social Science Institute, a very large and influential organization, created what is called a Department of Arts and Letters—a kind of informal academy, with power to split off whenever it is strong enough to do so. As one of the committee appointed to select the first hundred names, I have put down yours. It is now proposed by Stedman and Warner and Mabie to develop this annex into a separate institution with its own offices and by-laws. I'd like to have your aid in working out this plan."

This was my first knowledge of the enterprise and although I was rather vague about the charter under which it would operate, I agreed that the time had come for such an organization. "We have several authors' clubs and painters' clubs, but we have no *national* association of writers and artists. In a democracy like our own, we can not hope for an establishment by decree, and it seems to me the Social Science Institute has indicated the way of advance."

Howells asked me to see Hamilton Wright Mabie, who had accepted the temporary Secretaryship of the Institute— as it was finally decided to call it. "He is quite enthusiastically for it."

CHAPTER THIRTY-TWO

KIPLING RETURNS TO AMERICA

I

WHILE all my mornings were filled with work on my books and manuscripts, my afternoons were given to seeing my friends and doing whatever interested me. The month was rich in literary incident. For example—on the last day of January I saw the first performance of Herne's new play, "Griffith Davenport," a tense and painful evening. For the fourth time I shared the anxiety of an opening night. With him and Katharine I had suffered more keenly than with any other individuals outside my own family. With them I had endured the fear, the doubt, the agony of waiting which had been the invariable accompaniments of each new play's beginning; and now once again I was undergoing the familiar torture.

The daughters, Julie and Chrystal, whom I had known as tow-headed little girls, were now young ladies with real parts to enact (which they did very prettily), while their mother, looking much the same as when I first saw her, took the leading rôle with such grace and authority that she instantly won her audience. As for Herne himself, he was masterly in the title rôle, notwithstanding the distracting duties which fell to him as manager and producer. The play moved the audience powerfully and yet I confessed to a feeling of disappointment. I saw no future for it. It was too inconclusive, too fragmentary. It failed to clinch the nail. The audience went away admiring the Hernes but not in praise of the play. There was not enough of Herne in the writing. "He has been too loyal to the historical novel from which he has taken the story," they said, and they were right. The play was only a partial success.

As I was talking with John Phillips the following morning, McClure brought into the office a tall, dark, lean-faced youth whom he introduced as Booth Tarkington. "He is the author of that manuscript I gave you to read," he explained.

There was something in the quaintly ugly face of the young Hoosier which reminded me of Lincoln. "Your name really *is* Booth Tarkington," I said to him. "I thought it a pen name."

"Yes, Tarkington is my name and I can explain myself to you by saying that my aunt is Mary Jameson Judah, who has known you for many years."

This at once established a friendly understanding and we went away to lunch at The Players and to talk about Riley and other friends in Indiana. He confessed that he had been trying for five or six years to find acceptance of his manuscripts, and that my letter was one of the very first words of encouragement he had ever received.

"I got it just before McClure's wire of acceptance," he said with a happy smile.

He appeared a fine, serious, and very sensitive youth, sincere, gentle, and unspoiled. That he was exalted by McClure's praise was evident, but I conceded that he had a right to be exalted. His thin hands shook with emotion as he gave me the history of his novel. "I sent it to *McClure's* as a kind of final desperate venture. I had not been encouraged by my friends who had seen the manuscript, and when

I sent it away, I hadn't much faith that it would be even considered." As he said this, smiling across at me, I again caught something Lincoln-like in the modeling of his thin face.

"I don't think you need to worry any more about getting a reading," I responded from the standpoint of a middle-aged, established (insecurely established) author.

McClure published the novel; it was widely read and made Tarkington's name known to many thousands of readers. He took his place at once as one of the most imaginative and graceful of our young writers.

II

One of the editors who had helped to establish me was Edward Bok, whose *Ladies Home Journal* printed my novelette, "The Spirit of Sweetwater." Bok was at all times eager to welcome a story from me, although he was careful to say that it must be suited to his readers, an enormous number of women. He happened to be in town this day and as I was dated for a lecture in Philadelphia he said, "Why don't you go over with me and stay the night at Cyrus Curtis' house? He wants to know you, and so does Mrs. Curtis."

I accepted his suggestion, and as we rode over together I took occasion to name the various themes which I considered suited to his columns, and from them he selected "The Glittering Woman," a three-part story dealing with the dramatic material I had accumulated in my years of association with the Hernes. At the palatial home of Cyrus K. Curtis the head of The Curtis Publishing Company, I lived for a night in splendor inconceivable to me hitherto. Curtis was a small man, handsome and graceful. After a noble dinner, I went to my bed in a chamber fit for kings, and when I woke next morning I found that the house was in a wooded park glorious with new-fallen and still falling snow. It was not my world at all—it was the world in which sovereigns dwell and I went down the stairs to the stately rhythm of a pipe organ played by my host. As I listened to his music I could not relate him to the vast business which bore his name.

Bok had told me that Kipling was returning to America, and the New York papers confirmed the news by front-page accounts of his landing with his wife and two children. Nearly all the reporters mentioned his fur-lined overcoat and later papers said he had taken a suite of rooms at the "Grenoble," a small hotel near Carnegie Hall; and on my return to New York that afternoon I went up to call upon him. I had not seen him for five years, for he had been living in England, and my only news of him had been an occasional note; but he received me as if we had parted only yesterday. His reception room swarmed with visitors, mostly women, and somewhat appalled by the throng I hesitated about taking a seat. "Let me come again when you have fewer visitors," I suggested.

With a chuckle he replied, "I don't know when that will be! They come in endless streams. Come out into the hall; we can have a few words there."

That he was deeply gratified by this display of interest on the part of the public was evident. There had been much adverse criticism of him at the time of his leaving the States but all that was forgotten. The whole nation was ready to honor him.

He asked after Riley, Howells, Matthews, and other of our mutual friends, and agreed to lunch with me at the club for further talk. He was older in some respects, but still carried himself with boyish alertness. When I asked, "How are the books selling?" he replied with another chuckle, "Hugely!"

This led me to tell him the story of the Roxbury book-seller who at my suggestion stocked up on Kipling in 1892. "For a year or two he met me with reproachful glances, but I venture to bet he's all right now."

This seemed to amuse him, but he broke off to say, "I must go back to my other guests."

After leaving him I again went over to Herald Square to see how Herne's play was coming along. It was not drawing well and I was instantly back in the familiar atmosphere of anxious waiting. Once more I stood in the lobby as I had done with "Shore Acres" and later with "Margaret Fleming," watching the endless streams of people passing the doorway. Now and again one or two of them turned in as if to find shelter from the storm, rather than from interest in the play. Some of these would-be auditors were actors out of work hoping to find free seats. There was something pathetic in the manner of their timid approach to the manager—suave, cynical, and autocratic. Only now and then did he accept their extended cards, whereas I was eager to have them all go in and fill the house.

Herne's return to speculative producing seemed foolish to me, for it had plunged him once again into the morass of anxious toil from which "Shore Acres" had lifted him. The atrical folk are like that. They are seldom content to let well enough alone: "This time we are sure to win."

I talked of this and of Herne to Howells and as we were walking in Central Park. He was always interested in what Herne was doing, but agreed with me that this latest piece of writing was a mistake. "He should imagine his own plots and characters—he is too skillful and too imaginative to take some other writer's material."

I explained that this play was due to Herne's liking for Helen Gardner, the author of the "Unofficial Patriot," who was an intimate friend of his wife.

It was a glorious wintry day, with new-fallen snow covering the meadows in the park, and we both acknowledged the power of its associated memories. He was moved to reminiscence of early days in Ohio as I was reminded of later days in Iowa and Wisconsin. He loved this end of Central Park —it was his regular field of exercise—and I often joined him in a stroll, for there we could talk freely and without interruption.

He was ruddy with health that afternoon and full of plans for a book on Ohio which he had decided to write. "It isn't the one you have long urged me to do but I think you will like it," he explained apologetically.

On our return to the flat he returned to me my copy of an early edition of his poems, one which I had brought him several days before in order that he might inscribe his name on the flyleaf. On opening it, I was surprised and moved to find thereon an original poem addressed to me—lines which I here publish for the first time:

> It touched me more than I can say or ought
> (For still the heart is somehow wisely dumb),
> The other night, dear friend, to have you come
> Bringing this book of mine which you had bought,—
> For money talks, and yours was eloquent
> To me of liking for my rhymes, so true
> That if I could I would not wish to undo
> The effect for any gift-got compliment.

And in this book of mine, this book of yours,
I write my name and trust your love to keep
My drowsy fame from sinking off to sleep
While yours in lusty vigil long endures.

On February 1st came the first meeting of the National Institute, a meeting likely to be historic, for it was the first attempt at founding an American Academy. William Dean Howells and Charles Dudley Warner were the chief figures. Owen Wister, Charles G. D. Roberts, Augustus Thomas, Bronson Howard, and I also took an active part in the proceedings. Warner, who was made chairman, named Augustus and me as a committee to draft a constitution. Up to this time I had only slight acquaintance with Thomas, but I liked him and was glad of an opportunity to know him better. Only a few men were present, and all of us were thoroughly chilled, for the room was unheated. Nevertheless, it proved to be a far-reaching meeting.

Pursuant to instructions, Thomas and I met Dr. Holbrook Curtis at luncheon and took up the matter of the revision of the constitution of The National Institute of Arts and Letters. Curtis was a witty, attractive personality and the three of us had a delightful meal and put in an hour or two of work. Curtis, it appeared later, had been one of the prime movers of the Social Science Institute and it was at his suggestion that the literary and artistic section had been formed. "I am a physician and not a literary man or an artist," he explained.

On February 15, Holger Drachman, the Danish poet and critic who was visiting America, lunched with me at The Players. A big man, a handsome man, a giant in stature, he impressed me as a noble thinker with just the right feeling toward us and our writers, but he was sadly inarticulate in

English. He spoke wisely in all that he managed to make plain to me, but our talk necessarily ran turgidly in rather narrow channels. He began by saying, "I am told that you are a typical Western man and author and I wish to write an article about you." He glowed with enthusiasm when I touched on my faith in the future, and on certain altruistic beliefs which I hold. Despite his great bulk he was a singularly gentle and aspiring soul, a much greater man than I could arrive at by way of his broken English.

Some months later, a friend sent me a translation of the article which Drachman had written concerning our luncheon and I was amused and touched by its wording. I saw myself and my theories as they appeared when colored by Danish thought and Danish words. According to him I declared that our art and literature were in their first childhood—"We grope and copy, feeling our way but have an immense self-esteem." I had moods of feeling that way, but I don't remember saying so to him. I think he interpreted me in terms of his own impatient thought, for he was still more pessimistic about Danish art and literature. If his quotation was no more faithful than his picture of The Players' "lofty hall" I fear he was more the poet than the reporter. He was magnificent but not precisely true.

"The city was smothered in snow, and Zangwill, stormbound, proposed that I take him to call on Kipling whom he had never met. This I was glad to do, and we spent a lively hour with this marvelous young man who is the acknowledged spokesman of the English 'jingoists.' He gave us a brilliant statement of his merciless philosophy, but qualified it by reference to 'the white man's burden.' . . . 'The races who keep the dead out of their drinking water survive and those who don't—die. Which is as it should be. The white man's duty is to rule and sanitate.'

"To me he said, 'As for your Filipinos, make them work for you.'

"He was vivid, brilliant, and ruthless, and did not quite follow Zangwill's subtler wit—that is, he was just an instant longer in turning the corner, perhaps because of his 'white man's burden.' He argued that England's work was to civilize and regulate."

Zangwill sat with his big head sleepily swaying, his brain lightning swift, and his voice gentle and passionless. His position was in vivid contrast to that of Kipling, who saw little to reform in the white man's country and who insisted on reforming the brown races altogether, whether or not they wanted change.

One of his side remarks stuck in my mind. "I understand the native," he said. "My nurse was Hindustani. I spoke no English till I was six. I knew only Hindustani."

I remarked, "That explains your hold upon the lore of the natives."

He laughed as he replied, "I don't know how much it explains, but it is a fact. I didn't speak English till I was forced to do so by my father. Ours is the job of civilizing these savage and backward tribes," he summed up in effect. "Nothing is gained by coddling weak and primitive men. The law of survival applies to races as well as to species of animals. It is pure sentimental bosh to say that Africa belongs to a lot of naked blacks. It belongs to the race that can make the best use of it. I am for the white man and the English race."

At the end of Kipling's eloquent defense of the English as the chosen civilizers of the world, Zangwill remarked with gentle, reproachful, but humorous surprise, "Why, Kipling, you're almost Hebraic!"

That was precisely the paradoxical situation: Zangwill, the Jew, was the disciple of Christ; while Kipling, the Christian, was a follower of Gideon and the God of Battle.

As we came away Zangwill could talk of nothing else but Kipling's resemblance to the chieftains of David's time, the men who believed in smiting "hip and thigh," exterminating their enemies root and branch. I was opposed to Kipling's philosophy and so was Howells, with whom I discussed it; but I am not so sure that his view was not honester and more consistent than ours. Why should so much of the earth be given over to pitiless, filthy, half-formed savage races? So many billions of them have been slaughtered by their own kind. So many other billions have died like monkeys without the slightest value to the universe or their own kind. What does it matter whether such beings live or die? . . . My poor brain reels before such a problem and I long for Kipling's certitude.

Not long after this, Howells lectured on Socialism at the Social Reform Club, the first time, so far as I am aware, that any one had succeeded in bringing him to speak in public. With Kipling's argument still in mind, I was curious to hear what Howells would say. He surprised me. He gave a beautiful lecture, winning all hearts by his humor, his all-embracing altruism, and the grace and beauty of his diction. His voice carried unexpectedly well and his English was, as ever, quite faultless. He was Kipling's antithesis and I applauded his Christlike tolerance and sympathy. There was at times an almost apostolic earnestness in his voice as he pleaded for wider sympathy and deeper understanding of labor's problems. "It was a noble lecture, one of the finest I have ever heard. I shall be at him to speak more often." As I was going out I heard a workingman say, "That was a fine talk, but it was too short, that's all the fault I find with it." A woman said, "He is so genial. I had no idea he was like that."

Dining with Professor George R. Carpenter of Columbia a day or two later, I met for the first time William Vaughn Moody, the Chicago poet. I had heard something of him in college, but none of my friends knew him.

He was a saturnine individual, silent, entirely serious, and rather remote. I got very little out of him, and Carpenter, a genial host, was quite as unsuccessful. The poet may have been in an unusually taciturn mood, but he was to me a strange personality. He did not seem to be interested in what either of us said. He ruminated through the meal as though he were composing an epic.

III

As I stepped out of my door on East Twenty-fifth Street the morning of the 20th, I saw a small man wearing a light coat, alertly approaching, accompanied by a slender, self-contained young woman. Something in the man's compact figure was familiar—it was Kipling, and the woman was his wife. After a moment's greeting he said, "We're on our way to McClure's office. Can you tell me where it is?"

"Certainly—I'll go with you. It's only a step!" I replied.

As we walked along he spoke of the sudden turn to warm weather. "I have laid off my fur coat, of which the papers made so much," he added with a smile.

At the door of the big loft in which *McClure's Magazine* was printed, I left them and turned away. They were both in happy mood, rejoicing over the acclaim which still filled the press, and which had enormously increased the sale of his books. All the dislike of America which he had hitherto expressed went for nothing. He had entered upon a new era of wealth and honor.

As I was about to leave for the West, I considered it my duty to turn over the work of Secretary of the National Institute to some one who would be on the ground; and to this end I called upon Hamilton Wright Mabie in his office and gave him what records I had, telling him that I was to dine with Holbrook Curtis again and that I would ask him to surrender all his data.

The papers that morning all reported that Kipling was very ill with pneumonia, and Mabie said, "What a tragic end of his career that would be!" Much concerned, I stopped in at the Grenoble to inquire how the case stood. I found Jacacci, the art editor of *McClure's,* in the lobby. He said, "Frank Doubleday and I have just arrived. Frank has gone up to see Kipling and find out his condition."

When Doubleday came down his face was grave. "He's in a very critical stage of the disease. He has been unconscious part of the time to-day but is pluckily holding his own. The doctors have not given up. They are to employ oxygen and every other known resource, they say. It all came about from his laying aside his fur coat on one of our deceptively warm days. It appears that his little daughter is also ill and in the care of strangers. Mrs. Kipling, exhausted by the care of her husband, is unable to be with her."

It was a bitter and tragic change in Kipling's fortunes, and the whole world was in sympathy. All that day bulletins appeared almost hourly in the newspapers stating the progress of the battle and giving details of the treatment. Recalling him as I had seen him only a few days before, so happy and so alert, I experienced a chill foreboding. "What if he should go now?"

"Monday, February 27. I was afraid to take up a paper this morning for fear of finding a notice of Kipling's death. Happily he is reported to be holding his own and the use of oxygen has given a hope of his coming through. The whole of America is watching the struggle and many prayers are going up for his recovery."

For nearly two weeks his life was in danger and the whole nation shared the anxiety of the wife and others of his family. Bulletins continued to be issued as if for a great general, and when his doctors reported, "He will live!"—every one rejoiced.

During the very worst stage of his illness, his little girl died; but by order of the physicians her condition had been kept from him. He knew nothing of her death till after her burial, and when the time came to tell him, Frank Doubleday was chosen to speak the words. "It was the hardest task I ever undertook," said Doubleday, who had been in almost hourly attendance upon the sick man, "but it had to be done. I took a seat beside him and told the story in as few words as I could. He listened in silence till I had finished, then turned his face to the wall."

CHAPTER THIRTY-THREE

LITERARY PILGRIM SONS

I

In planning my trip to England I had in mind the procession of literary "pilgrim sons" (as Fuller had named them) who had made record of their joyous return to the homes of their ancestors: Longfellow, Emerson, Hawthorne, Lowell, Burroughs, Howells, James, Harte, Miller—all of whom had been most kindly received. Of these only Harte and Miller had carried with them the full flavor of the New World. All the others were scholarly, urbane variants of Carlyle, Tennyson, Dickens, or other British writers. Harte reflected at times the sentimental lyricism of Dickens, and Miller displayed a Byronic sonority; but underneath these obvious similarities ran a stream of original power.

In my lesser way I represented to my fellow craftsmen in England something which they considered valuable in a literature of the Western World. They classed me with Riley and Miller as a characteristic product of my environment—and led me to believe that Americanism was a very definite literary virtue. Without going so far as to hope for such a reception as that which Harte and Miller had received, I knew that I carried with me something like Miller's knowledge of the North American continent. On other scores I had no scholarship to match with that of Howells, no achievement to compare with Clemens, but I did know the

415

continent from Mexico to Alaska, and had mixed with the red men of Wyoming, and the miners of Colorado and Montana. I knew the people of every State in the Union. My journeys in pursuit of material for my life of Grant had immensely widened my knowledge of America. These were my claims to consideration.

In pondering the significance of the long line of American workers in the arts who had sought appreciation and approval in the Old World, I perceived that above and beyond any financial reward, they had hoped for the good opinion of London, for London not only represented "the judgment of posterity," but the wisdom of history. All our writers from Hawthorne to Harte had carried deep in their subconscious selves the mental isolation of pioneers. They were as provincial in thought as in material circumstance. Emerson leaned upon Carlyle and Kant. Hawthorne was a silent, deep-feeling son of Puritan England, and Lowell, notwithstanding his tart protest, was inwardly reverential—indeed, the smart of "a certain condescension in foreigners" came from its truth. At that time nobody read an American book for the reason that few of them were worth reading. Now that we are the dominant people of the globe, we can be quite honest about the pathetic beginnings of our art.

Why should we not admit to being pioneers? Provincialism is not precisely a crime—it is not entirely a weakness. Whitman and Emerson both made it a virtue in the writing of their books, but sought for their printed pages the commendation of their elders if not their betters in Europe. As the novelist of the mid-West, even if he finds publication and money reward in his native valley, looks longingly away to New York for a finer and more meaningful reward, so in 1899 we of New York and Boston still looked away to London and Paris for that higher distinction which only the master artists and historians of the mother countries could confer. Howells and Clemens had less reason for this feeling than any of our leading writers, but even they were glad of the good opinion of England. A degree at Oxford meant something like a patent of nobility even to these powerful chieftains in Western fiction. For them, for us, history lay to the East. After we had won the approval of our fellows, sometimes before we had gained that approval, we sought the aid of older communities in order that our honor at home might be increased. The praise of our native city meant much, but the praise of the Old World meant more.

Our musicians were still seeking honor in Germany and Italy, our playwrights hoping for a production in the Strand, our painters and our sculptors crowding the doors of the spring salon in Paris—when on that April day I sailed for Liverpool, another pilgrim son, back-trailing the course which my ancestor Peter Garland had taken nearly three hundred years before.

II

My summer in the wild Northwest was still fresh in my memory and but for the intervention of the Spanish War I should have been of interest in London both as subject of conversation and for use in fiction, but alas!—gold-seeking no longer interested people. My experience would not yield a single lecture date in England and could not be depended upon to earn a dinner. "The Trail of the Gold-Seekers," the volume of prose and verse which I had put together for Brett, was a foredoomed failure. People were tired of Yukon adventures and absorbed in the after-effects of the Spanish War. Aside from its verses (which I still value) my book was a stale report and no one read it then; it is an authentic bit of history now.

Notwithstanding George Brett's advance of royalty, I felt the need of money with which to make this trip, and so planned to make it pay for itself. Just before leaving Chicago I had plotted a travel story which would serve as a vehicle for my impressions. I called it "The Hustler," and actually read two chapters of it to Fuller, who liked it and said, "Go on with it." The plot was simple: a doctor who, in his vacations in Colorado, had met a prospector named Jim Mattison had joined him in the working of a mine. The story opens with the doctor's request—or demand—that Jim go to London and try to sell stock in this mine. Jim is appalled. "I'm no sailor," he says, "I can't see a girl shake a tablecloth without getting seasick."

This man, Jim Mattison, cattleman, trailer, prospector, was to go with me, in imagination, to London, whilst I reported his doings and sayings in the vernacular of the mountaineer, a vernacular which I knew very well.

This was over thirty years ago and the theme was not yet worn threadbare by "Uncle Tom in Paris," "So This Is London," and countless other later books and plays. There were still possibilities in the comment of a rough humorist like Jim Mattison, and I had hopes of making him pay my expenses as well as his own.

We were both seasick. The Scotch doctor on the steamer said I was the worst sailor he had ever known in his experience of nearly a quarter of a century. I ate one meal just after leaving Sandy Hook and another just as we sighted the green hills of Ireland. In no other known case had the boat's margin of profit been as large. For five days I lay in my berth saying, "Oh, why did I come?"—and Jim shared my sufferings. He also shared my delirious joy in the sight of something which did not creak and strain and climb and leap—"If I live to put my foot on solid earth again!"

The last day on the steamer was so tranquil that I was able to write a few letters. Knowing that my stay was to be short, I sent notes to Zangwill, Barrie, Kipling, and Shaw, giving Harper & Bros. as my address. James had written from the Continent and I had no hope of seeing him, but Sir Walter Besant, the head of the Authors' Society, was among those who had invited me to visit him.

Let no one imagine me a shining and triumphant pilgrim son, a worthy successor to Bret Harte, John Burroughs, or Joaquin Miller. I was a haggard, woebegone figure as I crept down the gangplank in Liverpool—but in my "Hustler" version I maintained as robust a humor as I could imagine; and immediately upon boarding the train for London, Jim perked up and made remarks concerning "the colt-like whinny" of the engine, and snorted with disdain of the coaches which were in truth descendants of the stagecoaches of the past.

I have written elsewhere of that first day in England and that first night in a little hotel near the station in London— "a hotel of brick and stone, thank God, which kept my bed from tossing in the air," and when next morning I walked out into the swarming, pounding, multitudinous streets of London, I was almost as bewildered as Jim confessed himself to be. "We must get the lay o' the land before we dive into *that* swamp," he said.

At my publishers, I found a note from Zangwill commanding me to report at once. This I was glad to do, for he was, after all, the one man in England who was unhesitatingly cordial. Barrie and Shaw were friendly, but Zangwill was instant in his hospitality.

He was living with his mother and sister in a small house in Kilburn, but his modest study owned a glowing fire of hard coal, a blessed comfort to me, for I had been cold ever since leaving New York. Israel's homely sympathy and humor warmed my heart. He was a fellow fictionist, and a cordial host. No doubt I exaggerated his importance in the London literary world, but that he was an outstanding figure can be proven by reference to the critical comment of that day.

With a gleam of fun in his brown eyes he said, "Now we must take up the question of an evening suit."

"Good Lord! I hoped you'd forgotten that."

"I have not and you must not. There is no time to be lost. The Authors' Society is having its annual dinner on Thursday and you are included among the guests as an overseas member. Come! I shall lead you to the tailor—at once."

In less than an hour I was being measured for a swallow-tailed coat while Zangwill fluttered about, highly amused, repeating the phrase, "Now we'll tame the cowboy—now we'll tame the cowboy."

Having in mind Howells' advice, I rejoiced in this invitation to a great literary banquet as an adequate excuse for conforming to the code. No one—not even Burroughs—could fail of understanding the power of such a mandate; and finding myself committed I went through to the end of the list of needfuls. I bought broad-bosomed shirts, studs, cuff links, gloves, and an opera hat; and when on the afternoon preceding the banquet I put them all on and looked at myself in the glass, I had a wordless sense of satisfaction. As

Zangwill had said, I could not tell myself from a lord—or a waiter.

It will not do to say that I approached this dinner with confidence. I was scared—I admit it—but I did my best to conceal my trepidation as I met Zangwill in the reception room of the hotel. He was politic. He looked me over without a word of comment, and led me about among the guests introducing me to all and sundry, confident, apparently, of my sustaining the part, surrendering me at last to Sir Walter Besant, who indicated my place at the speakers' table—an unexpected and rather terrifying honor. "I hope this does not carry with it the weight of a speech," I said.

"Oh, no," he replied almost too heartily. "You are a silent representative of our American membership."

My right-hand seatmate, a handsome, blond young man, was Henry Norman, a writer on the *Chronicle;* but the man on my left, a somber-visaged, bullet-headed man with gray hair, was not named to me, or if so, I failed to hear his name. Norman and I chatted easily, but the individual on the left was not interested in me, and as he was in the last chair of our end of the table, he sat in a silent glower, a look of savage resentment on his face. His indifference rather nettled me and leaning over toward Norman I muttered, "Who is the sour fat man on my left?"

"That is Henry M. Stanley."

Stanley! My boyhood's hero—the journalist, the great explorer, the man who knew more about darkest Africa than any other man. To myself I said, "This won't do. I must make Stanley talk. I must interest him." Turning toward him I said, "How do you pronounce the name of that deadly African fly—is it *tet*-sie or *teet*-sie?"

His face lighted up. I was on his ground. He could

reckon on my intelligence. He talked on easily, whilst I listened in absorbed interest and we were both a bit resentful when the gorgeous official behind the speaker announced with unction, "Me *Lords* and gentlemen—the honorable Lord Rosebery, presiding officer of the evening."

Rosebery, a smallish, smooth-faced man who looked a mere youth in the light of the lamps, presided with genial ease and introduced the speakers with understanding grace. I was deeply disappointed not to have Shaw or Barrie on the list, and the men who did speak left no distinct message in my ear. I occupied myself with trying to distinguish the authors seated below me, and with Norman's aid I singled out a few.

The one remark that I clearly remember was that made by Zangwill as we were on our way to the cloakroom. "Cowboy," he said as he nudged my elbow, "you wore 'em as to the manner born!"

III

A note from Barrie inviting me to lunch with him at the Garrick Club filled me with anticipation of a delightful hour, for in the two years since our meeting at The Players his position in English fiction had been advanced. His work had both broadened and deepened and my admiration for his plays and stories had grown with his growth. I considered him one of the few authors whose every new output was an important addition to literature.

Our luncheon at the Garrick was a very simple meal, and the only other guest was a black-bearded, black-eyed Scotchman of a type somewhat like my own uncles—the McClintocks. He was a swift and joyous talker, a noble monologuist. I have never heard a more continuous rhythmic roar of speech than that with which he filled our luncheon hour. His utterance was a flood, a torrent, a cascade, all in an English so colored by his Highland accent that I could scarcely follow him, and yet Barrie had introduced him as "the school inspector for the Hebrides Islands!"

I had looked forward to a talk with Barrie, but his part in the conversation was not impressive. Once he asked, "Garland, will ye have another roll?" and later, he succeeded in saying, "McFail, will ye pass the butter?" By this I do not mean to say that he was dour; he was just silent. He let McFail do the talking. Perhaps he had included McFail for that very purpose.

The last I saw of him that day was as he clasped my hand in parting at the door of the club. I watched him as he made off into the crowd, so inconspicuous in his gray suit and derby hat, that I could hardly believe him to be the most resourceful and imaginative fictionist in London. Strange, silent, imaginative Scot!

Kipling, with whom I lunched a few days later, had not been much changed, physically, by his illness, but the death of his little daughter had brought to him a graver outlook on life. He was distinctly less boyish. He retained his interest in "the States" and asked after Riley, Matthews, and others of his American friends, but was noticeably more remote. He was friendly, intellectually gay, but essentially secretive of his deeper self.

As I went about London, I began to see Gilder and all my New York associates from a new angle. They were a long way off to the people of an island with a thousand years of history, in a city swarming with writers and editors of its own. "It is a wonder that the English even know of us," I wrote to Fuller. "London seems to me a greater Chicago.

The historic is wholly submerged in the modern and commercial, and escapes notice until digged for. I go about alone—doing no deliberate sight-seeing, however—quite submerged in the English speech, seeing no Americans. I come and go in my heavy overcoat and Chicago hat—unnoticed and without a particle of friction. The policemen are exceedingly civil; so, indeed, are the bus drivers. My New York friends who warned me not to do this or wear that were talking nonsense. I am living here quite as I do in New York City. This hotel is about as big as the Everett and comically reminiscent of the boarding house out of which it sprang.

"I think I wrote you about my sea voyage. I am hardly recovered from it yet. I am cold all the time. The grate fires here are comical: two coals make a 'bedroom fire' and three lumps as big as oranges constitute a blazing 'sitting-room fire.' Fruit, except oranges, is very dear and poor; meat very good. Transportation is most primitive and *not* cheap when distance is considered. The finest building, almost the only *unified* structure I have seen, is the Parliament building, which is tremendously impressive looked at from the river. The city as a whole is formless, a jumble of gables, chimneys, blank walls, and harsh cornices. The whole impression is one of haphazard additions to an original village.

"An article in the *Star* last night blisters the annual art show here. 'It is for the most part beneath criticism,' the writer concluded. 'I regret that the soldiers and horses in the war pictures are not tin—then I could have played with them for hours.' He goes on to accuse the London public with a lack of taste in all things—a most amazing article to appear in a staid London paper. The exhibition *must* be bad to arouse such a rage. Sargent, it appears, carried off all the honors, and the critics seem grateful to him for being at least an English-speaking artist.

"Besant, when I lunched with him, ran on in similar vein, and so did Solomons the painter."

IV

Among my American acquaintances in London was Fay Davis, whose mother was the proprietor of the Boylston Place boarding house in which I spent my first winter in Boston. Her daughter, a long-legged girl of twelve or fourteen in those days, had miraculously become one of the best known actress on the London stage. As leading lady with George Alexander she was playing star parts in dramas by Pinero and Jones.

Our last meeting had been in a crowded Boston street car. While standing in the aisle, holding to a strap, I felt a light touch on my arm and turned to find a young girl at my side, whose face was lovely as a rose. It was Fay Davis, charmingly dressed, who called my attention to her mother sitting near me, well gowned and bonneted. With candid pride Fay told me that she had succeeded as a dramatic reader. "We have our own home, now, in Roxbury."

Since that meeting I had heard nothing of her other than a newspaper report that she had made a hit on the London stage. Naturally I was curious to hear the story of her triumph and when she wrote telling me that her mother was with her and wished to see me, I went in search of them.

Mrs. Davis met me at the door of a tasteful apartment adorned with pictures and filled with handsome furniture and while waiting for Fay to come in, we entered into humorous reminiscence of our days of poverty, and I permitted her to assume that I, too, was rich and happy.

In spite of the dark shadows and sordid associations of her days of worry in Boylston Place, Mrs. Davis was frankly homesick for America. "I don't belong here," she confessed, with a pathetic droop in her voice. "I stay only because Fay is happier here, and because she needs me. I love New England. All my people are there and it is hard for me to make friends here. The people are kind, but they are not like home folks. I'm lonesome."

In these words was revealed an insoluble problem. The daughter's desire to live in London—let us say her *need* to live in London—made of the mother an uneasy exile. Homesick in the midst of this pretty home, she presented, to my mind, the pathos of age uprooted. But when Fay came in, radiant, self-contained, beautifully clothed, and very gay, the situation was altered. Youth and beauty must be served.

During luncheon we had a homely talk on our humble past and afterward (presuming on my years) I went so far as to ask, "Why aren't you married?"

She laughed, and retorted, "Why aren't you?"

"Perfectly simple," I replied; "I can't afford it."

"Neither can I—and besides my managers won't let me. They say it is better 'business' to remain Miss." Here she became serious. "If I gave the time to a husband and a home which a wife ought, I couldn't do my work as an actress, and I am devoted to my profession—now."

Under all her banter ran a current of sadness. Successful, charming, and surrounded by admirers, she was not entirely happy. I went away with a feeling that she had not yet won content.

Here again, as in the case of Maude Adams, was evidence of the driving power of personality, an urge which had carried this sweet-faced girl from her mother's little boarding house to a leading place on the London stage. She was not a superlative actress and though beautiful was no more beautiful than some of her competitors—but she carried something in her heart and head which made for progress. "She won because she deserved to win," said Zangwill when I spoke of her to him.

She came to New York several years later in one of Shaw's plays, but I did not meet her, and for many years I have had no word of her, but as I think back into my dark days in Boston I see her eager face and hear her rich contralto voice as she read for me. I saw no shining future for her then and I am quite sure that to her mother I was only a poor teacher of literature, not yet able to afford a decent suit of clothes—and yet we each succeeded in different method and degree.

CHAPTER THIRTY-FOUR

SHAW AND HIS NEIGHBORS

I

IN 1899, George Bernard Shaw, just at the beginning of his great career as a dramatist, was, to me, one of the most interesting men in England. I had known of him first as a brilliant newspaper critic, a flaming Socialist, a cart-tail orator, and later as a most original dramatist. His speeches, letters, and amazing plays had made him a terror to the conservative and an incitement to the radical. Richard Mansfield had successfully produced "Arms and the Man" and "The Devil's Disciple"; and Miss Morgan's school of acting in Chicago had given a spirited reading performance of "Candida" with Taylor Holmes as the poet. But more provocative than all his plays were the letters which he had permitted Herbert Stone to publish in the *Chap-Book,* for they gave us the Irishman in his most Mephistophelian moods—I say "Mephistophelian" because the only portrait of him we had was one in which his eyebrows and beard were distinctly devilish in arrangement, and also because he took delight in mockery.

My admiration of his essays as well as of his plays had moved me to write him a letter of appreciation. His reply led to a correspondence and an invitation to visit him whenever I came to London. Hardly had I settled into my hotel on a corner of the Strand when a note came from him at

Hindhead, near Haslemere, asking me down to spend the week-end with him—a kindness not at all in character with his savage reputation.

As this was to be my first experience in English country life, I was in grave doubt about my costume. It will be remembered that I now possessed a swallow-tail suit and a tall hat, but as Shaw was reported to hate such garments I was undecided whether to leave my evening suit behind or take it along on the chance that Mrs. Shaw might have other guests in conventional garb. I also owned a long "Prince Albert" frock coat for afternoon wear, and still clung to a broad-brimmed hat. I was (from a mid-West point of view) well clothed; that is to say I was, in appearance, a blend of presiding elder and Wisconsin congressman, a powerful individual of thirty-nine, whose bearded face suggested that of General Grant.

I mention these details in order that my reader may anticipate the shock which Shaw was about to sustain, and also in order to measure the tolerance and good humor of all my English friends. In addition to these peculiarities, I suffered from the cold winds and carried a winter overcoat on my arm when not upon my back. Four months of the cold rains of Alaska had not been able to subdue me, but the chill winds of an English May had destroyed confidence in my vital machine. I walked in fear of pneumonia with an overcoat on my arm.

Behold me, therefore, a Western congressman, alighting from the train at Haslemere (a lovely little village in Surrey) carrying this overcoat and a bag, looking around for the carriage which Shaw had said would meet me.

The only vehicle in sight was a very smart cart drawn by a sturdy, well-groomed horse and driven by a man in a brown uniform. As I approached this very conventional turnout, the driver touched his hat and said, "For Mr. Shaw, sir?"

That he was surprised and displeased by my costume was evident, and the offhand gesture with which I tossed my bag into the cart positively shocked him. Accustomed as he must have been to strange guests at his master's house I was a new kind altogether. My broad hat, associated with a Prince Albert frock suit, was especially disturbing; and to make the impression worse, I said, with democratic heartiness, "You drive a fine horse, neighbor."

He drew away from me with a start of astonishment. My camaraderie distressed him. However I persisted in my questioning and at last drew from him the information that Hindhead was a colony of literary folk and that Conan Doyle, Grant Allen, and Mrs. Huxley were neighbors of the Shaws. "We shall soon pass Dr. Doyle's house on the left, sir," he volunteered.

As we rose I perceived that Hindhead was a group of summer homes occupying a long treeless ridge, and that Doyle's house was "at the head of a draw" as we say in the Rocky Mountains. On reaching the summit the man turned to the left along the hogback till he came to a large frame house which stood at the edge of the hill and overlooked the valley to the south. The entire landscape to the north was somber, barren, and strange. "It is called the black moor, sir," said the coachman. "And on that hill to the east there used to be a gibbet where they hung people."

As we turned in at the gate I saw a man sitting under an umbrella on the sunny side of a stone wall, writing on a pad resting against his knee.

Hearing the sound of wheels he rose and came toward

me, limping as he walked. He was tall, bearded, and dressed in a knickerbocker bicycling suit whose armpits were reinforced with patches of leather. This was Shaw, and as he greeted me I was amazed to find that his eyes were a sunny blue and his hair and beard blond, not to say "reddish" in color, and that his expression was not as "satanic" as his photographs had made it out to be. In fact he impressed me as a lank, sandy-complexioned Scot, not an Irishman at all. His voice and accent reminded me of my Scotch-Irish neighbors in Wisconsin.

He at once explained his limp and the patches of leather at his armpits my saying, "I've been on crutches. I fell from my bicycle a few weeks ago, and broke a bone in my ankle."

On entering the house, Mrs. Shaw, a handsome and kindly hostess, accepted me in the friendliest spirit notwithstanding the Wild Western effect of my dress. Perhaps she was more accustomed to her husband's socialistic friends than the coachman. "Don't dress for dinner," she said; "we are alone."

The house was spacious and the chamber to which I was led was handsome and overlooked the valley to the south. I had no sense of being in the home of a social disturber.

Shaw came to dinner in his bicycle suit, and while his wife and I ate heartily of a generous roast, he picked around among his dishes of chopped apples, beets, beans, and other vegetables. That he was a vegetarian I knew, but I learned with surprise that he drank neither wine nor coffee. He did not smoke or swear or talk slang, and was never coarse. His humor was so delightful that all my prejudices gave way to liking.

He was a tremendous talker, but I was glad to listen. His sharp thrusts at accepted absurdities, many of which I had never before questioned, kept me laughing. He explained, "People say I see everything upside down, but the opposite is the fact. I see things *as they really are*. Other people see them *as they once were* or as they *think* they are. They are the ones who see things bottom side up."

His teeth shone, his eyes glittered with fun. There was nothing cynical about him. Brilliantly wise and witty, he was at no time sour or malicious. His comic sallies, his sparkling paradoxes, were bewildering to me. He attacked all shams, all pretensions. He spoke of our habit of lynching negroes, and defined our cheap politicians with amazing knowledge; and when I, admitting the truth of all these, said, "But in spite of all these defects, we are getting along pretty well," he burst out, "You should be doing something more than 'pretty well'—you should be setting an example to the Old World. You should not be accepting and perpetuating the blunders and social crimes of monarchical Europe. You had a chance to discard the feudal land system of England and you failed of your opportunity. Henry George told you this. It was from him that I acquired my first impulse toward land reform." He spoke of his work in the Fabian Society. "I met Mrs. Shaw there," he explained. "We are both friends of the Webbs."

Never before had I listened to such a talker. His voice was beautiful and his brilliancy of phrase astounding. For four hours while we sat before his fire he talked, and yet, at the end of it, I could recall only here and there a line of that marvelous monologue. It was like watching a series of red and green and golden rockets flame by overhead, leaving no record on the skies. After I went to my room at midnight, I was moved to set down some part of it, but this is all I can now find: "If Shaw can talk like that on chopped apples and shredded carrots what would he do on a beefsteak!"

II

Immediately after breakfast, while Shaw was busy at his writing, I wandered out on the heath, studying the plants and the birds which I saw there. A small brown lark, something like our crested lark, was numerous, filling the air with a sweet twittering song; but I gave more thought to the gorse which appeared to be the primeval verdure, and on my return I asked Shaw whether these hills had ever been plowed.

"No, these common lands have never been tilled or changed in any way. They are just as they were when Cæsar came."

"What are those little singing birds out in the heather? They seem a kind of lark."

Shaw smiled. "Why, man, those are skylarks!"

"Skylarks! Those tiny twittering birds can't be Shelley's rapturous, heavenly singers?"

"But they are!" he replied with a laugh in his eyes. "The very same. But then," he added with the easy criticism of an Irishman, "the English skylark is a vastly overrated bird."

It was a lovely morning and as the dining room was full of sunlight, Shaw brought out his camera and took a snapshot of me at the breakfast table, and one in the garden while I illustrated the manner in which the farmers of the mid-West carry their heavy overcoats on a spring day—half on and half off their shoulders. These snapshots are before me as I write and enable me to substantiate Shaw's kindly humor.

As he had done all the talking the night before, so now

I was to have an inning, for when he learned that I knew something about "Red Indians," he asked me to tell him of them. I was in the midst of the story of Rising Wolf, a Cheyenne miracle worker, when he stopped me. "Grant Allen should hear that! He is keen on red men. Get your hat and coat and follow me."

Notwithstanding his lame foot he led the way briskly across the common to Allen's home and smilingly presented me as if I were a favorite nephew just returned from Canada. Having introduced me, and in a way explained me, he stood aside to listen. This may seem incredible to those who think of Shaw as a savage egotist, but that is what he did, taking pleasure, apparently, in seeing me win his friend's interest and respect.

When others speak of his "destructive bitterness," his "intellectual ruthelessness," I think of him as he appeared that day, smiling, friendly, courteous. His reputation as a cynic counted for nothing as I saw him in easy, genial intercourse with his neighbors. That they liked him as well as respected him was evident.

Grant Allen's books on Evolution were known to me and I was glad to meet him. He met me cordially and was not at all the typical Englishman, in manner or in accent. In truth he was almost American in speech, a thin, active man, keen-eyed and quick-spoken. After we had talked for some time on Red Indians he asked me if I were going to the Continent and when I said that I was he presented me a copy of a guidebook he had written and gave me some valuable advice concerning routes and scenes in Italy and France.

While we were still at Allen's, Conan Doyle came in and invited us all to Sunday midday dinner. I had met him several times in New York and Chicago and liked him. He was

Shaw's direct opposite in every way, a big, broad-shouldered athlete, typically British in form and spirit, fond of hunting and sports of all kinds—whereas Shaw took no interest in any game. "My only recreation is riding the bicycle," he said. "I abhor shooting and detest games of all kinds." Nevertheless, he and Doyle, if not intellectually congenial, were friendly.

Doyle was not a reformer, but we met on common ground when talking of tennis. He not only played tennis but was a member of the Authors' Cricket Team, and at the table we fell to discussing the relative merits of cricket and baseball. Naturally I stood up for the American game. "It is the most scientific ball game in the world," I declared. Doyle quite as loyally upheld cricket.

To prove my case for the scientific accuracy of baseball, I spoke of the curving of the ball in the air, a marvelous trick which our pitchers had developed in order to deceive the batsman. Doyle confessed that he had never seen the ball curve in the air—"and I have a doubt concerning it. We use what is called 'the break' of the ball from the turf, in cricket, but I can not see how a ball can alter its course while in the air."

"If I had a baseball," I said to him, "I would show you that it can be done, for I was once a pitcher for a baseball club and can still throw all the curves."

Doyle looked thoughtful. "I don't suppose there is a baseball in all England," he finally observed. "Would a cricket ball do?"

"It might," I said. "Let me see one and I can tell you whether it can be curved or not."

The moment I took the ball in my hand I realized that I had my work cut out for me, for the ball was heavier than a baseball and a little smaller; nevertheless, I would not admit defeat.

We adjourned to the tennis court where I measured off the ground, removed my coat, and rolled up my sleeves preparatory to the demonstration.

"Who's going to receive this ball?" I asked.

"I am," replied Doyle easily.

I looked at him with some doubt and said, "Not as you are, not with your bare hands."

"Oh, yes, I often receive the ball in cricket with bare hands."

"But, Doyle," I said, "it isn't done! It's dangerous. You may regret the experiment."

"Oh, no," he replied. "Let it come along; if it gets too hot for me I'll sidestep it."

Accordingly he took his position at the proper distance from the line I had drawn to represent the pitcher's box and I began throwing the outcurve. This is a comparatively slow ball and he not only was able to see it curve but stopped it rather neatly. After throwing two or three of these I said, 'Now, look out. I am going to throw the incurve which is very much swifter. It is likely to have a bone in it." He received this ball with a wince but gamely returned it to me. "Now in this one I expect to put all the steam I have," I explained to Doyle and those looking on; and with that warning I delivered the ball with all the force at my command. Doyle saw it coming, stepped aside, and let it go into the net.

"The demonstration is complete," he said.

It must be admitted that this was not a highly literary exercise for a group of celebrated authors to be engaged in, but I record it as it happened.

III

On the following morning Doyle and I rode into London together. We lunched together and at night he took me to a prize fight at his athletic club. "You should see a cricket match," he said. "There is a game on the Crystal Palace Green Wednesday, between the Authors and the Actors. Would you like to go?"

"I feel it my duty to do so," I replied. "It is a part of my education."

On Wednesday we met again and he took me to Crystal Palace Park, where I saw a typical English crowd and a typical English game. Hardly had we taken our seats when Barrie came poking along through the crowd, entirely alone, looking like some ten thousand other small men in bowler hats. No one recognized him, no one noticed him but Doyle and myself; and we were too far away to call to him. Somberly, slowly, he climbed to one of the highest seats, and there came to perch like a lonesome crow, peering dreamily out over the field. Doyle remarked this: "That's like him—he flocks alone."

Doyle then pointed out for me the most famous of the players, and was greatly pleased to learn that Grace, the great champion, was at bat. "You will see cricket at its best," he said. To me, however, it was a very monotonous game. For forty minutes, that man Grace did all the batting; and when they stopped for tea at 4:15, I pleaded another engagement and went back to my hotel. No one could have been kinder than Doyle, but cricket bored me.

Zangwill took charge of me on Thursday, and with him I saw the salon of the Independent Artists Association, a protesting group of younger men who regarded the Academy as "Old Hat" or at best merely correct or pretty. I felt quite at home in this atmosphere. It was another case of Youth announcing its contempt for Age.

Among others to whom Zangwill introduced me was Henry Harland, whom Howells always called my "rhyme" and for whom he had a genuine regard. Harland was a little of Zangwill's type, dark, lively of humor, and highly urban in sympathies and training. "You must come to dinner. I want to hear about Howells and others of my New York friends," he said.

I looked forward to that dinner with especial pleasure, for the weather was dark and chill and I was on the verge of admitted homesickness when Robert Barr, the Canadian novelist, came into my hotel one afternoon like a breeze from the Rocky Mountains. He was in the midst of cursing the English climate in good open-air style when a small, soft-footed man came down the hall like a blond ghost of Shakespeare. Barr started up. "Hello! There's Hall Caine. Come over here, Caine, I want you to know my American neighbor, Hamlin Garland."

Caine greeted me with mincing precision in a tone ludicrously flat when contrasted with Barr's good-natured roar. That the Manxman did not value me was evident, but as I didn't like his books, we were "horse and horse" as the gamblers say. His personality surprised and amused me. He was so small, so gentle to be the composer of the fierce and bloody volumes which bore his name. Doyle and Kipling and Shaw were like their books; but Caine was not in the least like "The Christian" or "The Manxman." His speech was precise, his face ascetic and refined, his hands effeminate. We parted to meet no more during my stay, although we continued to live at the same hotel. Barr had not succeeded in conveying to Caine an interest in me, and I did not blame him for keeping to the other side of the cañon.

Zangwill had me on his mind. His kindness was unremitting. One day he asked me if I had seen "Savage Africa." I answered, "No, what is it?"

"It is a kind of Wild West Show, which we English are having here in London this summer."

This "show" of African life and African history, which occupied a large enclosure in a suburb, moved me more than I cared to acknowledge. My throat filled with pity and my muscles grew tense with excitement when in mimic battle the wild songs of the warriors arose, and then as the appalling roar of the Maxim guns began, and I saw the naked blacks charging the British lines, I understood Zangwill's indignation. Here was the same sort of war on a naked race that we had made on the red men of America. With all that modern military science could do to aid them, the English had gone against these primitive blacks, driving them from the lands they long had occupied, aiming to change their leopard skins to rags and pith helmets just as we aimed to make the red Cheyennes over into the image of a Western tenant farmer. The missionary and the teacher following the flag complete the conquest.

After the "battle" I went into the enclosure where many of the negroes were camped in native fashion with huts and camp fires. A painted circular wall pictured the African landscape and the scene was most impressive as night began to fall. I secured a very clear concept of the huts and the green hills of a South African village. There was charm in its pastoral suggestion.

Still with Zangwill for a guide I visited Arthur Pinero

at his home in St. John's Wood. Pinero, who was one of the most successful dramatists of England, impressed me as a very frank, hearty, and candid character. He was medium sized, rather slender, and very bald over the entire front of his large head. Quick and precise of speech, he did not show his Jewish strain at all. In fact I should not have known him for a Jew had not Zangwill made it plain. It was this racial mixture perhaps which gave Pinero perspective on his English material, for he was not only prolific but victorious. It surprised me to hear him complain of "the commercial manager who considers art in the drama 'bloody rot'"; and when he added, "I came on the stage by way of a side street," I did not understand the allusion. His house, which fronted on Hamilton Terrace, was finely but not extravagantly furnished and he had every appearance of a solid success.

In lunching in the Temple with Albert Kinrose, I met Mrs. Clairmonte (George Edgerton), author of "Key-notes" and "Discords." I had never read a word of her writing but as a woman she interested me. She was amazingly frank in talking of herself and her work. Life had gone hard with her (according to her own statement) and she was extremely outspoken and bitter in admitting it. Nevertheless she gave me the impression of being essentially wholesome in thought, for she had her old father tottering about with her, and her care of him was fine and sincere. She was patient with him and tolerant of her absent husband, of whom she spoke with candor, as if he were a rowdy runaway boy. "The last time I heard of him," she calmly remarked, "he had shot a man in El Paso, Texas." She spoke of her lost beauty with sad candor, and left upon me the shadow of an approaching tragedy.

On the night of Henry Harland's dinner, I found my way to his apartment with some difficulty, and was late. He greeted me cordially, however, and at once set about amusing me, very much as Riley was accustomed to do. My evident appreciation of his humor put him on intellectual tiptoes and he became strenuously entertaining. He talked quite uninterruptedly throughout dinner, giving forth a most delightful series of shocking reactionary sentiments. As in my intercourse with Riley, I said nothing. My part was to laugh and applaud, delighted to have him go on.

He impressed me as a hybrid, neither American nor English, neither Jew nor Gentile. On this occasion he posed as a bitter conservative, opposed to all reforms and reformers and critical of American democracy; but I liked him and enjoyed his "goings on." I could not take his conservatism seriously, for all the women of his party drank and smoked, which was new and very "radical" to me.

He spent much time detailing the adroit methods by which he outwitted the various sheriffs who came to collect bills. He was especially funny in describing how in one case he engaged a constable in a political controversy in the drawing-room "whilst the piano was being salvaged down the back stairs." I accepted all this as a part of the evening's designed entertainment, but this story was not particularly funny to Mrs. Harland. The play of being "just a jump ahead of the wolf," as Henry pleasantly described it, was not so pleasing to her.

On the following morning, as I was on my way to the Parliament building, I chanced upon Gilbert Parker swinging along Pall Mall with a graceful step and air of happy possession. He had the look of a rich and popular man, and this in truth he was, for he had married happily, and was in Parliament. Nothwithstanding the wide gulf between his fortunes and mine, he greeted me as a fellow trailer and as we chatted he recalled with humorous comment our first meeting at the *Arena* office in Boston. After inviting me to call he walked on, leaving me with a better opinion of him than ever. He, too, had conquered London.

CHAPTER THIRTY-FIVE

AMERICAN EXPATRIATES

I

IT was with something of a shock that I had heard Howells admit his lack of contact with English men of letters. That I should know only four or five was natural, for I was an obscure young author; but Howells was one of the best known novelists of his day. "I do not know England well," he had said, "I have only made short stops there on my way to the Continent."

In this remark lies a hint of the situation in 1899: comparatively little literary and esthetic commerce between London and New York existed. In all matters of art we looked away to Paris, and for music and our musical judgments, to Germany. Furthermore, many of our writers still retained a feeling of resentment toward England. London patronized them as provincials. Conditions had changed since Lowell's essay on Old World condescension—as he himself as ambassador had learned; but some part of that patronization still lingered in the minds of book reviewers, and the English public welcomed American eccentricity as displayed in Mark Twain. For such Americans as they found amusing, they were hospitable. Very naturally and logically they wished the writers of America to be original. They were interested in Miller and Harte and Clemens for the reason that they had the tang of the far West in their writings, whilst we

443

as writers felt the need of Old World endorsement at the same time that we loudly proclaimed our intellectual independence. Our musicians still sought the approval of German masters, and our painters and sculptors strove for a place on the walls of the spring salon in Paris, just as our dramatists schemed for a London production of their plays and our actors dreamed of a season on the Strand—not for the money to be drawn from London but in order to strengthen their position at home.

All this, as we look back upon it from the year 1930 and across the changes following a world-shaking war, seems logical. As a grown-up nation we can admit our timid years. We *were* provincial so far as England was concerned—or if this word seems too blunt, we may call ourselves literary pioneers or esthetic squatters on new land. The longer I stayed in London the more clearly I perceived this relationship, just as in going from Dakota to Boston I came to an understanding of the patronizing attitude of Eastern critics toward Western writers, a patronization which was quite as plainly expressed in their over-cordial applause as in their captious criticism. There is no escape from this relationship. So long as history and scholarship center in cities, so long will the mother country be more authoritative than the colony. Politically free of the Old World, we still find ourselves dependent in affairs of the spirit. The weight of history, the wealth of tradition, must ever be on the other side of the water.

To make the case concrete; as I had sought the good opinion of Boston and New York critics, so now I hoped for a favoring judgment by English men of letters, and here was I, a son of Wisconsin, with only a few dollars in my pocket, wandering about London as Emerson and Burroughs and Miller had done, knowing only five or six writers, acknowledging my feebleness yet resenting any act of patronization. It is rather remarkable, however, that the few men with whom I was most at home had in them the seeds of long life. They are still the recognized masters of their arts after more than thirty years.

Howells had given me a note to Thomas Hardy, one to Bret Harte, and an especially valuable one to Mark Twain. "I don't know where Clemens is at this moment and I can not tell you where to find Harte, but if they are in London I am sure they will be glad to see you."

I had a special reason for seeing Clemens, for his firm had published General Grant's memoirs and I wished to clear up certain points concerning this important transaction. Harte had long been one of my high admirations. I regarded him as a leader (in point of power as well as of time) in the local-color school of fiction, which I was advocating as the most vital development of our literature. "Harte came East like a conquering prince in 1871," said Howells, "and was for six or eight years a friend of Lowell and Longfellow, and for a time acclaimed in England."

No one in London, however, could tell me anything very definite about him. He was not seen where Americans ate and drank and the gossip about him was not reassuring. Clemens, so my publishers told me, was in Austria. The only one of Howells' notes which I was able to present was the one to Thomas Hardy whom I found living in a small apartment in Kensington. At his invitation I had tea with him one afternoon.

He was in his late prime at this time and made a powerful impression on me. He was small and blond, with a fine head and full brown beard, more like a studious country doctor than a novelist, and his wife was equally plain. "We were both essentially country folk," he said. "My house is outside Dorchester which is only a little city. I am a justice of the peace," he added, with a faint smile. "I am hardly ever in London. I came up this time on my wife's account."

His lack of humor, his blunt, plain speech, his scientific outlook on the world all reminded me of Burroughs. His clothing was about like that which Burroughs wore when he came to town.

He spoke of America rather wistfully. "I'd like to see it," he said. "I have a great many readers over there and feel very friendly toward them, but I fear I shall never see them."

"You would be royally received."

"I know, I know! I'm afraid of that. I am afraid of New York. It's too rackety over there."

What he meant by this was evident. He dreaded the assaults of reporters, the din of receptions, the fatigue of dinners, and all that whoop and halloo with which every distinguished visitor was received. "I can not deny that you would find America 'rackety,' but part of that could be avoided. I hope you'll come."

He spoke of his home in Dorchester. "It is not on the sea. I never go to the sea even in the summer. I don't like it. It's too cruel. I prefer the moors. In olden times the people in these sea towns built the backs of their houses toward the water. They took no pleasure in looking out to sea—neither do I."

I came away from him with something like the feeling I had for Burroughs: "There is nothing egotistical or austere in his manner," I recorded among my notes.

II

One afternoon as Zangwill and I were having tea at Joseph Hatton's house, my attention was drawn to a man whose appearance was almost precisely that of the typical English clubman of the American stage. He was tall, and his hair parted in the middle was white. He wore gray-striped trousers, a cutaway coat over a fancy vest, and above his polished shoes glowed lavender spats. In his hand he carried a pair of yellow gloves.

"Who is that?" I asked of Zangwill.

"Don't you know who that is?" he asked. "That is your noble compatriot, Francis Bret Harte."

"Bret Harte!" I started at him in amazement. Could that dandy, that be-monocled, be-spatted old beau be the author of "The Luck of Roaring Camp" and "Two Men of Sandy Bar"? As I stared, I recalled Joaquin Miller in his little cottage high on the hills above Oakland, and marveled at the changes which the years had wrought in his expatriate fellow. I said to Zangwill, "I have a letter to Harte from Howells—present me."

Zangwill led me over to Harte and introduced me as an American writer with a note from Howells. Harte was politely interested. "Come and see me on Thursday," he said, and gave me his address which was near Lancaster Gate.

Although courteous, his manner was not winning and I hesitated about making the call. However, it was easier to go than to excuse myself, and on the afternoon he had named, I found my way to his "bachelor apartments" in Lancaster Gate. They seemed to me very ladylike, spic and span, and very dainty in coloring, with chairs of the gilded, spindle-legged perilous sort which women adore; and when Harte came in to greet me he was almost as aristocratic as the room. He was wearing the same suit with the same fancy vest but with a different tie, and from his vest dangled an English eyeglass. His whole appearance was that of an elderly fop whose life had been one of self-indulgent ease. His eyes were clouded with yellow, and beneath them the skin was puffed and wrinkled. Although affable and polite he looked and spoke like a burned-out London sport. I was saddened by this decay of a brilliant and powerful novelist.

Taking the letter which I handed him he asked me to be seated. Seating himself he read its two short pages slowly. At the close of it he sat for a few moments in silence. Then raising his glance he dropped his eyeglass and his English accent at the same time and said, "Tell me about Howells. Tell me of Tom Aldrich and all the rest of the boys."

My heart warmed to him. He was wholly the American. His voice and his words were not even Bostonian—they were Californian. Howells' words and something in my voice had not only awakened youthful memories but had strengthened a secret desire. His eyes as I talked became dreamy and his voice wistful, and at last I said, "When are we to see you again?"

"Never again, I fear. I *can't* go back now."

"You would have a splendid reception in California," I urged.

"I'm not so sure of that," he replied, a note of sadness in his voice. "I couldn't find *my* California. *My* California is gone. My friends are gone. The men who represented California to me are gone. No, I shall never go back. Sometimes I wish I had never come away."

In his mind, as in mine, he was an exile, an expatriate,

old and feeble and about to die, estranged from his family
and from all his American friends. He was poor and the
subject of gossip. His books were no longer in demand.
He had lived here too long, working over his memories of
California, and it was reported that he was living on the
bounty of a patron.

Twice I rose to go, but at his request resumed my seat.
"I want to hear more about the West," he said. "I seldom
meet anybody who knows Western America." It seemed
that I brought something precious, something which suggested to him the charm of his triumphant youth.

At last I took my leave. He opened the door for me and
still talking followed me down the steps to the sidewalk,
and there held me while he questioned me concerning Alden
and Stedman and Warner, his youthful companions and
friends. Finally, for the third time, I clasped his hand and
said good-by. On nearing the corner I was moved to turn
and glance backward. He was standing on the doorstep, his
hand on the railing, the sunlight on his bent head, making
his white hair gleam like silver. Such is the Bret Harte of
my memory and as I saw him last. He died a few years later,
almost forgotten by his native land.

III

Soon after my meeting with Harte I learned that Mark
Twain had returned to London, and I hastened to write him.
"There are several points in the 'Life of General Grant'
upon which I would like to have your comment."

He replied at once, inviting me to call upon him at his
hotel.

Up to this time I had never met him, although I knew a
great deal of him through his friends, and had heard him

speak several times. He had been living in Europe for four or five years and had been highly successful both as writer and lecturer. According to report, kings and queens had been quick to do him honor and many critics considered him to be the largest and most significant figure in American literature. His fame, based no longer upon his eccentricities but upon the rugged force and New World flavor of everything he said and wrote, was world-wide. I was keenly eager to see him and talk with him.

As I came upon him in a small but exclusive hotel in the West End, I was shocked by the changes which had come to him. His shaggy hair was white and a stoop had come into his shoulders. It appeared that in growing old he had diminished. He appeared smaller than I had remembered him on the platform, but his fine head and rough-hewn features were more impressive than ever before.

He had heard of my book on Grant, probably through Brander Matthews, but I think he would have been courteous without either of these aids. After putting his small hand in mine he motioned me to a chair and began to speak in the rhythmic drone which had been so large a factor in his success as an after-dinner speaker. It was made up of peculiar stresses difficult to describe, and was interrupted here and there by sudden pauses, corresponding to a dash in print—a most dramatic device, as when he wrote, "Be good—and you'll be lonesome." These, and a curious aloofness of glance (as though he spoke from out a mask) made it difficult for me to take his serious statements at their full value. Most people expected him to be funny, a fact which he was accustomed to curse regretfully. As he talked to me he appeared to forget me. He looked over my head at some far-off landscape. His eyes, hidden by his bushy eyebrows, were half closed and I saw them only occasionally. I was surprised to find them blue and keen.

I asked him if he had any objection to telling me how he came to publish the Grant memoirs and he replied, "None at all, but before you print it you'll have to get Mrs. Clemens' consent."

His story was something like this:

"One night as I was a-comin' away from the theater, I chanced to hear one man say to another, 'Do you know that General Grant is about to publish his memoirs?' And the other said, 'No; who is the publisher?' That was enough for me. I went the very next day to see the general. I found him in his library with his son, Colonel Fred. 'General,' I began, 'is it *true* that you are about to publish your memoirs?' 'It is,' he replied. 'I am at this moment considering an offer for the manuscript.' 'General,' I said, 'that interests me. Would you mind telling me exactly what that offer *is?*' 'Not at all,' he replied. 'The Century Company is willing to assume all the expenses and risk and pay me ten per cent on all copies sold.' 'Good God, general,' I exclaimed, 'you are *giving* them the book. You should have *three times* that amount.' . . . You know how modest the old general was; well, he showed that phase of his character now. 'Oh, no,' he answered, 'you are mistaken. I think they are treating me very handsomely. My book will not sell largely.'

" '*You* are the one mistaken, general,' I retorted. 'The book will sell largely, and just to show you how I feel about it, I will offer you twenty-five per cent royalty, and draw you a check for fifty thousand dollars advance royalty *right now!*' This staggered the old soldier, but he shook his head. 'That's very fine of you, Mr. Clemens, but I can't accept it. I am committed to these other men.' At this point Colonel

Fred put in his oar. 'Why, no, you're not, father. You're only *considering* their offer. You're under no obligation to them. You have a perfect right to lay Mr. Clemens' proposition over against theirs.'

"In the end I convinced the general that I was a publisher and not a philanthropist, and I got the book. I published it. It sold enormously, as you know—more than a half-million copies—and I had the high satisfaction of visiting the old commander on his deathbed at Mt. McGregor, when he could no longer utter a word or lift a hand, and of saying to him, 'General, there *is* in the bank in New York City—subject to *your* order or the order of Mrs. Grant—the sum of three hundred thousand dollars, and there'll be more—much more.'"

As he ended on this note of reminiscent emotion, I shared his conception of what that message must have meant to The Great Commander whose later days had been so quietly heroic, and so filled with mental and physical pain.

With this matter cleared away, Clemens fell into talk of his failure as a publisher. "I am going home soon—as soon as I have made a little more money. I am nearly clear of those obligations I assumed as a partner in Webster & Co.," he said, and this brought up the subject of his arrangement with his creditors. He cursed with heart-felt fervor and Oriental magnificence Charles Webster, "who chouselled me out of fifty thousand dollars, thus bringing about the ruin of my publishing house." With cold malignity he then said in level monotone, "For many years I have been writing a kind of diary in which I have set down from time to time exactly what I think of the men and women I have met. It can't be published while *I* am alive. It can't be published while *Mrs. Clemens* is alive. It can't be published while *any of the people mentioned* are alive; but when it *is* published, that blankety blank blank will turn in his grave!"

He ended with such deadly hatred in face and voice that I was able to share in some degree the disgrace he had been called upon to bear and the burden he had voluntarily assumed. In my notebook that night I outlined this conversation and added, "He has accomplished a tremendous task—A really great soul."

As I was going away I again said: "*McClure's Magazine* wants to print this story. Shall I send it to them?"

"Certainly. Go ahead! But they'll have to get Mrs. Clemens' O. K. on the proof."

The most curious sequel to this interview (which by the way Mrs. Clemens would not let us publish) is the fact that Webster, whom Clemens accused of "chouselling" him out of fifty thousand dollars, was not in any way connected with the business at that time. He had been ill and out of the firm for several years. The failure of the firm was due to Mark's own unwise investments in a typesetting machine. Albert Bigelow Paine, his biographer, told me this some ten years after this meeting, and added, "When I had convinced Clemens of his error he sat for a few moments in silence, then remarked in a musing tone, 'Albert, there *was* a time when my memory was reliable. There was a time when I could remember a great many things *that were so* and some that were *not* so—now I remember only the latter!'"

CHAPTER THIRTY-SIX

HENRY JAMES AT RYE

ALL through the early years of my stay in Boston, the critics and James reviewers invariably alluded to "Howells and James" as if they were a literary firm or literary twins. Usually they were thus named in a tone of resentment, as if representing a school of fiction unjustly in the ascendant. For no reason at all I had begun by sharing this resentment, but after I had read "The Minister's Charge" and "The Bostonians," I developed sincere admiration for them both.

It amused me then to wonder why they were thus bracketed, for they were not in the least alike, except in the broad sense of being students of manners rather than writers of romance. James was even then rather difficult to read, whereas Howells' pages were as limpid and flexible in flow as a brook. James concerned himself with stories of extraordinarily intellectual characters, people of the upper class, men and women whose deeds hinged on some psychologic subtlety, whereas Howells dealt with those of ordinary life—editors, business men, ministers, lawyers—reporting and analyzing their doings with such humor and insight that they are to-day exponents of New England social history. Nevertheless, people persisted in naming him and James in one breath as engaged in a combined assault on something which should be revered, not destroyed.

Howells often talked of James to me, quoting some of his

opinions with approval, and speaking of his books with delight. "We are friends of long standing," he said, "and when next he comes to New York, I shall contrive to have you meet him."

The opportunity did not offer during my life in Boston, and James remained a remote and rather awesome personality till in 1895, when he reviewed my "Rose of Dutcher's Coulée" in *Harper's Weekly,* speaking of it with surprising warmth of interest. Very naturally I wrote to thank him, and thus began a correspondence which continued at long intervals for three years.

His missives were hard to decipher, for he had the habit of writing completely to the bottom of the fourth page of his sheet and then criss-crossing it with diagonal lines, ending in some cases on the first page, thus bringing the signature and the salutation side by side. At other times he still further complicated his page by writing backward along the margins. Notwithstanding these complications, I enjoyed the matter of his notes so thoroughly that their illegibility was ignored, or rated only as an added interest. He never wrote aimlessly.

In one of these cryptograms, or palimpsests, he expressed a desire to have me visit him if I should ever come to England, and when I replied that I never expected to have money enough to cross the ocean, and asked in return, "Are you never coming to America?" he responded rather sadly, "I have no intention of doing so."

Now here I was leaving London with a letter of invitation in my pocket and Rye less than two hours away! "Come down on Saturday and spend Sunday with me," he had written, giving me the most minute directions as to trains.

As I looked back on the South Side of London that June

afternoon, it all seemed ugly, commonplace, and depressing. The railway ran to the southeast, bringing miles and miles of characterless streets into view, with acres of grimy roofs bristling with rectangular chimneys. It was about as inspiring as the West Side of Chicago, a wilderness of drab human dens and angular plots of verdureless ground.

The tragic significance of this congestion appeared as we came into the green countryside, overhung by a gray sky and swept by a clean wind from the east. Here was the real England, the England of our novels. While white uniformed cricketers were at play, girls lithely contended at tennis. Scullers were moving briskly along sluggish rivers thick with boats and crowded with gay young life. It appeared that all Surrey was out for a holiday, in a fresh, finished, unsoiled land, and yet the train was only a few miles out of the ugly, huge, and smoky town.

Glorious curving roads ran past embowered cottages. Wooded hills succeeded with comfortable farmsteads set among green pastures, while gray towers rising out of deep groves of elms and oaks suggested feudal manors. Tall roofs, lichen-spotted and black with immemorial soot, gave picturesque chimneys to the sky like clustered boles of close-growing trees. For an hour or more my ride through the country was a delight.

At Ashford I deflected to the south, and almost at once the land dipped into a succession of smooth, suave, coast-sloping meadows. Long-armed windmills peered over the hills. Sheep fed everywhere—sheep lately sheared and looking shivery and thin by reason of it. Thatched roofs, the kind I had seen in illustrations of old-time English novels, covered ancient homesteads very beautiful to look at, but very unsanitary to live in, I am told. The railway hedges were nicely trimmed. Faggots in bundles lay beside the cottages. Climbing roses covered the porches.

Soon all the meadows visibly descended to the sea beach, each slope covered with sheep. I could see the tidewater running in snakelike canals amid the flocks. Bent, sunburned shepherds were tending the lambs, each man in the immemorial English yeoman's smock.

Then came Rye, a town set on a height overlooking the ocean. The railway wound around the foot of this hill and stopped at a little depot on the west side. As I stepped from the car a portly, brisk, and smiling man met me—Henry James himself!

After a hearty handclasp he said, "It is only a short walk to my house and, if you don't mind, we'll make our way there on foot. My man will carry your bag."

As he led the way up a steep, narrow, cobble-paved street toward a compact, bristling cluster of old roofs and chimneys, I had a feeling that I was living a story. He was not in the least as I had expected him to be. He was cordial, hearty, almost commonplace.

The way became narrower until it was hardly more than an alley, walled by the most satisfyingly ancient brick dwellings and then, suddenly, the walk made a turn and left me facing an open white doorway and huge brass knocker. "Here it is," said James, "this is my house. It is a very small one, as you see, but of rather fine Georgian type. It is old. It dates from 1716."

It was indeed small, but in perfect taste. The hall was paneled in oak, but the rooms above were furnished in white. Many rare engravings hung on the walls, portraits of England's worthies, classical subjects, Italian scenes, and the like. The furniture was in keeping, and the entire effect charming and restful.

When I came downstairs James met me and led the way to his garden, which was spacious and surrounded by a high wall. A few trees shaded one corner, and roofs with odd angles overpeered on two sides. A steeple rose not far away and a little, cracked bell sounded. It was all so English, so remote that I can not do justice to it. It was the place for a recluse—a dreamer such as I understood James had become.

Taking seats, we began to talk on subjects which mutually concerned us and for a time James was hesitant, distressingly so. He groped for just the right word, but as we proceeded he grew less constrained. He told me how, almost by accident, he had found this house and that from the first moment he saw it he wanted it. "It had been lived in by one continuous family since its erection till a few years ago, when it fell into the hands of an old gentleman, a resident of this town. Upon his death the widow offered it for sale and I bought it and moved my few possessions down from London. I bought it as a refuge from the city, and I now spend the larger part of my time here. It is my home."

He went on to say that he found London more and more of a distraction, a whirlpool. "As I grow older, I go to it reluctantly in January usually, but only for a short time. Most of the year I live in Rye. Since the death of my sister I live here alone, and work, work incessantly."

In answer to my questions he told me much that was of interest concerning the history of Rye and Wynchelsea, which stands on the next hill to the south. "Both were ports at one time," he explained, "and rivals of London, but now they are left high and dry by the recession of the sea, a strange phenomenon. Rye, as you will see, is only a sleepy, curious, decaying little town, neither farm village nor sea town, and yet it possesses some of the characteristics of both."

He was curious about conditions of authorship in America —wanted to know more of the men whose books sold so enormously. He was amazed at my statement of the money certain writers made by their writings. He had no understanding of the midland America. Chicago was almost as alien to him as a landscape on Mars. He resented the self-satisfaction of the novelists who sold their hundreds of thousands of copies of superficial fiction. "I have never even heard of them," he said when I named two of the most successful.

It was natural that he should resent such upstarts; for he, to my mind, represented something fought for, something attained with care. He stood for culture, workmanship, style. In a quiet way he was intellectually contemptuous of commercial America. In all that he said he remained very human, very judicial, and very kindly. His large, pellucid, rather prominent eyes studied me tranquilly.

When I asked him what he was doing at the time, he replied, "I am putting a selective edition of my books into form for an American publisher."

He spoke of the placid quiet of his little town, of his kindly neighbors. "They are a great comfort to me, for I am a lonely man," he said. He spoke rejoicingly of the fact that there were only three wheeled vehicles in the village. "You noticed, perhaps, that the streets are grass-grown between the cobbles? Only now and then do I hear a footfall pass my door."

He alluded gratefully to my letters of appreciation of his stories. "I have for many years discharged my books into

America as into a hollow void," he admitted with somber inflection; "no word but yours has lately come back to me."

No doubt this was an exaggeration, and yet he meant that I should remember it as a confession.

He spoke of Howells with sincere love and appreciation. "He is an artist—always—but he has written too much, and so have I."

I then quoted Howells' remark, apropos of this criticism: "But what else am I to do?"

James instantly agreed. "Yes, we writers are lost without our pens in our hands."

He praised Owen Wister's work and commended Mrs. Wharton's "Valley of Decision," and this led up to his own fervid enthusiasm for Italy. He advised my hastening there at once. "Why study France?" he demanded; "France is only an imitation of Italy. Why waste time on the imitation when you can see the real thing?"

Precisely what he meant by this I could not determine, but I took it to mean that the historical remains of France were Roman. He could not have meant that France was in any modern sense an imitation of Italy.

A little farther on he spoke of his novel. "The Ambassadors," as the best of all he had written. "I am rewriting, not merely revising, my earlier books," he explained, and to this I could not respond with any enthusiasm. To me such work was a kind of wholesale deception—as well as a doubtful improvement. To relanguage a "Portrait of a Lady" would be but to blur its clear, original outlines. However, I did not say so at the moment, for it would have been obvious disapproval, and if my silence gave him that impression he did not remark upon it.

He referred to Thomas Hardy as a man who had lost his

power. Of his brother William James he spoke with affection. Several other American writers came in for his comment, which was never bitter nor ironic. He had a certain straightforward glance which made his words sound less harsh than they would look if printed. As he described his New York ancestry, I perceived that he was less remote than he had seemed to me hitherto. "I still read the New York journals and keep informed of New World politics in the mass!" he said.

He became very much in earnest at last and said something which surprised and gratified me. It was an admission I had not expected him to make. "If I were to live my life over again," he said in a low voice, and fixing upon me a somber glance, "I would be an American. I would steep myself in America, I would know no other land. I would study its beautiful side. The mixture of Europe and America which you see in me has proved disastrous. It has made of me a man who is neither American nor European. I have lost touch with my own people, and I live here alone. My neighbors are friendly, but they are not of my blood, except remotely. As a man grows old he feels these conditions more than when he is young. I shall never return to the United States, but I wish I could."

This may have been but a mood induced by his talk with me, but it filled me with a profound pity for this man, who, in spite of his great fame, was old and lonely. It brought back to my mind the feeling I used to have as I read his novels filled with expatriates, a feeling of emptiness and futility, an ache of resentment which I could never quite put into words. I knew the characters he depicted were mongrels, but I was never quite sure of his own attitude with respect to those who transferred their loyalty to France or England.

Whatever his mind had been, he now made it plain that he still loved the land of his youth and wished himself back in it and at home in it.

After our tea, which was served on a little table out under the trees, he took me to see the town, pointing out the most ancient of the buildings, well knowing that as a man from the plains of Iowa I would be interested in age-worn walls and door sills. He took me to the Old Mermaid Tavern, in which was a marvelous fireplace, as wide as the end of the room itself, with benches at the corners. Everybody we met seemed to know and like him; whether they recognized in him a famous author or not I cannot tell, but they certainly regarded him as a good neighbor. He greeted every one we met most genially. He was on terms with the postman and the butcher's boy. There was nothing austere or remote in his bearing. On the contrary, he had the air of a curate making the rounds of his village.

How beautiful, how far, how peaceful seems that small, crowded, lichen-covered town, as I recall it to-day! Its streets were like grass-grown alleys, and the graveyard which surrounded the old church was as lovely as a garden, with its graveled walks and its shrubs and vines. Ancient gates opened upon green meadows down below, meadows on which the sheep fed. Exquisite colors and quaint forms abounded in every direction, and yet it was not mine and did not satisfy Henry James—at least he had moments when he longed for the land of his birth. I understood his enthusiasms of the moment, but I understood also the hunger which he had voiced as we sat in his garden.

At seven o'clock we dined in his exquisite little dining room, and the dinner, which came on quite formally, was delicious. He had no other guest, but he presided at the service end of the table with quiet formality. The mahogany glistened with the care which had been lavished upon it, the silver was interesting and beautiful, and the walls of the room tasteful and cheerful—and yet I could not keep out of my mind a picture of him sitting here alone, as he confessed he did on many, many nights. To grow old even with your children all about you is a sorrowful business, but to grow old in a land filled with strangers is sadder still.

It was late when I went to bed that night, my mind filled with literary and artistic problems called up by his profound comment. The questions of National art, of Realism and Idealism, of New World garishness and crudeness, of its growing power and complexity—these were among the matters we had discussed. That James lived on the highest plane of life and thought was evident. He had no distractions, no indulgences. He permitted himself no loafing, no relaxation. He had not even the comfort of a comic spirit such as Clemens had. He was in earnest all the time—a genial earnestness, but an earnestness which could not be diverted.

I put down this statement in my record: "This man lives on the highest plane. No man of his time is nobler in his aspirations as an artist. He has put the best of his life, and in a sense he has put all of his life, into his art. Although elusive in its expression, his work is original. No other writer or school of writers has had a share in it."

We breakfasted in such comfort, so simple but so perfect as to form the most delightful luxury. The sun shone in at our window, the silver gleamed cheerily, the coffee was delicious, and James, immaculately clad and fresh and rosy again, presided at the opposite side of the table while his miraculous servants attended us.

At the close of our meal I said, "It is your habit to work in the morning—that I know, and I want you to keep to your routine. Don't permit me to interrupt your morning task."

"Very well," he said. "I will take you at your word, but first I want you to see my workshop."

His "shop" was a small detached building standing in the corner of the garden, and in the large room littered with books and manuscripts I found a smart young woman stenographer at work. James showed me the changes he was making in his earlier books—work which I did not approve, for he was rewriting these stories. In my judgment he was not bettering them; on the contrary it seemed to me he was transforming them into something which was neither of the past nor of the present. I think he was now aware of my disapproval, for he went on to explain that he found in the early versions many crudities which he could not think of allowing the future to observe—"if people ever take the trouble to look into my books," he added, with a note of melancholy in his voice.

After giving me elaborate directions concerning other landmarks of the region, he suddenly said, "But why should I not be your guide again? You do not come often. My work can wait."

My protesting availed nothing. Putting his secretary at another task he told me to come with him. "There are some other houses which I must show you. They are owned by some friends of mine and they will be glad to let you have a glimpse of them."

As he led me about the town, discovering for me delightful Georgian types of dwellings, the people everywhere greeted him with smiling cordiality. They liked and honored him, that was evident, and it gave me a keen sense of satisfaction to find him more and more neighborly, taking an interest in what his fellow citizens were doing and thinking. This phase of him was as surprising as it was amusing. To hear him asking after a child's health, or inquiring when Mr. Brown would return from London, was a revelation of the fact that, after all, he was more than half New England.

He sped me on my way to France with a hearty invitation to come and see him on my return, and I particularly urged him to come again to America, in order that we might show him the honor which so many of us were eager to pay, and also in order that we might profit by his criticism. To this he replied very thoughtfully, "I may do so, but I fear I shall not get so far as Chicago."

With this he gave me his hand, and I went away down the cobbled street on my way to Carcassonne and Pisa.

CHAPTER THIRTY-SEVEN

A GLASS OF OLD FRENCH WINE

I

As a part of my vacation, I had set aside a week or two for Paris, and a call upon a literary friend who lived in or near there. I made the crossing in June, and the change from the pale sunlight of England to the heat and light of France was almost like getting back to America. I surrendered myself with swift elation to the sights and sounds of a radiant French summer. For two weeks I gave my time to wandering into every nook and corner of Paris. I learned what the working people were like, and how they went about their early-morning tasks. I was interested in the historical buildings and the art collections, of course, but first of all I wished to gain a mental picture of the city's daily toil.

In this I was successful. As I close my eyes now, I can recall hundreds of dark little men in baggy trousers, joyously, noisily digging, hammering, lifting. I see them swabbing the streets at dawn. I sit again on one of the little iron chairs in front of a dusty café, eating rolls and strawberries which "Madame" serves with a smile of amusement at my Wisconsin accent. I dare again the villainous "coffee" which the toilers stop to drink before the larger cafés open. In the afternoon I sit on the grass in the parks, with scores of jolly picnicking families. I listen once more to the riotous yet good-humored arguments which start up like sudden storms

466

among the men seated upon the benches of the Trocadéro. Paris is a reality to me by reason of those days of observation.

I put some of these impressions into a letter to my father and mother:

"I have had a busy day in this great city. It is like New York, only greater. It is quite unlike London, and in many respects I like it better.

"I took a long walk to-day out to the great church of Notre Dame, past the Palace of Justice and the Tuileries. All around the Palace of Justice a cordon of police was drawn, resolute-looking fellows in blue uniforms. Things are getting warm again in the Dreyfus case and the authorities are alert. There is not a particle of danger of any trouble, but they want to be on the safe side. My room is very tasteful and bright. I am comfortably warm for the first time since I left Chicago.

"*Thursday Night.* I have just come in from the street which is filled with people applauding Major Marchand, the African explorer. The crowd was immense, good-natured, and very happy. For hours they waited, cheering on every pretext. They made a sound unlike any made by our people. It was high-keyed and continuous. A shrill roar which never intermitted, but was reënforced at times by a rhythmic clapping of hands and cries of *rat-a-plan, rat-a-plan,* in imitation of a drum, and at the last some one started the *Marseillaise.* To hear these people sing that wild and splendid hymn was a thrilling experience. It made my blood leap.

"The people were all, or most all, well dressed, and cries of *Vive l'Armée,* brought Marchand out. He is a fine-looking fellow with a black beard and a pleasant cast of countenance. He bowed again and again, but the crowd could not get enough of him. They were still there in immense numbers when I came away. I wish I could be here when Dreyfus is brought back. Excitement will be dangerously high, but these people can take care of themselves. In some ways they are more like Americans than the English. I must say I like the Frenchman on his own ground. He's quite a different man from the one who travels."

The only man I knew in all the city was Hermon MacNeil, the young sculptor who had accompanied me to the Hopi snake dance in 1895, and the only woman I knew was Th. Bentzon, "Madame Blanc," the French novelist and critic, who, as the guest of Alice French, had visited Chicago and St. Louis and knew many of my friends. She was living at Ferté Sous Jouarre, about forty miles out, and in accordance with a promise, I now wrote to her asking an opportunity to call.

She replied, "My brother, who is visiting me, and who speaks English, wishes to meet you. Will you not come down and stay the night with us? I am eager to talk of things American."

On the day named I took a train, which carried me into one of the quaintest and oldest of French villages. The Marne, a slow stream, more like a canal than a river, flowed peacefully through the town, and the life of the people, running as leisurely as the water, seemed a thousand miles from the city's boulevards.

M. Bentzon (a merchant from Martinique) met me at the station and led me to the ancient stone cottage in which he was spending the summer with his sister. His wife and two daughters, neither of whom could understand a word of English, studied me with frank curiosity, for they had never before met a man from the western United States. To them

I was a rare bird. The tones of my voice especially interested them, and when after dinner (at Madame Blanc's request) I read some of my dialect verses, they were all so delighted with the speech tunes of "Goin' Back To-morrow," that I was obliged to repeat it for them. My feeling was somewhat like that of the station agent whose harelip utterance so amused a small boy that his mother made frequent repetitions of her questions. Nevertheless, I was glad to give them pleasure.

One sad remissness on my part must be chronicled, however. At dinner a slender glass of wine was placed beside my plate, and as I had no taste for wines I left the glass standing untouched till Madame Blanc asked me if I did not care for it. "Oh, yes," I replied, "but I very seldom drink wine." Thereupon I took a mouthful of the lovely liquid and went on talking. For some reason my hostess seemed disappointed and so I finished my glass without delay. Then I learned what a *sauvage* I was, for she explained that it was a very old and very precious vintage which had been brought out in my honor!

Conscience-smitten and ashamed, I could only plead dense ignorance of liquors. "I can't tell the difference between ale and beer. I grew to manhood in a prohibition state and among very simple and abstemious folk. Please pardon my untutored palate."

She forgave me, but my blunder left me with a sore spot. Even now when I think of that dear lady hopefully putting her exquisite old wine beside my plate I am filled with mingled shame and regret.

We took a little walk about the village, and as we passed the dark, damp little stone cabins she said, "They are not much like your comfortable wooden homes in America."

"No. Our towns are utterly prosaic but every house has windows on all sides and a bathroom. There is nothing about our villages for an artist to paint, but their wooden houses are civilized."

"You are quite right," she said, "but only I can understand your feeling. I know your cottages with simple yards and furnaces and bathrooms. These hovels are darker and more uncomfortable than you can imagine by looking in at the doors. Change in France is slow. We are still medieval, that is true, but I rather like our lingering old customs."

"They go with the stone huts, that is true," I replied.

On Sunday M. Bentzon took me for a walk about upper Jouarre, which dated back a thousand years. He led me down into a crypt, which had been used as a refuge by the Christians of the eighth century. This gave me a still deeper sense of the far-reaching history of this small town. Some of it was here when Cæsar came his conquering way. Its people were direct descendants of the Cro-Magnon hunters of the hairy elephant, and yet, as a place to live, I preferred West Salem.

Madame Bentzon was the first French woman I had ever met and I found her almost as companionable as Alice French or Ruth McEnery Stuart. She was dark, rather stout, and a little beyond middle age, serious and kindly. I liked her quiet manner and rejoiced in her plan to be an interpreter of America to France. She knew American life in the small towns as well as in the cities and was catholic enough in judgment to admit its virtues. She understood our groups of local-color novelists, and saw in them something running parallel to the work of Mistral and Daudet—something rising from the soil.

II

On my return to my hotel, I was met by Zangwill, who had brought his mother and sister to celebrate in Paris, and so it happened that my last afternoon in the city was spent with him at the Longchamp races, a grandiose close to my outing in France.

It was the day of the Grand Prix, and the crowd was enormous. The flashing, rippling, rhythmic movement of regiments of cavalry, the ceaseless roll of carriages along the avenues, the incessant, hot snapping of cabmen's whips, the throngs of women in flower-like garments, the cool green woods fringing the drives, the delicious turf of the field, the broad mats of seated spectators (out of which thousands of gay, colored parasols shone, iridescent as bubbles of pink and blue and lilac), and a thousand other sights and sounds combined to make this an unforgettable hour. Nothing could have been farther away from the Skeena Valley in which I had camped the same day of the week just a year before.

It chanced that a demonstration against President Loubet took place while we were walking toward the track, but we saw nothing of it and we had no share in the excitement of the races, for as neither of us knew anything of the course we were only mildly interested when a group of mounted jockeys came romping along the turf. We imagined them out for an airing. Accustomed to the dusty race tracks of our county-fair grounds, I had no suspicion that this was the grand event I had come out to see!

As we were riding homeward in our little one-horse carriage, President Loubet came alongside in a noble landau, and when Zangwill rose and cheered, I joined him. Something in our appearance attracted the President's attention. He smiled and lifted his hat as if in greeting to a friend, a gesture which amused Zangwill. "He knew you were an American author. That hat of yours drew his salute."

"We'll let it go at that," I replied, "but I think it was your red Indian whoop that did it."

I was just beginning to know the city when I took passage for London—and home! My mother was waiting for me in Wisconsin and my conscience would not let me linger on in England, which was at its loveliest as I rode through it on my way back to Liverpool and my boat. This land so rich in human records produced in me a wistful greed. I wanted to include all its charm in my book of remembrance—a hunger made all the more poignant by the conviction that I should never see these velvet parks and towered hills again.

IN CONCLUSION

IT can not be said that my spring in England and my fortnight in France had been a social triumph or that they had made any great change in me or in my writing, but I had enjoyed a personal study of two great centers of human activity. "When any one speaks to me thereafter, of Paris," I made record, "I shall be able to visualize it. When the streets of London are named I shall be able (in most instances) to place them in their relationship to the Strand or to Regent Street and I had seen enough of English Country life to compare notes with others.

Furthermore (and to anticipate), the story which I had outlined before leaving Chicago was accepted by Gilder and published in the *Century Magazine,* and re-imbursed me for all my outlay. This manuscript and my evening suit, while not precisely spoils of conquest, were concrete evidences of my Old World invasion. Thereafter, formal dinners had no terrors for me. Safe within my social uniform I mixed indistinguishedly with the coal barons and college presidents of my native land.

Most lasting of all the pleasures of this vacation, however, were the meetings with the most admired of my fellow craftsmen. I knew Bernard Shaw and Thomas Hardy as hosts as well as great writers. I had renewed my acquaintance with Barrie and Kipling and I had formed several other new and valued friendships. I had talked with Mark Twain and Bret Harte and had gained a better knowledge of the charm which

473

held our ex-patriots year after year in the capitals of Europe. Acknowledging this charm, I knew that safety lay in flight. With no hope of ever seeing these shores again I sailed into the West as my ancestors had done nearly three hundred years before, treasuring all my pleasant experiences and willing to forget those which had been ugly and chill and drab. As another of America's literary pilgrim sons I freely acknowledge the educative value of my ancestral home.